MW00340650

Honor, Shame, and Guilt

Bulletin for Biblical Research Supplements

Editor

RICHARD S. HESS, Denver Seminary

Associate Editor

CRAIG L. BLOMBERG, Denver Seminary

Advisory Board

Honor, Shame, and Guilt

Social-Scientific Approaches
to the Book of Ezekiel

by

DANIEL Y. WU

Winona Lake, Indiana
EISENBRAUNS
2016

www.eisenbrauns.com

Library of Congress Cataloging-in-Publication Data

Names: Wu, Daniel, author.
Title: Honor, shame, and guilt : social-scientific approaches to the Book of
    Ezekiel / by Daniel Wu.
Description: Winona Lake, Indiana : Eisenbrauns, [2016] | Series: Bulletin
    for biblical research supplements ; 14 | Includes bibliographical
    references and index.
Identifiers: LCCN 2016006012 (print) | LCCN 2016007872 (ebook) |
    ISBN 9781575064376 (hardback : alk. paper) | ISBN 9781575064383 (pdf)
Subjects: LCSH: Bible. Ezekiel—Social scientific criticism.
Classification: LCC BS1545.55 .W82 2016 (print) | LCC BS1545.55 (ebook) |
    DDC 224/.4067—dc23
LC record available at http://lccn.loc.gov/2016006012

To my wife, Chrissie, my glory.

And to my boys, Liam, Archie, and Harry—
may you grow to become men of true honor.

Contents

Acknowledgments

This manuscript is a revision of my Ph.D. thesis, and it is due to the help of many others that it has now reached its current form. I am very thankful for the supervision of Dr. George Athas, my friend and now colleague at Moore Theological College. His warmth, care, humor, keen eye, and sharp mind made for a smooth and fruitful experience of research and writing. My secondary supervisor, Associate Professor Ian Young at Sydney University, also provided great support and important critical comments on my developing thesis. Dr. Yasmine Musharbash (Sydney University) and Dr. Yael Avrahami (Oranim College/University of Haifa) helped me become familiar with the fields of pschology and anthropology and with their application to biblical studies.

I am thankful for the encouraging and insightful comments of my thesis examiners, Professor Daniel Carroll (Denver Seminary), Professor Mark Boda (McMaster Divinity College), and Professor Daniel Block (Wheaton College), who also first suggested I submit my thesis to the BBR Supplement Series. I am also thankful for Dr. Richard S. Hess, the editor of the series, for accepting it for publication and for his perceptive, detailed editorial comments. Thanks also to the Eisenbrauns staff, and especially my editor, Amy Becker, for their warmth and work in preparing this manuscript for publication.

Many of the Moore College faculty gave generously of their time and expertise to help and encourage me on my way. I am especially grateful for the other members of the Old Testament department, Dr. Andrew Shead, Dr. Paul Williamson, and Dr. Michael Stead. Dr. Peter Bolt (New Testament) read and commented on the entire thesis with superhuman speed and accuracy, and Jane Tooher let me foist my ideas about honor, shame, and guilt on unsuspecting students in lectures. Dr. John Woodhouse, the Principal of Moore College during my studies, and Dr. Mark Thompson, the current Principal, also took a keen interest in my study, encouraged me warmly in it and, together with former Vice Principal Dr. Bill Salier, facilitated its completion by affording me time off normal duties early in my appointment to the faculty.

This work, and the experience of postgraduate study, would have been impoverished without the members of the Moore College Postgraduate Room. The value of the chats across the room, at lunch, or over coffee, cannot be overestimated, and the friendship among us made what could have been a potentially isolating experience one of joy and fellowship.

A huge note of thanks also must go to my church family at the time, Cherrybrook Anglican Church, where I worked as an assistant minister before and during postgraduate study. My Senior Minister, Rev. Gav Poole, was a source of unceasing support and flexibility. The late Alan Hohne was a strong voice encouraging me to consider pursuing further study in the first place, and he and many others from Cherrybrook provided prayers, encouragement, and financial support. My team of youth leaders picked up the slack of their minister dropping down to part-time work with heart-warming maturity, grace, and energy; their constant, thoroughly enjoyable peppering with biblical, theological, and ethical questions kept me on my toes.

Space does not permit me to thank many others who should be mentioned. However, I must include both my parents, Aldred and Janet Wu, and my parents-in-law, Richard and Glenda Brown, whose support and love at every level, and in every respect, were critical in what was at times a very challenging time of life.

My greatest thanks, humanly speaking, must go to my wife, Chrissie. For 7 out of our first 10 years of marriage, she had a full-time student for a husband. For most of the other 3, she had a husband who was thinking about it. For all that time, and beyond, she has been a constant joy, support, and source of strength. Without the help of others, this study would have suffered in quality. Without her love, encouragement, and self-giving service throughout, it would not exist. Thank God for you.

Foreword

When I was a youngster, growing up in northern Saskatchewan, Canada, my parents would often reprimand us directly with "Shame on you," or less directly with, "Aren't you ashamed of yourself?" And in the one-room country school I attended, if we misbehaved the teacher would regularly have us stand in the corner with our noses to the wall while our classmates snickered as they tried to continue their schoolwork. However, when I went off to university, I learned that the emotional and psychological problems my siblings and I faced were in fact attributable to the "guilt culture" in which we had been raised. Really? This was a time when the anthropological insights of Margaret Mead and the psychological/sociological proposals of Ruth Benedict were taking our campuses by storm, and the stereotypical labels of "guilt cultures" and "shame cultures" were taking root. I would not have intuitively labeled the environment in which I grew up as a guilt culture. Perhaps we were different from other Caucasian Canadians because my father had only recently immigrated from central Russia, while the attribution, "guilt culture," is commonly associated with western and northern Europe. More likely, it indicates that we should be more cautious about constructing and applying generalizing labels, at a psychological and, especially, at a cultural level. Indeed, as pointed out in this study, more recent cultural anthropology has exposed the serious shortcomings of the shame culture/guilt culture divide.

On the other hand, this does not mean that these labels are useless, or that they should be dispensed with completely. Whatever the flaws in method behind them, the concepts of honor, shame, and guilt seem persistently to underlie human life, experience, and relationships. As mentioned previously, I would not characterize my upbringing as arising from a guilt culture. But this does not mean that it was devoid of rules, or that there was no interest in developing a healthy conscience. My parents had extremely high ethical standards, which they sought to inculcate in us. Thus, binary labels such as "shame" and "guilt cultures" may still be heuristically valuable, but only if we are aware of the dangers of naive constructions and application that may blind us to the complexities of life on the ground. Indeed, for those of us involved in theological reflection, this ought to be familiar territory. We often look at epithets like Arminian and Calvinist as polar opposites, but many who characterize themselves as essentially Arminian share many theological convictions with John Calvin, and many Calvinists assent to beliefs held by Jacobus Arminius. The labels can helpfully communicate legitimate differences in content and emphasis, but simplistic polarization is misleading and can lead to unhelpful distortion of the facts.

In the same way, while biblical scholars welcome the benefits that social-scientific approaches offer to the hermeneutical process, we are not
immune to the seductive power of alien labels or the danger of disregarding evidence that undermines our method and conclusions. For decades,
we have read and sometimes unquestioningly accepted cultural analyses of
biblical texts that appear on the surface to have great explanatory power
in offering solutions to troubling passages. However, on closer inspection,
these often end up telling us more about the interpreter than about the interpreted text. To be sure, no interpretation is devoid of bias in the method
selected, the data chosen as significant, or the conclusions drawn. However,
the goal of interpretation by definition should be to clarify the meaning
and significance of the object/text interpreted. Therefore, great care is warranted if the exercise is to be most fruitful in advancing our understanding
of this ancient artifact.

We are indebted to Daniel Wu for his careful examination of the way
social-scientific approaches to biblical studies have influenced the discipline. He offers a very useful review first of the roots of the "guilt culture" and "shame culture" dichotomy in the social sciences and then of
how this dichotomy has been used in biblical studies. His assessment of
social-scientific approaches (SSA) is illuminating. On the one hand, conclusions derived from social-scientific research are highly valuable and have
alerted us to details in the text that we would not otherwise have seen. On
the other, he shows that interpreters are often so enamored with insights
from other fields that they impose them on the biblical texts, often against
the grain of the lexical and literary evidence. His own method builds a new
model of cultural analysis that seeks to be critically appreciative of those
who have gone before him but moves beyond old dichotomies (honor vs.
shame, shame vs. guilt) to provide a more sophisticated understanding of
the concepts and the manner in which they are related.

The author has wisely selected Ezekiel as the focus of his analysis. In
this book, the notions of honor, shame, and guilt feature prominently, and
here we also find some of the most shocking (and offensive) assertions related to honor, shame, and guilt. Texts such as Ezek 36:32 have caused both
consternation and bewilderment: "I want you to know that I am not doing
this for your sake, declares the Sovereign LORD. Be ashamed and disgraced
for your conduct, people of Israel!" (NIV). What sort of deity is this who
is concerned only about his own honor (cf. vv. 22–23) and who deliberately
shames his own people?

Through careful analysis of the key words for "honor" (כבוד), "shame"
(בוש), and "guilt" (עוה/עון), along with related expressions, Wu domesti-
cates the book's irascible lexical and conceptual challenges and clarifies
the prophet's rhetoric. In the end, he establishes that the book's concern is
not primarily psychological or anthropological but theological. His conclusions are significant. Wu demonstrates that Ezekiel is not an "erratic" in

the landscape of the Old Testament. He may have ministered in a troubled and troubling environment, and his prophetic activity is cast in unquestionably unique forms. But in the end, as for all the prophets since Moses, for Ezekiel:

1. "Honor is what Yhwh deems of worth, is indicative of right relationship with him, and is defined in accordance with and in appropriate response to his כבד, which is in turn derived from his own character of חסד ואמת."
2. "Shame is what in Yhwh's eyes fails/falls short of an appropriate response to his כבד and thus constitutes a fundamental breach of relationship with him."
3. "Guilt is the concrete expression of that failure, the transgression or distortion of the covenant terms that express and enable right relationship with the God of חסד ואמת." (p. 174)

In line with more recent cultural anthropology, Wu confirms from the biblical material that the notion that some societies may be characterized as "shame cultures," in contrast to others, which are "guilt cultures," is null and void. Perhaps shockingly to some, but as a welcome signal to others, he concludes that the truth is all cultures are both "shame" and "guilt cultures." The differences—which are still very real—lie in how these features are configured and related. In Ezekiel's profoundly theocentric worldview, Yhwh is honored and his people most blessed when they recognize and repent of their utter failure to live in appropriate response to his character, delight in the grace of forgiveness and restored relationship with him, and demonstrate that delight by anticipating the day when, renewed by his Spirit, they are enabled to live in accord with his will and his mission for them. This is the glory of Yhwh, and thus the glory also of his people. This theological truth, together with its powerful systematic, biblical theological, pastoral, and missiological implications, is as critical today as it was in the sixth century BC.

Daniel I. Block
Gunther H. Knoedler Professor of Old Testament
Wheaton College
April, 2016

Abbreviations

General

b. Sanh	Babylonian Talmud: Sanhedrin
D	D Source / Deuteronomist
DH	Deuteronomistic History
ESV	English Standard Version
H	Holiness Code
HB	Hebrew Bible
inf. cst.	infinitive construct
NASB	New American Standard Bible
NIV	New International Version
P	Priestly Code
RSV	Revised Standard Version
SSA	Social Scientific Approach(es) to Biblical Studies

Reference Works

AACOT	An American Commentary on the Old Testament
AB	Anchor Bible
AIIL	Ancient Israel and Its Literature
AJOT	*American Journal of Theology*
BDB	Brown, F.; Driver, S. R.; and Briggs, C. A. *Hebrew and English Lexicon of the Old Testament*. Oxford: Clarendon, 1907
BETL	Bibliotheca ephemeridum theologicarum lovaniensum
BibInt	*Biblical Interpretation*
BHS	Elliger, K., and Rudolph, W., editors. *Biblia Hebraica Stuttgartensia*. Stuttgart: Deutsche Bibelgesellschaft, 1984
BMCR	*Bryn Mawr Classical Review*
BZAW	Beihefte zur Zeithschrift für die alttestamentliche Wissenschaft
CAD	Gelb, Ignace J., et al., editors. *The Assyrian Dictionary of the Oriental Institute of the University of Chicago*. 21 vols. (A–Z). Chicago: Oriental Institute, 1956–2011
CBQ	*Catholic Biblical Quarterly*
CSSCA	Cambridge Studies in Social and Cultural Anthropology
CTL	Cambridge Textbooks in Linguistics
CurBS	*Currents in Research: Biblical Studies*
CV	*Communio viatorum*
DCH	Clines, D. J. A., editor. *Dictionary of Classical Hebrew*. 9 vols. Sheffield: Sheffield Phoenix, 1993–2014
DNTB	C. A. Evans and S. E. Porter, editors. *Dicionary of New Testament Background*. Downers Grove: InterVarsity, 2000
DOTPe	T. D. Alexander and D. W. Baker, Editors. *Dictionary of Old Testament: Pentateuch*. Edited by Downers Grove: InterVarsity, 2002
EQ	*Evangelical Quarterly*

FA	Frontiers of Anthropology
GKC	Kautzsch, E., editor. *Gesenius' Hebrew Grammar*. Translated by A. E. Cowley. 2nd ed. Oxford: Oxford University Press, 1910
HALOT	Koehler, L.; Baumgartner, W.; and Stamm, J. J. *The Hebrew and Aramaic Lexicon of the Old Testament*. Translated and edited under supervision of M. E. J. Richardson. 5 vols. Leiden: Brill, 1994–2000
HBM	Hebrew Bible Monographs
HTR	*Harvard Theological Review*
HUCA	*Hebrew Union College Annual*
IESS	David L. Sills, editor. *International Encyclopedia of Social Sciences*. New York: Macmillan, 1968
IJP	*International Journal of Psychology*
IJSSJ	Institute of Jewish Studies: Studies in Judaica
Int	*Interpretation*
IntJ	*International Journal of Psychoanalysis*
IPAL	The International Psycho-Analytical Library
JBL	*Journal of Biblical Literature*
JBPR	*Journal of Biblical and Pneumatological Research*
JBQ	*Jewish Bible Quarterly*
JETS	*Journal of the Evangelical Theological Society*
JFSR	*Journal for the Feminist Study of Religion*
JLSM	Janua linguarum Series Maior
Joüon	Joüon, P. *A Grammar of Biblical Hebrew*. Translated and revised by T. Muraoka. Subsidia Biblica 27. Rome: Pontifical Biblical Institute, 2006
JSNT	*Journal for the Study of the New Testament*
JSOT	*Journal for the Study of the Old Testament*
JSOTSup	Journal for the Study of the Old Testament Supplements
JTS	*Journal of Theological Studies*
KHZAT	Kurzer Hand-Commentar zum Alten Testament
LCL	Loeb Classical Library
LMRT	Library of Modern Religious Thought
LSAWS	Linguistic Studies in Ancient West Semitic
NDBT	B. S. Rosner et al., editors. *New Dictionary of Biblical Theology*. Downers Grove: InterVarsity, 2000
NICOT	New International Commentary on the Old Testament
NIDOTTE	Van Gemeren, W. A., editor. *New International Dictionary of Old Testament Theology and Exegesis*. 5 vols. Grand Rapids: Zondervan, 1997
NIVAC	New International Version Application Commentary
NR	*The New Republic*
NTPG	Wright, N. T. *The New Testament and the People of God*. London: SPCK, 1992
OD	*Oxford Dictionaries*. No Pages. Cited 10 November 2011. Online: http://www.oxforddictionaries.com
OTE	*Old Testament Essays*
OTRM	Oxford Theology and Religion Monographs
PTW	Preaching the Word
RBL	*Review of Biblical Literature*

RelSRev	*Religious Studies Review*
RT	*Religion and Theology*
RTR	*Reformed Theological Review*
SamP	*Samaritan Pentateuch*
SBL	Society of Biblical Literature
SBLDS	Society of Biblical Literature Dissertation Series
SBLSymS	Society of Biblical Literature Symposium Series
SBTS	Sources for Biblical and Theological Study
SBTSOTS	Sources for Biblical and Theological Study Old Testament Series
SDBH	R. de Blois and E. R. Mueller, editors. *A Semantic Dictionary of Biblical Hebrew*. No pages. Online: http://sdbh.org
SEEJ	*Scandinavian Evangelical E-Journal*
SNTSMS	Society of New Testament Studies Monograph Series
SPCK	Society for the Propogation of Christian Knowledge
SR	*Social Research*
SSI	*Social Science Information*
SSN	Studia semitica neerlandica
TDOT	Botterweck, G. J., and Ringgren, H., editors. *Theological Dictionary of the Old Testament*. Grand Rapids, MI: Eerdmans, 1974–2006
TLOT	Jenni, E., editor, and Biddle, M. E., translator. *Theological Lexicon of the Old Testament*. 3 vols. Peabody, MA: Hendrickson, 1997
ThWAT	Botterweck, G. J., and Ringgren, H., editors. *Theologisches Wörterbuch zum Alten Testament*. Stuttgart: Kohlhammer, 1973–2000
TynBul	*Tyndale Bulletin*
VT	*Vetus Testamentum*
VTSup	Supplements to *Vetus Testamentum*
WBC	Word Biblical Commentary
WC	World's Classics
WCJS	World Congress of Jewish Studies
WUNT	Wissenschaftliche Untersuchungen zum Neuen Testament
YLT	Young's Literal Translation
ZAW	*Zeitschrift für die alttestamentliche Wissenschaft*

Chapter 1

Introduction to the Study of Honor and Shame in the Book of Ezekiel: Emic A

Introduction and Orientation

In this study, I explore how the concepts *honor*, *shame*, and *guilt* function in the book of Ezekiel, as well as in the wider contexts of their general use in anthropological or social-scientific approaches to biblical studies (hereafter, SSAs).[1] My aim is to examine the meanings of and relationships between the key terms and concepts כבד, עוה, and בוש, as they appear in Ezekiel. I seek to do so in light of the use of these terms across the OT or HB,[2] and then to explore the implications of this analysis for the dominant contemporary definitions of honor, shame, and guilt in the fields of psychology and anthropology and their application to biblical studies.

Before commencing the study, some preliminary comments are in order. In this study, I will not offer a reconstruction or detailed discussion of the origin, provenance, or redaction of Ezekiel. Although an important area, it suffices for my present purposes to note two widely recognized points: first, that the final form of Ezekiel was taken as authoritative within the canon of a receiving community in the Second Temple era, which understood the whole book to be a rhetorical unit, that is, a communicative act; and second, that this canon was by and large what was accepted by Jesus and the Apostles in NT times, as evidenced by the NT documents' use and recognition of this canon as Scripture, and that a resulting canon of OT and NT has since then been accepted as the basis for Christian theological reflection.[3]

---

1. For an explanation of the term *emic* see pp. 21–29 below. I will discuss this in more detail in ch. 2. SSA usually denotes "Social Scientific Approaches to Biblical Studies" and, more specifically, the model of honor and shame endorsed by the group of scholars known as the Context Group.

2. Throughout this study, I will prefer the term OT, as a reflection both of my own convictions and of the fact that one of the catalysts for this study is the use of honor/shame concepts in debates on the meaning of the cross in the New Testament. Furthermore, unless otherwise indicated, all translations in this study are my own

3. On this front, see further Thomas Renz, *The Rhetorical Function of the Book of Ezekiel* (Boston: Brill Academic, 2002). Note that I am also bypassing the issue of whether or not the original function of a book is affected by its inclusion into a canon. For this

Additionally, while offering constructive suggestions on accessing the
"real" biblical world,[4] I will also attempt to remain aware of the difficulties inherent in speaking too determinatively about the cultural milieus and
concrete social and historical contexts that may be reflected in the text. On
this front, the rise of ideological criticism in particular has highlighted the
dangers in speaking too confidently about things "as they are." Words and
texts are much too able to function as avenues of power and/or oppression
at every stage of the communicative process, from generation to reception,
for us to ignore this issue.

On the other hand, a communicative act by its very nature requires an intent to be understood by another *at some level*, and so unless we are content
to dwell in the closed box of endless self-referential hermeneutics and/or
see deception (whether intentional or not) in every jot and tittle, we need to
establish some reasonable basis by which we can gain at least some genuine
access to the "reality" to which the text refers. In this, I will suggest that a
form of critical realism is one approach that can be fruitfully applied to the
issue.

Rationale, Précis of Methodology, and Outline of the Present Study

Ezekiel is chosen as the focus text in this study because of the particular
manner the book draws the main themes involved together. Ezekiel's major
visions concern the כבוד־יהוה, and the book is structured around its movements between Jerusalem and Babylon. Of prime importance is Yhwh's
concern for his reputation, expressed most powerfully through the recognition formula "Then they will know that I am Yhwh," the repeated refrain
of the book. Honor concerns are thus particularly pronounced in Ezekiel.

Ezekiel is also considered by many to be a catalyst for the rise of individualism in Judaism, Christianity, and wider Western culture, particularly
because of Ezek 18 and its prominence in critical study of the OT. In line
with this sort of emphasis, his prophetic proclamation emphasizes the guilt
(עון) of the Israelites before Yhwh, and he continually draws attention to
their misdeeds and transgressions of the covenant. I will review scholarship
on this passage in the next chapter, and explore the issue further in ch. 6 on
the notion of guilt in Ezekiel.

However, Ezekiel is also יחזקאל בן־בוזי הכהן and, as such, his sustained
emphasis—obsession, even—with defilement, impurity, and blood place
his proclamations in priestly and ritual categories. For Ezekiel, Israel has
not simply transgressed the covenant and so rendered themselves guilty;

---

discussion, see further John Barton, *Oracles of God: Perceptions of Ancient Prophecy in Israel
after the Exile* (London: Darton Longman and Todd, 2007).

4. I enclose "real" in quotation marks as an acknowledgment that, for example, a
work of fiction may refer to an imagined, rather than historical reality.

they have been defiled, become abominable, shamed, and stand in need of cleansing, restoration, and reacceptance.

In short, Ezekiel seems an appropriate choice of text for an examination of how the key terms and concepts involved in this study work and, further, in what manner they are related to each other, to God, and to his people.

My method for this study will be to conduct a contextual semantic analysis of the key terms for each of the main concepts involved (honor, shame, guilt), as they appear in the book of Ezekiel. Preceding the material chapters, I will give a review of research in the area so far and develop a fresh methodology for SSAs (chs. 2–3). In doing so, I will adopt the terminology and concepts "emic" and "etic," while articulating a new configuration of the terms as a model for engaging with the text of Ezekiel.

Three main material chapters (chs. 4–6) will analyze Ezekiel's key terms for honor (כבד), shame (בוש), and guilt (עוה). I will frame this analysis with a broad-sweep analysis of the terms in the body of the OT, to form the "concept spheres" within which the specific instances of each term in Ezekiel sit. At the conclusion of each of these chapters, I will return to the SSA model and reflect on how it informs and is informed by the analysis of Ezekiel just conducted. This will be the sustained pattern for the three main material chapters, although the variations in usage, frequency, and distribution of each key term will be reflected in a slightly different method of analysis in each case. I will examine כבד according to the clausal subject to which it is related, בוש sequentially by instance in Ezekiel, and עוה grouped by the grammatical constructions in which it appears.

Following the main analysis, I will conclude the study by drawing together the implications and contribution of the analysis of Ezekiel and applying them to the development of SSA models into the future (the "derived etic").

One final note is that my method for this study incorporates a particular application of the emic-etic distinction, which is articulated in ch. 2. Given that the main focus of the study is OT, I have removed the original "outer frame" of the thesis, which situated the study within my own contemporary setting (as an Australian within the Reformed, Evangelical Christian tradition), and then concluded by applying its findings to that same setting. However, being aware of and articulating the researcher's own interests is a critical factor in my formulation of emics and etics. As such, I have appended the original introduction and conclusion of the thesis to the end of this study, for the reader's interest (in the terminology I use throughout the study, these would be labeled "emic A" and "emic A1").

Chapter 2

Anthropological Approaches to Biblical Studies: Imposed Etic

Review of SSAs in Biblical Studies

This study seeks to engage with the recent interest in SSA in biblical studies, particularly those utilizing classic anthropological labelling of cultures (individualism/collectivism, guilt/shame), as a hermeneutical key to the Bible.[1] Before embarking on the main study, however, it is worth recognizing that SSAs have long played a key part in critical studies of the OT. Ezek 18, for example, played a central role in the early 20th-century debate over individual vs. corporate judgment in the OT.[2] I will trace the use of SSAs in biblical studies, using Ezek 18 as a case study and springboard into a survey of the more recent SSAs. I will then suggest my own method, which seeks to be critically appreciative of previous study in the area.

"First Wave" SSAs: Ezekiel 18—
Shattering the "Now-Rotten Collectivism"

The Developmental View:
H. Wheeler Robinson and Corporate Personality

At the beginning of the 20th century, H. Wheeler Robinson proposed that the ancients saw themselves in terms of "corporate personality," with

---

1. By "recent," I mean the last 30 or so years, in which social-science methods features heavily in studies of the Bible. Although beginning from works in anthropology, there have also been significant developments in the related disciplines of psychology and sociology. Some significant examples that commonly appear in biblical studies include Clifford Geertz, *The Interpretation of Cultures* (New York: Basic Books, 1973); Charles Taylor, *Sources of the Self: The Making of the Modern Identity* (Cambridge: Harvard University Press, 1989); Thomas J. Scheff, *Microsociology: Discourse, Emotion and Social Structure* (Chicago: University of Chicago Press, 1994); Margaret Mead, *Coming of Age in Samoa: A Study of Adolescence and Sex in Primitive Societies* (Melbourne: Penguin, 1954); Ruth Benedict, *The Chrysanthemum and the Sword: Patterns of Japanese Culture* (Boston: Houghton Mifflin, 1946). It is also worth mentioning at this point, however, that I will also argue that the issues surrounding individualism and collectivism are complex, and there have been several alternatives to the paradigms of the above scholars throughout the last half-century. I will explore the development of the terminology and concepts in the next chapter.

2. A full list of references on the topic is given in Gordon H. Matties, *Ezekiel 18 and the Rhetoric of Moral Discourse* (SBLDS 126. Atlanta: Scholars Press, 1990), 113–14 n. 2.

blessing or judgment experienced in spheres of solidarity; whether in terms of household, tribe, or nation.[3] Over time, however, there grew within Israel an increasing movement or away from corporate personality toward an emphasis on the individual as a moral agent, catalysed especially by the Babylonian Exile.[4]

The figures most strongly associated with this apparent rise of individualism are Jeremiah and Ezekiel. In the face of national collapse, solace was sought in the collectivistic "sour grapes" proverb (Jer 31:29; Ezek 18:2). Indeed, more than solace, it was a veiled accusation of injustice on YHWH's part, or resignation to an immutable, cosmic "cause and effect."[5] The sins of their fathers had caused their expulsion. This attempt to use YHWH's own character against him forced a bold new innovation from the prophets. As von Rad put it, Ezekiel "completely shatters the now rotten collectivism [and] drags the individual out of this anonymity into the light."[6] From now on, one stood or fell not on the basis of the merits of previous generations but individually before God.

Critiques of the Developmental View:
J. R. Porter and John Rogerson

The Developmental View described above lies behind much of mainstream OT scholarship.[7] However, significant critiques have now been

---

3. H. Wheeler Robinson, *The Christian Doctrine of Man* (3rd ed.; Edinburgh: T. & T. Clark, 1926), 8; idem, "The Hebrew Conception of Corporate Personality," in *Werden und Wesen des Alten Testaments: Vorträge gehalten auf der internationalen Tagung alttestamentlicher Forscher zu Göttingen vom 4.–10. September 1935* (ed. P. Volz, F. Stummer, and J. Hempel; BZAW 66; Berlin: de Gruyter, 1936), 49.

4. Considerable effort has gone into examining the exact stimuli for this movement. Besides Robinson, see, for example, I. G. Matthews, *Ezekiel* (AACOT; Philadelphia: American Baptist Publication Society, 1939), xxiii–xxiv; John Merlin Powis Smith, "The Rise of Individualism among the Hebrews," *AJT* 10 (1906): 251–66. Smith suggests that just about every aspect of Judah's existence—social, economic, political, ethical, *and* religious prepared the way for individualism (p. 253). The Exile, however, is especially key, not simply because of Judah's national dissolution, but also because of its resulting contact with the "advanced" Babylonian civilization (p. 261).

5. So Walther Zimmerli, *Ezekiel: A Commentary on the Book of the Prophet Ezekiel, Chapters 1–24* (ed. F. M. Cross et al.; trans. R. E. Clements; Hermeneia; Philadelphia: Fortress, 1979), 378; Rodney R. Hutton, "Are the Parents Still Eating Sour Grapes? Jeremiah's Use of the Māšāl in Contrast to Ezekiel," *CBQ* 71/2 (2009); Daniel I. Block, *The Book of Ezekiel: Chapters 1–24* (Grand Rapids: Eerdmans, 1997), 561. Note that Block rejects the Developmental View, although he sees the proverb as reflective of the Deuteronomistic Historian's view of history.

6. Gerhard von Rad, *Old Testament Theology*, vol. 2: *The Theology of Israel's Prophetic Traditions* (trans. D. G. M. Stalker; San Francisco: Harper & Row, 1965), 394; cf. Matthews, *Ezekiel*, 63: "[Ezekiel 18] is the classic expression of the dogma of individualism."

7. Besides Hutton's article, see the survey in T. Desmond Alexander, *From Paradise to the Promised Land: An Introduction to the Pentateuch* (2nd ed.; Grand Rapids: Baker Academic,

raised on several fronts. In a 1965 article examining OT legal practice, J. R. Porter cast doubt on Robinson's suggestion of "psychical unity," on which corporate personality was founded.[8] Shortly afterwards, John Rogerson extended Porter's critique by highlighting the dependence of Robinson's "corporate personality," on Maine and Lévy-Bruhl's theory of evolutionary development in human society, before subjecting it to devastating critique.

According to the theory, which became dominant in anthropology in the early 20th century, human society evolved from a primitive, prelogical stage, in which one saw oneself simply as part of one's social group, to a more advanced understanding of the self as a discrete, autonomous moral being.[9] Drawing on the work of Evans-Pritchard,[10] Rogerson demonstrates how the problematic assumptions made in this cross-cultural anthropological theory were carried over and imposed on the OT text *a priori*, resulting in Robinson essentially finding what he wanted to find, but only by doing great violence to the biblical evidence he used.[11]

Joel Kaminsky

Joel Kaminsky argues further that the Developmental View is both "historically inaccurate and theologically problematic."[12] He suggests that the strong notions of corporate responsibility, and the lack of pronounced individualism in the postexilic editing of D and the DH, implies "an inappropriate evolutionary bias at work" in the Developmental View.[13] In other words, Kaminsky exposes a cultural elitism inherent to the Developmental

---

2002), 7–61; Baruch Halpern, "Jerusalem and the Lineages in the Seventh Century BCE: Kinship and the Rise of Individual Moral Liability," in *Law and Ideology in Monarchic Israel* (ed. B. Halpern and D. W. Hobson; JSOTSup 124; Sheffield: Sheffield Academic Press, 1991), 11–107; Howard Eilberg-Schwartz, *The Savage in Judaism: an Anthropology of Israelite Religion and Ancient Judaism* (Bloomington: Indiana University Press, 1990).

8. J. R. Porter, "Legal Aspects of the Concept of Corporate Personality in the Old Testament," *VT* 15/3 (1965): 361–80. It should be noted that Porter still held to a form of the Developmental View, but it was his work that largely opened the door for questioning of the foundations of the paradigm. For further comment, see Joel S. Kaminsky, "The Sins of the Fathers: A Theological Investigation of the Biblical Tension between Corporate and Individualized Retribution," *Judaism* 46/3 (1997): 320.

9. J. W. Rogerson, "The Hebrew Conception of Corporate Personality: A Reexamination," *JTS* 21/1 (1970): 1–16; idem, *Anthropology and the Old Testament* (Oxford: Blackwell, 1978), 47; Lucien Lévy-Bruhl, *Primitive Mentality* (trans. L. A. Clare; London: Allen & Unwin, 1923); Henry Sumner Maine and Carleton Kemp Allen, *Ancient Law: Its Connection with the Early History of Society and Its Relation to Modern Ideas* (WC 362; London: Oxford University Press, 1931),

10. E. E. Evans-Pritchard, *Theories of Primitive Religion* (Oxford: Clarendon, 1965).

11. Rogerson, "Hebrew Conception," 13.

12. Kaminsky, "Sins of the Fathers," 322. See also his *Corporate Responsibility in the Hebrew Bible* (Sheffield: Sheffield Academic Press, 1995).

13. Kaminsky sees D anf DH as distinct; ibid., 30–138. Cf Rogerson's review of Wellhausen's dependence on the Developmental View (*Anthropology and the Old Testament*, 27);

View, in its bias toward individualism as the most advanced and moral view of the self.[14] Furthermore, his observation that both individual and corporate outlooks exist in every strata of biblical material is a devastating blow to the foundations of the Developmental View.[15]

Paul Joyce and Gordon Matties

The most concentrated works on Ezekiel 18 in recent times have come from Paul Joyce and Gordon Matties.[16] As the two reach similar conclusions, I will focus on Joyce, who draws heavily on Lindars's distinction between criminal law and divine retribution to suggest the basic logic of the latter: a current situation of adversity implies prior guilt.[17] In light of Judah's attempt to "pass the buck" of responsibility, Ezekiel adapts the language of legal "test-cases" to leave the Judeans with no room to maneuver; there is nowhere to look for blame but themselves.

Importantly, however, Joyce insists that this use of Priestly case-law indicates that Ezekiel is *not* expressing a new individualism. In fact, the chapter reinforces Israel's collective responsibility for the Exile.[18] If anything, the moral independence of *generations*, not individuals, is in view, and the chapter is designed to foster *national, as well as individual*, repentance.[19]

Likewise Sean M. Warner, "Primitive Saga Men," *VT* 29 (1979): 325–35, who finds similar anthropological foundations in Gunkel's dating of oral sources.

14. Kaminsky, "Sins of the Fathers," 325.

15. Kaminsky proposes that the two perspectives on judgment (individual and corporate) are important correctives to each other. For example, he takes Ezek 18 to be an expression of God's "strict justice," which needs softening by recourse to other passages that emphasize God's mercy (ibid., 326). However, the language of "corrective" may be too strong at this point. In the case of Ezek 18, *both* justice *and* mercy feature in Yнwн's treatment of his people and, further, are placed alongside each other quite seamlessly (Ezek 18:19–32). It should also be noted that the passage presents several exegetical difficulties (written in Ezekiel's typical—or perhaps better *a*typical—rambling style; cf. Daniel I. Block, "Text and Emotion: A Study in the 'Corruptions' in Ezekiel's Inaugural Vision (Ezekiel 1:4–28)," *CBQ* 50 (1988): 418–42).

16. Paul Joyce, *Divine Initiative and Human Response in Ezekiel* (Sheffield: JSOT Press, 1989); Matties, *Ezekiel 18*. For more of Joyce's work, including his wider work on collectivism and individualism in the OT, see also Paul Joyce, "The Individual and the Community," in *Beginning Old Testament Study* (ed. J. W. Rogerson; London: SPCK, 1998), 77–93; idem, "Ezekiel and Individual Responsibility," in *Ezekiel and His Book: Textual and Literary Criticism and Their Interrelation* (ed. J. Lust; BETL 74; Leuven: Leuven University Press, 1986), 317–21; idem, "Individual Responsibility in Ezekiel 18?" in *Studia Biblica 1978: Papers on the Old Testament and Related Themes* (ed. E. A. Livingstone; JSOTSup 11; Sheffield: JSOT Press, 1978), 185–96.

17. Ibid., 37–38; cf. Barnabas Lindars, "Ezekiel and Individual Responsibility," *VT* 15 (1965), 452–67.

18. Ibid., 36.

19. Idem, "Individual Responsibility," 194; idem, *Ezekiel: A Commentary* (New York: T. & T. Clark, 2007), 140. Matties seems to prefer a slightly more equally balanced interdependence between individual and generational perspectives in the chapter (*Ezekiel 18*,

The developments of Joyce and Matties are a good point of departure for "first-wave" SSAs on Ezek 18. This is especially because they represent a healthy advance in the use of anthropology in OT studies. Whereas, for older studies, anthropology tended to come to the fore, "distilled" from the text of Ezek 18, newer studies have demonstrated a move toward more chastened and provisional SSAs and attempted an integration of both individual and collective (or community) perspectives present in the text.

"New Wave" SSAs: Exposing Cultural Blinkeredness, Honor, and Shame

SSAs have experienced something of a renaissance since the 1980s, in large part due to the significant work of the Context Group.[20] Though focused primarily on NT studies, there has also been a slow but steady trickle of works investigating the OT.[21] The catalyst for the Context Group's growth was Bruce Malina's 1981 *The New Testament World: Insights from Cultural Anthropology*. I will therefore begin this section with a review of his work before giving briefer reviews of other scholars in the area. In so doing, I will seek first to present the Context Group's work in a positive light, before introducing some voices of caution.

147–49). Antti Laato and Walter Brueggemann have also suggested that the three generations described in vv. 5–19 ought to be taken to describe three of the last kings of Judah—Josiah, Jehoiakim, and Jehoiachin/Jeconiah. Akin to Joyce, Ezek 18 thus leaves the door open for the repentance and restoration of Jehoiachin's generation (A. Laato, *Josiah and David Redivivus: The Historical Josiah and the Messianic Expectations of Exilic and Postexilic Times* [Stockholm: Almqvist & Wiksell, 1992], 358; Brueggemann, *An Introduction to the Old Testament: The Canon and Christian Imagination* [Louisville: Westminster John Knox, 2003], 206–7). In so doing, both follow Herntrich's "historical perspective" on the chapter (Volkmar Herntrich, *Ezechielprobleme* [Giessen: Alfred Topelmann, 1933], 103; cf. Alfred Bertholet, *Das Buch Hesekiel erklärt* [KHZAT 12; Freiburg: Mohr, 1897]). Zimmerli, on the other hand, consciously argues against this sort of reading and suggests a "hypothetical" reading (Zimmerli, *Ezekiel 1–24*, 377; cf. Joyce, *Ezekiel*, 139). Nevertheless, both historical and hypothetical readings also reach the same conclusion—that generational, rather than individual, responsibility is in view.

20. Some representative recent works from the Context Group (besides those I will sepcifically review) include edited volumes from the group: Anselm C. Hagedorn et al. eds., *In Other Words: Essays on Social Science Methods and the New Testament in Honor of Jerome H. Neyrey* (Sheffield: Phoenix Press, 2007); Philip F. Esler, ed., *Ancient Israel: The Old Testament in Its Social Context* (London: SCM, 2006); Bruce J. Malina and John J. Pilch eds., *Social Scientific Models for Interpreting the Bible: Essays by the Context Group in Honor of Bruce J. Malina* (Boston: Brill, 2001). For the origin and development of the Context Group, see Philip F. Esler, "The Context Group Project: An Autobiographical Account," in *Anthropology and Biblical Studies* (ed. L. J. Lawrence and M. I. Aguilar; Leiden: Deo, 2004), 46–61.

21. E.g. Shane Kirkpatrick, *Competing for Honor: A Social-Scientific Reading of Daniel 1–6* (Leiden: Brill, 2005); Timothy S. Laniak, *Shame and Honor in the Book of Esther* (Atlanta: Scholars Press, 1998); Ronald A. Simkins, "'Return to Yahweh': Honor and Shame in Joel," *Semeia* 68 (1994): 41–54.

Bruce Malina

Malina begins by observing that mainstream biblical interpretation has come almost exclusively out of a modern, Western, individualistic world-view, which is very different to the Bible's original cultural context. Thus, cross-cultural comparison must be performed in order to avoid "ethnocentric anachronisms"—imposing modern, individualistic perspectives onto an ancient text that may have meant something completely different in its own social context. [22] Malina's conviction, drawn from the anthropology of John Peristiany and Julian Pitt-Rivers's 1965 volume *Honour and Shame*, is that the biblical world was, and continues to be a "Mediterranean," and, therefore, collectivistic, honor/shame culture. [23]

In societies such as these, the goal of life was the acquiring of honor, defined as "the assertion of worth and the acknowledgment of that worth by others." [24] Honor thus forms a sort of social rating system that guides interactions with others based on one's relative place within social groupings. It is, in the terms Malina uses, a "pivotal value," present in all human interactions. [25] From this basis, Malina puts forward several models, or building blocks, of honor/shame culture:

1. *Anti-Introspective Self*
2. *Agonistic Interaction/Challenge-Riposte*
3. *Limited Good/Zero-Sum Exchange*
4. *Dyadic or Group-Oriented Personality*
5. *Sexual Division of Labor*

---

22. Bruce J. Malina, *The New Testament World: Insights from Cultural Anthropology* (Louisville: Westminster John Knox, 1993), 12. Malina is not the first to recognize this in biblical studies; Krister Stendahl, "The Apostle Paul and the Introspective Conscience of the West," *HTR* 56 (1963): 199–215, for example, is an interesting anticipation of renewed interest in SSAs to biblical studies. The thesis is in fact a variation of Lessing's "ugly, broad ditch," separating modern and ancient worlds; cf. Gotthold Lessing, *Lessing's Theological Writings: Selected and Translated by Henry Chadwick* (ed. and trans. Henry Chadwick; LMRT; Stanford: Stanford University Press, 1957), 55.

23. John G. Peristiany ed. *Honour and Shame: The Values of Mediterranean Society* (London: Weidenfeld & Nicolson, 1965). Malina's modelling of the biblical world also draws on other significant studies in anthropology, most notably, Benedict, *Chrysanthemum and Sword*; Mary Douglas, *Purity and Danger: An Analysis of the Concepts of Pollution and Taboo* (London: Routledge and Kegan Paul, 1966). Two further volumes by Pitt-Rivers and Douglas are also worth mentioning as influential contact points between cultural anthropology and Biblical Studies: Pitt-Rivers, *The Fate of Shechem, or, The Politics of Sex: Essays in the Anthropology of the Mediterranean* (Cambridge: Cambridge University Press, 1977); Mary Douglas, *Leviticus as Literature* (Oxford: Oxford University Press, 1999).

24. Malina, *New Testament World*, 31. Malina gives a fuller explanation of honor as "the socially proper attitudes and behavior in the area where the three lines of power, gender status and religion intersect."

25. Ibid., 28.

It is worth noting at this point that, although Malina reintroduces individualism and collectivism as interpretive keys, his use of the terms is, at least at first glance, appreciably different to first wave, evolutionary SSAs, in two regards. First, great effort is taken to present collectivist cultures in an even-handed light, with the continued urge not to impose contemporary, individualistic perspectives onto the text. Second, where the trend in older studies was to see an evolution from collectivism to individualism, Malina sees collectivism persisting as the dominant Mediterranean "cultural script," from biblical times to the present day.

Zeba Crook

Crook's 2004 *Reconceptualising Conversion* constructs a fresh understanding of the subject from within the conventions of patronage and benefaction. [26] In this light, conversion is best viewed not as an existential/psychological crisis but as the (human) client entering into this sort of relationship with the (divine) benefactor. [27]

Crook's key contribution to this study, however, is his work on the idea of the "Public Court of Reputation" (drawn from Pitt-Rivers's seminal essay; hereafter, PCR). [28] In a subsequent article, Crook suggests that Malina's original model, while largely correct, mistakenly started with the individual in attempting to define honor. [29] In a collectivistic society, however, the actual meaning of honor is completely determined by the PCR, the body that defines and upholds the central value system of the particular social group under consideration. As Crook defines it: "the collectivistic and relentless PCR . . . the first, last and only arbiter of honorable and shameful behavior." [30]

---

26. Zeba A. Crook, *Reconceptualising Conversion: Patronage, Loyalty, and Conversion in the Religions of the Ancient Mediterranean* (BZAW 130; Berlin: de Gruyter, 2004). Crook makes extensive use of Seneca's *De beneficiis* in building his case. See also idem, "Reflections on Culture and Social-Scientific Models," *JBL* 124/3 (2005): 515–20.

27. Crook's work bears some similarity to Mendenhall's classic study of Deuteronomy as a suzerain-vassal treaty; see George E. Mendenhall, *Law and Covenant in Israel and the Ancient Near East* (Pittsburgh: Presbyterian Board of Colportage of Western Pennsylvania, 1955). Crook has also explored the similarities and differences between "patronage" and "covenant" in the ancient world. See further Crook, "Reciprocity: Covenantal Exchange as a Test Case," in *Ancient Israel: The Old Testament in its Social Context* (ed. P. F. Esler; London: SCM, 2005), 78–91.

28. Pitt-Rivers, *Honour and Shame*, 27.

29. Zeba A. Crook, "Honor, Shame, and Social Status Revisited," *JBL* 128/3 (2009), 591–611. The examples Crook lists that render Malina's original model problematic are the variations in exactly what constitutes honor and shame, the participation of women in honor discourses, and interstatus challenges to honor.

30. Crook, "Honor Revisited," 599. Cf. the important work of David Arthur DeSilva on the notion of the PCR: "Despising Shame: A Cultural-Anthropological Investigation of the Epistle to the Hebrews," *JBL* 113/3 (1994): 439–61; idem, *Despising Shame: The Social Function of the Rhetoric of Honor and Dishonor in the Epistle to the Hebrews* (Atlanta: Scholars

Crook then argues that there are several PCRs in any social context (Crook cites the examples of Cynics, Judeans, and Jesus followers), all "competing" for the right to define what honor and shame actually are.[31] This allows one to see that even PCRs that appeal to a divine source nonetheless continue to be fully embedded within the framework of agonistic honor. For Crook, this is the key in solving the problems with the honor and shame model.[32]

The notion of the PCR—or, more accurately, several competing PCRs—is a very important development in the field, one that I will explore at length throughout this study. While I will take issue with Crook's particular articulation of the concept, there is much to commend his work on it, and the insistence that the actual meanings of honor and shame (and, I will argue, guilt) are dependent on the particular "courts of reputation" in play, in any given social setting.

Old Testament Studies by the Context Group

Although the main emphasis of the Context Group's work lies in New Testament studies, there have been a growing number of forays into the Old Testament. Among them are a number of articles in *Semeia* 68 (1996, devoted to social-scientific criticism of the Bible) focused on the OT/HB, as well as an entire later volume of the same journal devoted to "the social world of the Hebrew Bible" (1999).[33] As there have been no major explorations by the Context Group specifically focused on Ezekiel, I will briefly

---

Press, 1996); idem, "Honor and Shame," in *Dictionary of New Testament Background* (ed. C. A. Evans and S. E. Porter; Downers Grove: InterVarsity, 2000); idem, "Honor and Shame," in *Dictionary of the Old Testament: Pentateuch* (ed. D. W. Baker and T. D. Alexander; Downers Grove: InterVarsity, 2003). While DeSilva's work resonates with that of the Context Group in several respects, it also stands apart in significant ways, as exemplified in Malina's strident criticisms of his work. In his review of DeSilva's monograph (Malina, "Review of *Despising Shame: Honor, Discourse, and Community Maintenance in the Epistle to the Hebrews*," *RBL* 116/2 (1997): 378–79) he states, "the author is singularly uninformed when it comes to the social sciences . . . he dabbles in honor and shame sanctions and structures of patronage, but offers no indication of a general understanding of social systems, institutions, and values, much less of the specifics of social sanctions and patronage that form the burden of his contribution."

31. Ibid., 598.

32. Ibid., 610.

33. Ronald A. Simkins, et al., "The Social World of the Hebrew Bible: Twenty-Five Years of the Social Sciences in the Academy," *Semeia* 87 (1999) 123–44. Earlier, Dianne Bergant, "'My Beloved Is Mine and I Am His' (Song 2:16): The Song of Songs and Honor and Shame," *Semeia* 68 (1996): 23–40; Simkins, "Return to Yahweh," *Semeia* 68 (1996): 41–54; Gary Stansell, "Honor and Shame in the David Narratives," *Semeia* 68 (1996): 55–79. Other important studies in the area include Lyn M. Bechtel, "Shame as a Sanction of Social Control in Biblical Israel: Judicial, Political, and Social Shaming," *JSOT* 49 (1991): 47–76; idem, "The Perception of Shame within the Divine-Human Relationship in Biblical Israel," in *Uncovering Ancient Stones: Essays in Memory of H. Neil Richardson* (Winona

review the most relevant for the current project: Timothy Laniak's 1998 exploration of Esther.[34]

Laniak uses the Context Group's honor and shame model in a socioliterary reading of the story, replacing the traditional "sin-judgment-repentance-restoration" pattern with "honor granted-challenged-vindicated-enhanced." Laniak begins with a semantic analysis of כבד as the basic honor root in the OT, in four overlapping "conceptual spheres"—substance, status, splendor and self—then uses these as the sociological categories through which the story of Esther is viewed.

Laniak's major contribution to this study lies in his example of marrying "top-down" (social-scientific) and "bottom-up" (semantic) approaches in refinement of the modelling enterprise. Furthermore, his semantic analysis of יקר/כבד (and its SSA antonym, כלם) is a helpful example of seeking to construct the concept from within the boundaries of the OT itself. I will engage at length with Laniak's semantic analysis of כבד in ch. 4.

Critiques of the Context Group

From the survey above, it is clear that the Context Group's contribution to biblical studies is tremendously important, not only in the application of anthropological methodology to the Bible, but also in the hermeneutical questions it raises and seeks to answer. However, for all the benefit to be had, several scholars have raised significant shortcomings in the Context Group's research. In this section, I will survey four key critiques of the Context Group, before presenting a fresh methodological approach that both appreciates the gains and dangers in the honor and shame model.

Michael Herzfeld

In an important 1980 article, Michael Herzfeld warned of mediterraneanism's two tendencies toward "massive generalisations of 'honor' and

---

Lake, IN: Eisenbrauns, 1994), 79–92; T. M. Lemos, "Shame and Mutilation of Enemies in the Hebrew Bible," *JBL* 125/2 (2006): 225–41.

34. See Laniak, *Shame and Honor in Esther*. For other sustained Context Group studies on the OT, see Kirkpatrick, *Competing for Honor;* Philip F. Esler, *Sex, Wives, and Warriors: Reading Old Testament Narrative with Its Ancient Audience* (Eugene, OR: Cascade, 2011).

There have been some limited explorations of the themes of honor and shame in Ezekiel: e.g., Johanna Stiebert, *The Construction of Shame in the Hebrew Bible: The Prophetic Contribution* (London: Sheffield Academic Press, 2002), 101–12; Margaret S. Odell, "The Inversion of Shame and Forgiveness in Ezekiel 16.59–63," *JSOT* 56 (1992): 101–12; John T. Strong, "Egypt's Shameful Death and the House of Israel's Exodus from Sheol (Ezekiel 32.17–32 and 37.1–14)," *JSOT* 34/4 (2010): 475–504. However, honor and shame themes are usually discussed insofar as they support more primary interests (e.g., the significance of gender issues and presentation, as in S. Tamar Kamionkowski, *Gender Reversal and Cosmic Chaos: A Study on the Book of Ezekiel* (London: Sheffield Academic Press, 2003).

'shame.'"[35] The first was an excessively "top-down" or deductive approach, neglecting significant cultural variations in favor of making studies "fit" the constraints of a generic model.[36] The second was the use of imprecise glosses such as "honor" and "shame" importing and imposing alien meanings onto often-complex, specific native terminology.[37] For Herzfeld, this did not render the enterprise bankrupt, but was a stark warning against the dangers of misleading results from inadequate construction and/or application of models.[38]

Herzfeld's article did not arise in specific response to the work of the Context Group—his article focused on cross-cultural anthropological studies of contemporary Greek-speaking cultures, and, in any case, the first edition of Malina's *New Testament World* did not appear until the following year. However, several scholars have noted that his warnings have by and large gone unheeded by Malina and his associates. As such, the Context Group model of honor and shame has tended to fall prey to Herzfeld's concerns.[39]

---

35. Michael Herzfeld, "Honour and Shame: Problems in the Comparative Analysis of Moral Systems," *Man* 15/2 (1980): 349.

36. Such use of models may be likened to the famous "Procrustean bed," chopping off or stretching the specifics of the evidence to fit the terms and framework of the model.

37. Ibid., 339–40. He illustrates the point using Brögger's study of a south Italian cultural group: "Many of the local terms for moral values correspond closely to English-language cognates: obvious examples include *onore*, *rispetto* and *egoismos* . . . [but they] maintained that honor (*onore*) only concerned the sexual conduct of the female members of the household as reflected on its male members, and they would use the term respect (*rispetto*) in other contexts. This statement only makes sense when we realize that the 'translations' of the Italian terms are unavoidably inexact. South Italian *onore* clearly operates in a manner markedly different from the Victorian English sense of 'honor' as a man's ideal comportment towards unrelated women" (ibid., 340).

38. Ibid., 349.

39. See, for example, the invited responses of anthropologists to the papers in *Semeia* 68: John K. Chance, "The Anthropology of Honor and Shame: Culture, Values, and Practice," *Semeia* 68 (1994): 142; Gideon M. Kressel, "An Anthropologist's Response to the Use of Social Science Models in Biblical Studies," *Semeia* 68 (1994): 159. Chance engages particularly with Jerome Neyrey's paper on the Gospel of John as a clear example of this tendency. See also Yael Avrahami, "בוש in the Psalms: Shame or Disappointment?" *JSOT* 34 (2010): 297; Louise Joy Lawrence, *An Ethnography of the Gospel of Matthew: A Critical Assessment of the Use of the Honor and Shame Model in New Testament Studies* (WUNT 2/165; Tübingen: Mohr Siebeck, 2003), 33; Timothy J. Ling, "Virtuoso Religion and the Judean Social World," in *Anthropology and Biblical Studies: Avenues of Approach* (ed. L. J. Lawrence and M. I. Aguilar; Leiden: Deo, 2004), 227; Markus Bockmuehl, "Review of Bruce Malina, *The New Testament World: Insights from Cultural Anthropology (Third Edition, Revised and Expanded)*," *BMCR* (2002), n.p. [cited 26 August 2011]. Online: http://ccat.sas.upenn.edu/bmcr/2002/2002–04–19.html; Mario I. Aguilar, "Changing Models and the 'Death' of Culture: A Diachronic and Positive Critique of Socio-Scientific Assumptions," in *Anthropology and Biblical Studies*, 310

F. Gerald Downing

In an insightful 1999 article, Downing casts significant doubt on two of the foundational elements of the Context Group's research: first, the supposed all-pervasiveness of honor; second, its indecipherability to Western culture.[40] Downing instead demonstrates both that the honor is only pivotal where it can be shown to be and also that it is a concept quite native to Westerners, albeit perhaps under different terms (such as *respect* or *embarrassment*).[41]

Perhaps the most devastating facet of Downing's critique, however, is his observation that the Context Group's work stands at odds with the very anthropologists the model was generated from.[42] Indeed, in a follow-up publication, Peristiany and Pitt-Rivers make clear how *Honour and Shame* was, in their impression, grossly misapplied. In particular, they objected to conceiving of the Mediterranean as a "culture area," they did not subscribe to the "shame culture/guilt culture" distinction, and they had never intended their specific descriptions of honor and shame in various settings to become a prescriptive model for cultural analysis of the "Mediterranean personality."[43]

Like Herzfeld, however, Downing does not suggest abandoning the method. Instead, he urges for a more cautious use of, built on demonstration, rather than assumption, of honor's primacy.[44] One of my goals, therefore, will be to demonstrate the relative importance or, alternatively, *lack* of importance of honor and shame (and guilt) in the passages examined.

---

40. F. Gerald Downing, "'Honor' among Exegetes," *CBQ* 61 (1999): 55.

41. Downing (pp. 59–60) cites Peristany, "Introduction," in *Honour and Shame* (ed. J. G. Peristiany; London: Weidenfeld & Nicolson, 1965), 10: "some societies make much more constant reference than others to forms of social evaluation." For examples of Western tendencies, see Malina, *New Testament World*, 63–89; Jerome H. Neyrey, *Honor and Shame in the Gospel of Matthew* (Louisville: Westminster John Knox, 1998), 14–34; Philip F. Esler, *The First Christians in Their Social World: Social-Scientific Approaches to New Testament Interpretation* (London: Routledge, 1994), 19–36; Crook, *Reconceptualising Conversion*, 13–52.

42. Ibid., 58–59. See also Chance, "Anthropology of Honor and Shame"; Seth Schwartz, *Were the Jews a Mediterranean Society? Reciprocity and Solidarity in Ancient Judaism* (Princeton: Princeton University Press, 2010), 23–24; Harold W. Attridge, "God in Hebrews," in *The Forgotten God: Perspectives in Biblical Theology. Essays in Honor of Paul J. Achtemeier on the Occasion of His Seventy-Fifth Birthday* (Louisville: Westminster John Knox, 2002), 208. See also Charles E. Carter, "A Discipline in Transition: The Contributions of the Social Sciences to the Study of the Hebrew Bible," in *Community, Identity, and Ideology: Social Science Approaches to the Hebrew Bible* (ed. C. E. Carter and C. L. Meyers; SBTSOTS 6; Winona Lake, IN: Eisenbrauns, 1996), 23–29.

43. John G. Peristiany and Julian Alfred Pitt-Rivers, introduction to *Honor and Grace in Anthropology* (ed. J. G. Peristiany and J. A. Pitt-Rivers; CSSCA 76; Cambridge: Cambridge University Press, 1992), 5–6.

44. Downing, "Honor," 73 (emphasis original).

Louise Lawrence

In her 2002 *An Ethnography of the Gospel of Matthew,* Lawrence identifies three weaknesses in the Context Group's projects: problems with research methodology, problems of an outdated view of culture, and problems of reification.[45] The first and second of these have been discussed in the sections on Herzfeld and Downing. However, it is worth noting her analysis of Pitt-River's typology of honor, which considers the third set of problems.[46]

Lawrence draws on Pitt-Rivers's distinction between two types of honor.[47] "Honor Precedence" correlates to Malina's definition of honor as "ascribed" or "acquired.[48] "Honor Virtue," on the other hand, relates to the individual's internal value system, whether that be conscience, or a divine figure as the ultimate arbiter of honor.[49] This distinction, according to Lawrence, is a key piece in the honor "puzzle" that is missing in the Context Group's conception of honor.[50]

Perhaps the most important contribution Lawrence makes is to highlight Honor Virtue as a distinct value orientation to Honor Precedence.[51]

---

45. Lawrence, *Ethnography of Matthew*, 7–36. Lawrence notes the movement within anthropology away from "culture" as a fixed and definable object of study to a more fluid, dynamic social process. Lawrence does seek to balance her presentation with the caveat that both micro- and macro-scale dynamics are needed. By "reification," Lawrence means the error of treating an abstract concept as though it were a concrete reality.

46. Lawrence, *Ethnography of Matthew*, 29–30; idem, "'For truly, I Tell You, They Have Received Their Reward' (Matt 6:2): Investigating Honor Precedence and Honor Virtue," *CBQ* 64 (2002), 687–702.

47. Julian Alfred Pitt-Rivers, "Honour," in *IESS* (ed. D. Sills and R. Merton; New York: MacMillan, 1968), n.p. [cited October 4 2011]. Online: http://www.encyclopedia.com/doc/1G2–2045000526.

48. Lawrence, *Ethnography of Matthew*, 29.

49. Ibid., 30.

50. Pitt-Rivers does not actually use the term *Honor Virtue* in his *IESS* article (whereas he does use *Honor as Precedence*). The section that Lawrence cites is rather titled "Honor and the Sacred." However, the term as a parallel to *Honor Precedence* is apposite.

51. Crook ("Honor Revisited," 598) takes exception to this distinction, arguing that Honor Virtue is Honor Precedence simply redirected toward a different PCR. His critique, however, is undermined by its syllogistic nature. Crook essentially argues that, because ancient culture was collectivistic, and in a collectivistic society all honor is agonistic, "claims to virtue are fully embedded within an agonistic system of Honor Precendence." In fact, Crook's statement demonstrates exactly the weakness in the Context Group's methodology that Lawrence points out—the inability, almost in principle, for anything to lie outside, or contradict, the abstract model. From a slightly different perspective, this sort of view, in effect, sees theology simply as a subset of anthropology. For an analysis and critique of this view, see Kevin Vanhoozer, "Human Being, Individual and Social," in *The Cambridge Companion to Christian Doctrine* (ed. C. E. Gunton; Cambridge: Cambridge University Press, 1997), 158–88 (see esp. 159). See also the sustained debate between Lawrence and Crook on the issue: Louise Joy Lawrence, "Structure, Agency and Ideology: a Response to Zeba Crook," *JSNT* 29 (2007): 277–86; Zeba A. Crook, "Structure

The effect of this is to legitimate—perhaps even necessitate—a move beyond anthropology alone, to include *theology*, in articulating a biblical document's presentation of honor. This is especially so in the light of Peristiany and Pitt-Rivers' argument that anthropological study of honor must move beyond itself to deal with the sacred, and, in particular, the notion of (divine) grace.[52] As such, Lawrence's recognition of a unique and transcendent *Divine* Court of Reputation is highly appropriate.

To extend Lawrence's point further, for the purposes of this study, it should also be noted that Herzfeld's call for specificity applies also to theology. The distinctions in ancient conceptions of deity are well documented, as are the resulting theology and ethics of those cultural groups.[53] As such, merely to include "the divine" in a formulation of Honor Virtue is insufficient. Instead, the specific character and relationship of the divine figure(s) to the cultural group involved also needs careful articulation. This is especially so for Ezekiel, whose presentation of Yhwh's character is often claimed to be at odds with "mainstream Yahwism." Discussion of Ezekiel's continuity and discontinuity with the rest of the OT, then, will form a significant part of this study.

Johanna Stiebert

In her 2002 revised doctoral thesis, Johanna Stiebert criticizes Context Group scholars for privileging the social dimension of shame and argues that psychological considerations are an integral part of honor and shame

---

Versus Agency in Studies of the Biblical Social World: Engaging with Louise Lawrence," *JSNT* 29 (2007): 251–75; idem, "Method and Models in New Testament Interpretation: A Critical Engagement with Louise Lawrence's Literary Ethnography," *RelSRev* 32 (2006): 87–97.

52. Compare: "It is above all its relation to the ultimate source of the sacred within each individual that brings honor into the religious sphere" (Peristiany and Pitt-Rivers, introduction, 2).

53. See John H. Walton, *Ancient Near Eastern Thought and the Old Testament: Introducing the Conceptual World of the Hebrew Bible* (Nottingham: Apollos, 2007); Mark S. Smith, *The Origins of Biblical Monotheism: Israel's Polytheistic Background and the Ugaritic Texts* (New York: Oxford University Press, 2001); Robert Karl Gnuse, *No Other Gods: Emergent Monotheism in Israel* (JSOTSup 241; Sheffield: Sheffield Academic Press, 1997); Louis H. Feldman, "Jewish Proselytism," in *Eusebius, Christianity and Judaism* (ed. H. W. Attridge and G. Hata; Detroit: Wayne States University Press, 1992); John H. Walton, *Ancient Israelite Literature in Its Cultural Context: A Study of Parallels between Biblical and Ancient Near Eastern Texts* (Grand Rapids: Zondervan, 1989); Herbert Brichto, *The Names of God: Poetic Readings in Biblical Beginnings* (New York: Oxford University Press, 1998); Molly Whittaker, *Jews and Christians: Graeco-Roman Views* (Cambridge: Cambridge University Press, 1984); Gerhard F. Hasel, "Polemic Nature of the Genesis Cosmology," *EQ* 46 (1974): 81–102; Richard S. Hess, *Israelite Religions: An Archaeological and Biblical Survey* (Grand Rapids: Baker Academic, 2007); Augustine, *The City of God* (trans. M. Dods; Peabody, MA: Hendrickson, 2009).

in the Bible.[54] Stiebert raises the impact of theology and ideology on SSA and argues that a gaping hole in these studies is the character of YHWH and his impact on the model.[55] For Stiebert, YHWH is both the source of honor and the generator of shame in the prophets, which makes him "difficult to accommodate" in the model.[56] I will extend this theological critique especially in my analysis of כבד in ch. 4.

With regard to ideology, Stiebert takes a strongly poststructuralist view on the opacity of the provenance and cultural context of the biblical texts.[57] Following R. P. Carroll, she criticizes overconfident claims of reconstructing original social settings and instead urges an acknowledgment of personal bias (that is, ideology) in research as a more fruitful way forward in scholarship.[58]

Stiebert's conclusion is a helpful reminder of the difficulty in recovering the "original" prophet, author, text, community, and so on, and exposes the tendency of many Context Group scholars to speak far too easily and confidently of the ability of the honor/shame model to reconstruct biblical culture accurately. On the other hand, the radical poststructuralism that she advocates may be overstated and may not actually reflect the conclusions she herself presents.[59] I will engage with the interface between text and history and the extent to which we may speak of the "native" meaning of the text in the outline of my own method later in this chapter.

Yael Avrahami

In her 2010 *JSOT* article, Avrahami takes up Herzfeld's call for terminological precision in response to the Context Group.[60] She undertakes

---

54. Stiebert, *Construction of Shame*. For studies on the evidence for the psychological dimension of human thought and activity in the OT, see Barbara M. Leung Lai, *Through the 'I'-Window: The Inner Life of Characters in the Hebrew Bible* (HBM 34; Sheffield: Phoenix, 2011); Michael Carasik, *Theologies of the Mind in Biblical Israel* (New York: Peter Lang, 2005).

55. Stiebert, *Construction of Shame*, 84.

56. Ibid., 108.

57. Ibid., 2–3.

58. Stiebert, *Construction of Shame*, 111; cf Robert P. Carroll, "The Myth of the Empty Land," *Semeia* 59 (1992): 79–93; idem, "Textual Strategies and Ideology in the Second Temple Period," in *Second Temple Studies*: vol. 1: *Persian Period* (ed. P. R. Davies; JSOTSup 117; Sheffield: JSOT Press, 1991), 108–24.

59. Stiebert, for example, cites Beardslee in advocating "the futility of reconstruction": "[Poststructuralism's] function is rather to lead readers to live without absolutes, in a world of processes that is not directed toward a goal." Cf. William A. Beardslee, "Poststructuralist Criticism," in *To Each Its Own Meaning: An Introduction to Biblical Criticisms and Their Applications* (ed. S. R. Haynes and S. L. McKenzie; Louisville: Westminster John Knox, 1993).

60. "[Context Group] scholars do not attempt to explain the nuanced 'shame roots', or the possible contrbution of such explanation to the understanding of the alleged cultural notions of honor and shame"; Avrahami, "בוש in the Psalms," 297.

a thorough semantic study of the instances of the root בוש (the predominant shame root in SSAs) in the psalms, emphasizing immediate context and semantic field over comparative philology.[61] Beginning with a broad analysis of synonyms and antonyms, followed by examination of the root's use in several psalms, Avrahami concludes: "the meaning of בוש has to do with the experience of a disconnection between experience and reality. בוש is avoided when reality matches expectations. In other words, בוש is the experience (or causing) of disappointment."[62]

Avrahami draws two important implications from her study. First, the meaning of בוש as "disappointment" is much broader than "shame." She thus cautions against too quickly translating instances as "shame," with all its contemporary anthropological and/or psychological baggage. Second, there are actually no honor roots that appear in as a direct synonym or antonym to בוש in the OT. Avrahami does note that "worthlessness" (the wider semantic field to which בוש belongs) is an antonym to כבד, and "through this contrast that בוש is indirectly linked with honor."[63] However, the lack of specific instances in which the two are directly related raises signifcant doubt over the binary contrast between honor and shame in the OT.[64]

Avrahami's critique is an excellent example of how the evidence that may be derived from the text "pushes back" against the contemporary models with which the text is approached. This is an important inclusion in developing a more satisfying SSA than the honor/shame model, and I will seek to incorporate it into the approach of this study.

Seth Schwartz

In his 2012 *Were the Jews a Mediterranean Society?* Schwartz launches a stinging critique against the Context Group's "clumsy" appropriation of Mediterranean cultural anthropology.[65] Schwartz further argues that the Torah's prescriptions, social, and ethical injunctions "constitute Mediterraneanism's nearly perfect antithesis." YHWH, the possessor of true honor, was the only one to whom the Israelites were to relate by bonds of dependence. Thus, solidarity, rather than reciprocity (the foundation of mediterraneanism) was to characterize Jewish society.[66]

However, for Schwartz, these significant weaknesses do not discount the value of these studies as a heuristic tool, "offering fuel for structural comparison."[67] Schwartz's own method is to view the honor/shame con-

---

61. Ibid., 299.
62. Ibid., 308.
63. Ibid., 302.
64. Ibid., 303.
65. Schwartz, *Mediterranean People*, 23–24. Schwartz is referring to *Honour and Shame*.
66. Schwartz, *Mediterranean People*, 26–27.
67. Ibid., 24–25. Schwartz also says, "Let me state matters more strongly: for anyone working on the social and cultural history of the ancient Jews, mediterraneanism cannot be ignored" (p. 22).

struct as a Weberian ideal type, against which the continuity and discontinuity of actual situations (as described in literature), may be assessed.[68] Indeed, Schwartz's final position is that reciprocity- and solidarity-based norms, "though in principle opposed to one another, in practice were interdependent."[69]

Schwartz concludes by suggesting that, in these investigations of cultural groups through their literature, anthropology and hermeneutics are both indispensible and inseparable.[70] (Social) history is more complex than an abstract model can capture, so rather than squeezing the evidence to fit the mold, a better strategy is to let the evidence stand out in stark relief against the model. To illustrate: if the modeling process adopted by the Context Group can be likened to a shape-sorter, whereby finding the right "mold" allows the pieces to proceed, perhaps Schwartz's approach is more like a "spot the difference" page: the model provides an incomplete template against which to observe both similarities and differences.[71] This sort of approach allows us to move from abstract models to examination of wider evidence in more accurately giving account of historical realities.

Schwartz is very aware of the dangers of naive historical positivism and admits that getting at "real history" is a very difficult thing, given the paucity of archaeological evidence available to us. As a result, he comes to a sober, and critical conclusion: that texts are themselves historical artifacts and so must form an integral part of historical investigation. However, because of their nature *as* texts, the hermeneutic processes involved in approaching them must also be taken seriously. By treading carefully between a naive historical positivism and a blanket scepticism regarding ancient texts, a more fruitful use of them may be made in historical investigation.[72]

Honor and Shame:
Initial Gains and Dangers in the Model

Initial Gains in the Model

It is helpful to pause and summarize the discussion so far. The literature review demonstrates that there are both great gains and dangers in SSAs utilizing the honor/shame model. In terms of gains, I suggest three main benefits. First, and most broadly, these studies have elucidated how an alternative model of social organization (individualistic vs. group oriented) can challenge the assumed meanings and significance of words and actions

---

68. Schwartz's primary texts are Ben Sira, Josephus, and the Jerusalem Talmud.

69. Ibid., 29–30.

70. Ibid., 166.

71. I apologize if this example seems a little facetious, but as the father of three young children, one of my significant cultural contexts is the world of children's toys and activities, and the parallel seems rather apt. It is also interesting to note the extent to which academia can sometimes resemble toddlerhood!

72. Ibid., 175–76.

in the biblical documents.[73] Second, the Context Group has raised awareness of the importance of honor, or social worth, in human life. This is a
good corrective to the philosophical individualism that can undergird much
biblical research, and highlights the emphasis on relationships in biblical
material. Third, the Context Group has helpfully articulated the "distance"
between the modern researcher and the ancient world they study. This distinction between "outsider" and "insider" perspectives (in technical terms,
etic and emic) can enable researchers to become observant of their own
part in the process of interpretation and, hopefully, further foster honest,
open, and more accurate scholarship.

Initial Dangers in the Model

On the other hand, some major flaws in method and application have
been identified, which need to be heeded. First, there is a tendency for the
model to be applied deterministically, with little regard for significant variation in indigenous terminology and conceptuality. Second, there is also a
tendency to excessive separation between modern and ancient worlds, rendering the latter virtually incomprehensible without the lens of the honor/
shame model. Third, there is a lack of attention to the place that YHWH
occupies within (and outside) the human honor/shame system, and what
impact this has on the application of the model to biblical documents.

There are some further associated weaknesses to the Context Group's
work that are worth mentioning as a bridge to moving forward in the area.[74]
Fourth, then, some studies assert, rather than argue for, the validity and in-
dispensability of the model for biblical interpretation, and demonstrate a
frustrating lack of serious engagement with criticism.[75] Laniak, for example,
names several critics but fails almost entirely to address their concerns.[76]
His only statement is the puzzling inference, "to the concern of Lever and
Herzfeld that the umbrella term 'honor' is too ambiguous, we must con-
tend that the biblical counterpart כבד is even *more* elastic and multivalent."[77]

---

73. See John H. Elliott, "On Wooing Crocodiles for Fun and Profit: Confessions of
an Intact Admirer," in *Social Scientific Models for Interpreting the Bible: Essays by the Context
Group in Honor of Bruce J. Malina* (ed. B. J. Malina and J. J. Pilch; Leiden: Brill, 2001), 11–12;
Crook, *Reconceptualising Conversion*, 199–250, on the meaning of πίστις as "fidelity" rather
than the more traditional "faith."

74. Although this list is somewhat distinct from the initial three points, for the sake
of clarity I will continue the enumeration, rather than beginning it again.

75. E.g., P. J. Botha, "Isaiah 37.21–35: Sennacherib's Siege of Jerusalem as a Challenge
to the Honour of Yahweh," *OTE* 13 (2000): 279: "[The honor/shame model is] a *sine qua
non* for understanding . . . almost every chapter of the entire Old Testament."

76. Laniak cites Herzfeld and Kressel; and Unni Wikan, "Shame and Honour: A Con-
testable Pair," *Man* 19/4 (1984): 635–52; Bertram Wyatt-Brown, *Southern Honor: Ethics and
Behavior in the Old South* (New York: Oxford University Press, 1982); A. W. H. Adkins,
Merit and Responsibility: A Study in Greek Values (Oxford: Clarendon, 1960).

77. Laniak, *Shame and Honor in Esther*, 31–32. See also Kirkpatrick, *Competing for*

This, however, effectively hands the problem Herzfeld raised straight back to him as if it were the solution!

Fifth, even when some concession to critiques is given, the impact that this has on the application of the system seems at best superficial.[78] Crook, for example, acknowledges that anthropological study has now recognized the false dichotomy between structure and agency.[79] However, his conclusion reverts to the default view of the ancient Mediterranean as "a collectivistic culture (as opposed to an individualistic one)," which operates on "mostly structure" and thus completely minimizes any sense of the dialectic so tantalisingly raised mere paragraphs before.[80]

The sixth, final weakness in the Context Group's work that I will draw attention to here comes in their use of the terms *emic* and *etic*. In the predominant Context Group usage, the etic perspective is taken to be the "modern, Western individualistic" outlook, while the emic perspective is the "ancient, Mediterranean collectivistic" outlook.[81] However, the concepts and terms are complex, and require fuller and more careful formulation. To this task I now turn.

Emics and Etics: Method for the Study

Emics, Etics, and the Importance of Clarity

The emic/etic distinction is terminology developed and coined by linguist Kenneth Pike and popularized in anthropology especially by Marvin Harris.[82] Márta Cserháti gives an excellent summary of the distinctives:

> The terms "etic" and "emic" . . . are indeed the truncated versions of the distinctive linguistic categories phonemic and phonetic. A phonemic analysis examines the significant sounds in a given language, those complex sounds that differentiate meaning in the language and build up the words of the language. The phonetic representation of the sound units in a given language is a system of cross-culturally useful notations based on an outsider's attempt to transcribe and compare these sounds in relation to a system of written characters

---

Honor, 27, who notes Chance, Kressel, and Downing's critiques but simply moves on to his analysis without comment or engagement.

78. E.g., Esler, *Sex, Wives and Warriors*, 35–76; Strong, "Egypt's Shameful Death," 476. Esler has given the most sustained and balanced interaction with critics of the Context Group, but though he concedes several points of weakness in the model, his analysis is largely unaffected and the model remains unchanged after analysis.

79. Crook, *Reconceptualising Conversion*, 256.

80. Ibid.

81. E.g. Jerome H. Neyrey, *Paul, in Other Words: A Cultural Reading of His Letters* (Louisville: Westminster John Knox, 1990), 12.

82. Kenneth L. Pike, *Language in Relation to a Unified Theory of the Structure of Human Behaviour* (JLSM 24; The Hague: Mouton, 1971); Marvin Harris, *Cultural Materialism: The Struggle for a Science of Culture* (New York: Random House, 1979). For a more recent survey of the field, see also Kenneth L. Pike, et al., *Emics and Etics: The Insider/Outsider Debate* (FA 7; Newbury Park: Sage, 1990).

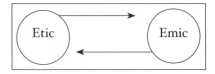

Fig. 1. Cserháti's etic-emic schema.

that can be used in the study of all languages. According to Pike, the "etic viewpoint studies behavior as from outside of a particular system, the emic viewpoint results from studying behavior as from inside the system."[83]

The application to anthropological study of the Bible is immediately apparent and offers researchers a manner of clarifying and potentially overcoming ethnocentric blind spots in approaching biblical interpretation that is both clear and profound.

At first glance, privileging an emic approach (as Pike advocated) would seem to be the preferred option for biblical researchers to gain "closer" access to the meaning of the Bible. Neyrey, for example, suggests that we can avoid naively imposing modern, Western values onto the biblical documents, by attempting to enter the native thought and culture in which the texts were written.[84]

However, while the sentiment is correct, the issue is not so simple. As Cserháti cautions, without an etic "control," readings can be equally naive, trapped within a possibly erroneous construct. Thus, emic and etic are in fact complementary perspectives: the emic seeks to investigate the particularities of an individual culture, while the etic seeks to discern regularities across cultures that enable fruitful comparison.[85]

Cserháti concedes that "etics" are in reality the emic perspective of the scientific community.[86] However, she defends the use of "science" as a useful tool for accountability and proposes that, by oscillating between emic and etic perspectives, a fruitful "derived etic" can be attained from the comparison.[87]

This discussion highlights the care needed, with the underlying theories in science, anthropology, and theology needing clarification.[88] A basic ex-

83. Márta Cserháti, "The Insider/Outsider Debate and the Study of the Bible," *CV* 50/3 (2008): 314.

84. Neyrey, *Paul, in Other Words*, 13; cf. Crook, *Reconceptualising Conversion*, 51; Marcus J. Borg and N. T. Wright, *The Meaning of Jesus: Two Visions* (San Francisco: Harper, 1998), 226.

85. Cserháti, "The Insider/Outsider Debate," 317.

86. Ibid., 315, 319. Cserháti engages particularly at this point with the work of John Milbank, *Theology and Social Theory: Beyond Secular Reason* (Oxford: Blackwell, 2006), 110. For a humorous illustration of the emics of the scientific community, see Frederick Crews, *The Pooh Perplex* (Chicago: University of Chicago Press, 2003); idem, *Postmodern Pooh* (Evanstone: Northwestern University Press, 2006).

87. Cserháti, "The Insider/Outsider Debate," 320.

88. This is the point of Craffert's insightful article on the subject; Pieter F. Craffert, "Is the Emic-Etic Distinction a Useful Tool for Cross-cultural Interpretation of the New

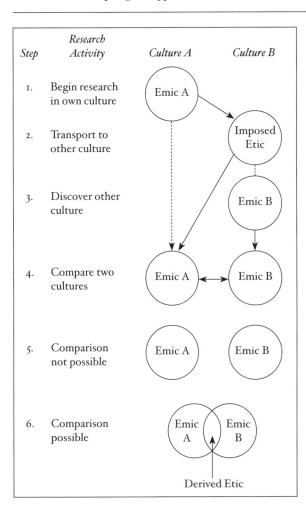

Fig. 2. Berry's derived etic.

ample of this is the need to distinguish, but not polarize, the key terms. As Cserháti notes, "both etic and emic can be either subjective or objective; nor is it identical to the insider/outsider dichotomy, because insiders of a culture can be at the same time observers, while not all outsiders are observers at the same time."[89]

Given the above discussion, I suggest that SSAs may be advanced by including not simply an acknowledgement but an *incorporation* of the

Testament," *RT* 2 (1995): 14–37. Craffert traces the history of the terms in an effort to uncover the various philosophical and methodological presuppositions that lie behind their usage in differing historical contexts and debates. The warning is helpful and is indicative of a wider concern for self-awareness and criticism as the tools are used.

89. Cserháti, "The Insider/Outsider Debate," 315. See also the discussion on terminology and usage between Pike and Harris in *Emics and Etics*, 13–83.

researcher's own emic perspective into the research process. It is insufficient to speak simply of etic and emic as dichotomous approaches, or even as two extremes of a continuum, between which we oscillate.[90] Cserháti in fact touches on where progress can be made at two points, although she does not pursue them in the article.

The first is the more trivial and can be dealt with briefly. Where Cserháti advocates "oscillation" between emic and etic, I suggest "recursion" as a better choice of terms. The reasons for this are that there are more than two perspectives that need to be acknowledged (as stated above), and that the research process may be seen as a repeated, operationalized procedure (as argued below), in which the best parallel to oscillation is recursion.[91]

The second point, therefore, is the recognition that the researcher undertakes their study from within their own emic point of view, complete with interests, sensitivities, and blindspots that are particular to their own subculture.[92] As such, where Cserháti's schema could be represented diagramatically as in fig. 1, a more accurate depiction would include *two* emic perspectives: *both* that of the researcher *and* that of the entity being researched. Cserháti implicitly acknowledge this in using the term *derived etic*, developed by John Berry.[93] Berry's research is especially helpful with regard to this study, and so I will briefly review his work, before developing it for use in my own model.

The Contribution of J. W. Berry to Cross-Cultural Comparison

According to Berry, a "derived etic" is to be distinguished from an "imposed etic."[94] Key to this, however, is this recognition of two emics: the researcher's own culture and that of the object of study. Berry's representation of this can be seen in fig. 2.[95] My contention is that the inclusion of the researcher's own cultural perspective and self-interest is a necessary but heretofore largely missing factor in the Context Group's work on honor and shame.

---

90. As Hymes suggests in Dell H. Hymes, "Emics, Etics, and Openness: An Ecumenical Approach," in Pike et al., *Emics and Etics*, 120–26.

91. As the distinction may not be immediately apparent, I should clarify what I mean by each term. By "oscillation," I mean the common understanding of a sustained back-and-forth movement between two positions, as suggested by Cserháti. My use of recursion is drawn from its meaning, for example, in computer programming. A recursive program contains a looping procedure, which repeats several times before supplying a final result. Consider, for example, a program that is designed to give the sum of the numbers leading up to a user-inputted number; if the user enters 3, the program will begin at 3, then add 2, then 1, to give the result 6.

92. Cserháti, "The Insider/Outsider Debate," 319.

93. Ibid., 320.

94. J. W. Berry, "Imposed Etics-Emics-Derived Etics: The Operationalization of a Compelling Idea," *IJP* 24 (1989): 721–35.

95. Ibid., 730.

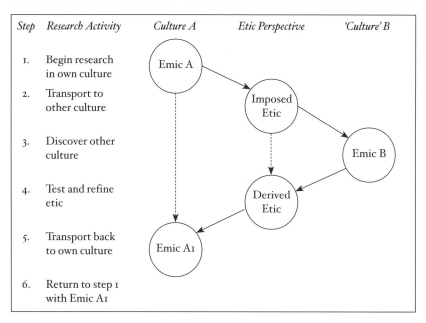

Step	Research Activity	Culture A	Etic Perspective	'Culture' B
1.	Begin research in own culture			
2.	Transport to other culture			
3.	Discover other culture			
4.	Test and refine etic			
5.	Transport back to own culture			
6.	Return to step 1 with Emic A1			

Fig. 3. Modified version of Berry's derived etic.

It should be noted that Berry's model is drawn from the area of cross-cultural analysis, primarily with regard to cultures that are contemporary and accessible to the researcher: their own, and the other.[96] Obviously, a more satisfying cross-*cultural* analysis would include more than textual evidence; to use Geertz's term, it would involve a "thick" description. Biblical studies SSAs thus encounter particular challenges, because we lack access to most of the "thickness" of a living culture.[97]

As such, because the window into "the biblical world" is the biblical text itself, our SSA models must be at the same time more limited (because we do not have the same breadth of data to draw on), and broader (because we have both more tools to analyze texts than anthropological categories alone, and also potentially proceed from differing presuppositional and methodological principles) than those of cross-cultural anthropology in general.[98] My contention is that models must therefore revolve primarily

96. Or, more accurately, drawn from linguistics as a sub-branch of anthropology.

97. An interesting parallel to this can be seen in step 5 of Berry's diagram. In the case of cross-cultural analysis, there may be cultures that are so unlike each other that a fruitful comparison of concepts or the like is not possible.

98. There are, of course, difficulties in accessing the sociohistorical realities of "the biblical world" (Which? When? Whose?)—hence the quotation marks. This is especially so when one takes into account the rise of "ideological criticism" in recent times (although this area too is fraught with difficulty); see further James Barr, *History and Ideology*

around literary study of the Bible as an artifact of an ancient culture, if we are to have a robust attempt at an emic view of the text and, consequently, be open to a truly "derived" etic.[99]

Thus, while we necessarily begin with imposed etic cultural models, they must be able to be rigorously tested within the matrix of literary study. The deductive model must at some point "sit under" the inductive process of contextual-semantic exegesis, otherwise the "etic" is as much a closed hermeneutic circle as the "purely" emic approach, and remains an imposition on the text, rather than a genuine derivation from it.

Developing Berry's Framework for Cross-Cultural Comparison

In this regard, a modified version of Berry's operationalization, suitable for SSAs, may be suggested as follows (fig. 3).[100] The researcher begins from within their own culture (step 1) and uses the tools and concepts from their emic perspective (emic A) to formulate an initial/imposed etic (step 2). The imposed etic is then brought to bear on the biblical text, as a means of attempting to come as close to the meaning indigenous to the text as possible (step 3). However, as the text is analyzed and understood "in its own terms" (emic B), the imposed etic is modified, or perhaps even discarded in favor of a derived etic that reflects a more accurate understanding of the other culture (step 4). Finally, the derived etic is applied to the researcher's own emic and variously affects, confirms, contradicts, and nuances their original perspective (emic A1). This modified perspective is then "carried over" to become the initial "emic A" in the subsequent iteration of the research process.

---

in the Old Testament: Biblical Studies at the End of the Millennium (Oxford: Oxford University Press, 2000); Tina Pippin, "Ideology, Ideological Criticism, and the Bible," *CurBS* 4 (1996) 51–78; and the interchange between Davies and Watson in Philip R. Davies, *Whose Bible Is It Anyway?* (London: T. & T. Clark, 2004); Francis Watson, "Bible, Theology and the University: A Response to Philip Davies," *JSOT* 71 (1996): 3–16. Perhaps, given the literary nature of the artifact, it may be better to speak of the thought-world (or worlds) of the author/redactor/community/canon.

99. I am aware that I am adopting a certain view of texts and history that may not be shared by all. However, as Berry has helpfully put it, "unless one subscribes to total subjectivity in science (e.g., 'You have to be one to understand one'), there is always the possibility that an outsider can eventually 'discover native principles' and 'grasp the native's point of view'. . . . If this position is accepted, then a researcher is in a position to do emic work" (Berry, "Imposed Etics," 289). For a more philosophical approach to a similar question, see William A. Dembski, "The Fallacy of Contextualism," *Themelios* 20 (1995): 8–11.

100. There may be wider application than biblical studies. For example, it may be potentially fruitful in exploring the relationship between systematic theology and exegesis. In fact, the process is fairly generic and could be used across a broad spectrum of research.

A key contribution of conceptualizing the research process in such a way can be seen in light of statements by some SSA scholars, equating "individualism" or "psychological categories" with "etic," and "collectivism" or the honor/shame model with "emic."[101] Review of their work, however, has demonstrated that the honor/shame model cannot be equated with emic B. It is, rather, an alternative imposed etic, generated from the emic A of a researcher who has incoporated cross-cultural anthropology into their own framework. In fact, in several respects the very concept of an emic view of an ancient culture is an artificial construct, given that there are no real participants to observe, assess, or confirm its accuracy.[102]

Despite this caveat, it is still useful to retain the term *emic*, and the ideal that lies behind it. McCutcheon's clarification is helpful: emic B is not so much an insider's *actual* views but rather an outsider's attempt to reproduce, as faithfully as possible, a native's own descriptions of their production of sounds, behavior, beliefs, meanings and so on.[103] This sort of definition preserves the "otherness"—in a positive sense—of the text over the researcher, and thus upholds the communicative intent of its author/community, as worth pursuing as an entity in its own right.[104]

At this point, of course, we enter the realms of ideological criticism, with which I will briefly engage in due course, under the categories of "coherence" and "correspondence."[105] However, it is sufficient to note for now, following Renz, that there are both a solid sociohistorical setting for much of Ezekiel (the book) within the community of second-generation

---

101. E.g., Neyrey, Crook and Wright, as discussed above.

102. Cf Russell T. McCutcheon, *Studying Religion: An Introduction* (London: Equinox, 2007), 51–53.

103. Ibid.

104. As Schwartz notes on investigating ancient texts, "the historicity of the tale is debatable, the fact that someone told it, fixed its form, and eventually wrote it down is not: it is true by definition, and so constitutes a much firmer foundation for the production of a historical account than either positivistic investment in the story's truth or blanket skepticism about it" (Schwartz, *Mediterranean People*, 175). Schwartz's argument here may also assist in a chastened reconstruction of the idea of "original meaning," or "authorial intent," which has been so effectively questioned in postmodern philosophy; e.g., Friedrich Wilhelm Nietzsche, et al., *The Will to Power* (New York: Vintage Books, 1968); Stanley Fish, *Is There a Text in This Class? The Authority of Interpretive Communities* (Cambridge: Harvard University Press, 1980); Jacques Derrida and John D. Caputo, *Deconstruction in a Nutshell: A Conversation with Jacques Derrida* (New York: Fordham University Press, 1996); Jacques Derrida, *Of Grammatology* (Baltimore: Johns Hopkins University Press, 1998); Michel Foucault et al., *The Politics of Truth* (New York: Semiotext(e), 1997). For one commendable attempt at such an exercise, see Kevin Vanhoozer, *Is There a Meaning in This Text? The Bible, the Reader, and the Morality of Literary Knowledge* (Grand Rapids: Zondervan, 1998).

105. For an introduction to the issues involved, see Barr, *History and Ideology*; David J. A. Clines, *Interested Parties: The Ideology of Writers and Readers of the Hebrew Bible* (JSOTSup 205; Sheffield: Sheffield Academic Press, 1995).

Babylonian deportees and a discernible rhetorical function to the final form of the book accepted as authoritative by the canonical community.[106] In other words, there are both correspondence and coherence aspects in the text of the book itself that enable us to speak about the emic perspective of the book with more precision than if one or both were less apparent.

What is required to construct a solid attempt at emic B, then, is:

1. A clear articulation of the model used and its terminology
2. Sound justification of the that make up the approximation of emic B
3. A willingness to let the evidence break and reform the initial model
4. An acknowledgement of the limiting factors involved in the particular study

Conceptualizing the process of biblical research as per fig. 3 is helpful in several respects. First, acknowledged incorporation of the researcher's biases and self-interests should be an integral part of a robust SSA. While self-interest has sometimes (with good reason) been seen as a hindrance to scholarship, this is not inevitable.[107] A proper inclusion of self-interest in the research process (emic A), potentially allows researchers to be more open to critique and dialogue, aware that there will be limits, blind spots and weaknesses in their own perspective, while also recognizing that they may be perceptive to the same in others.[108]

Second, recognizing the provisionality of the imposed etic used to access the biblical text can foster a genuine attempt to *under*-stand the object of study. In other words, an imposed etic with its own inbuilt "breakability" can foster a more deliberate attempt to approach the text on its own terms, as far as possible, in the hope that a more accurate model (derived etic) may emerge on the other side of the process.

Third, the final step in the diagram highlights and seeks to include the postmodern revival of the pragmatic aspect of "truth."[109] Particularly key here is the notion that legitimate interpretation of a text *includes its utility by the reader/reading community*.[110] Furthermore, this utility may well differ

---

106. Ibid., 1, 9–11, 249.

107. E.g., Davies' argument against "faithism" in the academy (*Whose Bible?* esp. chs. 1 and 2).

108. In its original form, I articulated the emic A and emic A1 of this study (i.e., the initial self-interests that drove me to it, and the resulting modifications to them) as the introduction and conclusion to the dissertation. This was a self-conscious attempt to step through my own methodological model. In its current form, these have been integrated into a single appendix, following the main SSA study.

109. One thinks of Richard Rorty's famous summary of truth as "the way we do things around here"; cited in Charles Taylor, "Rorty and Philosophy," in *Richard Rorty* (ed. Charles Guignon and David R. Hiley; Cambridge: Cambridge University Press, 2003), 179.

110. See further George Lindbeck, *The Nature of Doctrine: Religion and Theology in a Postliberal Age* (Philadelphia: Westminster, 1984); Kevin Vanhoozer, *The Drama of Doctrine: A Canonical-Linguistic Approach to Christian Theology* (Louisville: Westminster John Knox, 2005).

from interpreter to interpreter, according to their respective self-interests, and even differing occasions.[111]

For example, one may read a Jane Austen novel in order to analyze a certain literary device used, as an expression of the social concerns of a certain period of history, or to explore the nature of romance. All could be scholarly studies of Jane Austen, and yet they each approach the text with a different initial framework (imposed etic) which in turn restricts (or focuses) the data scrutinized to access the original meaning (emic B) of the text, according to their respective interests. Likewise, the derived etics (appreciation for the literary device, discussion of the role of marriage in the late 18th / early 19th century, or reflection on the nature of love) would be tailored according to the researcher's original interest.[112]

In terms of application to biblical studies, this is a helpful recognition that a pure interpretation is an illusion, as any act of interpretation modifies the original data in some way (otherwise, the only faithful interpretation would be replication). Thus, the goal in biblical studies should not be to escape the "culture gap" between us and the biblical world, but to embrace it. An articulation of the researcher's interests (as outlined above) will hopefully facilitate clarity in explaining the research process involved, the claims being made as to the significance of each step, and the coherence and legitimacy of the foundations, tools, and application of technology to them.[113]

In the case of Ezek 18, for example, the conceptualization allows the scholar to recognize *both* that the notions of individualism and collectivism, as used in modern anthropology, are not emic to the chapter *and* that one may still make fruitful use of them, if we are careful to articulate for what interests, or step(s) in the process they are being used. Problems arise when the researcher fails to see or acknowledge the emic distance involved (between emic A and emic B), and simply assumes or imposes their own

---

111. Cf Claude Levi-Strauss, "Structuralism and Ecology," *SSI* 12/1 (1973): 7–23, who argues that the entire research process happens within the emic of the researcher. While I do not agree with his argument in full (that attempts at forming an etic, or articulating emic B are simply illusory), his point regarding the importance of recognizing bias and self-interest in research is sound.

112. Cf. the range of hermeneutical approaches outlines in Kevin J. Vanhoozer, ed., *The Cambridge Companion to Postmodern Theology* (Cambridge: Cambridge University Press, 2003); also Colin E. Gunton, ed., *The Cambridge Companion to Christian Doctrine* (Cambridge: Cambridge University Press, 1997).

113. This discussion raises in turn the issue of epistemology and its overlap with anthropology. From an epistemological point of view, my modified version of Berry's operationalization is built on a form of Critical Realism that, as its name suggests, seeks to hold together both Realism and Perspectivalism. For further exploration of Critical Realism in the context of Christian theology and mission, see Paul G. Hiebert, *Missiological Implications of Epistemological Shifts: Affirming Truth in a Modern/Postmodern World* (Harrisburg: Trinity Press International, 1999); Harvie M. Conn, *Eternal Word and Changing Worlds: Theology, Anthropology, and Mission in Trialogue* (Grand Rapids: Zondervan, 1984).

particular etic onto the text. This is, for example, a major problem with the Evolutionary View critiqued earlier in this chapter.

We should bear in mind, however, that as the emic distance between the interests of the researcher and the text grow wider, the care taken in each step of the process becomes more critical. One may even reach a version of step 5 in Berry's operationalization (lack of comparable cultural features render cross-cultural comparison impossible), and the gap between emic A and emic B renders the reading of the text illegitimate.[114] However, the conceptualization seeks to maximize the use of diverse research tools, while at the same time being aware of their limitations and the modifications that may be necessary to make, according to the task and interests at hand.

To this we can also add that an acknowledgment of the limitations of the etic framework actually allows it to be utilized and appreciated for what it is—a partial and limited perspective—which can then be strengthened by other (also partial and limited) perspectives. For example, as Schwartz states, "the fact that the Torah's prescriptions constitute mediterranean-ism's nearly perfect antithesis requires an explanation."[115] Likewise, recognizing that an emphasis on the "collectivistic" aspects of biblical culture can provide a helpful *addition to*, rather than replacement of, a Western, individualistic perspective can give us a healthier orientation in appreciating the complex, integrated nature of personality and ethical responsibility evident in the biblical material.[116]

Fourth, the conceptualization helps in moving the deductive/inductive methodology debate forward. Avrahami, for example, sees a foundational problem in the Context Group's method being deductive rather than inductive. She argues that these scholars start from the "field of notions" or "values," and then proceed to "find" them in the text, rather than an inductive investigation generating a more nuanced definition of terms.[117] However, while I agree with her basic critique, the opposition between deductive and inductive, and the importance of starting point are in fact not necessary. As already demonstrated, *both* inductive (which has affinities to the emic perspective) *and* deductive (which has affinities to the etic perspective) approaches are necessary in a robust process of research and understanding; it is not a case of either-or but rather both-and.[118]

---

114. Possible examples of this include attempts to psychoanalyze Ezekiel and his prophecies as symptomatic of psychosis, schizophrenia and/or misogyny/misandryny due to childhood sexual abuse, as in David J. Halperin, *Seeking Ezekiel: Text and Psychology* (University Park: Pennsylvania State University Press, 1993); Edwin C. Broome Jr., "Ezekiel's Abnormal Personality," *JBL* 65 (1946): 277–92.

115. Schwartz, *Mediterranean People*, 26.

116. See Robert A. di Vito, "Old Testament Anthropology and the Construction of Personal Identity," *CBQ* 61 (1999): 235–38, for an example of such an approach, that helpfully avoids polarization between individualism and collectivism.

117. Avrahami, "בוש in the Psalms," 296–97.

118. This is a further reason why a "recursive" SSA model is suggested.

The real weakness of the scholars Avrahami takes issue with is not so much that their method is deductive, as that the deductive aspect of their research—their imposed etic—is often not open enough to correction. Indeed, one could argue that *all* research starts deductively (that is, from emic A, and the resulting imposed etic), and therefore that the important thing to focus on is not so much where one starts (although that may be helpful in orienting the researcher to the object of study), but the rigor, clarity, and transparency of the overall research process that finally matters.

To conclude this section, let me reflect briefly on why this discussion is so key to the current project. To some readers, much of the foregoing may seem fairly obvious: "Isn't all this just 'research?'" (as it has been put to me in discussion). In some ways, the answer is "yes!"—I am simply outlining and clarifying the principles that lie behind seeking to understand an object of study. However, the *manner* in which I have attempted to do so results from what I consider to be a necessary response to the Context Group's proposals as to how cross-cultural models and methods are to be utilized.

The Approach of This Study

Thick Interpretation

Utilizing anthropological models seeks to move us toward a "thick interpretation," a term coined by Ken Stone in applying Geertz's "thick description" to biblical studies. This is a helpful distinction, as ethnography proper, which includes empirical observation of "live culture," is an impossibility for biblical scholars. As such, cultural analysis of biblical societies must be conducted by a careful interplay between *literary discourse* and *cultural assumptions*.[119]

Stone's point is apposite, given that a text, while a product of a particular culture, is not itself a pure expression of that culture. Rather, as already observed, texts are artifacts of a culture—and so not only describe, but inform, develop, challenge, undermine, or even produce culture. Obviously, then, the more background informants of a text we can draw on, the "thicker" and, in principle, the more accurate our reading.

Contextual Semantic Analysis

Stone's analysis focuses on narrative texts and hence his reading strategy focuses on "narratology," following the work of Mieke Bal.[120] In the case of Ezekiel, however, we are dealing in the main not with narrative but with

---

119. Ken Stone, *Sex, Honor and Power in the Deuteronomistic History* (JSOTSup 234; Sheffield: Sheffield Academic Press, 1996).

120. Mieke Bal, *Narratology: Introduction to the Theory of Narrative* (2nd ed.; Toronto: University of Toronto Press, 1997); idem, *Death and Dissymmetry: The Politics of Coherence in the Book of Judges* (Chicago: University of Chicago Press, 1988). The term *narratology* refers to the attempts of structuralists to develop a "poetics" of narrative literature,

(poetic) prophecy. Further, I am not seeking to examine the suitability of the honor/shame model to account for social behavior as described in the text. Rather, following Avrahami, I am seeking to examine the contextual meaning of the terms themselves, in their sematic and literary relationships.

Rather than analyzing the book for "story" elements, then, I will focus on a robust method of semantic analysis of key vocabulary. The exercise, however, will be more than simply a word study in that, like Schwartz, I will relate the analysis to the honor/shame model as the imposed etic, in order to produce a derived etic model of the meanings of the terms and, critically, their relationship.

To examine Ezekiel, I will combine a form of *intertextuality* with *canonical* and *biblical theology*, as a foil against which the anthropological model of honor and shame may be cast. As each of the three terms requires clarification to be useful, I will briefly outline what I mean by each.

Intertextuality has been widely used in biblical studies.[121] As Hays observes, however, the term has become diffuse and imprecise, and in application.[122] I will not enter this discussion at depth in the present study.[123] For my purposes, it is sufficient to note that the prophets saw themselves as standing in continuity (of some sort) with the Torah, and thus intertextual practice, or "inner-biblical exegesis," is prevalent throughout the OT.

My use of canonical theology follows logically from this.[124] While outside sources were utilized by the biblical authors (e.g., the etiologies in Gen 10:9 and 22:14, or the adaptation of ANE creation accounts), canonical material dominates the category. The canon is its own primary intertext. I will take the broader usage of each of the key terms in the OT as the primary background against which to locate Ezekiel's understanding and use.

On the other hand, canonical (final-form) criticism is situated within the realm of synchronic analysis. As Stead has noted, however, research in hermeneutics seems to have moved beyond older structuralist oppositions—synchronic vs. diachronic—to a recognition that they are comple-

---

perhaps the most well-known example being Seymour Chatman, *Story and Discourse: Narrative Structure in Fiction and Film* (Ithaca: Cornell University Press, 1978).

121. The term comes from Julia Kristeva, *Desire in Language: A Semiotic Approach to Literature and Art* (Colombia: Columbia University Press, 1980).

122. Richard B. Hays, foreword to *Reading the Bible Intertextually* (ed. R. B. Hays et al.; Waco, TX: Baylor University Press, 2009), xi. See further idem, *Echoes of Scripture in the Letters of Paul* (New Haven: Yale University Press, 1989); Michael R. Stead, *The Intertextuality of Zechariah 1–8* (London: T. & T. Clark, 2009); Michael A. Fishbane, *Biblical Interpretation in Ancient Israel* (Oxford: Oxford University Press, 1988); John Barton, *Reading the Old Testament: Method in Biblical Study* (London: Darton, Longman, & Todd, 1996); ibid., "Introduction: Exegesis, Eisegesis, Intergesis," *Semeia* 69–70 (1995): 7–18; as well as the articles in the same issue (vols. 69 and 70 were published together).

123. For a fuller discussion, see Stead, *Intertextuality of Zechariah*.

124. The foundational works in canonical criticism are Brevard S. Childs, *The Book of Exodus: A Critical, Theological Commentary* (OTL; Philadelphia: Westminster, 1974); idem, *Old Testament Theology in a Canonical Context* (Philadelphia: Fortress, 1986).

mentary methodologies. One *can* restrict examination to one or the other, depending on the purpose of the research, although I would wish to argue that this cannot be done in totality or in a mutually exclusive fashion, without warping the object of study.[125]

This leads to the final part of analytical triangulation, biblical theology. Earlier work in this discipline has been heavily criticized.[126] However, a more robust version, developed especially in the work of Graeme Goldsworthy, may be seen as the diachronic counterpart to canonical theology.[127] Furthermore, integrating the two into a semantic study allows us to recognize conceptual relationships, and suggest directions of conceptual dependence between canonical books and themes, even if, in terms of actual historical development, this is difficult to do.[128]

Constructing Indigenous Definitions

One of the major goals of the contextual semantic analysis is to heed Herzfeld's warnings to avoid the imprecision of English language glosses obscuring the meaning of indigenous terminology. An example of this, which I will engage at length with in the following chapter, is Laniak's semantic analysis of כבד, in which he attempts to cast the entire semantic range of the root under the umbrella of "honor." My process in the three main analytical chapters will thus be to frame Ezekiel's specific use of key terms (that is, Ezekiel's diachronic place within the development of the biblical theological narrative of the OT) with a broader, OT-wide semantic study of the key terms (that is, a synchronic integration of the key term's scope of meaning within the canon). I will then employ a similar stategy for בוש and עוה in the subsequent chapters.

History and Hermeneutics

The approach I am advocating, which seeks to account best for the issues of cultural interpretation raised above, rests on as a form of critical realism.[129] This stream of philosophical engagement seeks to move beyond

---

125. Stead, *The Intertextuality of Zechariah 1–8*, 16–39.

126. Barr, *Semantics of Biblical Language*; idem, *The Concept of Biblical Theology: An Old Testament Perspective* (London: SCM, 1999).

127. Graeme Goldsworthy, *Gospel and Kingdom: A Christian Interpretation of the Old Testament* (Rydalmere: Crossroad, 1994); idem, *Christ-Centred Biblical Theology: Hermeneutical Foundations and Principles* (Nottingham: Apollos, 2012).

128. For a critique of the mainstream Documentary Hypothesis dating of OT texts, see Hess, *Israelite Religions*, 46–59. For a critique of linguistic dating of texts, see Ian Young et al., *Linguistic Dating of Biblical Texts* (2 vols.; London: Equinox, 2008); cf. the response in Cynthia Miller-Naudé and Ziony Zevit, eds., *Diachrony in Biblical Hebrew* (LSAWS 8; Winona Lake, IN: Eisenbrauns, 2012).

129. For an introduction to the topic, see Margaret S. Archer, *Critical Realism: Essential Readings* (New York: Routledge, 1998); Roy Bhaskar, *Reflections on Meta-Reality: Transcendence, Emancipation, and Everyday Life* (Thousand Oaks: Sage, 2002); idem, *Dialectic: The*

the impasse of modern positivism and postmodern idealism, by attempting to hold together ontological/historical realism (it assumes that a real world exists independently of human perception and opinion), and a critical epistemology (it examines the processes by which humans acquire knowledge, and acknowledges that this does not have a literal, one-to-one correspondence with reality).[130]

A helpful corollary of this recognition is to heal the split between "coherence" and "correspondence" views of truth, while maintaining a helpful distinction between them. Applied to a text, this is our warrant to "sit loose" on models, and seek to build a reading based more on internal "coherence"—the network of literary relationships (vocabulary, syntax, and themes) that make the text a unified communicative entity in its own right.[131]

On the other hand, a recognition that the biblical text arose in, and "corresponds" to, a concrete situation in history, allows us to seek historical and ideological causes for the appearance and acceptance of the communicative entity and its intent. In the case of Ezekiel, the task is made somewhat simpler because its abundance of references to historical events and dates. As such, if we can say with some reasonable confidence that the book is situated reasonably closely to the events it describes, we can then investigate its relationship to what else we can know of its historical and cultural setting from other, comparable sources.

Critical realism is not without its own critics, and I am wary of claiming too much under its banner, especially in terms of "realism's" implicit claim for authority.[132] However, if applied carefully and cautiously, it can be a helpful tool in the attempt to overcome both naive positivism and excessive skepticism.[133] Indeed, we are left no choice but to make such an attempt, for as Rorty (among others) has demonstrated, knowledge is ultimately and irreducibly an *ethical* activity. It is therefore incumbent on researchers to make sure that we know *responsibly*—which includes attempting, as far as possible, to hear an author's communication *as they would want it to be heard*, before we offer our own assessments and labels.

Pulse of Freedom (New York: Verso, 1993). For its use in biblical and theological studies, see Kevin Vanhoozer, *Is There a Meaning in This Text*; N. T. Wright, *The New Testament and the People of God* (London: SPCK, 1992); Bernard Lonergan, *Method in Theology* (London: Darton, Longman, & Todd, 1973); Thomas F. Torrance, *Theological Science* (Edinburgh: T. & T. Clark, 1996); Conn, *Eternal Word*; Hiebert, *Missiological Implications*; John M. Frame, *The Doctrine of the Knowledge of God* (Grand Rapids: Presbyterian and Reformed, 1987).

130. Hiebert, *Missiological Implications*, 69.

131. It should also be said, however, that this activity is done with the clear understanding that even such tools as grammar and syntax are, at best, contemporary approximations of how language could have worked for that particular text.

132. See, for example, Stephen Kemp, "Critical Realism and the Limits of Philosophy," *European Journal of Social Theory* 8/2 (2005): 171–91.

133. As, for example, in the cases of Schwartz, Torrance, Wright, and especially Vanhoozer.

To return to a previous statement, use of a text is not necessarily abuse, *but it may be*. Readers and researchers must pay careful attention to their tendency not to listen hard enough before speaking, to assume mastery over the subject. The critical realism I am advocating seeks to move toward this by recognizing the *reality* of the text—it exists independently of me, my perceptions, and my opinions, and thus my perceptions and opinions of it are subject to its objectivity.

Method: Contextual Semantics as Gateways to Cultural Concept Spheres

Given all of the above, my method will be to examine the gains and dangers of applying an honor/shame framework to the reading of Bible, as articulated by scholarship such as that of the Context Group. In order to do this, I will first analyze the *breadth* (or range) of meaning for each of the main Hebrew roots taken by SSAs to indicate the pivotal values of honor and shame in the Bible—כבד for honor and בוש for shame. In light of the fact that SSAs make a claim against a guilt culture reading of the biblical text, I will also analyse the root עוה for the notion of guilt.

In so doing, I am not seeking to present an exhaustive lexical/semantic analysis; for that, the reader is better served consulting the relevant reference works and monographs.[134] Rather, building on these, I aim to present a contextual analysis that is sufficiently thorough to examine the ways the usage of the roots (first in a broad brushtroke coverage of the OT as a whole, then in Ezekiel's specific usage of the terms) relate to SSA notions of honor, shame, and guilt.

Following this, and in order to provide further *depth* and perspective on the notions of honor, shame, and guilt, I will also include further coverage of other Hebrew roots in Ezekiel that are associated with the concepts: הדר, יקר, and צבי for honor; חרף, כלם, and קוט for shame; and חטא, אשם, and פשע for guilt. Due to space limitations, these will necessarily be summary in nature, although I will seek to provide extended discussion where especially relevant.

Finally, I will bring the honor/shame model to bear on the analysis as an "ideal type" of biblical culture against which to compare the matrix of values at work in the text.[135] In so doing, I will also provide a critique of

---

134. Besides the standard lexicons and semantic dictionaries, see further James Barr, *The Semantics of Biblical Language* (London: Oxford University Press, 1961); Donald A. Carson, *Exegetical Fallacies* (Grand Rapids: Baker, 1996). For more recent developments on lexicography and semantic analysis of Biblical Hebrew, see William Croft and D. A. Cruse, *Lexical Semantics* (CTL; Cambridge: Cambridge University Press, 1986); idem, *Cognitive Linguistics* (CTL; Cambridge: Cambridge University Press, 2004); Stephen L. Shead, *Radical Frame Semantics and Biblical Hebrew: Exploring Lexical Semantics* (Leiden: Brill, 2011).

135. Schwartz, *Mediterranean People*, 166.

the Context Group's model and, as an extension of this, I will also include terminology usually associated with guilt in the analysis, in order to assess the validity of the suggestion that behavior in the ancient world (and thus the cultural *milieu* of the biblical writers) was governed *externally,* by honor and shame (that is, collectivistic), more than it was governed *internally*, by guilt (that is, individualistic), and to advance discussion on the portrayal of God in the book of Ezekiel and the categories of relationship to him that undergird its rhetoric.[136]

The basic pattern of each chapter examining the key terms may be laid out as follows:

1. Introduction and examination of OT usage of key term
2. Examination of specific usage in Ezekiel of key term and concepts
3. Examination of other conceptually associated terms in Ezekiel
4. Construction of a tentative emic (B) view of key term
5. Examination of areas of agreement and disagreement with SSA model
6. Conclusion and contribution of the analysis to the key concept

One final clarification is pertinent at this point. In light of the above review and methodology, I will continue to use the terms *honor*, *shame*, and *guilt* in this study, but without necessarily accepting the interpretive framework of the models of which they are normally part. For example, "reputation" is clearly an honor concept, but one need not accept the Context Group's agonistic honor/shame model in its entirety, to confirm its presence or importance in a particular setting. To clarify this matter further, it may be helpful first to outline the historical development of shame in psychology and anthropology before commencing the detailed study. To this I now turn.

---

136. E.g., Crook, *Reconceptualising Conversion*, 51.

Chapter 3

Shame (and Guilt) in Recent Study: Imposed Etic

Shame in Recent Study

As is clear from the preceding chapter, the concept of shame has played an important role in SSAs, particularly in the last 30 years.[1] However, as is also clear, the terms and concepts that have been developed and utilized in the area are by no means established or unified; rather, a survey of the relevant material shows considerable variation and confusion in definitions and application. Given the foundational place of shame in the imposed etic of SSAs, it would serve us well to unravel the threads of the discussion, to gain as much clarity as we can before attempting to bring the research to bear on the biblical text.

Broadly speaking, the rise in prominence of shame in biblical studies can be traced to two related streams of studies in humanities: psychology and anthropology. It is not my intention to rehearse the developments in detail; that has been adequately explored by others.[2] Instead, I will give a summary and assessment of a few key contributions related to the use of shame in biblical studies, as an orientation to the analysis in the following chapters.

Shame in Psychology[3]

The most sustained research on shame has been conducted in the realm of the psychology of emotions. *Oxford Dictionaries* defines it as "the painful feeling of humiliation or distress caused by the consciousness of wrong or foolish behavior."[4] However, the constant, complex, and diverse range of studies, in the cognitive, physiological, and social factors indicate the need for a fuller exploration of the concept.

---

1. As well as in theological and missiological studies. See the appendix for further detail.

2. See especially Bechtel, "Shame as Sanction"; idem, "Perception of Shame"; Stiebert, *Construction of Shame*; Crook, *Reconceptualising Conversion*.

3. For this section, I am indebted to Geoff Broughton's work on shame and restorative justice, which was the subject of many discussions across the room in our time together in the Moore College postgraduate room. Geoff's thesis now appears as *Restorative Christ: Jesus, Justice, and Discipleship* (Eugene, OR: Pickwick, 2014).

4. S.v. "Shame," *OD*.

D. L. Nathanson

One of the landmark enquiries into the exact nature and definition of shame in recent times was conducted by D. L. Nathanson.[5] Building on the insights of experimental psychologist Silvan Tomkins,[6] Nathanson made the distinction between *emotion*: "characterized by some combination of thoughts and *somatic feelings,*" and *affect*, the hard-wired, physiological response to the various stimuli that result in an emotion.[7] In other words, affect is the physical "raw material" behind an emotion (as a biologist might study it), while emotion is the complex integration of affect, cognition, memory, culture, and so on that constitute a moving personal experience. For Nathanson, this distinction is key in understanding the complexities of the concept and its many and varied manifestations.

In grounding his theory in concrete life, Nathanson drew on Tomkins's "eureka" moment as a parent of a newborn infant in the 1940s. In responding to the normal communication of the baby's distress, Tomkins realized that the newborn could have no understanding of why it was crying, lacking any concepts or ability to identify the experience. Instead, the baby's own central nervous system was triggered, resulting in crying. Of course, as the baby grew, it would begin to form associations with sensory perception, memories, patterns of behavior, and the ability to articulate and identify the experience, which would become components of emotion.[8] As Nathanson summarizes, "affect is biology, emotion is biography."[9]

Nathanson (following Tomkins) went on to identify nine basic affects in human physiological makeup: interest-excitement, enjoyment-joy, surprise-startle, distress-anguish, anger-rage, fear-terror, dismell, disgust, and finally, shame-humiliation.[10] According to Nathanson, shame is somewhat unique in the above list, in that it can only be properly understood in light of the other affects, particularly the positive ones of interest and joy. For Nathan-

---

5. Donald L. Nathanson, *Shame and Pride: Affect, Sex and the Birth of the Self* (New York: Norton, 1992). See also idem, ed., *The Many Faces of Shame* (New York: Guilford, 1987). This section includes material from a review essay of *Shame and Pride* by Richard Ostrofsky, *Affect Theory, Shame and the Logic of Personality*, n.p. [cited June 6 2012]. Online: http://www.secthoughts.com/Misc%20Essays/Shame%20and%20Personality.htm.

6. Silvan S. Tomkins and Bertram P. Karon, *Affect, Imagery, Consciousness* (4 vols.; New York: Springer, 1962).

7. Nathanson, *Shame and Pride*, 37–38 (emphasis original).

8. Ibid., 57–58.

9. Ibid., 50.

10. Nathanson suggests that the label "enjoyment-joy" may be slightly misleading, as it has nothing to do with what is commonly called "having fun"; rather, it describes the pleasurable release of psychic tension that leads to a reduced level of neural activity, often expressed physically in a smile or bodily relaxation. In some ways, it is more like the *denouement* of the interest affect: *interest* stirs you up, while *enjoyment* calms you down. Nathanson defines "dismell" as the physical reaction to a sharp or unpleasant smell.

son, the reason for this is that *shame is essentially an interference with the pleasures associated with the "positive affects."*[11]

According to Nathanson, shame is triggered "any time desire outruns fulfilment," with its purpose to "protect an organism from its growing avidity for positive affect."[12] The physiological indicators of shame include eyes and face averted and downcast, lowered eyelids, drooping head, or even entire body. In terms of affect theory, then, shame is a biological capability to terminate positive experience, for whatever reason, when other negative affects fail to do the job: "a physiological mechanism of renunciation—a literal turning away from what is otherwise attractive and desirable."[13]

Nathanson goes on to make some crucial observations about shame, so defined. First, shame is more "primitive" (in a positive sense) than an actual emotion (under which category it is usually discussed) and, as such, classifying it as an affect enables greater accuracy in understanding the phenomenon. In support of this, Nathanson notes that shame-affect can be observed in infants, even though they lack the concepts of self and, consequently, self-esteem, that are necessary in speaking of shame as an emotion. Before it is an emotion, then, shame is the physiological response alerting the organism that a positive affect has been blocked or impeded in some way.

Second, shame is somewhat unique among the affects, in that while the other negative affects arise directly in response to an object—"turned outwards," so to speak—the shame affect, in and of itself, requires no such external stimulus. "In shame, there is no turning outward of energy and action; rather there is collapse inward."[14] As such, shame is distinguished from the other affects in that it "is a programmed response to an impediment to preexisting affect when there is every reason for that preexisting affect to continue!" It is thus "an auxiliary to the positive affects, rather than a true innate affect in the sense of the first six." On the other hand, Nathanson still counts it among the affects because "it bears all of the properties of the other affects."[15]

Third, Nathanson folds "guilt" under the umbrella of the family of shame emotions.[16] While he notes that the two feel different, he justifies his categorization with two main arguments: that no separate physiological mechanism (affect) has been found for guilt, and that guilt appears to be simply shame concerning an action.[17]

---

11. Ibid., 72.

12. Ibid., 140.

13. Ostrofsky, *Affect Theory*.

14. Ibid.

15. Nathanson, *Shame and Pride*, 138.

16. Nathanson includes more than guilt feelings in the category: embarrassment, humiliation, mortification, and discouragement are also identified as "depending mostly on our lifetime experiences of shame affect," ibid., 145.

17. Ibid., 144.

There are great strengths to Nathanson's work that are potentially beneficial to our understanding of the concepts involved in בוש and כלם. First and foremost, by extending the range of shame research beyond study purely of the (psychocognitive) emotions and into (biological) affect theory, Nathanson heightens our sensitivity to the physiological symptoms and foundation of emotional responses.[18] This is helpful in light of recent studies that seek to minimize the significance, or even presence, of psychology and emotion in the Bible and its portrayal of people on the basis of anthropological models.[19] Incorporating affect theory into the discussion may indicate that, rather than biblical characters lacking a developed sense of individual agency or inner-personal psychological states, the divide between "inner" and "outer" worlds, so overpronounced in Western thinking since the Cartesian absolutizing of the mind in isolation to all else, is simply less extreme.

Barbara Leung Lai, for example, has attempted to demonstrate the plausibility of accessing the "inner life" of biblical characters through the biblical text, by integrating psychological, literary, and philosophical perspectives into her reading of the (literary) characters of Daniel, Isaiah, and YHWH.[20] More explicitly, the example of Middle Eastern cultures, where inner emotional states are often reflected more explicitly in external, physical phenomena than in Western cultures, may speak at least of the plausibility that, in biblical descriptions of ritualized emotional activity (mourning practices, for example), social scripts may be a vehicle for, rather than a denial of, individual emotional expression.[21]

---

18. As Nathanson states, "the innate affect [of shame-humiliation] is a physiological mechanism, a firmware script that guarantees the operation of functions that take place at a number of sites of action. The script for shame is dependent on the integrity of certain structures in the central nervous system, on many chemical mediators that transmit messages, and on the organising principle stored in the subcortical brain as the affect program. No matter what shame or any other affect 'means' to us, it is essential to keep in mind that we are dealing first and foremost with a mechanism that is initially free of meaning" (ibid., 149).

19. E.g., Crook, *Reconceptualising Conversion*, 13ff.

20. Leung Lai, *Through the 'I'-Window*.

21. It may be helpful to add two supporting statements to this point. First, it should further be noted that Western, individualistic societies also have social scripts for expression of emotion. Second, as a caveat, external, public expressions of emotion in non-Western cultures may or may not match what the person is feeling "inside," just as in a Western setting someone may lack an external expression of an internal emotional state (for example, at least some of the often over-the-top public wailing in the state funerals of Mao Zedong and Kim Jong Il may have been "for the sake of appearance" rather than truly reflective of an individual's feelings toward their ruler, given the damage and misery to the lives and families of some of those present, caused by each of them). However, the point remains that even without a necessarily full-orbed description of interior psychological states, it is reasonable to suggest that we may have some genuine access to the inner thought and emotional life of biblical characters through the text.

Second, on a related note, Nathanson attempts to link shame with the nature of humanity as a social animal. In line with the evolutionary model of human emotion that characterizes post-Freudian psychoanalysis, Nathanson concludes that shame has become intimately tied to our identity, as the border between a person's outer and inner worlds. As such, "to the extent that man is a social animal, shame is a shaper of modern life."[22] Whether or not one follows the implications of Nathanson's Darwinian evolution of human sociality, he is correct to say that "man" *is* a social animal.[23] Hence, it is no surprise that shame should figure so strongly in biblical texts, both within human culture and before God. It is especially in this regard that biblical research utilizing SSAs are a helpful addition to the available ammunition in the biblical interpreter's cache.

Third, according to Ostrofsky (in a review of Nathanson's work), affect theory has superceded both major schools of theoretical and clinical psychology: psychoanalysis and behaviorism. With regard to psychoanalysis, it sees the mind not as a buildup of internal pressures, but as a "self-programming computer pre-equipped with 'firmware' routines [that is, affects]," which develop as they are experienced in encounter with others.[24]

With regard to behaviorism, Ostrofsky suggests that affect theory overcomes the somewhat inbuilt naivety of behaviorism's maxim that "behaviors that bring pleasure or avert pain are 'reinforced,'" by including the complex interaction of affect and behavior: "any positive affect can reinforce a behavior, while any negative affect can extinguish it.... People, we know, can learn to like (and dislike) the strangest things. Human beings suddenly become as complicated, as individual, as difficult to predict, as we know ourselves to be." Ostrofsky goes on to suggest that "between behaviorism and cognitivism, affect theory would appear to have a foot in both camps, combining the scientific rigor of one with the explanatory power of the other."[25]

Fourth, also according to Ostrofsky, affect theory has implications for philosophical paradigms, especially in its identification of shame as the foundational affect in human psychology. For if affect is hard-wired biologically, rather than being solely socially constructed, then a "human nature" exists, and value judgments (which are triggered especially by shame) are

---

22. Nathanson, *Shame and Pride*, 149.

23. The difficulty with "survival of the fittest" in this context is that it is essentially anti-relational. One could argue, of course, that sociality is simply a means to increase the odds of survival ("safety in numbers"), but it is on the whole a rather inadequate explanation of the complexity and profundity of the social nature of human existence to view others simply as a means to the end of ensuring my continued existence.

24. Ostrofsky, *Affect Theory*, n.p. Ostrofsky does temper this comment with "to be sure, both drive and attachment remain important concepts, but without their former sovereignty. In their place, affect now plays the central role, determining the "color" (so to speak) of incoming sensation, and whether it will be admitted to consciousness at all."

25. Ibid.

not simply learned but can be "scientifically" assessed. As Ostrofsky concludes, "A science of anthroplogy is possible after all—though whether we really want one is another question."[26]

Neil Pembroke

On the other hand, as helpful as Nathanson's work is, it has not gone without criticism, some of which is, frankly, scathing. Pembroke, for example, suggests that there are serious questions to be raised in Nathanson's affect model, especially in terms of its depiction of the relationship and (lack of) distinction between shame and guilt, due to the limits of the affect system. According to Pembroke, the dictates of the model force guilt, embarrassment, shyness, inferiority feelings, and so on to be understood simply as a variant of shame, which flies in the face of substantial empirical and clinical studies indicating that these are all distinct emotions.[27]

Essentially, Pembroke argues (although not using the language) that the Tomkins/Nathanson affect system is a closed hermeneutic circle, an imposed etic that never goes through a thorough enough process of testing and refinement to proceed to a derived etic. As a result, the distinction between the two concepts is squashed into the mold of the nine-affect model that was initially constructed, with no real possibility of escape.

Pembroke instead follows psychoanalytic theorist Susan Miller (who in turn follows Erik Erikson),[28] in suggesting that early contact between the two "developmental lines" of shame (having to do with self-esteem) and guilt (having to do with the generation of conscience) are the cause of the two being mistakenly dissolved into each other by the likes of Tomkins and Nathanson. Instead, Pembroke sees shame as an early response to parental over-control which, in childhood development "atrophies" into guilt, or conscience: the generation of self over-control, driven by the lingering need to avoid parental disapproval.[29] While one may question the validity of Freudian developmental patterns of emotions/neuroses, nonetheless his critique of Nathanson raises the significant question of whether affect theory is in fact the best way in which to understand the distinction and relationship between shame and guilt.

---

26. Ibid.

27. Neil Pembroke, *The Art of Listening: Dialogue, Shame, and Pastoral Care* (Grand Rapids: Eerdmans, 2002), 150–51. Pembroke's own critique may extend too far in the other direction. I will seek to articulate a more careful path between the overlap between shame and guilt and what distinguishes them from each other.

28. Susan Miller, "Shame as an Impetus to the Creation of Conscience," *Int J Psychoanal* 70 (1989): 231–43; Erik H. Erikson, *Childhood and Society* (London: Vintage, 1995).

29. Pembroke, *Art of Listening*, 150–51. Pembroke illustrates this transition using the case of a young man brought up with a strict code of moral conduct being confronted with a liberal lifestyle at university. The man initially feels shame at his "straight" lifestyle, begins to behave like his friends, and then feels a burden of guilt at rejecting his family values.

Christopher Lasch

One of the main issues the discussion above highlights is whether or not shame and guilt are distinct (Pembroke) or sit under the same family of emotions (Nathanson). However, the continued division in the psychology community may point to a deeper problem in the area. Christopher Lasch, for example, has roundly criticized Nathanson and others (including those whom Pembroke draws on), for entirely oversensationalizing shame as *the* neglected, even actively suppressed psychological issue.[30]

Lasch does agree that Western society has a deep problem with shame, but claims that researchers are symptomatic of it, rather than part of the solution. In his critique of prominent works in the area, Lasch suggests two related areas in which shame researchers have lost their way: in viewing shame as the opposite of self-esteem, and the manner in which researchers attempt to distinguish between shame and guilt.

In terms of viewing shame as the opposite of self-esteem, Lasch begins his critique by calling the bluff of shame researchers. In a culture where nothing shocks us anymore, the suggestion that shame has been "kept in the closet" is simply implausible. Rather, in such a culture "the only thing forbidden . . . is the inclination to forbid." Lasch notes that even Nathanson admits, shame has become "more than a little 'trendy.'"[31] Lasch then clarifies the key question: "Instead of asking how we can lift the conspiracy of silence supposedly surrounding shame, we should ask why it gets so much attention in a shameless society."[32]

Lasch sees part of the answer in the double meaning of shame: it refers *both* to a decent respect for privacy, *and* to the fear of disgrace. According to Lasch, the first meaning is scarcely mentioned, as "an exaggerated sense of propriety obviously doesn't rank very high on the scale of contemporary social problems." In other words, Western society is characterized not so much by "shame," as "shamelessness." By failing to recognize this, most usage and research equates shame simply with fear of disgrace. Lasch decries the manner in which "even that has lost its moral resonance: shame, these days, refers to whatever prevents us from 'feeling good about ourselves.'" In Lasch's words, shame has become "merely the opposite of self-esteem."[33]

Lasch argues that the root cause of this is a narcissistic individualism running rampant through (American) society. There is an almost universal

---

30. Christopher Lasch, "For Shame: Why Americans Should Be Wary of Self-Esteem," *NR 207* (1992), n.p. [cited June 7 2012]. Online: http://www.newrepublic.com/book/review/shame-why-americans-should-be-wary-self-esteem#; idem, *The Culture of Narcissism: American Life in an Age of Diminishing Expectations* (New York: Norton, 1991). For a critique of Lasch's thesis, see Charles Elliott, *Memory and Salvation* (London: Darton, Longman, & Todd, 1995).

31. Lasch, *For Shame.*

32. Ibid.

33. Ibid.

belief that people's psychological problems come from conforming to society's standards, rather than setting their own goals. The consequence of
this, according to Lasch, is an inversion of what shame is: "Formerly shame
was the fate of those whose conduct fell short of cherished ideals. Now
that ideals are suspect, it refers only to a loss of self-esteem." Lasch cites
Steinem's "revolution from within": self-esteem/"empowerment" requires
casting off shame, because shame makes people feel "intrinsically sinful"
and unworthy." Lasch then draws the straightforward implication: "Clearly
shame loses much of its moral content when it becomes merely the opposite of self-esteem."[34]

Lasch then turns his sights onto the second problem with shame research: the manner in which researchers attempt to distinguish shame from
guilt (so Pembroke). Though noting the appeal of conceptual clarity, Lasch
accuses theoreticians of overplaying the difference between them, with
the consequence that both became trivialized: "guilt loses the suggestion
of conscientious self-condemnation [and becomes legalistic], while the element of self-condemnation in shame comes to be viewed merely as an un-
fortunate byproduct of unrealistic expectations."[35]

We will have cause to return to Lasch's assessment later in this chapter
and in the next. Interestingly, however, Lasch traces the current day confusion in psychology to its relationship to the shame/guilt culture anthropological studies of the 20th century. Indeed, his analysis is borne out in some
of the anthropological biblical studies already reviewed in this study:

> The story [of the unhelpful distinction between shame and guilt] begins in the
> 1930s, when comparative studies of socialisation patterns prompted anthro-
> pologists to distinguish between shame cultures and guilt cultures. Shame,
> they argued, sets up a purely external sanction for good conduct, whereas
> guilt internalizes a sense of right and wrong. This interpretation soon proved
> untenable, but speculation about shame, which passed from anthropology to
> psychology, continued to be dominated by the effort to distinguish it from
> guilt.[36]

It should be noted further that the cultural anthropologists Lasch refers to
(e.g., Margaret Mead and Ruth Benedict) themselves depend on psychoana-
lytical categories. In other words, the concepts seem to have gone through
a sort of "double refraction," from the psychology of the individual (via
Freud), through to the broad characterization of cultural sanctions of social
anthropology, and back into clinical/therapeutic psychology. In so doing,
the weaknesses noted by Lasch seem to have not only become part of the
assumed edifice of shame scholarship, but also seem to have been magnified
in the process, and made a slight distinction into an overblown dichotomy.

---

34. Ibid.; Gloria Steinem, *Revolution from Within: A Book of Self-Esteem* (London:
Corgi, 1993)
    35. Ibid.
    36. Ibid.

Cairns, who shares Lasch's concerns regarding shame scholarship, sums up the critique well. He argues that although an abstract distinction between who we are and what we do may be tenable and can often be distinguished phenomenologically by virtue of the different associations and connections, the failure of popular usage to provide an adequate distinction in various settings indicates that there is a significant area in which *no effective difference between them exists.* The most that can be said about the difference between shame and guilt is the slight shift of ideation in moral evaluation between "*I* should not have done that," to "I should not have done *that*." As he concludes: "such a shift clearly does not amount to much; it certainly does not amount to a distinction between a concept that is fundamentally non-moral and one that is, or between one that is solely concerned with external sanctions and one that is based on individual conscience."[37]

It is clear from the above that, in terms of the study of shame from a psychological perspective, while there is broad agreement as to its nature as an affect/emotion, there is also a great deal of variance in attempting to define exactly what it *is*. There is also significant debate concerning the relationship between shame and guilt, with the overall impression that the field is deeply divided and in a state of flux.

Clearly, it would be unwise to dispense with the psychological approach completely. Even if the emic distance between the pre- and post-Freudian worlds were so great that no fruitful comparison could be made, psychological study has so influenced *our* terminology and conceptual world that, at a minimum, it would still illumine the researcher's own emic, a factor of no small importance in and of itself (even if only for the sake of critique). However, given that embarrassment, humiliation, social sanction and the like do seem to be sustained conditions of human existence globally and throughout history, we should expect to be able to utilize at least some aspects of psychological research as part of our initial etic.

In light of the above, the most constructive way forward would seem to be not to settle too quickly on one definition or model of shame over and against another nor to reject psychological research into the area wholesale. Instead, I will seek to incorporate appropriate insights, while at the same time "sitting loose" on definitions that may be prematurely restrictive.[38]

---

37. Douglas L. Cairns, *Aidōs: The Psychology and Ethics of Honor and Shame in Ancient Greek Literature* (Oxford: Clarendon, 1993), 25–26. As with Lasch, I will return in more depth to Cairns's work, as there is much to gain from both in critiquing both the psychological and anthropological views of shame that have been utilized in biblical studies and Christian theology.

38. Cairns points us in this direction in his summary of psychological research on shame: "This discussion of shame and guilt, of course, is subordinate to our study of *aidōs*, a concept from a language which has no words covering exactly the same range as either shame or guilt. Yet *aidōs* is continually characterized by classical scholars in terms of shame, and in terms which presuppose a sharp and self-explanatory distinction between shame and guilt. Thus the foregoing analysis seems to me worthwhile . . . beacuse

In other words, using psychological research on shame as a springboard to closer reading of the text of Ezekiel may help us to begin to ask the questions that will move us toward an emic and then properly derived etic view of the concepts involved in the shame terminology he uses.

Shame in Anthropology

Ruth Benedict and Margaret Mead

Before proceeding, however, there is a further link in the history of research that needs to be explored. The criticisms of Lasch and Cairns in psychology lead us to the relationship it has with shame research in anthropology (to which most recent SSA studies on shame are indebted). This is especially crucial when one takes into account that some SSA studies posit a fundamental dichotomy between anthropological and psychological perspectives, dismissing (or at least minimizing) the psychological aspect in the Bible, without recognizing the very dependence the anthropological model has on psychological terms and concepts.[39]

Benedict, for example, was attempting to give an account of the wartime behavior of Japanese to a somewhat puzzled Western audience in the aftermath of World War II and introduce Americans to "Japanese culture." Mead sought to free Western society from conservatism by appeal to Samoan society in which, she claimed, sexual freedom, uninhibited by the repressive restraints of marriage and the modern, Western nuclear family, was the norm.[40] Both, however, adopted the psychological distinction between peoples directed primarily by external, public, "shame-based" sanctions, and those directed primarily by internal, private, "guilt-based" ones.

Both Benedict and Mead (not to mention Freud) have come under heavy attack for their methodology, the quality and reliability of their research, and the implications that they have drawn from them.[41] That there is such a

---

it indiactes that even if we do choose to characterize *aidōs* in terms of shame, this does not commit us to the view that *aidōs* involves mere observance of external sanctions and has nothing to do with any sort of internalized standard" (ibid., 26).

39. Besides *The New Testament World*, see also Crook, "Honor Revisited"; and especially idem, *Reconceptualising Conversion*, 1–11.

40. Benedict, *Chrysanthemum and Sword* (esp. p. 225, where her explanation of cultural difference is put explicitly in Freudian terms); Mead, *Coming of Age*. Mead's discussion is placed within the wider banner of the nature/nurture debate. As Franz Boas writes in the foreword to the book: "The results of [Mead's] painstaking investigation confirm the suspicion long held by anthropologists, that much of what we ascribe to human nature is no more than a reaction to the restraints put on us by our civilisation." What is especially noteworthy about this is that there is a fascinating (and somewhat ironic) affirmation in Boas's statement, namely, that even in attempting to characterize Western culture as an individualistic culture, Boas and Mead actually identify that *social sanction*—"the restraints put on us by our civilisation"—is the driving force behind a guilt culture.

41. M. R. Creighton, "Revisiting Shame and Guilt Cultures: A Forty-Year Pilgrimage," *Ethos* 18/3 (1990): 170–307; Derek Freeman, *The Fateful Hoaxing of Margaret Mead: A*

sustained body of research effectively undermining the work of such key figures in the development of the dominant paradigm in the area of shame research casts significant doubt on the viability of the entire characterization.

On the other hand, the fact that there is ample evidence that there are several cultural groupings for whom the opinions of their social groupings *does* seem a more powerful motivating and evaluative force than an explicit and independent "inner voice," combined with the historical pedigree that has built up around the concepts, mean that some benefit may still be obtained from the research and models, albeit chastened by the counterevidence.

Douglas Cairns

This approach certainly rings true of one of the most comprehensive and stinging critiques of the shame/guilt distinction in the context of biblical studies: Cairns's inquiry into the use of αἰδώς in classical Greek literature.[42] Although he focuses on "the psychology and ethics" involved in the term, Cairns devotes almost his entire introduction to a searching analysis and critique of Benedict, Mead, and other significant anthropological voices in the area of shame and guilt culture research.

Cairns first demonstrates the problematic nature of positing a hard and fast distinction between the emotions of shame and guilt. While acknowledging that there are instances in which each label alone may be appropriate, Cairns demonstrates how quickly the distinction breaks down in practice. At the heart of his critique is the observation that the supposedly separate realms of guilt (having to do with the violation of an internalized prohibition) and shame (having to do with failure to live up to a valued self-image) quickly blur into one another. As Cairns views it, shame involves a negative evaluation of the self *in light of some specific shortcoming*, and guilt arises from an act that creates a *discrepancy between self-image, and conduct*.[43]

Cairns then applies this observation to Benedict and Mead's anthropological model, noting the key place the separation of guilt and shame play in their research. Once the fundamental divide is lost, however, the entire

---

Historical Analysis of Her Samoan Research (Boulder: Westview Press, 1999); idem, *Margaret Mead and Samoa: The Making and Unmaking of an Anthropological Myth* (Canberra: Australian National University Press, 1983); idem, *Paradigms in Collision: The Far-Reaching Controversy over the Samoan Researches of Margaret Mead and Its Significance for the Human Sciences: A Public Lecture Given at the Australian National University on October 23, 1991* (Canberra: Research School of Pacific Studies–Australian National University, 1992); E. Michael Jones, *Degenerate Moderns: Modernity as Rationalized Sexual Misbehavior* (San Francisco: Ignatius, 1993); Richard Webster, *Why Freud Was Wrong: Sin, Science and Psychoanalysis* (London: HarperCollins, 1996); idem, *Freud's False Memories: Psychoanalysis and the Recovered Memory Movement* (Southwold: Orwell, 1996); Gertrude Himmelfarb, *Marriage and Morals among the Victorians: Essays* (London: Faber, 1986).

42. Cairns, *Aidōs*.

43. Ibid., 24.

construct collapses, because "at all stages both shame and guilt possess an internalized component, and neither is one differentiated from the other by the fact that that it may occur before a real audience, a fantasy audience, or before oneself."[44]

Cairns goes on to a close examination of Benedict's work, and his assessment is devastating: her admission that Japanese society was not a "true shame culture" but a shame culture "with an admixture of guilt" belies the untenability of the distinction. Cairns notes that Benedict's work actually demonstrates the exact reverse of her claims: "how both acute concern for the opinion of one's fellows and the capacity to act on the basis of internalized standards are instilled by that nations' emphasis on honor, status, and reciprocal obligation."[45] In other words, the Japanese that Benedict studied are, like all humans across the globe and throughout history, are driven by *both* external, social sanctions, and internal, unconditional convictions.

Cairns traces the theoretical basis of Benedict's work back to Mead,[46] and finds in her work a key failure to distinguish between shame as a (subjective) state of mind and shame as an (objective) state of affairs.[47] Cairns highlights Mead's use of the phrase "fear of shame," which Cairns notes must mean "fear of disgrace," or "fear of *being shamed*." The result of this clarification, however, is that Mead's definitions collapse in on themselves, as the external sanction has, for all intents and purposes, become an internalized one. As a result, the whole shame/guilt antithesis becomes a contradiction in terms.[48]

Following the thread even further, Cairns goes on to observe that the shame/guilt antithesis, in its more complex form, has more to do than simply the difference between external and internal sanctions. He finds instead that the characterization "guilt culture" put forth by Mead is in fact a product of her (and the entire psychoanalytic enterprise's) particular socialization, and a flawed presupposition that guilt and conscience—the supposed origins of internalized sanctions—can only exist in societies where children are raised by parents who stress absolute values (good and evil), hypostasized in the figure of the fatherly deity.[49]

In other words, Cairns argues, the very characterization of guilt and shame cultures relies on an underlying *a priori* framework that, in the end, only a society that relies on Protestant, Anglo-American methods of parenting can be said to emphasize internal sanctions.[50] This is essentially

---

44. Ibid., 27.
45. Ibid., 28.
46. Margaret Mead, *Cooperation and Competition among Primitive Peoples* (London: McGraw-Hill, 1937).
47. Cairns, *Aidōs*, 30.
48. Ibid.
49. Ibid.
50. Ibid.

because the definitions are completely, self-referringly circular—"guilt" is what characterizes the Western mode of sanction, and hence those cultures which operate according to the Western mode of sanction are "guilt" cultures. As a result, the evidence in non-Western cultures for internalized sanctions, guilt-like behavior, and the notion of personal "conscience" has been largely ignored or overlooked, simply because they don't usually look like they do in white, middle-class American society.[51]

Once so exposed, the arbitrariness of such constructions is clear. *All* societies, generally speaking, feature adults using external sanctions in an attempt to instill cultural values in the next generation; values that are expected to become internalized as the norm for their children, because they were internalized at some stage for their parents. In other words, all societies construct and feature what anthropologists label as "guilt" characteristics; they are not reserved for or exclusive to Western societies.[52]

To this we might add that an additional question mark over the distinction is raised when we consider that, functionally, both "shame" and "guilt" cultures alike provide the growing child with primarily external sanctions which are expected to be appropriated into internal ideals; all that has happened in a "shame culture" (if we may follow the parameters of the model for a moment) is that the set of elements in the "authoritative moral body" has been expanded, from the parents alone (in a guilt culture) to the kinship group, community or society as a whole (in a shame culture).

Cairns concludes that, given that the entire basis of the shame/guilt culture distinction is groundless, there isn't actually much use for the antithesis, as it cannot be used to distinguish helpfully between societies. He is also unwilling to use them even as an abstract model (in other words, an initial/imposed etic), given this was not the intention of the antithesis, nor has it traditionally been used that way. More substantially, however, Cairns's second objection is that the categories are too wide and imprecise and can only end up with the rather redundant conclusion that all societies are rather complex in the combination of social and psychological factors that go into their makeup.[53]

On the other hand, Cairns does recognize that the concepts of shame and guilt, if more carefully articulated and sensitively applied, can still be useful in researching the significant differences between our social setting and ancient Greek society. In this regard, Cairns suggests that the heightened sense of feeling under the scrutiny of others (and even oneself), which would seem to be a particular characteristic of societies where social status and roles are more clearly defined and consciously adhered to as a default, renders plausible the suggestion that people in these societies come to

---

51. Ibid.
52. Ibid., 35.
53. Ibid., 42–43.

see their actions from the viewpoint of the "other" in a more pronounced way.[54]

Despite this concession, Cairns still feels there is ultimately little to be gained by the continued application of the antithesis. Instead, he urges that a more careful articulation of *both* the similarities *and* the differences between cultures is a far more fruitful way forward in cross-cultural research.[55]

The critique is certainly a *tour de force*, one that scholars not only working directly in the field but also those who appropriate the terms and concepts in supporting statements for their own area of research (as is increasingly occurring in biblical studies) need to take into serious account. Indeed, for myself, as a person whose ethnicity originates in a so-called shame culture, it is fascinating to reflect on the manner in which Cairns's analysis rings true, at least in the experience of some of my personal friends, family, and acquaintances who share my Chinese heritage. For, though it is true that Chinese society and communities exert considerable pressure on families and individuals by means of "external sanctions," it is equally true both that, as in "guilt cultures," the role of the *parents* in instilling and enforcing sanctions in children is particularly pronounced, and that the sanctions are expected to be *internalized* by children in what equates to a sense of morality.

Cairns's work also leads us to three related conclusions of vital importance to this study. First, he stresses the *relational* nature of shame-awareness, in which self-evaluation is brought into frequent and explicit relationship with that of other people.[56] This is an important point to make, especially in light of the older characterization of the prophets as "rugged individualists." Far from this being the case, as Stiebert notes, "in the Major Prophets . . . shame vocabulary is most prevalent."[57] Their sustained use of *relational* terminology, including shame, indicates that they understood themselves in thoroughly social terms.

Second, Cairns points out repeatedly that shame and guilt are not antithetical, but share an intimate (although sometimes distinguishable) relationship. This recognition not only helps overcome the problems with the cultural dichotomies that many contemporary SSAs are built on, but also helps overcome the philosophical split between act and being that can lie behind it. In other words, just as we cannot ultimately separate shame and guilt into external and internal sanction, it is also problematic to posit a notional separation between being (who I am) and act (what I do).[58]

---

54. Ibid., 45–46.

55. Ibid., 47.

56. Ibid.

57. Stiebert, *Construction of Shame*, 1; cf. idem, "Shame and Prophecy: Approaches Past and Present," *BibInt* 8 (2000): 255–75.

58. The parallel terms in psychology are "self" and "agent," or in Freudian terms, ego-ideal and superego. On Freud's understanding of shame and guilt, see further Sigmund

We can extend this further by recognizing that, by implication, just as with shame, so *guilt* is ultimately relational.[59] In the case of the Bible, "transgression" (עוה/פשע/חטא) is not simply the breaking of an internalized prohibition or even an abstract moral code, it is doing "what is forbidden in any of *Yhwh's* commands" (Lev 4:2). Moreover, as the commands of Yhwh are often tied to his self-giving relationship to his people (e.g., Exod 19:1–5), sustained and willful transgression of the commands is taken to be indicative of the rejection of Yhwh himself: "Ah, sinful nation, a people loaded with iniquity, a brood of evildoers, children given to corruption! They have forsaken Yhwh; they have spurned the Holy One of Israel and turned their backs on him" (Isa 1:4).

As expressed especially in the prophets, the issue that brought Israel under Yhwh's condemnation, then, was not so much their failure to perform the sacrifices prescribed in the Torah. Rather, in Isaiah (for example), the heart of the matter was Israel's rejection of Yhwh, of which their continual breach of *torah* was simply symptomatic (Isa 1:1–13, 27–28). I will explore the relational aspect of guilt, and how this is affected by Yhwh's role as "the Judge of all the earth" (Gen 18:25) further in ch. 6.

Third, Cairns highlights the complexity of meaning in the usage of αἰδώς/αἰδέομαι—it can mean both "I feel shame before" and "I respect."[60] Cairns notes that the two meanings are obviously related, but nonetheless distinct categories of thought. Given that such a key "shame" word can convey these distinct senses at least opens the door to a wider range of possibilities in translating Hebrew "shame" words with greater sensitivity, and awareness that there may be a broader range of concepts involved than simply "shame notions."[61] On this front, it is helpful to note some further recent contributions to the field that will aid in "clearing the air" in discussing the topic.

Freud, *The Ego and the Id* (ed. J. Strachey; trans. J. Riviere; London: TIPL 12; Hogarth Press and the Institute of Psycho-Analysis, 1962).

59. For a presentation of this perspective, see Herant A. Katchadourian, *Guilt: The Bite of Conscience* (Stanford: Stanford General Books, 2009). Katchadourian's chapter on "Guilt and Relationships" is particularly illuminating, in which he states: "It takes two to play the guilt game. However, studies of guilt in human relationships are relatively new. This is partly due to the Freudian heritage of emphasizing the *intra-psychic* rather than *interpersonal* aspects of psychological conflicts" (pp. 63–64).

60. Cairns, *Aidōs*, 3.

61. It would significantly strengthen the case if instances of "shame" terminology in the Hebrew Bible were rendered by αἰδώς/αἰδέομαι in the LXX. However, the only instance of the term appears in Prov 24:23, where it is used for פנים. Most instances of בוש/כלם are translated with αἰσχύνη, which seems to sit more comfortably within the realms of "shame" concepts. Prov 24:23: "to show partiality in judging is not good," is still of interest, because the idiom הַכֵּר־פָּנִים ("to show partiality": literally, "to give regard/pay attention to face") is translated with αἰδεῖσθαι πρόσωπον. This usage clearly reflects Cairns's second translation "I respect" and indicates that the term was felt to be appropriate to use in translating a Hebrew concept of respect or esteem.

New Contributions

In the wake of rising awareness that earlier models are insufficiently accurate to analyze ancient conceptions of shame, several new contributions have made positive advances in the field. Before proceeding with analysis of "shame" terminology in Ezekiel, I will briefly state the most helpful ones that have not yet been raised in this chapter, as a means of broadening the set of tools we have at our disposal when we come to analysis of the text.[62]

Johanna Stiebert

Stiebert's work, already referred to in this monograph, is the most comprehensive on shame in the major prophets. For Stiebert, who draws on Cairns, shame in the prophets bridges both anthropology and psychology: it is used both in the context of social control and also as an internalized self-restraining mechanism. Stiebert argues that the prophets drew on shame language as a means of ensuring social stability, in the face of utter crisis.[63]

Stiebert's chapter on Ezekiel focuses mainly on chs. 16 and 23, in which she utilizes the categories "antilanguage" ("the languages of antisocieties seeking self-consciously to create a different kind of society from the one which either has been or is dominant, [which] are often characterized by extremity")[64] and "deviance amplification" ("a social group wishing to promote and enforce its agenda will distort and exaggerate that which it labels deviant with a view to justifying and bringing about its containment")[65].

While I question whether such categories are the most appropriate parameters for analyzing the chapters, Stiebert's conclusion is sound: in the prophetic writings "right" behavior is associated with the person of YHWH, mediated through his Torah. As such, "the role of Yhwh requires more attention in the analyses of shame language in the Hebrew Bible."[66]

In terms of this study, Stiebert makes two fundamental points that move discussion forward. First, that "shame" language in the prophets does not easily fall into the clean-cut distinctions set up in psychology and anthropology. Second, that the character of YHWH needs to be given more prominence in OT shame research.

David Konstan

In a 2003 article, David Konstan analyzed another significant Greek term for shame, αἰσχύνη.[67] Konstan found, importantly, that ancient Greek

---

62. Although aspects of some may have been raised in a slightly different context in previous chapters.

63. Stiebert, *Construction of Shame*, 170–71.

64. Ibid., 151.

65. Ibid., 172.

66. Ibid.

67. David Konstan, "Shame in Ancient Greece," *SR* 70 (2003): 1031–62; see also idem, *The Emotions of the Ancient Greeks: Studies in Aristotle and Classical Literature* (Toronto: University of Toronto Press, 2006).

and Roman sources "did not have distinct terms for what we call shame and guilt, and they seem to have made do with one concept where we recognize two."[68] Furthermore, he observes that in Aristotle, αἰδώς and αἰσχύνη have distinct, though clearly related usages. According to Konstan (who also follows Cairns), αἰδώς is always used in a prospective or inhibitory sense, while αἰσχύνη is both prospective and retrospective, thus "signifying equally 'shame' and a 'sense of shame.'"[69]

Konstan's key observation is that lexicographers have thus tended to classify the two senses of shame as distinct: "shame" as an emotion, and "sense of shame" as an ethical trait. However, Konstan argues that classical Greek had no such distinction, and cites Aristotle's definition as a way forward: "Let *aiskhune*, then, be a pain or disturbance concerning those ills, either present, past or future, that are perceived to lead to disgrace, while shamelessness is a disregard or impassivity with regard to those things."[70] Konstan concludes that both senses of shame are a single concept. There is in fact nothing to disambiguate, "what varies is simply the timing of the perceived ills."[71]

The obvious corollary of this, in light of Aristotle's definition, is that shame's opposite is simply "shamelessness" (ἀναισχυντία), "a failure of sensitivity to the relevant kinds of ills, whether past, present or future." This has the additional benefit of eliminating the need to differentiate two meanings of shamelessness (positive and negative). Rather, it is simply an insensibility to all evils that result in disgrace (whether retrospective or prospective). People who are shameless (that is, who have no shame) will obviously lack the restraint to prevent themselves from committing such acts.[72]

There is an immediate relevance in this conceptual clarification for this study. One of the key difficulties in Ezekiel is the thorny issue of "shame in restoration" (Ezek 16 and 36). The call, "be ashamed and disgraced for your conduct" (Ezek 36:32), has proved resistant to both approaches: in the anthropological model, restoration should eliminate shame, while in the psychological approach, it casts Yʜwʜ as psychologically abusive, perpetually holding past transgressions against his people. That αἰσχύνη is used to translate בּוֹשׁ in both chapters in the LXX provides us with alternative avenues of interpretation that may help resolve some of these issues.

Deonna, Rodogno, and Teroni

In response to the view of shame that sees it as an inherently negative, undesirable psychological concept, Deonna, Rodogno, and Teroni (2011)

---

68. Idem, "Shame in Ancient Greece," 1032.

69. Ibid., 1037.

70. Aristotle, *Rhetoric* 1383b.2–4 (Freese, LCL); cited (as 1383b.12–14) in Konstan, "Shame in Ancient Greece," 1040.

71. Ibid., 1041.

72. Ibid.

defend shame as a necessary and, in fact, beautiful part of the human emotional makeup.[73] To do so, they draw a key distinction between the shame someone has or feels and the act of shaming that is undertaken to incite such feelings.[74] This leads the authors to argue that shame itself is not inherently problematic in human psychology. The issue, rather, is *being shamed for irrational, or immoral reasons*: In other words, if shame is always associated with being shamed for illegitimate reasons, then it is no wonder that the emotion has been (mis-)understood to be completely negative and undesirable.[75]

Instead, the authors develop Aristotle's idea of prospective shame (that is, the ability to simulate future, shame-inducing activities). They conclude that this notion of shame is in fact an invaluable tool for both avoiding these situations and, importantly, on the positive side, for constructing parameters for life in accordance with the values one holds.[76] This shame is thus a "semi-virtue," which reflects both the subject's attachment to the relevant value (the "virtue") and the failure to uphold it (the "semi-"). Furthermore, by extension, because our sense of shame is not present solely in actual experiences of shame, it can in fact be seen as a "full blown virtue, *as long as we endorse without hesitation the values that sustain it.*"[77]

This line of thinking is both penetrating and illuminating in view of the confusion generated in discussions on the topic of shame. In essence, the authors argue that shame is, in and of itself, a morally *neutral* category. It is in fact the *particular values that underlie the causes of shame* in any given situation that determine whether it is a good or a bad thing. If the values that cause shame in a person or society are immoral, pathologically irrational, or detrimental to positive relationship, then shame (as the failure to attain to such values) may be said to be negative or detrimental. However, if the values are *virtues*, then shame (and especially prospective shame) in this regard can be said to be both essential and positive. This has obvious application to the study of biblical texts, and may provide resources in engaging with Ezekiel's radical theocentricity, and the deep connection in the book between shame, cultic, and moral terminology.

Yael Avrahami

As already reviewed in this monograph, Yael Avrahami has made an important contribution to our understanding in translating the key Hebrew shame word for shame, בוש as "disappointment," rather than "shame."[78] Avrahami's study is illuminating in several respects, but especially so in re-

---

73. Julien Deonna, et al., *In Defense of Shame: The Faces of an Emotion* (Oxford: Oxford University Press, 2011).

74. Ibid., 155.

75. Ibid., 43.

76. Ibid., 178.

77. Ibid., 178–179 (emphasis mine).

78. Avrahami, "בוש in the Psalms."

lating shame to honor. For Avrahami, the link is rather indirect (in contrast to some significant SSA works, which continue see them as polar opposites), as בוש belongs to a wider semantic notion of "worthlessness" which, as a whole, stands as an antonym to the root כבד ("to be heavy/important/honored.")[79]

The key to Avrahami's essay, as I have noted, is that בוש is thus defined as "the experience of a disconnection between expectations and reality . . . in other words, בוש is the experience (or causing) of disappointment."[80] Avrahami's definition draws us back toward a psychological definition of shame as a failure to live up to an ideal, although here the ideal is not so exclusively intrapsychic as in many psychological formulations. Rather, it can be applied more broadly to "external" situations and circumstances, including that of social status. However, Avrahami draws attention to the *theological* emphasis of the word in the psalms, which is sustained throughout the OT: "In the Psalms, בוש commonly describes an opposite experience to divine help and response. The confidence in such help is the confidence that בוש will not be experienced."[81]

Christopher Lasch

I have already outlined the main thrust of Lasch's article, but one point I raised previously in brief I will now expand on. An important strand of Lasch's historical argument is the disconnection of shame and guilt from *theology* (which Lasch usually refers to under the more generic rubric of "religion"). According to Lasch, through the work of scholars such as Piers and Singer, followed by Lynd, the idea of guilt progressed (or perhaps regressed) from a close association with sin, through the concept of crime, to the rather banal sense of anything considered to be unconventional conduct.[82]

This transition also marked a fundamental change in the theological and philosophical conceptions involved in both guilt and shame. Previously, sin and guilt had been associated both with violating the moral law and failing to keep faith with God. It thus had to do not simply with specific actions but also with a sustained disposition of the will in rebellion against God and right human order. In Lynd's secularized version of guilt, however, it became reduced to a somewhat irrational fear of punishment for violation of community standards, that is, taboos.[83]

It is, however, Lasch's conclusion that I wish to highlight at this point, as it is rather surprising in the context of a contemporary, secular, academic

---

79. Ibid., 302.
80. Ibid., 308.
81. Ibid., 302. Note here also the overlap with Aristotle's "prospective" shame, whereby when Yнwн acts, בוש is avoided.
82. Lasch, *For Shame*, n.p.
83. Ibid.

context, particularly given that Lasch himself wrote from a self-consciously secular perspective:

> At its best, psychoanalytic theory exposes the moral and existential dimension of mental conflict; but even then it cannot compete with religion. Wurmser's book on shame, a work in the grand tradition of psychoanalytic speculation, reminds us that psychoanalytically informed interpretation can reclaim ageless moral wisdom and deepen our understanding of it. Reading Wurmser, we see why shame and curiosity have always been so closely linked in people's minds, why shame ought to evoke feelings of awe and reverence, and why it refers, above all, to the irreducible element of mystery in human affairs.
>
> But this very depth of moral understanding, so compelling at the level of moral theory, can also render psychoanalysis useless not only for therapeutic purposes but also as a guide to the conduct of life. The more it infringes on the territory once occupied by religion, the more it invites unflattering comparisons with its rival. Can psychoanalysis really do anything for people who suffer from an inner conviction of "absolute unlovability"? Maybe religion is the answer after all. It is not at all clear, at any rate, that religion could do much worse.[84]

Of note in the above quote is the clear link he sees between a "right" (or at least satisfying) understanding of shame and guilt, and an ultimate reference to the divine being: for Lasch, we need God to understand both guilt and shame (and, indeed, the relationship between them) properly.

Shame and Guilt: Clarifying the Concepts

In summary, it is interesting to note that problematic analyses of shame, as discussed throughout this project, seem to be characterized by various binary oppositions. In psychology, the primary polarity is shame vs. guilt as the fundamental motivating or ethical force in a person's life. In anthropology, the corresponding opposition is shame vs. honor. In fact, there is a further binary opposition that arises from the distinctive interests of psychology and anthropology: shame as subjectively experienced emotion (the emphasis in psychology) vs. shame as external social sanction (the emphasis in anthropology). Further, it is consistently taken to be an exclusively negative phenomenon in both psychology and anthropology spheres.

The inadequacies of these bipolar and exclusively negative characterizations of shame should be fairly clear by this stage, and there is increasing recognition of the need to move beyond simplistic schemata to a more satisfying account of the complexities involved in the concept. People are not motivated by *either* shame *or* guilt; nor is shame simply the negative mirror image of honor. Rather, shame operates in a complex interaction between internal, subjective emotion and external, social sanction. It can be both a

---

84. Ibid. Lasch is referring to Léon Wurmser, *The Mask of Shame* (Baltimore: John Hopkins University Press, 1981).

negative and positive phenomenon and can come in response to both moral and nonmoral stimuli.

From this conclusion, it seems reasonable to view both shame and guilt as part of a common concept sphere denoting an actual or potential ascription of disconnection between expectation and reality. This ascription may be given by God, the community, the person themselves, or whatever other evaluative entity (or combination of entities) is relevant. The disconnection between expectation and reality may have variously to do with self-perception or ideals, community values, a legal code, and so on. It may be actual (as in the case of an indictment or social sanction) or potential (as in the case of "positive shame," as a sensitivity to appropriate ethical conduct).

It is also reasonable enough to distinguish various aspects of the overall concept and, given the history of research in the area, to continue to give these aspects the labels that have been applied to them (that is, shame relating to the self, and guilt relating to agency, as in contemporary formulations). If we choose to do so, however, we must be careful to maintain their interconnectedness and not to impose false dichotomies or isolate one aspect from others in the shared concept sphere, as contemporary formulations are wont to do.

When we include Herzfeld's calls to pay heed to particularization, it is unsurprising that such an inquiry will become quite a complex affair.[85] However, the purpose of the foregoing discussion has been to clear the air, such that the *unnecessary* complexities generated by forcing words and concepts into rather ill-fitting models and concepts may be avoided as much as possible and as much clarity gained as we are able to. Indeed, given the confusion that is evident in shame research, both contemporary and biblical, it has been necessary to devote a much more significant portion of this study to it than was originally envisioned. My hope is that we are now a great deal freer to examine exactly what may or may not be involved when the words are used.

---

85. As echoed, with regard to research into shame, in Konstan, "Shame in Ancient Greece," 1032–34.

Chapter 4

Honor in Ezekiel: Emic B Part 1

כבד *in the Old Testament*

Malina's model of honor (along with shame) as the pivotal value in the Mediterranean have become widely accepted in biblical scholarship. Some scholars, including those within the Context Group, have sought to refine the model but usually defend the original, with subtle additions or modifications.[1] The preceding comment is not necessarily intended as a slight; rather, it demonstrates the longevity of the model, an indication of both its plausibility and continued applicability.

I have previously outlined Malina's model and its definition of honor. However, it will be helpful for the ensuing discussion to give a brief restatement of the concepts involved in the notion, distilled under the headings "Honor as Socially Acknowledged Worth," "Honor as Relational," "Honor and Limited Good," "Honor Precedence," and "כבד and Honor." Following this, I will engage more fully with Timothy Laniak's work on the semantics of honor in Esther, before examining Ezekiel's use of the concept and its implications.

The Anatomy of Honor in Mediterraneanism

Honor as Socially Acknowledged Worth

At the heart of Malina's model lies the oft-quoted definition: "Honor is the value of a person in his or her own eyes (that is, one's claim to worth) *plus* that person's value in the eyes of his or her social group. Honor is a claim to worth along with the social acknowledgement of that worth."[2] There are two important implications arising from this initially simple statement. First, the "substance" of honor—what honor actually *is*—is encapsulated in the idea of *worth* or *value*. Second, the key factor in assigning or dispensing

---

Author's note: The broad semantic studies in this chapter and the subsequent two have utilized the information obtainable in the standard lexicons and dictionaries of the OT (*TDOT, NIDOTTE, TLOT, HALOT, BDB, DCH*, etc.) as a general guide. However, I have attempted to supplement these (where relevant) with newer insights, and am presenting the data in a form framed and affected by the recent SSA research into the dynamics of honor and shame.

1. For example, Esler, *Sex, Wives and Warriors*; Crook, "Honor Revisited."
2. Malina, *New Testament World*, 31.

honor—the authorizing agent that makes honor "real"—is *social acknowledgement*: "A person's claim to honor requires a grant of reputation by others before it becomes honor in fact."[3] As we shall see in our analysis of Ezekiel and the wider body of the OT, this basic definition is both the great strength and the great weakness of the Context Group's model as applied to the Bible.

Honor as Relational

One important corollary of the anthropological model of honor put forward by the Context Group is a renewed emphasis in biblical studies on the importance of relationality in understanding human life. As Malina points out, some modern approaches have so stressed individual agency that the importance of "structure" in understanding the texts has been minimized or lost.[4]

By contrast, an awareness of the dynamics of honor that are more apparent in non-Western societies leads to a view that, rather than beings in independent isolation, humans in these societies are transparently dependent on the "other" for virtually everything—identity, value, purpose, and place in the larger scheme of things. In this chapter, I will argue that the use of honor language in Ezekiel (and the rest of the OT) confirms the notion, in that it sees human life as inherently relational and dependent on the estimation of the other (the PCR). However, it also significantly modifies it, in that human PCRs, while present, are nonetheless supplanted and relativized by the DCR: the "Divine" Court of Reputation.

Honor and Limited Good

A third tenet of the Context Group's model is the insistence that in non-industrialized/consumer societies, honor, like everything else, is seen as a "limited good" and that, therefore, individuals and groups are constantly competing in a "zero-sum" honor game. In this game, when one party gains honor, another party must lose honor. Life is thus a series of agonistic challenges to one's (or one's group's) honor, and responding to these challenges to defend and increase honor.[5]

It is important to note that there are exceptions to this general pattern in Mediterraneanism, for example, in the notion of the "in-group" or "family" (where members work co-operatively for the sake of the group's honor). However, it is also worth noting that such studies can underplay in-group loyalty breakdown, with tensions and betrayals occuring within these groupings (as seen, for example, in the conduct of Jesus' disciples in Mark 8–10, and in Judas's betrayal).

---

3. Ibid., 33.
4. Ibid.
5. Ibid., 34.

The idea of honor as a limited good is one of the cornerstones of the model that has been appropriated by the scholarly community at large.[6] I will thus seek to test this fundamental premise of the model by close examination of Ezekiel's well-established "radically theocentric" perspective and presentation of the כבוד־יהוה as the nexus of his understanding of the concept of honor.

Honor Precedence

I have already made note of the debate between Zeba Crook and Louise Lawrence, over Pitt-Rivers's typology of honor. For Crook, the notion of "Honor Virtue," distinct from agonistic "Honor Precedence," does not sit comfortably within the Context Group's model. Instead, Crook sees "Honor Virtue" simply as "Honor Precedence," with a shift in PCR the only difference (from the public at large to a smaller community of faith). It is worth noting that this is a somewhat inevitable consequence of defining honor as a limited good: if honor is absolutely limited in its supply, then even deities must be subject to its machinations.

This in turn raises the obvious question of whether or not YHWH in the book of Ezekiel is as subject to the agonistic honor game as any other entity; for Crook, the answer is clearly "yes." Indeed, deities are in fact *dependent* on the human PCR for their very existence. Crook supports his view by Martial's epigrams concerning the Roman pantheon: "He does not make gods who sculpts sacred faces into gold or marble; he makes gods who asks of them" (8.24.5–6).[7]

While Crook's argument has persuasive elements, and his assessment of Greco-Roman deities being dependent on human supplicants for their continued existence is valid (there are no Zeus worshipers today), his attempt to include all deities under the same umbrella is at least worth questioning, if only for the fact that there *are* a good number of YHWH worshipers. One may wish to argue on different grounds for the existence or nonexistence of YHWH, but the logic of his argument fails at at least at this point. In this chapter, then, I will utilize the distinction between "Honor Precedence" and "Honor Virtue," while acknowledging the helpful aspects of Crook's suggestions.

------

6. E.g., the innocuous reference in Ben Witherington III, *Is There a Doctor in the House: An Insider's Story and Advice on Becoming a Bible Scholar* (Grand Rapids: Zondervan, 2011), 14: "If America were still an honor and shame culture" or the more explicit reference in John P. Dickson, *How Christian Humility Upended the World* (Australian Broadcasting Association, 2011), n.p. [cited October 27 2011]. Online: http://www.abc.net.au/religion/articles/2011/10/27/3349673.htm; cf. idem, *Humilitas: A Lost Key to Life, Love, and Leadership* (Grand Rapids: Zondervan, 2011), 83–95.

7. Martial, *Epigrams* 8.24.5–6 (Shackleton Bailey, LCL); cited in Crook, "Honor Revisited," 604.

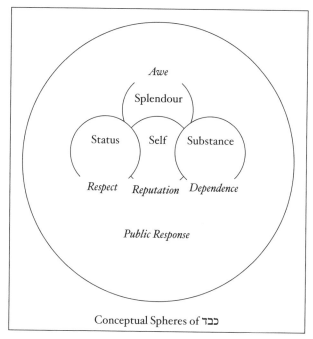

Conceptual Spheres of כבד

Fig. 4. Laniak's semantics of honor.

כבד *and Honor*

The above discussion raises the basic issue of how the root כבד should be understood in Ezekiel, and how it is related to notions of honor. In order to begin our investigation into these matters, I will engage with Laniak's recent study of the semantics of honor, as a foil against which to explore Ezekiel's contribution to the matter.

Laniak's Semantics of Honor

Laniak's 1999 *Shame and Honor in the Book of Esther* contains the most developed Context Group study on the semantics of honor in the OT to date.[8] Laniak takes כבד as "the most comprehensive honor root" and builds a representation of the range of meanings of כבד under the four headings *substance, status, splendor,* and *self*. He does this both for clarity, and as the four sociological categories on which his study is based (fig. 4).[9]

There are great strengths in Laniak's work, and several aspects of his exploration of כבד are helpful. Perhaps the greatest of these is his attempt to give a simple and unified account of the root and show the interconnectedness of its various meanings. Further, Laniak seeks to ground his categories in actual OT usage rather than simply to assume them. Also, importantly,

---

8. Ibid.

9. Ibid., 17–23. Illustration reproduced from p. 21.

Laniak acknowledges that כבד has both *objective* and *subjective* dimensions — that is, כבד can exist without being recognized (that is, ascribed or acquired). This is an important point, and one that does not seem to receive enough attention in many honor/shame analyses of the Bible.

However, despite this recognition, Laniak defaults to the standard Context Group position that the "substance" of honor is in its recognition, and that this is reflected throughout in the Bible.[10] While this is partially correct, a closer investigation of the actual use of the terms, both in Ezekiel and in the rest of the OT, suggests the need for a more developed and particularized approach to understanding the concept.

Jobes's review of Laniak's work is a helpful stimulus toward a way ahead, in this regard. She points out that lack of actual evidence of honor and shame codes in Persia, in combination with Laniak's overly broad categories, significantly minimize the usefulness of his methodology for providing new exegetical insights. Furthermore, she suggests that the detailed historical research required to articulate the distinctive cultural expressions of the concepts render them largely inaccessible by modern sociological theory.[11]

Aside from raising the more common critiques of the Context Group's research, Jobes's article is especially valuable in raising the need for relevant contemporary historical sources, if one seeks to validate the honor/shame code as reflective of actual, historical sociological patterns and realities. In fact, her observation exposes the fragile basis of OT studies utilizing the honor/shame model. This has occasionally been acknowledged in individual studies, but, as with other critiques, seems not to have made much impact on the confidence with which the model is endorsed.[12] In other words, until enough relevant ANE data are gathered and assessed, the suggestion that the OT is written in and from the perspective of an honor/shame culture largely analogous to that developed from Greco-Roman sources several centuries later remains simply that.

---

10. Ibid., 22.

11. Karen H. Jobes, "Review of Shame and Honor in the Book of Esther," *RBL* 2 (2000): 273–75.

12. Kirkpatrick concedes: "the [Context Group] model of honor . . . depends on modern-day anthropological studies and has been adapted for use in the ancient world primarily by New Testament scholars . . . [based on] cultural scripts in the ancient Greek rhetorical tradition. Unfortunately, nothing comparable has been identified in the Aramaic literature of the Persian period, nor in the Hebrew literature of the ancient Israelites and Judeans specifically" (Kirkpatrick, *Competing for Honor*, 28–29). He attempts to justify the honor/shame model by arguing that there is a transparent patron-client relationship between Yʜwʜ and Israel in the OT, and that the final form of Daniel was influenced by 2nd-century BC Hellenism (ibid., 30–31). The second argument is plausible, but the first seems circular, given that the patron-client relationship is itself dependent on assumptions of an honor/shame construction. Perhaps a more tentative suggestion with regard to its validity, as illustrative of a possibility, rather than justification of a methodological foundation, would have been appropriate.

However, while this aspect of Jobes's critique is immensely helpful, her statement that the generalizations of the honor/shame code render it ineffective in granting new exegetical insights into the text is overstated. As argued previously, taking the honor/shame model as an imposed etic allows one to recognize its value as a reading strategy and highly plausible *preliminary* framework, which can facilitate a more sensitive attempt at constructing a plausible conceptual framework for understanding כבד in Ezekiel, to which I now turn.

Honor and Shame: Lack of Evidence and Steps Forward

The lack of primary evidence of ancient honor codes sets important parameters for OT SSAs. As Stone notes, these studies often seem to become mired in the difficulties of accessing the real history behind the text, which has led to a relative neglect of symbolic and ideological questions.[13] However, if we view the biblical texts as artifacts of ancient culture and thus at the same time both history *and* historiography, then the possibility of making progress in our inquiries is opened, via careful, subject-specific literary analysis.[14]

To this may be added a judicious use of canonical theology. As Conrad, for example, has recognized, meaning is generated by the interplay of both text and reader but is also constrained by an encoded *intentio operis* (following Umberto Eco) within the text itself.[15] This, if not pressed too far, allows us to further ground our hermeneutic process in real history. While we do not have ancient honor codes to compare, we *do* have a body of texts that was accepted as authoritative within a community of faith, and in the case of Ezekiel, in close historical and cultural proximity to the time and circumstances to which it refers.[16] We can therefore legitimately examine themes across the OT as comparative data to reconstruct the cultural conceptions behind their use.

כבד *in the Old Testament*

The Hebrew root most commonly translated as "honor" in SSAs is כבד, which has the basic meaning "to be heavy." Its usage in the OT and ANE

---

13. Stone, *Sex, Honor and Power*, 29. Stone draws on James Barr, *The Scope and Authority of the Bible* (London: SCM, 1980), 1–17.

14. Stone's categorical distinction is that between the raw historical events ("history") and how they have been recorded by the interested parties ("historiography")

15. Edgar W. Conrad, *Reading the Latter Prophets: Toward a New Canonical Criticism* (JSOTSup 376; London: T. & T. Clark, 2003), 1–30. Conrad adopts a minimalist position with regard to Israelite historiography, but whether or not the reader accepts this, the manner in which he develops it is a helpful step forward in the area of hermeneutics.

16. For a discussion on the difficulties of the concept of Canon, see George Aichele, "Canon as Intertext: Restraint or Liberation?" in *Reading the Bible Intertextually* (ed. R. B. Hays et al.; Waco, TX: Baylor University Press, 2009), 139–56.

literature encompasses a wide range of related meanings that are both physically and metaphorically linked to this basic concept. Given the nature of the root, a variety of suitable semantic frameworks could be applied to the word.[17] My own structure is drawn from Laniak's recognition that the term may be used in situations where there are one or both of what I label "substantive" and "responsive" aspects.[18] In other words, there are some instances of כבד that refer to the actual properties of the object, irrespective of the perceptions of others, while others refer to the action or disposition of a party in response to the object.

The Substantive Aspect of כבד

Weight/Substance/Density/Severity

The basic meaning of כבד ("to be/become heavy"), is used in both physical and metaphorical senses in the OT. The physical sense can be found, for example, in Ezek 27:25, the "heavy cargo" of Tyre carried by the ships of Tarshish. Likewise, the elderly Eli is described as "a heavy man" (1 Sam 4:18), while Absalom's hair is described as "heavy" (200 shekels' worth), resulting in the need to have it cut (2 Sam 14:26). It is also possible that the use of the nominal form כבד for the liver (Exod 29:13) derives from its being considered the "weightiest" organ.[19] Tied in with heaviness is also *density/ denseness*, such as in the thickness of the fiery cloud surrounding Mt. Sinai in Exod 19:16.

Metaphorically, the notion of heaviness is often used in the context of an oppressive or difficult burden. 1 Kings 12:11 speaks of the "heavy/-ier yoke" that Solomon brings on the people of Israel, while in Exod 5:9, Pharaoh presses the Israelites further into forced labor. However, the word may also be used without any particular sense of oppressiveness, as in Exod 18:18, where Moses's role in settling disputes in the Israelite community is simply too much work for one man to reasonably do: "The work is too heavy for you; you cannot handle it alone."

"Heaviness" is also used of parts of the body that are disabled or unable to function properly. In Gen 48:10, כבד is used to describe Israel's failing eyes, while in Exod 4:10 Moses resists appearing before Pharaoh on the basis of his "heavy mouth and heavy tongue." Using the same phrase, YHWH tells Ezekiel that he is not being sent to foreigners with "heavy tongue" (Ezek 3:5). In this instance the phrase is paralleled with עמקי שפה, "unfathomable speech," and thus the sense here is not so much (lack of) eloquence (as in Exod 4:10) as the notion of incomprehensibility.

---

17. Besides Laniak, see for example the entries on כבד in *TDOT, NIDDOTE,* and *SDBH.*

18. Cf the parallel terminology of "fact" and "sentiment" in Pitt-Rivers, "Honour."

19. S.v. "כבד," *TDOT.*

In an extension of physical and mental disability, the heart (לב, or ears אזן) can be said to be "heavy" in terms of their orientation to Yhwh and his word. The overwhelming concentration of this sort of כבד in this sense appears in the context of Pharaoh's refusal to release the Israelites and the resulting plagues (Exod 7:14, 8:11, 28, 9:7, and so on). In these cases, כבד is used in parallel with חזק (e.g., Exod 4:21, 7:13) and conveys Pharaoh's determined, stubborn unresponsiveness to Yhwh and refusal to submit to his word. In subsequent parts of the OT, including Ezekiel, the language is applied to Israel's own obstinate rebellion against Yhwh (e.g., Isa 29:13; cf. לב חזק, Ezek 2:4; 3:7).[20]

An interesting junction of heaviness and honor concepts comes in the use of כבד to denote "severity." Genesis, for example, records at least two instances of "heavy famine" (רעב כבד, Gen 12:10, 41:31), while several of the plagues of Exodus (flies, pestilence, hailstorm, and locusts) use כבד in the same sense (one could also say that there is significant overlap in the spheres of meaning of כבד here: because there are so many insects/dead livestock, the suffering is "severe"). What is intriguing in the context of the Exodus is the repeated insistence of Yhwh throughout the narrative that "I will gain glory (אכבדה) through Pharaoh," the vehicle of which is the "heavy" plagues that Egypt is afflicted with. In this usage, there are clear overtones of "honor," including the concepts associated with the honor/shame model. Agonistic contest, reputation, awe, call for loyalty, and so on, seem to all be at stake in the rescue of the Israelites out of Pharaoh's hand.[21]

In a similar vein, several passages speak of the "heavy hand" of Yhwh to express the distress of being under the judgment of God (Job 23:2; Ps 32:4). The sin of Sodom and Gomorrah is also said to be "grievous" (כבדה מאד) in Gen 18:20, while the idea of severity also lies behind descriptions of battles as "fierce" (Judg 20:34; 1 Sam 31:3).

Perhaps the most noteworthy passages featuring the meaning "severity" are the so-called Ark Narrative (1 Sam 4–6; 2 Sam 5–7), which seem to be constructed around a play on words with כבד.[22] In 1 Sam 4, for example, the Israelites attempt to use the ark of the covenant, the main locus of the כבוד יהוה as something of an amulet in battle with the Philistines.

The result, however, is disaster: the Israelites are defeated, the sons of Eli are killed and the ark is captured by the Phillistines. At the news of the

---

20. For further discussion on the importance of recognition of Yhwh in the OT, see Walther Zimmerli, *I Am Yahweh* (ed. W. Brueggemann; trans. D. W. Scott; Atlanta: John Knox, 1982), 1–28.

21. On the theme of the plague narrative as a revelation of Yhwh's character, see Childs, *Exodus*, 149–51, 169–77; Moshe Greenberg, "The Thematic Unity of Exodus 3–11," *WCJS* 4/1 (1967): 151–54.

22. See further Robert Alter, *The David Story: A Translation with Commentary of 1 and 2 Samuel* (New York: Norton, 1999), 27–31; John Woodhouse, *1 Samuel: Looking for a Leader* (PTW; Wheaton: Crossway, 2008), 100–110.

ark's capture, Eli falls off his chair and his neck is broken, "because he was an elderly man, and heavy (כבד)." In response, the daughter of Saul perishes in childbirth, but not before giving her son the name אי־כבוד ("Where is the glory?") with the explanatory comment "the כבוד has departed from Israel." The implied answer to the question comes in 1 Sam 5, as the Philistines are made subject to the "heavy" hand of Y<small>HWH</small> (ותכבד יד־יהוה) in a somewhat similar fashion to the Egyptian plagues, beginning with the dismemberment of Dagon in a "contest of gods" reminiscent of Y<small>HWH</small> and Pharaoh in Exodus.[23] As with the Exodus plagues, the victory reputation of Y<small>HWH</small> among the nations is prominent.

Possessions/Wealth/Abundance

Closely linked to the concept of weight, כבד is also used to denote possessions and, by extension, wealth. Judges 18:21 uses the nominal כבודה in the plain sense of "possessions," while Gen 13:2 describes Abraham's wealth in terms of "abundance of possessions": "Abraham became very wealthy (כבד מאד) in livestock and in silver and gold." The same meaning is found in Exod 12:38, in which "large herds" of livestock are given to the Israelites in the Exodus, while Balak promises to "handsomely reward" (כבד אכבדך) Balaam with silver and gold in Num 22:17–18. Esther 5:11 is especially clear: "Haman boasted to them about his *vast wealth* (כבוד עשרו)." This use of כבד suggests that wealth was primarily construed as the abundance and/or value of the possessions that someone held. Such a close association would be fairly intuitive, especially in the context of a non- or semi-monetary society.

The notion of abundance also often appears in descriptions of armies or entourages as "mighty" or "large" (Gen 50:9; Num 20:20; Judg 1:35). Furthermore, in these and other instances there is a clear overlap in meaning between "size" or "number," and "strength." This is especially prominent when כבד is used adjectivally in the phrase חיל כבד, a "great/huge army" (2 Kgs 18:17; Isa 36:2; although cf. 1 Kgs 10:2; 2 Chr 9:1, where it describes the size, wealth and majesty of the Queen of Sheba's [nonmilitary?] entourage).

Significance/Status

Often associated with abundance and strength is "significance," "greatness," "dignity," and "power." This is especially the case with those who are of importance or high status, who are (fittingly) held in high regard. Thus, Joseph instructs his brothers: "Tell my father about all my glory (את־כל־ כבודי) in Egypt," by which is meant his significance and administrative authority over the country, as well as the resulting status in the eyes of the community: "God has made me lord of all Egypt" (Gen 45:9). In a similar vein, Abishai is כבד over "the three" because of his particular military prow-

---

23. For further discussion on the association between mutilation and honor/shame concepts, see Lemos, "Shame and Mutilation."

ess in battle (2 Sam 23:18–19). Closely connected again is the statement in Judg 1:35 that "the power of the house of Joseph increased" (ותכבד יד בית־יוסף).

In this concept sphere, כבד is often associated with the vocabulary of "elevation," "lifting" and "exaltation," both physically and in terms of social standing or esteem. In Hannah's song, for example, we are told that YHWH "raises (מקים) the poor from the dust and lifts (ירים) the needy from the ash heap; he seats them with princes and has them inherit a throne of honor (כסא כבוד)" (1 Sam 2:8).[24] Likewise in Prov 4:8, the reader is exhorted: "Exalt [Wisdom], and she will raise you up, she will honor you if/because you embrace her (סלסלה ותרוממך תכבדך כי תהבקנה)." Unsurprisingly, YHWH is to be exalted above all, as is appropriate to his nature as God over all: the Levites declare, "Stand up and praise YHWH your God, who is from everlasting to everlasting. Blessed be the name of your glory (שם כבודך), and may it be exalted (ומרומם) above all blessing and praise" (Neh 9:5) Likewise, the refrain, "Be exalted (רומה), O God, above the heavens, and let your glory (כבודך) be over all the earth," rings through several of the Psalms (57:6, 12, 108:6, 113:4 in a modified form).

It is in this concept sphere that we come closest to the idea of "honor" as set forth by the Context Group. However, it is important to maintain the distinction (often glossed over) between "actual" honor, and the recognition of that honor, especially when it comes to the character of YHWH. In the example of Neh 9:5 above, it is *because* YHWH is "from everlasting to everlasting" that his name is to be blessed and exalted.

Splendor/Magnificence

כבד can also have the sense of visible radiance, or magnificence, often in relation to the display of wealth. The princess bride is said to be "all glorious (כל־כבודה)" in her gown interwoven with gold (Ps 45:14). The queen of Sheba visits Solomon with "a great caravan (בחיל כבד מאד)," which is then further decribed in terms of its "camels carrying spices, large quantities of gold, and precious stones" (2 Chr 9:1). Likewise in Esther, for 180 days Xerxes "displayed the vast wealth (עשר כבוד) of his kingdom and the splendor and magnificence of his greatness" (Esth 1:4).[25]

---

24. Cf. Alter, *The David Story*, 11, who draws on Polzin's argument that "the early chapters of 1 Samuel [are] a grand foreshadowing of the fate of the monarchy with the old and failing Eli, who will die falling off his chair or throne, as a stand-in for the Davidic kings." Alter's comment is significant for the manner in which it highlights the overlapping concept spheres of כבד as "honor/exaltation" in Hannah's song, and Eli as "heavy" and, by implication, unresponsive to YHWH. See further Robert M. Polzin, *Samuel and the Deuteronomist: A Literary Study of the Deuteronomic History*, part 2: *I Samuel* (San Francisco: Harper & Row, 1989).

25. The most developed study of honor themes in Esther is Laniak, *Shame and Honor in Esther*.

The idea of splendor can also be extended to persons themselves, not simply their regalia. In Ps 8, YHWH is said to have made humanity (represented under the corporate notions of "man" and "son of man") "a little lower than the heavenly beings, and crowned (him) with glory (כבוד) and honor." Once again, YHWH himself is the expression of splendor *par excellence* in the Bible. In the Exodus narrative, the description of the כבוד־יהוה stresses his awesome and spectacular appearance, "like a consuming fire" (Exod 24:17). In a more indirect association, "the heavens declare the glory of YHWH" (Ps 19:1).

It is in the prophets, particularly in the visions of Ezekiel and Isaiah, however, that we have the most full-orbed descriptions of a person's splendor, in the כבוד־יהוה.[26] Here I will focus on Isaiah, and save more focused coment for Ezekiel's visions. In Isa 6:1–4, Isaiah sees YHWH

> seated on a throne, high and lofty, and the train of his robe filled the temple. Above him were seraphs, each with six wings . . . and they were calling to one another, "Holy, holy, holy is YHWH Almighty, the whole earth is full of his glory." At the sound of their voices the doorposts and thresholds shook and the temple was filled with smoke.

Isaiah's vision is noteworthy not simply for its spectacular description, but for the close association of "glory" and "holiness," that is characteristic of YHWH's portrayal in the Scriptures. YHWH's glory, in this case, is the awe-inspiring manifestation of his holiness. Moreover, this link is not unique, but is common throughout the OT. Ps 29:2 is another intriguing example of the relation of these concepts: "Ascribe to YHWH the glory due his name; worship YHWH in the splendor of his holiness." What is of particular note in Ps 29:2, however, is the explicit reference to the "name" of YHWH, which forms a bridge between the "splendor" aspect of כבד and the next concept sphere, "name" or "character."

Name/Character

כבד is used several times in association with an entity's name (שם).[27] By far the most common subject in these cases is YHWH, but not exclusively. In Isa 62:2, for example, restored Jerusalem is told: "The nations will see your

---

26. For a more sustained exploration of the theme of a person's glory/splendor, especially with regard to the intriguing notion of YHWH's body and its relationship to human embodiment, see Benjamin D. Sommer, *The Bodies of God and the World of Ancient Israel* (New York: Cambridge University Press, 2009), 1–4.

27. It goes almost without saying that the relationship of "name" (שם) to "presence/*kabod*" (כבוד) has been and continues to be a linchpin of critical OT scholarship. Most often, the two terms are taken as representative of sharply divergent theological traditions and conceptions of deity in the HB. A sustained exploration of this topic lies well beyond the scope or thrust of this study. However, recent studies on honor and shame have highlighted the close, harmonious association between a person's "name" and their "honor" in the relevant fields of inquiry. It seems a reasonable axis of inquiry, therefore,

righteousness, and all kings your glory; you will be called by a new name that the mouth of YHWH will bestow."

There are also several other examples where כבד is not directly used in conjunction with שם, but the concept is clearly in view. In Gen 11:4, one of the motives for building the Tower of Babel is "so that we may make a name for ourselves and not be scattered over the face of the whole earth." In line with honor themes, the text also possibly indicates that the ill-fated project was ultimately an attempt to usurp the right of YHWH to rule over them and provide their significance and security. This is perhaps reflected in the blessing of Noah's son, Shem (שם, Gen 9:26), and also in YHWH's calling of Abram: in contrast to the builders' attempt to make a name for themselves, YHWH declares in his blessing of Abram, "*I* will make your name great (ואגדלה שמך)" (Gen 12:2).[28]

It is also well attested in the Bible that a person's name is often reflective of, or even generated by, their moral character.[29] After being tricked out of both the inheritance and blessing by his brother, for example, Esau laments, "Isn't he rightly named (קרא שמו) 'Deceiver' (יעקב)?" Nabal's treatment of David is summarized aptly by Abigail: "He is just like his name—his name is Fool (נבל שמו), and folly goes with him (נבלה עמו)" (1 Sam 25:25). Likewise in the Othniel narrative (Judg 3:7–11), Israel's oppressor is כושן רשעתים—"Cushan of Double Wickedness."[30]

The definitive instance of the connection between name/character and כבד in the OT is the person of YHWH.[31] A key example of this, Ps 29:2, has already been mentioned, where the vocabulary of "glory" (כבוד), "name" (שם), "splendor" (הדרה) and "holiness" (קדש), are all integrally tied together (see also Lev 10:3; Isa 58:13; Ezek 28:22). However, though the core idea of "holiness" is the generic concept of separation, its biblical use as a descriptor for YHWH focuses on *his ontological and qualitative/ethical distinctiveness:* "I am God (אל), and there is no other; I am God, and there is none like me" (Isa 46:9).[32] The rationale for Israel's obedience to Torah was, accordingly,

---

to explore the literary link between the terms synchronically across the canon, even if diachronically, it is a more complex matter.

28. Cf Gordon J. Wenham, *Genesis 1–15* (Waco, TX: Word, 1987), 239–40, 242–46. See also John H. Walton, *Genesis* (Grand Rapids: Zondervan, 2001), 374–79, who suggests that the tower was a *ziggurat*, and thus "the offense in this passage, then, is . . . [that] it went beyond mere idolatry; it degraded the nature of God by portraying him as having needs" (p. 377).

29. S.v. "שם," *NIDOTTE, TDOT , DCH.*

30. See Barry G. Webb, *The Book of Judges* (Grand Rapids: Eerdmans, 2012), 159, who argues that the name is pseudonymous.

31. The connection between them (and other aspects of כבד) is seen most clearly in the Exod 33–34 theophany, but given that I will suggest that the episode forms something of a nexus of meaning for כבד in the OT, I will reserve examination of this passage until later in this chapter.

32. *Pace* Otto's suggestion, drawn from the more generic idea, that the concept was essentially a nonrational, and thus nonethical, experience of the numinous: Rudolf Otto,

to demonstrate Yhwh's superiority to all other gods, in the superiority of
life under his rule:

> This will show your wisdom and understanding to the nations, who will hear
> about all these decrees and say, "Surely this great nation is a wise and under-
> standing people. What other nation is so great as to have their gods near to
> them the way Yhwh our God is near to us whenever we pray to him? And what
> other nation is so great as to have such righteous decrees and laws as this body
> of laws I am setting before you today?" (Deut 4:6–8).

The above passages are consistent with the overall thrust of holiness language in the OT, especially when this language is applied to Yhwh's people.
The fundamental call on Israel that they "be holy, as I am holy" (Lev 19:2) is
applied in both cultic and ethical contexts throughout the canon (not just
in P/H). The consistent stress of holiness language falls on the distinctive,
theologically driven conduct of Israel in comparison to the nations that
they are to displace in the Land: [33] "You must not live according to the cus-
toms of the nations I am going to drive out before you. . . . You are to be
holy to me because I, Yhwh am holy, and I have set you apart from the
nations to be my own" (Lev 20:23–24, 26). [34] The foundation of this specificity of meaning for holiness can be traced back to the introduction to the
Mosaic Covenant in Exod 19–20 (besides the major themes of "separation"
and "distinctiveness," see the references to קדשׁ in Exod 19:4–6, 10, 14, 22,
23; 20:8, 11). [35]

In summary, Israel's holiness was the Torah-driven, distinctive pattern of
social, ethical, and cultic life (that is, morality) designed to express something of the distinctive person and character of the God that is worshiped:
"Be holy, because I, Yhwh your God, am holy" (Lev 19:2). [36] Accordingly,
Yhwh's character is spelled out in the rest of the OT in terms of what could
be termed "moral perfection": "I will proclaim the name of Yhwh . . . his
works are perfect (תמים פעלו), and all his ways are just (כל־דרכיו משפט). A
faithful (אמונה) God who does no wrong (אין עול), upright and just (צדיק

---

*The Idea of the Holy: An Inquiry into the Non-rational Factor in the Idea of the Divine and Its
Relation to the Rational* (Harmondsworth: Penguin, 1959). See also s.v. "קדשׁ," *NIDOTTE,
HALOT.*

33. Cf. the numerous references to holiness, by and large consistent with the Priestly
presentation, in Deuteronomy: 5:12; 7:6; 12:26; 14:2, 21; 15:9; 23:15; 26:15, 19; 28:9; 32:51. For
a sustained discussion of the use of holiness concepts in the OT from a canonical/biblical
theological perspective, see Jo Bailey Wells, *God's Holy People: A Theme in Biblical Theology*
(JSOTSup 305; Sheffield: Sheffield Academic Press, 2000).

34. For further discussion on the relationship between cult and ethics, see Leigh M.
Trevaskis, *Holiness, Ethics and Ritual in Leviticus* (Sheffield: Phoenix Press, 2011). I will return to this topic in ch. 5 of this study.

35. Although *SamP* has שׁמר for קדשׁ.

36. See further the discussion on the use of holiness language in the Pentateuch and
its connection to Israel's ethical life in Wells, *God's Holy People*, chs. 1–3.

וישֵׁר) is he" (Deut 32:4); cf. הָאֵל תָּמִים דַּרְכּוֹ (2 Sam 22:31; Ps 18:31); יהוה ...
אֱמוּנָה אֹמֶן (Isa 25:1).[37]

Before moving on to the "responsive" aspect of כבד, I wish to make one
final important addendum to the above discussion, in relation to honor/
shame studies. It should be noted that in contrast to the Context Group's
insistence on the *recognition* of honor being the decisive factor in its reality, the stress in the OT seems to lie on the *substantive* aspect of honor as
critical. As Stiebert comments in her analysis of Isaiah, "Honor is depicted
as a quality only Yhwh owns and bestows."[38] Or, as di Vito puts it, "Moral
competence belongs only to Yhwh. Only his appraisal determines the significance of an action."[39] If this is the case, then the appropriate response
to YHWH is *not* constitutive of his honor—that is his by definition. What is
at stake is whether or not humanity acknowledges him and is thus honored
by him in turn or rejects him and is condemned. The PCR, while present at
points in the biblical texts, is finally and in reality subject to the DCR (e.g.,
Isa 2:11–17; 4:2; Joel 2:11; Mic 4:1; Zech 14:9).[40]

The "Responsive" Aspects of דבכ

The responsive aspects of כבד can be summarized in the overlapping
ideas of *Reverence/Respect, Reward,* and *Repute.* As stated above, the range
of these instances is more limited in scope than the substantive, and particularly concentrated around the "honor" concept cluster.[41] I will work
through each in turn, noting some examples that correspond to the substantive aspects discussed above, before tying both substantive and responsive aspects together.

Reverence/Respect

כבד often involves fear and/or reverence, both via the root itself and
in response to it. Moses warns, "if you ... do not revere (ירא) this glorious

---

37. Cf. s.v. "Honor and Shame," *DOTPe,* 431–32. The "moral perfection" of YHWH has
been hotly discussed, especially with regard to how he is presented in Ezekiel. I will discuss this issue further in ch. 6, in considering the notion of "justice" and its relationship
to YHWH.

38. Stiebert, *Construction of Shame,* 88.

39. Di Vito, "OT Anthropology," 235.

40. One of the complicating issues that is relevant to this discussion is the nature of
biblical eschatology. It is the promissory/inaugurated/now-and-not-yet of judgment and
vindication by YHWH that both gives rebellious humans scope to "play the honor game"
in the period before the decisive judgment falls and allows YHWH himself to partake in
this sort of human activity, while also not being subject to its mechanisms.

41. This unbalanced distribution of susbtantive and responsive aspects gives us another insight as to why the Context Group's taxonomy of honor, exemplified by Laniak,
falls short of a satisfying semantic study—Laniak tries to force the word to do work that
it is simply not cut out to do, for the balance of ideas is simply not weighted according to
what the model demands.

and awesome name (את־השם הנכבד והנורא)—YHWH your God" (Deut 28:58). The Philistines send the ark away "for death had filled the city with panic (היתה מהומת־מות); God's hand was very heavy (כבדה מאד) upon it." Ps 22:24 describes the appropriate response of those "who fear YHWH" (יראי יהוה) in the overlapping calls to "praise" (הללוהו), "honor" (כבדוהו), and "revere" (וגורו) him.

These occurrences demonstrate that, while not completely congruent, כבד and ירא overlap significantly.[42] Perhaps the key reference associating כבד and reverence comes in Mal 1:6, where YHWH indicts the priests for showing contempt towards his name in the undertaking of their ministry: "A son honors (יכבד) his father and a servant his master. If I am a father, where is my honor (כבודי)? If I am a master, where is my fear (מוראי)?" The verb יכבד, in the initial couplet, is first repeated in its cognate nominal form (כבודי), as the appropriate response to paternal relationship, then expanded by a parallel use of מורא, "fear," as the appropriate response to the master-slave relationship. A similar concept is in view in Josh 7:19, where Joshua calls on Achan to "give glory (שים־נא כבוד) to YHWH," that is, to revere YHWH's authority and character enough to confess his theft of booty from Jericho.

The example of Mal 1:6 is important in discussing this aspect of כבד. In this verse, by virtue of its correspondence to מורא, it is clearly expressive of an internalized attitude of heart.[43] This is significant in light of the Context Group's perpetuation of the older anthropological polarization of collectivistic/externally driven and individualistic/internally driven societies, and points us toward a more accurate, integrated view of the dynamic between the psyche and the social in ancient Israel.

Laniak, for example, sees the command to honor one's parents as a command to provide financial assistance, due to the Context Group's tendency to downplay psychological connotations for the sake of emphasizing external, social expressions.[44] However, this seems rather forced and unnecessarily restrictive. Certainly, financial care of one's aged parents may be included, but the meaning of the term (and therefore the command) in context encapsulates much more than this. The prohibitions on cursing one's parents (Exod 21:17), sleeping with one's mother (Lev 18:7), and the command in Lev 19:32 to "rise in the presence of the aged [and] show respect (הדר) before the elderly," are clear examples where (internal) attitude of heart is of prime importance.

---

42. They are not congruent, because fear does not always come in response to honor, nor is what is feared always perceived as worthy of honor.

43. Cf. Isa 66:2, "This is the one I esteem: he who is humble and contrite in spirit, and trembles at my word." Here there is expressed both an internal attitude of "spirit" (רוח) and external expression of the inner reality, (trembling), although even then one could argue that this has a heavily metaphorical flavor.

44. Laniak, *Shame and Honor in Esther*, 18.

This is not to suggest that internal "honor" *doesn't* have appropriate external, social expressions. An attitude of reverence, or fear, presumably *should* lead to appropriate actual expression, which may well include providing financial assistance for one's parents. As such, no parent should be destitute in Israel, in large part because their years of provision in caring for their children *should be* responded to in like kind. Likewise, the service of discipline and rearing a child *should be* responded to with obedience and awe, as it is a weighty matter to be responsible for growing, shaping, and protecting the life of another (cf. Prov 23:22, "Listen to your father, who gave you life, and do not despise (אל־תבוז) your mother when she is old"). Thus, when כבד has to do with fear and reverence, both internal attitude and external expression may be in view in varying proportions, according to the context.

Reward

Corresponding especially to the substantival use of כבד for riches is the concept of reward. Balak promises to Balaam: "I will reward you handsomely (כבד אכבדך מאד)" (Num 22:17, 37; 24:11). Solomon likewise is promised "wealth, riches, and honor (עשר ונכסים וכבוד)," although, ironically, as a reward for *not* asking for them (2 Chr 1:12).

The use of כבד for reward can also extend beyond monetary considerations. Already in 2 Chr 1:12, honor is both tied to wealth and riches, and as such, is to be seen in the category of reward. Its use here, however, also seems to encompass the more abstract connotations of reverence and repute. Likewise, Manoah says to the messenger of YHWH, "What is your name, so that we may honor you (וכבדנוך) when your word comes true?" (Judg 13:17). The psalmist declares, "YHWH bestows favor and honor" (חן וכבוד יתן יהוה, Ps 84:12), while in Prov 4:8 the reader is exhorted regarding wisdom, "Esteem her, and she will exalt you; embrace her, and she will honor you (תכבדך)."

Repute

Reputation is often at the forefront in the biblical examples of כבד, especially (as I have already discussed) when it appears in the context of *name*. Abishai's acts of valor result in his being "held in greater honor than the three" (2 Sam 23:19). In response to Michal's derision of his decision to dance, David replies, "By these slave girls you spoke of, I will be held in honor (אכבדה)" (2 Sam 6:22). This presumably includes the new reputation of the undignified king "disrobing in the sight of the slave girls of his servants as any vulgar fellow would!" (2 Sam 6:20). In response to Balaam's rejection of his envoys, Balak "sent other princes, more numerous and more distinguished than the first (רבים ונכבדים מאלה)" (Num 22:15). Reputation is also included in the warnings of Ps 49:11–19, against the ungodly rich:

> Their tombs will remain their houses forever … though they had named lands after themselves … do not be overawed when a man grows rich, when

the splendor (כבוד) of his house increases, for he will take nothing with him when he dies, his splendor (כבוד) will not descend with him . . . he will join the generation of his fathers, who will never see the light.

Reputation is also accorded to those of virtuous character. In Prov 11:16, "A kindhearted woman (אשת־חן) gains respect (כבוד), but ruthless men gain only wealth," while in 1 Sam 9:6 Saul's servant describes Samuel as "highly respected" (נכבד), because "everything he says comes true."[45]

It should be noted at this point just how much not only the substantive, but also the responsive aspects of כבד overlap, such that sometimes they are virtually indistinguishable.[46] However, the categories are worth retaining because of the distinctive application to YHWH, for while it is inconceivable that one could reward YHWH (as YHWH is both the giver and owner of everything), it is completely appropriate that his reputation should be acknowledged and magnified. Accordingly, the OT is replete with examples of כבד where the knowledge and reputation of YHWH's name is the clear focus.

As one might expect, this theme comes into particular relief in the psalms (whose focus is praise of YHWH), and the Prophets (where a critical disruption in the appropriate relationships between YHWH and his people has occurred). A few examples are enough to paint the picture: "Be exalted, O God, above the heavens, let your glory (כבודך) be over all the earth" (Ps 57:6); "All the nations you have made will come and worship before you, O Lord, they will bring glory (ויכבדו) to your name" (Ps 86:9); "Declare his glory (כבודו) among the nations, his marvellous deeds among all peoples!" (Ps 96:3); "YHWH Almighty planned . . . to bring Tyre down . . . to bring low the pride of all glory and to humble all who are renowned on the earth (כל־נכבדי־ארץ)" (Isa 23:9); "Therefore in the east give glory (כבדו) to YHWH, exalt the name of YHWH, the God of Israel, in the islands of the sea" (Isa 24:15); "For the earth will be filled with knowledge of the glory of YHWH (כבוד־יהוה), as the waters cover the sea" (Hab 2:14).

From the above references it is clear that there is a strong link between name, reputation, and כבד, which is especially significant in Ezekiel. Furthermore, in these instances, the concepts of knowledge and name have relational overtones. Knowledge of a name often indicates the establishment of (or intent to establish) a relationship, in which one party expresses authority over another. For example, the cry of the man possessed by an

---

45. Prov 11:16 provides an interesting juxtaposition of concepts, in that כבד can also be used of wealth, which is often associated with honor. However here wealth is *dis*honorable because of the scurrilous means by which it is gained. This again demonstrates the difficulty of seeing "honor" as the overarching categorial "bucket" to encapsulate the meaning of כבד.

46. Furthermore, the distinction between substantive and responsive aspects is also sometimes hard to define. For example, when Abraham becomes "heavy" with possessions in Gen 13:2, it is reasonable to suggest that his reputation also increased, and perhaps that he became more respected/revered as a "man of substance."

evil spirit in the Capernaum synagogue, "What do you want with us, Jesus of Nazareth? Have you come to destroy us? I know who you are—the Holy One of God!" (Mark 1:24), is not a simple statement of recognition but an attempt to wrest power from Jesus by revealing knowledge of his identity as "the Holy One of God."[47] Likewise in the OT, the persistent ascription in Yhwh's acts of judgment and salvation are that "you may know that I am Yhwh" (Exod 10:2; 31:13; Josh 3:7; Isa 43:10; 45:3). Again, the statement is not simply one of standing in awe at Yhwh's power but implies a recognition of his authority, with a call to the hearers to respond in submission and loyalty.[48]

Exodus 33–34 as the "Nexus" of כבד in the Old Testament

Perhaps the clearest and most significant association of כבד with the character of God comes in the interchange between Yhwh and Moses in Exod 33–34, following the Golden Calf incident. I will conclude my initial examination of כבד with this passage both because it demonstrates *in situ* several of the major aspects of the concept, and because it seems to be a nexus of meaning for the term in the OT, which is echoed in key formulations of the revelation of Yhwh.[49]

Possibly with a sense of desperation at Israel's spectacular failure to keep Yhwh's covenant, and seeking assurance of his continued presence and protection, in Exod 33:18 Moses makes the appeal: "Now show me your glory (כבודך)." The ensuing episode contains several key points relevant to understanding the concept of כבד in this passage, which are presented as follows:

1. כבד is used synonymously—or more accurately, predicatively—with "goodness" (טובי): Yhwh's glory *is* his goodness (33:18–19).[50] The declaration

---

47. William L. Lane, *The Gospel according to Mark* (Grand Rapids: Eerdmans, 1974), 74–75; Robert H. Gundry, *Mark: A Commentary on His Apology for the Cross* (Grand Rapids: Eerdmans, 1992), 76.

48. Paul R. Williamson, "Promises with Strings Attached: Covenant and Law in Exodus 19–24," in *Exploring Exodus: Literary, Theological and Contemporary Approaches* (ed. B. S. Rosner and P. R. Williamson; Nottingham: Apollos, 2008), 96–102; Childs, *Exodus*, 401–402; Barry G. Webb, *The Message of Isaiah: On Eagles' Wings* (Leicester: Inter-Varsity, 1996), 175–76.

49. Fishbane, for example, notes that the key terms of Exod 34:6–7 "recur as the organising principle in a host of psalms," while Dozemann notes its use in the Book of the Twelve. See Fishbane, *Biblical Interpretation in Ancient Israel*, 347; Thomas B. Dozeman, "Inner-Biblical Interpretation of Yahweh's Gracious and Compassionate Character," *JBL* 108/2 (1989): 207–23. In terms of its use in the NT, see James M. Hamilton, *God's Glory in Salvation through Judgment: A Biblical Theology* (Wheaton: Crossway, 2010), 355–551. Cf. Hos 2:19; Joel 2:13; Jonah 4:2; Mic 7:18–20; Nah 1:3; Pss 40:11–13, 18; 78:38; 79:5–6; 99:8; 111:1, 117; 145:7–10; John 1:14, 18; Rom 3:23–26.

50. The predicate nominative here is not a convertible proposition but rather a subset proposition. "Goodness" is a subset of "glory" or, more accurately, it is a particular (and, here, central) expression of the wider concept of Yhwh's glory.

in 34:6–7 then explains what is meant by the vague term "goodness," in terms of Yʜᴡʜ's character: he is "the compassionate and gracious God, slow to anger and abounding in love (חסד) and faithfulness (אמת)."[51] This observation does not deny the strong association between כבוד and Yʜᴡʜ's presence (or, as per Sommer's suggestion, his "body"); that theme is clearly present in the passage. However, the emphasis lies not in Yʜᴡʜ's physical description, which is left rather vague, but rather on his character, which is made quite explicit.[52]

2. The passage makes significant connections between Yʜᴡʜ's "goodness," the visible splendor of his manifestation, his own person, his name, and his (moral) character.[53] This is indicated in particular by the use of עבר and its various subjects in the passage. In Exod 33:19, Yʜᴡʜ says he will cause "all my goodness (כל־טובי)" to pass before Moses. In 33:22, on the other hand, it is first the visible manifestation of Yʜᴡʜ's glory (כבדי), then Yʜᴡʜ himself (עברי) that will pass by. In 34:6, it is still Yʜᴡʜ himself that passes by, but the emphasis shifts away from the physical manifestation to

---

51. The term טוב is broad in meaning, and does not often relate to moral/ethical concepts: *BDB* and *HALOT* have the gloss "good things," often referring to prime produce of the land (e.g., Gen 45:18), choice goods (e.g., 2 Kgs 8:9) or prosperity in general (e.g., Job 20:21). It can also refer to positive disposition, often in conjunction with possession of "good things" (e.g., Deut 28:47). Both lexicons take the occurrence in Exod 33:18 to have the rare meaning (Yʜᴡʜ's) "beauty" (cf. Hos 10:11; Zech 9:17). The visible splendor of the theophany is an undeniably significant aspect in the episode, as Moses' request for Yʜᴡʜ to "show" him his glory indicates. On the other hand, a close reading of the passage suggests that the sense of טוב here extends beyond a simply physical phenomenon to include the notion of character. I will explore this extension especially in point 2.

52. Interestingly, Sommer sees the passage as "an anthology of conflicting traditions regarding the presence of God and how humans relate to it," which "an ancient Israelite editor crafted . . . by collecting originally independent texts in order to pose a debate concerning a single theme" (Sommer, *Bodies of God*, 4). Sommer draws on a previously published paper in support of this argument, in which he suggests that such crafting of competing sources in diachronic perspective "invites rereading and rumination, so that a verse can emerge now in one setting, now in another, carrying a particular meaning here and its opposite there. Like a set of mirrors, it encourages the reader to notice how elements of the text reflect on each other. Even more, it resembles a kaleidoscope. It is full of divergent views, so that the reader need only turn it and turn it to see that all of them are in it" (idem, "Reflecting on Moses: The Redaction of Numbers 11," *JBL* 118 (1999): 624). The point is powerful, and helpful, whether or not one accepts as clear a conflict between the accounts that Sommer proposes.

53. I enclose "moral" in parentheses because the emphasis in the passage does not lie on Yʜᴡʜ's morality *per se*, but rather on his nature as "compassionate and gracious . . . slow to anger, abounding in love and faithfulness," and also his authority to forgive and to judge. However, the sustained language of "faithfulness" (reflected especially in the terms חסד and אמת), as well as the basis of judgment (ונקה לא ינקה) have at least strong moral overtones, and can be taken as analogous to what contemporary Westerners might call "justice" or "morality." I will explore the notion of Yʜᴡʜ's justice further in ch. 5.

the verbal proclamation that takes place. That this is the case in YHWH's *actual* passing by Moses suggests that his declaration in Exod 34:6–7 is the focal point of the passage.[54] It is YHWH's character as the "gracious" and "just" God that is brought to the fore.[55]

As noted previously in this chapter, most major historical-critical studies of the OT have focused on the *disjunction* between the *shem* and *kabod* traditions and their respective conceptions of YHWH's presence.[56] While I am not here seeking to denigrate the historical-critical enterprise or its value in the academic study of the OT and its provenance, from the perspective of honor/shame studies, a synchronic reading of the text in its final form (with an exploration of how the terms and concepts involved in שם and כבוד can be seen as mutually illuminative, rather than mutually exclusive, for example) is of more immediate value for the purposes of this study.[57]

3. The passage is set within a discussion between Moses and YHWH that appeals to the tie between YHWH's reputation and his people "How will anyone know that you are pleased with me and your people unless you go with us? What will distinguish us from all the other people on the face of the earth?" (Exod 33:16). That YHWH replies in terms of "maintaining love to thousands . . . [yet] punishes the children and their children for the sin of the fathers to the third and fourth generation" is at least consistent with the idea of a growing reputation. This is in turn strengthened by the subsequent dialogue in 34:10–14, where "the people you live among will see how awesome (נורא) is the work that I, YHWH, will do for you."

In summary, the sustained overlap of concepts involved in the theophany suggests that the final form of the text displays an intimate connection between YHWH's "honor" and splendor with his character, expressed essentially as his justice and mercy. In Exod 33:18–34:7, YHWH's glory is his goodness, and his goodness is his love and faithfulness (חסד ואמת), seen both in his forgiveness and justice in judgment. Furthermore, the widespread use

---

54. Cf. the verbal conjugations and temporal markers in each occurrence of עבר: אעביר (*yiqtol*, Exod 33:19), בעבר (*inf. cst.* + ב, Exod 33:22a), עד־עברי (*inf. cst.* + 1 c.s. suffix, Exod 33:22b), ויעבר (*wayyiqtol*, Exod 34:6).

55. This does not minimize the importance of the visible aspect of YHWH's כבוד in the section: cf. Moses' face "was radiant because he had spoken with YHWH . . . [and the Israelites] were afraid to come near him" (Exod 34:29–30). Rather, it simply indicates a close relationship between YHWH's טוב, his כבוד, and his character.

56. Gerhard von Rad, "Deuteronomy's Name Theology and the Priestly Document's 'Kabod Theology,'" in *Studies in Deuteronomy* (London: SCM, 1953), 37–44; Tryggve N. D. Mettinger, *The Dethronement of Sabaoth: Studies in the Shem and Kabod Theologies* (Lund: Gleerup, 1982); cf. Sommer, *Bodies of God*, 4.

57. For a sustained interaction and critique of "name" and "glory" theologies from a historical-critical perspective, see J. Gordon McConville, "God's 'Name' and God's 'Glory,'" *TynBul* 30 (1979): 149–63; Sandra L. Richter, *The Deuteronomistic History and the Name Theology: lᵉšakkēn šᵉmô šām in the Bible and the Ancient Near East* (BZAW 318; Berlin: de Gruyter, 2002).

of the terms throughout the OT suggests that they formed something of
a "summary" of Yhwh's character, and what his reputation was to be built
around (e.g., Num 14:18; Neh 9:17; Ps 26:3; 86:15; 115:1; 117:1–2; Mic 7:20; Joel
2:13; Jonah 4:2).[58]

Excursus: כבד *and Hypostasis*

Before moving to examine Ezekiel, it is worth pausing to consider the
relation of von Rad and Mettinger's alternative explanation of כבד to the
current study.[59] Von Rad suggested the use of *kabod* as characteristic of an
older, more primitive conception, with the deity locally present in the tab-
ernacle. The Deuteronomist, however, relocated Yhwh to heaven, leaving
only "the Name" as a forwarding station for Israel (Deut 12:1–28).[60] "The
Name" thus "verges on a hypostasis," a "quality" of a deity that has become
a quasi-independent entity in and of itself.[61] The deuteronomic "Name"
theology was in turn replaced by P's *kabod moed* theology, in which the כבוד־
יהוה was said to dwell in the Holy of Holies, with Ezekiel forming the bridge
between the two traditions, with the innovation of the mobile throne coming to rest in Jerusalem.

Tryggve Mettinger developed von Rad's suggestions by examining the
occurrences of designations for Yhwh. Mettinger put forward the suggestion that the title יהוה צבאות, representative of Zion theology, was replaced
by Ezekiel's conception of the mobile throne, as an explanation of why Jerusalem was able to be defeated: God had abandoned his dwelling because

---

58. The importance of Yhwh's חסד ואמת has been increasingly recognized in theological and biblical studies. From the perspective of systematic theology, see further Graham A. Cole, *God the Peacemaker: How Atonement Brings Shalom* (Nottingham: Apollos,
2009), 33–52; J. B. Webster, *Holiness* (Grand Rapids: Eerdmans, 2003), 40; Hamilton, *God's
Glory*, 53–59, 101–7. From the perspective of biblical studies, see further James Nogalski,
"Recurring Themes in the Book of the Twelve: Creating Points of Contact for a Theological Reading," *Int* 61/2 (2007): 125–36; Dozeman, "Inner-Biblical Interpretation," 207–23;
Fishbane, *Biblical Interpretation*, 347; Alan Cooper, "In Praise of Divine Caprice: The
Significance of the Book of Jonah," in *Among the Prophets: Language, Image and Structure
in the Prophets* (ed. P. R. Davies and D. J. A. Clines; Sheffield: Sheffield Academic Press,
1993), 144–63; Raymond C. Van Leeuwen, "Scribal Wisdom and Theodicy in the Book
of the Twelve," in *In Search of Wisdom: Essays in Memory of John G. Gammie* (ed. L. G. Perdue et al.; Louisville: Westminster John Knox, 1993), 31–49. In summary, as Childs states:
"The frequent use through the rest of the Old Testament of the formula in v. 6 by which
the nature of God is portrayed . . . is an eloquent testimony to the centrality of this understanding of God's person" (Childs, *Exodus*, 612).

59. See von Rad, "Name Theology," 37–44.

60. Ibid., 39.

61. Ibid., 38; cf S. Dean McBride's definition, cited in John T. Strong, "God's *Kabod*:
The Presence of Yahweh in the Book of Ezekiel," in *The Book of Ezekiel: Theological and
Anthropological Perspectives* (ed. M. S. Odell and J. T. Strong; SBLSymS 9; Atlanta: SBL,
2000), 73.

of the people's sin.[62] Mettinger pushes further than von Rad and defines "the Name" explicitly as a hypostasis.[63]

John Strong notes that, while both von Rad and Mettinger suggest that "the Name" is a hypostasis that guards YHWH's transcendence and freedom, neither do the same for the יהוה‎־כבוד. Strong goes on to argue that von Rad and Mettinger were both mistaken in seeing Ezekiel's mobile throne as an innovation and break from Zion theology; rather, viewing the כבוד־יהוה‎ as another hypostasis meant that Ezekiel could maintain the idea that YHWH himself was still enthroned in Jerusalem, while he sent his כבוד‎ into the unclean parts of the world to fight his battles against Chaos for him.[64]

Despite some ongoing influence, Name Theology has largely fallen by the wayside in recent research. Searching critique has found a distinct "Name" theology impossible to maintain in Deuteronomy. Furthermore, in other key passages (e.g., Exod 33–34), "Name" and *kabod* are so integral to the passage that neither can be removed without the sense of the passage being lost.[65] To this we can add that the close link between כבוד‎ and שם‎ established by SSAs presents a further critique, not only to von Rad and Mettinger, but also Strong's suggestion that כבוד־יהוה‎ likewise indicates a hypostasis of YHWH.

Indeed, Strong's argument, besides relying on von Rad and Mettinger, seems also to depend on some rather idiosyncratic translations. For example, Strong translates Isa 6:3: "Holy, holy, holy is Yahweh Sabaoth, *but* his Glory (*kabod*), the fullness of the whole earth."[66] The verse, however, is asyndetic, with no explicit connective joining its halves (קדוש קדוש קדוש‎ יהוה צבאות מלא כל־הארץ כבודו‎). While asyndeton may communicate disjunction, it hardly does so by default, as the most "unmarked" connective.[67] Strong's translation of Ps 97:6 also seems rather forced, as he takes a continuation form (*weqatal*), and translates it as a disjunctive form: "The heavens proclaim his righteousness, *but* all the peoples see his glory," without any clear contextual indicators that would justify such a rendering. In both cases, one would expect that if such a deliberate contrast were intended,

---

62. Mettinger, *Dethronement of Sabaoth*, 109.

63. Ibid., 130.

64. Strong, "God's *Kabod*," 73.

65. For further discussion, see Peter T. Vogt, "Centralization and Decentralization in Deuteronomy," in *Interpreting Deuteronomy: Issues and Approaches* (ed. D. G. Firth and P. Johnston; Downers Grove: IVP Academic, 2012); idem, *Deuteronomic Theology and the Significance of Torah: A Reappraisal* (Winona Lake, IN: Eisenbrauns, 2006); Michael Hundley, "To Be or Not To Be: A Reexamination of Name Language in Deuteronomy and the Deuteronomistic History," *VT* 59 (2009): 533–55; Richter, *Name Theology*; Ian Wilson, *Out of the Midst of the Fire: Divine Presence in Deuteronomy* (Atlanta: Scholars Press, 1995).

66. Strong, "God's *Kabod*," 74 (emphasis mine).

67. For more on the function of asyndeton, see J. C. L. Gibson, *Davidson's Introductory Hebrew Grammar—Syntax* (Edinburgh: T. & T. Clark, 1994), 177–80; Joüon §177; Steven Runge, *Discourse Grammar of the Greek New Testament: A Practical Introduction for Teaching and Exegesis* (Peabody: Hendrickson, 2010), 17–27.

a more explicit disjunctive construction would have been used (such as a fronted nonverbal element). As such, the wedge between YHWH and his glory that Strong drives feels forced.

In support of his position, Strong cites the refrain found in several psalms: "Be exalted, O God, above the heavens, let your Glory be over all the earth" (e.g., Ps 57:6), as evidence of an earthly hypostasis.[68] However, it seems more straightforward to suggest that the verse is simply stating that YHWH rules over both realms of creation—heaven and earth—and that it is precisely by virtue of his being enthroned in heaven that his ruling presence is able to "radiate" to all parts of the earth. Moreover, in the light of honor/shame studies, the strong separation between "Name" and "Glory," and between both of these and the person being spoken of, is difficult to maintain.[69]

Strong does, however, make some valuable points in his article, especially in highlighting the function of the construction כבוד־יהוה in expressing the paradox of the vision of the invisible God.[70] In the semantic study of כבד presented above, I have not included the concept of *presence*, which may seem a rather glaring omission, especially given the fact that the construction כבוד־יהוה so often refers to the physical manifestation of the deity.[71] The reason I have not done so is that, as frequently as the construction denotes the physical manifestation of YHWH and as important as the concepts involved are, the notion of presence is not encoded in the term כבוד itself.[72] Thus, while I would argue that the manifestation of YHWH is indeed glori-

---

68. Ibid., 80.

69. On this note, Luc's statement, "A major teaching in the priestly circle where Ezekiel came from was the holiness of God, in which Yahweh's name and glory played a significant role. For Ezekiel, however, Yahweh's name was more important than his glory," is puzzling to say the least, and seems to be a false dichotomy that is imposed on the concepts. Indeed, it is important to note against both Luc and Strong that the final chapters of Ezekiel stress the organic connection between YHWH, his name, and his glory. It is only after the כבוד יהוה returns to take up residence in the city and the restoration of creation flowing out from the now reoccupied temple that the city is worthy to bear the name יהוה שמה (Ezek 48:35). See Alex Luc, "A Theology of Ezekiel: God's Name and Israel's History," *JETS* 26/2 (1983): 137.

70. Strong, "God's *Kabod*," 81.

71. See further Pieter de Vries, *De heerlijkheid van JHWH in het Oude Testament en in het bijzonder in het boek Ezechiël* (Heerenveen: Groen, 2010), 151–54; idem, "The Glory of YHWH in the Old Testament with Special Attention to the Book of Ezekiel," *TynBul* 62 (2011): 151–54; idem, "Ezekiel: Prophet of the Name and Glory of YHWH—The Character of His Book and Several of Its Main Themes," *JBPR* 4 (2012): 94–108. De Vries largely agrees with Strong regarding the notion of hypostasis and sees this as a precursor to the Incarnational/Trinitarian language of the NT. While an intriguing idea, I am unpersuaded as to its likelihood, given the strong Yahwistic/monotheistic perspective expressed by the exilic and postexilic prophets. Cf Joyce (*Ezekiel*, 19): "[In Ezekiel] there is only room for one God who runs the affairs of the world as a whole. Implicit here are the nascent claims of monotheism as well as universalism, themes that would be articulated more explicitly in Isa 40–55 later in the exile."

72. E.g., how YHWH can be present both in heaven and on earth simultaneously.

ous, and (against Strong) that כבוד־יהוה indicates the presence of YHWH himself, not merely a *hypostasis,* the idea of "presence" *per se* is not necessary to its primary semantic payload in the same manner as the other aspects covered in the semantic study above.[73]

The Use of כבד in Ezekiel

I now move to an examination of the instances of כבד in Ezekiel. There are 26 examples of כבד in Ezekiel: 6 in chs. 1–3, 10 in chs. 4–24, 3 in chs. 25–32 and 7 in chs. 33–48. Given the scope of the project in examining three major concept spheres ("glory," "shame," "guilt") and their interrelations, my examination will focus mainly on the examples of כבד, with only passing reference to other glory/honor related terms and concepts.[74] This is not ideal, but is necessary in keeping the project manageable.

In Ezekiel, כבד is used in relation to the three main literary entities of the book—YHWH, the nations and Israel/Judah.[75] I will examine each of them in turn. Though the intuitive order to proceed in would be YHWH, Israel/Judah, and the nations, I have placed my examination of Israel last because there is only one appearance of a form of כבד used in relation to Israel/Judah (Ezek 23:41, the rare nominal form כבודה "throne/luxurious thing").

כבד *and* YHWH

כבוד־יהוה

The most common context in which כבד appears in Ezekiel is in the theophanic construction כבוד־יהוה, 9 times in the book.[76] The similar construction כבוד אלהי ישראל, unique to Ezekiel, appears 5 more times, while

---

73. Cf. Sommer's argument for YHWH himself having a "body" (*Bodies of God,* 145–74), as an alternative to a separate hypostasis. On the notion of "presence," a stronger case can be made for particularly anthropomorphic vocabulary such as פנים to have an encoded idea of presence. In Exod 33:14, YHWH tells Moses, "My Presence (פני) will go with you." In reply, Moses says, "If your Presence (פניך) does not go with us, do not send us up from here. How will anyone know that you are pleased with me and with your people unless *you* go with us (בלכתך עמנו)?" (emphasis mine). The parallelism reinforces the point: to have YHWH's "face" is to have YHWH's presence. Whether it is necessarily encoded in כבד, however, is less likely.

74. For a fuller semantic study, including a catalog and analysis of תפארת, יקר, הוד, הדר, and תהלה, see de Vries, *De heerlijkheid van JHWH.* I will follow a similar pattern in the following chapters, focusing on בוש and עון, respectively.

75. In terms of the nations, the term is used with respect to various individual nations that are under scrutiny, but for our purposes these may be examined together. Although canonically speaking, Babylon is the arch-nemesis of YHWH and his people, in Ezekiel it is peripheral to the action. Strikingly, Babylon is absent from the list of nations judged in Ezek 25–32, and although the Babylonians are described at points as the agents of God's wrath on the Israelites, "they are incidental to the book entirely . . . they are just tools [in YHWH's hand to punish Israel/Judah]"; William A. Tooman, "Ezekiel's Radical Challenge to Inviolability," *ZAW* 121 (2009): 511.

76. Ezek 1:28; 3:12, 23; 10:4, 18; 11:23; 43:4, 5; 44:4.

there is also one example of כבוד alone that is a clear parallel to the standard construction: "The כבוד־יהוה was standing there, ככבוד that I had seen by the Kebar River, and I fell facedown"(Ezek 3:23). [77]

The initial vision, culminating in Ezekiel's declaration "This was the appearance of the likeness of the glory of Yнwн (הוא מראה דמות כבוד־יהוה)" (Ezek 1:28), is foundational to the book and its message. As many have noted, Ezekiel emphasizes the mobility of Yнwн's glory, while the movements of the book (which may be characterized by, variously, uncreation-recreation or judgment-restoration) are mirrored by the movements of the theophany away from Jerusalem (chs. 8–11) and back again (chs. 43–44). [78] It is the initial vision, however, which is the key to communicating the significance of Yнwн's appearing, with many of the subsequent references only immediately describing the movements of the theophany. [79]

In his commentary, Block notes six things of theological significance that the theophany expresses: (1) Yнwн's transcendent glory, which emanates from his being, [80] (2) his transcendent holiness, [81] (3) his sovereignty, (4) his interest in his people, (5) his presence among the exiles (and especially with Ezekiel), and (6) the impending judgment of Yнwн. [82] To Block's points we may add several relevant observations. First, while some have argued against the presence of creation motifs or traditions in Ezekiel, too much in the description of the כבוד־יהוה is reminiscent of Gen 1–3 to easily dismiss the connections. [83] Further, there is a mixture of Israelite and

---

77. For the construction כבוד אלהי ישראל: Ezek 8:4; 9:3; 10:19; 11:22; 43:2. The closest parallel phrase is Josh 7:19, where Joshua calls on Achan to "Give glory (כבוד) to Yнwн, the God of Israel, and give him the praise (תודה)."

78. Iain M. Duguid, "Ezekiel," in *New Dictionary of Biblical Theology* (ed. T. D. Alexander and B. S. Rosner; Leicester: Inter-Varsity, 2000), 229; John F. Kutsko, *Between Heaven and Earth: Divine Presence and Absence in the Book of Ezekiel* (Winona Lake, IN: Eisenbrauns, 2000), 78.

79. This is not to say that the movements themselves do not convey something of importance; they certainly do. However, their importance derives particularly from what is expressed in the initial vision, which is "carried over" into the subsequent references: "the glory of Yнwн was standing there, *like the glory I had seen by the Chebar river*" (3:23). "And behold there the Glory of the God of Israel, *like the vision that I saw on the plain*" (8:4, emphasis mine).

80. In contrast to the gods of the nations, whose images needed constant polishing.

81. Which Block understands primarily as "distinction," as does this study.

82. Block's list actually stands at seven, but his final point applies to contemporary readers in the context of Christian ministry. As such, it is not included in my list, which relates to ancient textual matters; Block, *Ezekiel 1–24*, 107–9.

83. The links are even more likely if a canonical perspective is granted, and the connections extend beyond the vision into the commissioning of Ezekiel in ch. 2, where "breath" (רוח) enters Ezekiel and sets him on his feet, anticipating the "resurrection" of Israel in ch. 37. See further Duguid, "Ezekiel," *NDBT*, 229. For arguments against creation motifs, see David L. Petersen, "Creation and Hierarchy in Ezekiel: Methodological Perspectives and Theological Prospects," in *Ezekiel's Hierarchical World: Wrestling with a*

wider ANE iconography in the description. However, given Ezekiel's famed "radical theocentricity," it is likely that, as Block argues, rather than taking a mythological interpretation, the use of the ANE motifs is a polemic choice—commenting on Yʜwʜ coming "from the north" (צפון). As Block writes, "Yahweh is free to come from any direction he pleases, even the purported home of the storm deity," indicating his sovereignty over the Babylonian pantheon.[84]

If the above is true, then it is no wonder that Ezekiel falls on his face when he sees it (1:28), for he is confronted with the awesome splendor of the Creator himself. However, it is important to note that the theophany not only calls up creation motifs, but is also reminiscent of the Exodus theophanies in (amongst others) its reference to the visible splendor and fire, its intimate manner of discourse between deity and prophet, and even perhaps the inability to apprehend the glory directly.[85]

Bringing honor concepts to bear on the passage enhances and further illumines the significance of what is communicated through the vision. In my semantic study, I noted that glory and honor finally belong to Yʜwʜ. If Ezekiel is interweaving into his visionary report echoes of the Genesis creation accounts as well as of the Exodus theophanies, this reinforces the primacy of the substantive aspect of כבד with respect to Yʜwʜ. He is glorious, "his eminence radiates from his very being,"[86] by virtue of being Creator (Genesis; cf. 1 Sam 2:8), Redeemer, and Judge (Exodus). These main themes will go on to be the lifeblood of Ezekiel's prophecies.[87]

There may be further honor overtones in what immediately follows. As noted previously, Ezekiel's response of prostration in 1:28 reflects a natural

---

Tiered Reality (ed. S. L. Cook and C. Patton; SBLSymS 31; Atlanta: SBL, 2004), 169–78; Madhavi Nevader, "Creating a *Deus Non Creator*: Divine Sovereignty and Creation in Ezekiel," in *The God Ezekiel Creates* (ed. Paul M. Joyce and Dalit Rom-Shiloni; LHBOTS 607. London: Bloomsbury, 2015), 55–70.

84. See Block, *Ezekiel 1–24*, 90–98; Stephen L. Cook, "Cosmos, *Kabod*, and Cherub: Ontological and Epistemological Hierarchy in Ezekiel," in *Ezekiel's Hierarchical World*, 179–97. Cf a similar argument with respect to Gen 1 by Hasel, "Genesis Cosmology." Further reinforcing this point is Hab 3:3, where Yʜwʜ comes from yet another direction, Teman in the South.

85. Ezekiel's idiosyncratic phraseology "the likeness of the appearance of Yʜwʜ's glory" may not simply be because the prophet is overwhelmed by the sight (although this seems likely; for more detail, see Block, "Text and Emotion"). It may also be reflective of Yʜwʜ's word to Moses, "No one can see my face and live" (Exod 33:20). Where Yʜwʜ placed Moses in the cleft and covered him with his hand, Ezekiel's vision may have been similarly "clouded" to protect the prophet. For sustained explorations of the intertextual links between Exodus and Ezekiel, see Rebecca G. S. Idestrom, "Echoes of the Book of Exodus in Ezekiel," *JSOT* 33 (2009): 489–510; Henry McKeating, "Ezekiel the 'Prophet Like Moses,'" *JSOT* 61 (1994): 97–109.

86. Block, *Ezekiel 1–24*, 106.

87. Zimmerli, *Ezekiel 1–24*, 123–24.

response to a vision of such overwhelming awe, but would have also been recognized as an appropriate posture of submission toward an enthroned monarch. [88] In the command of YHWH to "stand up on your feet," Greenberg also suggests that "the biblical visionary must be in possession of himself in order to receive the divine word . . . [in contrast to pagan prophets, in which] consciousness was obliterated." [89]

The rest of the instances of אלהי ישראל / כבוד־יהוה (vv. 8–11, 43–44) mainly concern the movements of the theophany with respect to the Jerusalem temple, and several scholars have suggested that these movements may also express concerns for honor. Most scholars argue for a balanced movement away from the temple (signifying abandonment to judgment, vv. 8–11) and back into it (signifying restoration, vv. 43–44). [90] For scholars making use of social-scientific criticism, however, the abandonment has the added dimension of a shaming mechanism. Lyn Bechtel, for example, suggests that ANE peoples believed that the gods would shame their people as a means of controlling their behavior if displeased with them. In particular, the power and disposition of the gods were tied to the rise and fall of nations—a nation's god was believed to march at the head of its army, and victory over another nation was attributed to the god's superior power. By contrast, the enemies were believed to have been abandoned by their god, who had either been angry at the people, or bowed before the superior power of the conquering nation's god. [91]

Viewing divine abandonment in light of honor and shame studies thus adds significant depth to our understanding of the passages. It helpfully emphasizes the centrality of YHWH's concern for his honor and reputation in all that he does. It also demonstrates the importance of the covenant relationship between YHWH and his people, particularly in his promises to "dwell" with his people, and that they should "bear his name" (Exod 20:7). Furthermore, it gives a good account of the perceptions of human-divine relationship, as something akin to patronage.

There are, however, some caveats that must be borne in mind, lest the patron-client model with its underlying notions of honor and shame are

---

88. Mayer I. Gruber, *Aspects of Nonverbal Communication in the Ancient Near East* (Rome: Pontifical Biblical Institute, 1980), 187–251; Block, *Ezekiel 1–24*, 115.

89. Moshe Greenberg, *Ezekiel 1–20: A New Translation with Introduction and Commentary* (ed. W. F. Albright and D. N. Freedman; AB 22; New York: Doubleday, 1983), 62.

90. E.g. idem, "Divine Abandonment: Ezekiel's Adaptation of an Ancient Near Eastern Motif," in *The Book of Ezekiel: Theological and Anthropological Perspectives*, 15–42; Kutsko, *Between Heaven and Earth*, 1; Margaret S. Odell, *Ezekiel* (Macon: Smyth & Helwys, 2005), 119, 125, 496–500.

91. Bechtel, "Perception of Shame," 82; cf. David A. Glatt-Gilad, "Yahweh's Honor at Stake: a Divine Conundrum," *JSOT* 98 (2002): 63–74; Morton Cogan, *Imperialism and Religion: Assyria, Judah and Israel in the Eighth and Seventh Centuries B.C.E* (Missoula: SBL, 1974), 11–12. The key evidence for such a perspective is the Mesha Stele.

applied without paying enough attention to the particulars of the biblical texts. This is especially necessitated by those texts that Baumgarten calls "orphan passages," that simply do not fit the model.[92] In other words, while there are several aspects and dynamics within the text that seem to fit well with the model, there are also several that do not.

For example, William Tooman has argued against the "standard view," suggesting instead that the temple and city have long been abandoned by YHWH at the time of Ezekiel's visions, and that in Ezek 8–11 the theophany is revisiting the temple in order to execute judgment.[93] Whether or not one accepts his argument regarding the direction of movement, there is no question that he is correct in assigning the destruction of the city directly to YHWH. As Glatt-Gilad himself points out,[94] in Ezekiel, YHWH himself actively judges his people (a fact that is strengthened by Ezekiel's initial sign-act, taking on the part of YHWH in besieging the model city), rather than simply abandoning it to foreign powers. Block likewise notes that while there are common elements with ANE divine abandonment texts, "on the other hand, his vision of Yahweh's departure could no more fit the pattern of the religious beliefs of the native Mesopotamians than could the representation of Yahweh in his temple [that is, no images of Yahweh, in contrast to ANE religions]."[95]

Furthermore, what is striking is the complete absence of shame terminology in regards to YHWH or his name in the book.[96] Never is YHWH "shamed" (YHWH is never the subject of בוש, כלם, or חרף in Ezekiel). The closest associated terminology is the language of "defilement" (טמא, for example, Ezek 43:7–8) or "profanation" (חלל, for example, Ezek 36:20) of his name. While these can be associated with the concept of shame, the issue in Ezekiel is not so much that YHWH's place in the social pecking order of deities is in jeopardy (as is often the manner in which SSA scholars argue). Rather, as Avrahami has shown with regard to בוש in the Psalms, "it has to do with . . . a disconnection between expectations and reality. בוש is

---

92. Albert I. Baumgarten, "Prologue: How Do We Know When We Are On To Something?" in *Sects and Sectarianism in Jewish History* (ed. S. Stern; *IJSSJ* 12, eds. M. J. Geller, et al.; Leiden: Brill, 2011), 3–19.

93. Tooman, "Inviolability," 498–514. The challenge in accepting Tooman's argument is whether it can overcome the balance of movement away from and back to the temple, which seems such a powerful structuring element in the book. On the other hand, supporting Tooman's argument is Ezek 43:3, referring to the vision of the כבוד יהוה returning to take up residence in the restored Jerusalem: "The vision I saw was like the vision I had seen *when he came to destroy the city* and like the visions I had seen by the Chebar River, and I fell facedown." See further Tooman's discussion, including the textual issues on (507–8).

94. Glatt-Gilad, "Yahweh's Honor," 74.

95. Block, "Divine Abandoment," 42.

96. Incidentally, this is why I am addressing the issue in this chapter, rather than the chapter on "shame."

avoided when reality matches expectations."[97] Given Ezekiel's view of the utter sovereignty of Yнwн, however, it would be even more accurate to put it as בוש is avoided when *expectations* match *reality*.

That this is the case is not only evident from the manner in which the use of כבוד־יהוה emphasizes the "substantive" aspect, the splendor of Yнwн's own being, but also in the fact that it is not simply his name that he has concern for, but his *holy* name. In other words, Yнwн's impetus for acting is so that he be recognized and responded to as is appropriate to the reality (to adopt Avrahami's phraseology) of his character.

The preceding observation resolves a further issue to do with the presentation of Yнwн in honor and shame studies on Ezekiel; the seeming oversight on the part of Yнwн with regard to the effect that the Exile has on his reputation. Some scholars have made much of this seeming conundrum, with Schwartz being especially scathing in his assessment of Ezekiel's portrayal of Yнwн:[98]

> By pouring out his wrath upon his people and casting them out of their land, Yнwн fully expects to get the satisfaction of seeing justice done.... Once the exile has taken place, however, this plan backfires. The moment the nations get a look at the exiled Israelites, Yнwн realizes the colossal error he has made.... He becomes obsessed with the dishonor suffered by his reputation.[99]

However, this may be a case of applying a social-scientific model in a manner ill-fitting with the object of study. One immediately apparent problem with the interpretations offered is that they hinge on Yнwн being both rather dim-witted, and also (in the case of Schwartz) explotatively (and vindictively) self-aggrandizing. In such presentations, Yнwн's "honor" is simply equated with the supposed ancient obsession with agonistic Honor Precedence.

If, however, the links between glory, holiness, and character explored in the broad semantic study above are valid (which is at least plausible, given that there are significant links between Ezekiel and Exodus), a different picture can be argued for, even granting the unique and disturbing starkness of Ezekiel's presentation of Yнwн.[100] In line with the descriptions of judgment and restoration of ch. 36 in particular, it is possible to see *both* the judgment *and* the restoration of Israel as driven by Yнwн's character of "the gracious and compassionate God ... [who] does not leave the guilty unpunished," and the reality (at least from Ezekiel's perspective) that the

---

97. Avrahami, "בוש in the Psalms," 308. I will discuss the relationship between shame and defilement more comprehensively in the next chapter, here it is sufficient to simply note it.

98. E.g. David A. Glatt-Gilad, "Yahweh's Honor at Stake: A Divine Conundrum," *JSOT* 98 (2002): 63–74; Baruch J. Schwartz, "Ezekiel's Dim View of Israel's Restoration," in *The Book of Ezekiel: Theological and Anthropological Perspectives*, 43–67; Bechtel, "Perception of Shame," 79–92.

99. Schwartz, "Dim View," 57–58.

100. I will explore this further, particularly in ch. 6.

only appropriate final state of affairs occurs when this is recognized by all and sundry, when expectation (or acknowledgment) matches the reality that YHWH is the Creator and Lord of all.

The above can be supplemented by noting that, for Ezekiel, one way of expressing the goal of YHWH's actions is שלום (for example, Ezek 37:26), the restoration of blessing and harmonious relationship between Creator and creation (Ezek 47–48; cf. Gen 1:1–2:3). It is therefore significant that once the כבוד־יהוה returns to the city to take up residence, the water of life flows out from the temple such that creation is restored and renewed in terms that are highly reminiscent of Gen 2.[101]

Other Uses of כבד *with* YHWH *as Subject*

The remainder of Ezekiel's uses of כבד reinforce the notions expressed in the titular construction that were explored above. In Ezek 28:22, YHWH states of Sidon, "I will gain glory (נכבדתי) in your midst. They will know that I am YHWH, when I inflict punishment (שפטים) on her and show myself holy (נקדשתי) within her." The language is reminiscent of YHWH's contest with Pharaoh in the Exodus narratives, and again the concepts of glory, judgment, and holiness are closely connected.

In Ezek 39:13, YHWH's victory over Gog and Magog is described as "the day I am glorified" (יום הכבדי), and "a memorable day" (והיה להם לשם). However, this glory does not consist simply in his victory and supremacy among the nations. It also includes the vindication and acknowledgment of his character, with regard to the nations, and especially within Israel: "I will send fire on Magog and on those who live in safety on the coastline, and they will know I am YHWH. I will make known my holy name among my people Israel. I will no longer let my holy name be profaned, and the nations will know that I, YHWH, am the Holy One in Israel" (Ezek 39:6–7).[102]

A similar sentiment is expressed a few verses later in 39:21, "I will display my glory among the nations, and all the nations will see the punishment I inflict and the hand I lay upon them. From that day forward the house of Israel will know that I am YHWH their God." Here, however, the link with YHWH's character is more explicit: the glory of YHWH is expressed particularly in his role as judge, executing "my judgment" (משפטי). The word is unavoidably forensic in category, and "because all true authority is God's and he shall ultimately act as judge of the world in the last great assize, he is *shophet* preeminent."[103]

---

101. See further Cole, *God the Peacemaker*, 19–22; Stanley E. Porter, "Peace," in *New Dictionary of Bibilcal Theology* (ed. T. D. Alexander and B. S. Rosner; Leicester: Inter-Varsity, 2001), 682–83.

102. Zimmerli, commenting on the phrase שם קדשי in Ezek 20:39, also ties the recognition of YHWH to his merciful character expressed in Ezek 18:32: "Yahweh does not will the end of those who were apparently sentenced to death, but desires rather that they should repent" (Zimmerli, *Ezekiel 1–24*, 416).

103. S.v. שפט, *TWOT*.

כבד *and the Nations*

There are three appearances of כבד in Ezekiel that have the nations as their subject: Ezek 21:26, 27:25, and 31:18. In 21:26, on his way to be the instrument of Yʜwʜ's judgment on Jerusalem, "The king of Babylon will . . . cast lots with arrows, he will consult his idols, he will examine the liver." Here כבד appears in nominal form, and reflects the common usage of the liver for divination practices. As such, there are no honor concepts or overtones are obviously present.

In Ezek 27:25, the fall of Tyre is lamented (קִינה) by first cataloging the trade relations of the Phoenician city, before declaring disaster on it: "The ships of Tarshish serve as carriers for your wares, you are filled with heavy cargo (ותמלאי ותכבדי מאד) in the heart of the sea." The immediate meaning of כבד here is the common overlap of abundance and wealth, as is clear from v. 12. There may also be more explicit echoes of honor-related concepts in the wider section. Ezek 28 goes on to explain the reason for Tyre's downfall: the success and amassed wealth of trade has led the king of Tyre to think that he can rival God (Ezek 28:5). In the following lament, this is expanded using the hapax noun יפעה, "shining splendor": "Your heart became proud on account of your beauty, and you corrupted your wisdom because of your splendor (יפעתך)" (Ezek 28:17).[104]

The use of כבד and its synonyms here has several important implications for this study. First, the prophecy uses creation/Eden imagery to cast Yʜwʜ as the creator of Tyre, and thus responsible for its glory.[105] However, although the point is made in highly figurative terms, it is no less powerful: not only does Judah's glory come from its God Yʜwʜ but so does Tyre's—despite the fact that Tyre does not acknowledge Yʜwʜ as its god. In other words, Yʜwʜ is seen as the universal creator God, the possessor and dispenser of glory, and it is by virtue of this fact that he is Tyre's rightful judge in her misuse of his gift (28:11–19).[106]

In this observation, there is a powerful statement on the view of honor presented here, that would seem to stand in stark contrast to the model of agonistic honor precedence. A similar sense may be expressed, for example, in Prov 25:27: "It is not good to eat too much honey, nor is it honorable to seek one's own honor (אכל דבש הרבות לא־טוב וחקר כבודם כבוד)."[107] As

---

104. S.v. יפעה, *HALOT*.

105. However, compare the arguments against Ezekiel's appropriation of Israel's creation traditions in Nevader, "*Deus Non Creator*"; Petersen, "Creation and Hierarchy."

106. Walther Zimmerli, *Ezekiel 2: A Commentary on the Book of the Prophet Ezekiel, Chapters 25–48* (ed. P. D. Hanson and L. J. Greenspoon; trans. J. D. Martin; Hermeneia; Philadelphia: Fortress, 1983), 94.

107. The Hebrew of Prov 25:27b is notoriously difficult, given the ambiguity of the construction in general, and especially the meaning of כברם. See Bruce Waltke, *The Book of Proverbs: Chapters 15–31* (NICOT; Grand Rapids: Eerdmans, 20015), 307–8; 336–37, for further discussion, especially his argument that the term means "weighty matters." If,

Peristiany and Pitt-Rivers comment in *Honor and Grace in Anthropology*, "in concentrating upon a social explanation of honor [in *Honour and Shame*] . . . most of us . . . had been to some extent blind to its intimate connection with the realm of the sacred," and a little later, "Honor has a kind of congenital relationship with grace which challenges our previous view of it as primordially a matter of social structure."[108] However, in the case of Ezekiel we are pushed even further: for if YHWH is the source, giver, and judge of honor, then in order to move towards an emic perspective on Ezekiel, "honor" must be defined first and foremost *theologically*, and then, as a derivation from this, anthropologically.[109]

Second, consequently, we see reinforced here the notion that the PCR is ultimately and eschatologically subject to the DCR—though Tyre has exalted itself in the its own eyes and the eyes of the nations, that perception does not match YHWH's reality. In Ezekiel's terms, "In the pride of your heart you say, 'I am a god: I sit on the throne of a god in the heart of the seas.' But you are a man and not a god, though you think you are as wise as a god" (Ezek 28:2).

In the oracle against Egypt of ch. 31, Pharaoh (as the personification of Egypt) is likened to the Assyrians, who are in turn likened to the Cedar of Lebanon which outshines "all the trees of Eden" (31:9).[110] The passage is replete with exaltation themes: "Who can be compared with you in majesty (בגדלך)?" (31:2); "The cedars in the garden of God could not rival it . . . no tree in the garden of God could match its beauty . . . the envy of all the trees of Eden in the garden of God" (31:8–9); "Which of the trees of Eden can be compared with you in splendor (בכבוד) and majesty (ובגדל)?" (31:18). Quite clearly, then, honor concepts are present here, as well as something approaching a patronage structure in the dependence of nature/the nations on Assyria *cum* Egypt, "All the birds of the air nested in its boughs, all the beasts of the field gave birth under its branches; all the great nations lived in its shade" (Ezek 31:6).[111]

---

however, the meaning "honor" can be maintained, the sense of an illegitimate seeking of honor (or, perhaps more accurately, a seeking of illegitimate self-honor) in the verse is clear. Downing ("Honor," 63–65), also has an interesting discussion of the parallel concept of κενοδοξία ("false/empty honor") in ancient Greek thought.

108. John G. Peristiany and Julian Alfred Pitt-Rivers, *Honor and Grace*, 2–3.

109. By "first and foremost," I obviously do not mean a *chronological* order in constructing a model of honor: our initial etic is anthropological in nature. Instead, I am speaking of *logical* order, in that what has first priority logically supplies the parameters for understanding the concept overall.

110. The tree symbolism here does not seem to draw on the "Cosmic Tree" theme in the ANE, the tree of life in Eden, or any other distinctive tree ideology: "It is surprising how free of specific political references the description is" (Zimmerli, *Ezekiel 25–48*, 146).

111. While something like patronage structure is expressed in these verses, a full-blown social structure cannot be extrapolated from the language; it is both too transparently

כבד *and Israel*

There is only one example of כבד in Ezekiel that has Israel as its main referent. In 23:41, Judah/Oholibah is characterized as a prostitute, sitting on "an elegant couch (מטה כבודה)." Although coming in the context of the dishonorable action of Israel/Judah, here כבד itself does not have any major detectible honor themes, aside from it being a description of a luxury item.[112]

Other "Honor"-Related Terms in Ezekiel: רדה, רקי, יבצ

Of other main honor-related roots in the OT,[113] three (הדר, יקר, צבי) appear in Ezekiel. הדר appears twice (Ezek 16:14, 27:10). In Ezek 16:14, it is used positively, as a descriptor of YHWH's adornment of orphan Israel to become the unrivalled beauty of the nations. הדר is used in conjunction with several other terms in the surrounding verses that are related to the semantic sphere of כבד, including honor concepts. Reputation is in view (her name "went out among the nations"), as is the splendor and beauty given to Israel by YHWH (v. 14). This beauty included the display of great wealth (vv. 10–13) and was a sign of YHWH's covenant love and commitment to her (that is, the expression of his character in his relationship to Israel, vv. 8–9).

In Ezek 27:10, הדר is used of the array of shields and helmets of Tyre's mercenary army, which "gave you splendor (המה נתנו הדרך)." Again, the term shares several aspects of meaning with כבד that are related to honor, as analyzed in the broad semantic study in this chapter—visible magnificence is explicit, with further connotations of reputation and size (of the multiethnic army) in the description. Further, given the nature of the prophecy, the notions of substance and significance are also likely. The size and scope of Tyre's armies seem to testify to the city's substance and permanence, and leads to the nations looking to it for the source of כבד, by virtue of its place as the center of world trade. However, it will be brought to ruin, its substance shown to be as nothing (Ezek 27:26–36).[114]

The word יקר, the most prominent honor term in Laniak's study of Esther, is used in a much more straightforward fashion in its three appearances in Ezekiel (Ezek 22:25, 27:22, 28:13). In all three instances, the word

---

metaphorical and unidirectional to support a zero-sum reciprocity; all that is being noted here is the primacy that Assyria held among the nations that has come to naught.

112. According to Greenberg, "the unique adjective . . . presumably corresponds to the meanings of the noun *kabod*. . . . In this context *opulent* must mean something like 'covered in glorious cushions,' or 'glorified and adorned with beautiful spreads'"; Moshe Greenberg, *Ezekiel 21–37: A New Translation with Introduction and Commentary* (ed. W. F. Albright and D. N. Freedman; AB 22A; New York: Doubleday, 1997), 486.

113. Collins lists seven: ארד, הדר, הוד, נצח, יקר, פאר, and צבי. S.v. כבד, *NIDOTTE*.

114. Greenberg notes the irony in the imagery, and its use of the semantic range of כבד: "The focus [of the oracle] is entirely on the contrast between the past (in reality present) glory of Tyre and its lamented (in reality future) downfall . . . the sinking of the ship (vs. 26) is ominously juxtaposed (vs. 25) to its being weighted down with merchandise" (Greenberg, *Ezekiel 21–37*, 571).

simply means "valuable/precious" (stones), and thus stands most closely related to the "wealth" aspect of כבד. Any honor-related connotations are implicit, rather than explicit.

There are five examples of צבי in Ezekiel (Ezek 7:20; 20:6, 15; 25:9; 26:20). Three have the meaning "beautiful" (referring to jewelry in 7:20 and fertile land in 20:6, 15), while the final two have stronger honor associations, having to do particularly with the status of the nations in view. In Ezek 25:9, YHWH responds to the Moabite derision of Judah's fall, put specifically in terms of profanation/loss of holiness: "Look, the house of Judah has become like all the other nations" (Ezek 25:8). [115] The fall of Moab is then cast in terms of poetic justice in vv. 9–10: YHWH will "expose the flank of Moab," beginning at Beth-Yeshimoth, Baal-Meon, and Kiriathaim, which are described as צבי ארץ, "the glory of (that) land." [116] The final result of YHWH's judgment is that the Moabites (along with the Ammonites) "will not be remembered among the nations" (Ezek 25:10). As Moab has profaned the glory of YHWH's land, mocking Judah as if it were nothing of note among the nations, so Moab will become nothing among the nations, its disassembly beginning with its own glory.

Ezekiel 26 describes the fall of Tyre, with honor concerns present in the context. As with Moab, Tyre's boast over Jerusalem: "I will prosper, she has been ruined! (אמלאה החרבה)" (v. 2), is given as the reason for YHWH's judgment: as Greenberg comments, "[Tyre's] boundless self-exaltation, epitomized in her ruler's apotheosis, has entrenched on God's prerogative and sealed her doom. Thus Ezekiel's concern over God's injured majesty . . . retains its centrality in his oracles against Tyre." [117] In v. 17, the coastal princes lament the fall of "the city that was praised (העיר ההללה)" for its strength. In v. 20, its fall is expressed in terms of death and burial; she will go down to "the pit" (בור) and "dwell in the land below" (הושבתיך בארץ תחתיות). As the final step in the process, YHWH declares: ונתתי צבי בארץ חיים. The phrase is rather difficult to render into English, [118] but the sense is clear: Tyre's beauty/splendor will not descend with her to the pit, but will be given to another, still living nation.

In summary, other honor-related terms used in Ezekiel fall within a similar semantic range to כבד, with a particular concentration around physical splendor, wealth, reputation, and significance/power. Several concepts

---

115. Cf. Greenberg: "Moab's offense is to deny Israel's incomparability . . . Moab infers from Israel's fall that Israel's destiny is no different from any other—by implication, that to be YHWH's people confers no special status" (ibid., 526).

116. Zimmerli notes that the use here is similar to the description of Canaan as the "glory" of all lands (Ezek 20:6) and suggests that the ascription צבי ארץ indicates that these are the "most important cities" of the Moabite territory (Zimmerli, *Ezekiel 25–48*, 15).

117. Greenberg, *Ezekiel 21–37*, 541.

118. As indicated by the BHS apparatus. Zimmerli notes that this phrase is distinctly Ezekiel's (Zimmerli, *Ezekiel 25–48*, 39).

usually associated with Mediterranean honor and shame *are* present, but as with כבד they are conditioned by their relationship with (or determination by) Yʜᴡʜ and especially tied to Judah's appointed status as the holy representative of Yʜᴡʜ's glory among the nations.

Constructing an Emic View of כבד in Ezekiel

The Range of Meaning of כבד in Ezekiel

From the examination of specific examples of כבד in Ezekiel, we have seen that Ezekiel's use of the term covers several of the main categories raised in the semantic study. There are instances where כבד does not involve honor: the liver in divination practices, or to describe splendor and wealth, but without any honor concepts being necessarily involved. On the other hand, honor is a central concern for Ezekiel, and this is reflected in the most significant uses of כבד in the book.

By far the most common usage is as the classic designation of the theophany (כבוד יהוה). However, for Ezekiel it is much more than simply a designation; he intricately weaves the divine attributes into the particulars of the vision itself, replete with overtones of honor. As such, the overall meaning not only of the vision but of the book itself is unmistakable: "The center of Ezekiel's theology is the glory of God . . . as Yahweh acts for the sake of his name, saving to show mercy and judging to show holiness, that all might know that he is Yahweh."[119]

The other examples that have significance with respect to honor are the references to the fate of the ships of Tarshish (and through them the fate of Tyre), and Assyria, the cedar of Lebanon (and, by parallel, Egypt). In the case of the ships of Tarshish, more than simply expressing the physical weight of the cargo (although this it does indeed do), honor concepts can be detected both in the use of כבד itself, as well as in the subject matter of the broader passage. Similarly, exaltation and splendor are in view with regard to the judgment on Egypt. In both cases, the usage stretches across several of the semantic concept spheres of כבד, with wealth, splendor and exaltation foregrounded against the backdrop of honor, which is in turn especially focused on Yʜᴡʜ as its source and arbiter.

Wider Reflections

Ezekiel and Exodus 3–14

The association of Ezekiel with Moses has been increasingly recognized in recent scholarship, including the suggestion that Ezekiel may have been taken to be the "prophet like Moses" of Deut 18:15.[120] Within this field of

---

119. Hamilton, *God's Glory*, 228; cf. Walther Zimmerli and K. C. Hanson, *The Fiery Throne: The Prophets and Old Testament Theology* (Minneapolis: Fortress, 2003), 106.

120. See McKeating, "Prophet Like Moses," 108; Jon Douglas Levenson, *Theology of the Program of Restoration of Ezekiel 40–48* (Missioula, MT: Scholars Press, 1976), 37–49;

study, Idestrom's work on the connections between Ezekiel and Exodus are particularly relevant. She notes that "both books emphasize the theme of coming to know who the Lord is through his divine acts, whether in judgment or salvation."[121]

Block has further noted the significance of the Recognition Formula, "they/you will know that I am Yʜwʜ" in both books, as well as its shared significance as the ultimate outcome of judgment. Speaking in regard to Ezekiel's distinctive use of the formula in Yʜwʜ "turning his sights" onto his own people, Block states, "underlying Ezekiel's usage [of the Recognition Formula] is a keen awareness of the traditional exodus narratives . . . just as the deliverance of his people from Egypt centuries earlier had been intended to impress the Israelites, the Egyptians, and the world with the presence and character of Yahweh, so too will his acts of judgment on a rebellious people."[122]

The parallels between Exodus and Ezekiel provide a further perspective on honor concepts in the OT. Recognition of Yʜwʜ plays a vital role in the Exodus narratives, especially in the account of the plagues. Exod 5:2 recounts Pharaoh's inital response to Yʜwʜ's command: "Who is Yʜwʜ that I should obey him to let Israel go? I do not know Yʜwʜ (לא ידעתי את־יהוה)." This statement sets the framework for the ensuing action, whereby both Israel (via deliverance) and Egypt (via judgment) "will know that I am Yʜwʜ" (Exod 6:7, 7:5).

The term כבד also plays a significant role in the narratives: Pharaoh, for example, "hardens" his heart (ויכבד פרעה את־לבו, Exod 8:28; cf. Exod 7:14; 8:15; 9:7, 34) against Yʜwʜ and his commands. However, the narrative emphasizes Yʜwʜ as the true owner of כבד. It is he who ultimately makes Pharaoh's heart "hard" (כבד) (Exod 10:1, 14:4; cf. 14:17), and who unleashes the "heavy" plagues against Egypt (Exod 8:20; 9:3, 18, 24; 10:14). Israel, meanwhile, "plunders the Egyptians" and leaves, כבד מאד with posessions and livestock (Exod 12:35–38).

The most critical references to כבד in the narratives come, however, in Yʜwʜ's stated purpose in the enterprise. As the decisive defeat of Pharaoh

---

Idestrom, "Echoes of Exodus," 489–510. For an argument against this association, see David L. Petersen, "The Ambiguous Role of Moses as Prophet," in *Israel's Prophets and Israel's Past: Essays on the Relationship of Prophetic Texts and Israelite History in Honor or John H. Hayes* (ed. Brad E. Kelle and Megan Bishop Moore; LHBOTS 446; London: T. & T. Clark, 2006), 311–24.

121. Idestrom, "Echoes of Exodus," 496; cf. Alexander, *Paradise to Promised Land*, 166: "There can be little doubt that the most important theme running throughout the book of Exodus is that of knowing God. Not only does the text highlight the different ways in which God may reveal himself, but it also focuses on those attributes which lie at the very heart of his nature: his sovereign majesty, his holiness, his awesome glory, his power to perform wonders, his righteousness and his compassion."

122. Block, *Ezekiel 1–24*, 38–39; cf. Idestrom, "Echoes of Exodus," 498 n. 41: "The Recognition Formula is not at all prominent in the rest of the Pentateuch in comparison to the book of Exodus."

approaches, three declarations are made that "I will be glorified (ואכבדה) by Pharaoh and all his army, and the Egyptians will know that I am YHWH" (Exod 14:4; cf. 14:17, 18).

The parallels with Ezekiel are abundantly clear, and helpful in giving perspective on the developments of the themes in Ezekiel. Both Exodus and Ezekiel have in common the themes of knowing YHWH through his acts of judgment and deliverance. Both also emphasize the primacy of acknowledging YHWH as the source and owner of all כבד, and the removal of any and all obstacles to that acknowledgment. Both stress the importance of tying these to YHWH's character of faithfulness to his covenant. All these condition what is meant by כבד in both Exodus and Ezekiel and, consequently, the meaning of "honor" as a subset.

On the other hand, Ezekiel demonstrates a development of themes in the Exodus narratives. As Idestrom (following Evans) notes, Ezekiel's use of the Recognition Formula is radical because, unexpectedly, it is directed against Judah.[123] Thus, while in Exodus the Recognition Formula applied to Israel "in a wholly positive way, to speak of Yahweh's deliverance of Israel and his blessing upon her,"[124] in Ezekiel it is also used of YHWH's judgment on his people.

This distinctive use indicates that, for Ezekiel, Israel's rejection of YHWH is akin to that of Pharaoh's (and the other nations')—they are also "hard of heart" (וחזקי־לב) against YHWH and his glory in such a manner that if they are to be delivered again, they must first undergo judgment (Ezek 2:4). This is obviously a major issue, which that will be explored in the subsequent chapters. At the very least, though, we can observe even at this point that for Ezekiel, Judah's situation in Exile is symptomatic of a cataclysmic rupture to the covenant relationship between YHWH and his people, or even its complete dissolution.

Furthermore, the scope of judgment in Ezekiel extends well beyond Egypt, although Egypt is still in view. The outward spiral of nations under judgment (Ezek 25–32), along with the proto-apocalyptic Ezek 38–39, indicates that YHWH is not to be viewed as a localized, tribal deity but as uniquely sovereign over all. It is not simply Pharaoh and Egypt, but now "the nations will know that I am YHWH (וידעו הגוים כי־אני יהוה)" (Ezek 36:23). For Ezekiel, then, recognition of YHWH's כבד, the sustained emphasis in the Exodus narratives, is now to be acknowledged by all nations.

Ezekiel and the Sinai Theophany (Exodus 33–34)

If, as I have argued, Exod 33–34 has a significant intertextual relationship with Ezekiel's theophanies, then a further implication is that in Ezekiel's

---

123. Idem, "Echoes of Exodus," 498; John Frederick Evans, "'You Shall Know That I Am Yahweh': Ezekiel's Recognition Formula as a Marker of the Prophecy's Intertextual Relation to Exodus" (Th.D. diss., University of Stellenbosch, 2006).

124. Ibid., 206.

presentation of the mobile throne, the emphasis does not lie simply in the overwhelming splendor of YHWH's appearance. Rather, the echoes of Exodus suggest that the YHWH whose כבד appeared to Ezekiel by the Chebar river is the same YHWH who by and for his כבד delivered his people from Egypt through judgment.[125] This in turn forms something of a template for Judah's present (to Ezekiel) deliverance from Babylon: it will likewise come through the manifestation of YHWH's כבד in judgment and salvation.

Seeing a significant connection between the Sinai theophany and Ezekiel's vision of the כבוד־יהוה also potentially further informs the motivations for YHWH's actions in the latter book. In Ezekiel, YHWH *does* act for his honor. However, if it is plausible that the character creed formulation lies in the thought-world of Ezekiel's time, then this may condition and constrain the interpretation of YHWH's acts. In Ezekiel YHWH variously acts as *both* judge and deliverer.[126]

In the character creed (Exod 34:6–7), YHWH is likewise ... אל נשא עון, פקד עון, and רב־חסד ואמת. In other words, the character of Ezekiel's YHWH *can* be seen in terms consistent with other OT contexts where the formula recurs. What varies in such a canonical reading of the person of YHWH (and this variation is perhaps most pronounced and extreme in Ezekiel) is the degree to which each aspect of נשא עון ... פקד עון is emphasized or elaborated on by the various writers. Thus, the nations can be judged and destroyed for YHWH's כבד (e.g., Ezek 28:22), while Judah can be both judged *and* delivered, also for YHWH's כבד (cf. the movements of the כבוד־יהוה in Ezek 8–11, resulting in judgment, and Ezek 40–48, resulting in restoration).

This is an important recognition, as some significant contemporary assessments of Ezekiel's portrait of YHWH are vitriolic in their tone. Schwartz, for example, argues that Ezekiel's view of restoration, consistent with his view of the relationship between YHWH and Israel, "has nothing to do with love." Rather, it is solely because he is unable to bear the stain on his reputation should their absence from the land continue, that he acts to bring them back into the land. Moreover, Israel is thus locked into a perpetually abusive relationship—unable to leave again, try though they might—as YHWH cannot allow their sinfulness to be displayed to the nations.[127]

Such a perspective, however, may be a somewhat unfair representation of Ezekiel's YHWH. Schwartz seems to assume that Ezekiel's stress on YHWH as אל פקד עון excludes the possibility that he might be at the same time אל נשא עון. A fuller-orbed perspective of YHWH's כבוד, informed by the echoes of Exodus traditions in Ezekiel, helps us to understand how Schwartz's view may go awry. YHWH's concern for his honor and reputation in Ezekiel thus may not need to be seen so strictly in isolation from the more comprehensive

---

125. Cf. Zimmerli, *Ezekiel 1–24*, 124; Greenberg, *Ezekiel 1–20*, 51.
126. Sometimes simultaneously.
127. Schwartz, "Dim View," 66–67.

understanding of his כבוד expressed in the character creed.[128] As this issue
also informs the notions of shame and guilt in Ezekiel, I will return to address the view that Schwartz is representative of in the following chapters.

Imposed Etic and Emic B Part 1:
Agreement and Disagreement

The study above bears out a simple conclusion, but one whose implications are often overlooked. In Ezekiel, Yʜwʜ's honor becomes something
of an all-consuming obsession: not only is he is the owner, source, and ultimate judge of what is truly glorious, but his honor becomes virtually the
sole motivating factor in his acts of judgment (both on Israel and the nations) and salvation. Bringing the research to bear on the Context Group's
suggested model of honor and shame, we can confirm that there are significant areas of agreement, where the model has opened up new avenues of
understanding. On the other hand, there are also significant areas where the
biblical data stretches and perhaps even breaks the espoused model. Some
such areas are outlined below.

Areas of Agreement

Acknowledgment of Yʜwʜ's כבד

From the examination of Ezekiel, it is clear that an overriding concern
for Yʜwʜ is that his name be acknowledged, especially in Israel, but also
among all the nations. Ezekiel's God is not distant or emotionless and al-
truistic, nor is he nonjudgmentally benevolent. He is the covenant-making,
covenant-keeping God, who is determined that his name should be glorified
by all in a manner consistent with that covenant. The Context Group has
drawn attention to the importance of honor being recognized, and this has
been a helpful move forward in understanding the perspective expressed in
the Bible and, in particular, Ezekiel.

In this sense, it could be said that honor—more specifically, Yʜwʜ's
honor—is indeed a pivotal value in Ezekiel, central to his concerns, above
the restoration or re-establishment of Judah.[129] However, in accordance
with Herzfeld's caveat, this statement must also be tempered by particularization with regard to Yʜwʜ and his character, as well as its place within the
sweep of the wider semantic range of כבד.

Honor and Human Relationality

The Context Group also draws attention to the importance of social
bonds in human life and significance. The insistence of Malina's "call and
response" of honor (the worth that someone has in their own eyes plus the

---

128. Cf Zimmerli's discussion on the use of the recognition formula in Ezekiel (*I am
Yahweh*, 96).

129. Ibid., 88.

recognition of that honor by others) points to an important, but sometimes neglected strand of biblical teaching. Human life, according to the Bible, is not individualistic (at least not in the sense it is commonly used today, reflective of Enlightenment rationality and a view of the subject as an independent, autonomous entity). Rather, we are relational creatures, and the Context Group's renewed attention to the social dynamics reflected in the text is a welcome addition to the quiver of approaches in this strand of biblical studies.

Emphasis on honor also extends human ethical directives beyond simply seeking to avoid juridical crime: "I haven't hurt anyone," as some vulgar versions of Western ethics would have it. To hold to such an ethical basis reflects a limited view of the nature and purpose of human life, and takes insufficient account of our relationality. Rather, the biblical material *does* reflect a concern to live with an appropriate sense of honor: the command to honor one's parents, and above all to honor God illustrates this perspective. That SSAs have drawn attention to the importance of honor dynamics in the ancient world and the Bible is again a helpful development, not only in seeking to understand that world, but also in critiquing and correcting ours.

Areas of Disagreement

Honor and YHWH

While the centrality of honor is an area of agreement, it is also an area of disagreement when it comes to the person of YHWH, especially in the text of Ezekiel. At points, YHWH does appear to "play the honor game," as reflected in his concern to be acknowledged by both Judah and the nations.[130] However, as Stiebert has noted, because YHWH is the owner and ultimate dispenser of honor, he also "stands outside" the system, and is not finally subject to its dictates. As she states: "the figure of Yhwh complicates matters, as his presence renders social processes more opaque than transparent. Is he, for instance, another player, an ideological sweep or distortion, or a value system?"[131] I have therefore sought to articulate how true honor, according to the Bible, springs from its place in relation both to the wider semantic range of כבד, and to the character of YHWH.

Thus, while the Context Group model of honor may "cohere" as a symbolic system, and at points may resemble the dynamics of the biblical material, it ultimately shares the limits of its anthropological foundations. Accordingly, its "correspondence" to the theologically defined כבד in the Bible is tenuous. Indeed, as we have seen in the previous chapter, the problems with the model run deeper still, and thus for all its strengths and helpful aspects, it ultimately falls short of a satisfying explanation of honor concepts in general, and biblical ones in particular.

---

130. As indicated by the prevalence of the recognition formula.
131. Stiebert, *Construction of Shame*, 166.

Honor Precedence and Honor Virtue

The Mediterranean model of honor and shame, as Crook has observed, ultimately folds all honor under the umbrella of agonistic "Honor Precedence." This in turn depends on the conception of all goods, including honor, as being a limited commodity. As a result, even God/the gods must partake in and be finally subject to exchanges of honor. Lawrence, building on the insights of Pitt-Rivers, has helpfully distinguished between "Honor Precedence" and "Honor Virtue," and this distinction is confirmed by analysis of the biblical material.

Once again, the critical factor in the equation is the person and character of YHWH. The distinction between the two forms of honor springs from the uniqueness of YHWH as both transcendent and immanent, involved in the world (and its "honor games") and yet above it. As such, the view of honor as a "zero-sum game" put forward by the Context Group is of limited value in the biblical material. Although there may be suggestions of such forms of exchange (in Ezekiel, for example, the restoration of Judah coincides with the judgment on the nations that held her in derision), the "zero-sum" mechanism is not the best explanation of the data. Rather, nations are elevated or judged simply on the basis of their response to YHWH (or his people). Presumably, if the nations had mourned over the fall of Jerusalem, or themselves turned to YHWH, they too would have escaped his judgment. There is no "balancing the books" of honor in view in this regard.[132]

Honor, the PCR, and the DCR

SSAs have highlighted the prominence of the PCR(s) in determining and dispensing honor. This has been an extremely helpful development and an area that warrants further development. However, as the concept has been framed almost exclusively by the Mediterranean honor/shame model in practice, it stands in need of significant modification to account for the biblical material in a satisfying manner.

The foundational ideas behind the PCR, as mentioned above, are that the PCR is the body that has authority to determine what is deemed honorable, and dispense that honor to whom it sees fit. An extension on these ideas is the existence of multiple PCRs in whatever social context is in view. While these are all valid points in and of themselves, the place of YHWH is, again, critical in analyzing the biblical documents. By virtue of his position as the ultimate source, owner, and giver of כבד, he is the ultimate standard against which all created honor is to be measured, and it is his to determine and dispense honor. Thus, in partial agreement with the Context Group model, there *is* a sense in which honor must be recognized to be real. However, ultimately it is recognition by YHWH that counts—the DCR, stands above and reigns supreme over all other PCRs.

---

132. For further reflection and critique of honor and "zero-sum" exchanges, see Lawrence, *Ethnography of Matthew*, 181–221.

As a result of this, the character of Yʜwʜ sits rather uncomfortably in the honor/shame model, for (*pace* Crook) he is not ultimately dependent on others for his כבד to be realized. Ezekiel does not present Yʜwʜ as one deity jostling for position amongst many, dependent on human recognition for his continued existence. The כבוד יהוה is depicted as sovereign and free in its movements, independent of—*ruling over*—the affairs of humanity. As such, the "real," substantive aspect of his כבד is unaffected by Judah's failures; it remains constant and true. It is simply the responsive aspect that has been disrupted by humanity's rejection of him, and is restored by his subsequent actions.

Conclusion

My methodological review and analysis has so far explored the concepts involved in both the English "honor" (in the context of SSAs) and the BH כבד. The analysis has demonstrated that כבד is a broader concept than honor, which can be seen as one aspect of its semantic range. I have suggested, therefore, that the traditional, theological term *glory* remains a more satisfying basic rendering of the word into contemporary English, as it captures a wider sweep of its semantic sphere.[133]

The analysis has also demonstrated that the concept of honor is ultimately vague, needing its content "filled out" according to the authoritative body that is relevant to the context (that is, the PCR/DCR). Thus, for Malina, "honor" is defined as "a claim to worth along with the social acknowledgment of worth."[134] The key issue, then, is *what constitutes "worth"*? For the Context Group, that content is filled out according to the PCR constructed by the Mediterranean model; a model, we have seen, with both great strengths and weaknesses in attempting to provide a satisfying characterization of ancient social dynamics. For Ezekiel, on the other hand, the answer to the question of what constitutes "worth" is simple: Yʜwʜ himself and, derivatively the response to him that is appropriate for his creatures.[135] However, this cannot be finally understood without reference to its fundamental disruption within the scheme of Ezekiel's prophecy, for Yʜwʜ's כבד does not appear in a vacuum but comes to light in the context of Israel's failure and Exile. In the following two chapters, I will explore the key terms Ezekiel uses to express this disruption, בוש and עון.

---

133. That is, the categories covered in the semantic analysis above. Etymologically, "glory" is derived from the Latin *gloria*, which does sit more firmly within the concept of "honor." However, its usage in contemporary English most often expresses something of a transcendent feel, hence its particular association with religious terminology and especially the divine.

134. Malina, *New Testament World*, 31.

135. This is hinted at in Lawrence's definition of honor: "conferral of status before a significant other" (Lawrence, *Ethnography of Matthew*, 297).

Chapter 5

Shame in Ezekiel: Emic B Part 2

בוש *in the Old Testament*

In the previous chapter, I noted that the basic concept behind the root כבד, "heaviness," is widely agreed on. When it comes to בוש, however, the situation is not so clear cut, and I have already outlined the various problems in rendering the Hebrew root as "shame." Moreover, as Avrahami's analysis of בוש demonstrates, it rarely (if at all) appears in direct conjunction with the vocabulary of honor roots.[1] The issue at hand, then, is to find a suitable replacement as a basic concept in English that is able to convey as accurately as possible the sense of the Hebrew.

Avrahami's own suggestion revolves around a disconnection between expectations and reality: "בוש is the experience (or causing) of disappointment."[2] Such a definition is specific enough to be useful in encapsulating a semantic range, while also generic enough to allow for the contextual factors that give rise to "various shades" of meaning in usage: frustration, failure, lack of trust, and so on.[3] A survey of the use of בוש in the OT bears this conclusion out, as well as the fact that the word can also, in certain contexts, mean what contemporary English speakers would define as "shame."

Disappointment

Avrahami has already demonstrated the prevalence of the concept of disappointment in the meaning of בוש throughout the OT. Of particular note, however, is the sustained demonstration that "disappointment" often fits the meaning of בוש, where "shame" seems, on reflection, somewhat forced. This is clear, for example, in the case of Jer 2:36: "You will be disappointed (תבושי) by Egypt as you were disappointed (בשת) by Assyria." That disappointment accurately captures the sense of בוש here is strengthened by the following verse, in which the object of בוש is the "trust" (בטח) for deliverance that Israel put in the foreign nations, rather than in YHWH. בוש thus refers primarily to disappointed hope, due to a savior who has failed or will fail to deliver what is hoped for or trusted in.[4]

---

1. Avrahami, "בוש in the Psalms," 303. Besides her published work, this section is also indebted to personal discussions with Avrahami on the topic.

2. Ibid., 308.

3. Ibid.

4. See also Isa 19:9; 20:5; 30:5; 42`:17; Jer 48:13; 51:17; Ps 22:6; 25:2, 3, 20; Job 6:20.

It should be noted that the majority of references to בוש have, accordingly, to do with the appeal to or hope in an entity of greater authority or power than the supplicant. This is sometimes a foreign nation, but more often than not it is a deity. In most OT contexts, the only legitimate source of this confidence is said to be YHWH himself.[5] Hence Israel's reliance on foreign nations (Egypt and Assyria) can be described in terms of בוש, as seen above.

However, it is also the reason why the gods of the nations are also associated with the term. In Jer 51:17: "every goldsmith is disappointed (הביש) with his idol, for his image is a falsehood (שקר), and there is no breath in them." Likewise, the use of בשת as synonym of Baal (Jer 11:13; Hos 9:10), in conjunction with כזב ("to lie, deceive," Isa 28:15, 17; Amos 2:4) and שקר ("to deal falsely with," Jer 3:23; 5:2, 31) suggests that the primary meaning of the word in such usage is "something false or incapable, which cannot be trusted. בשת is a disappointing entity."[6]

Dismay/Disillusionment/Despair

The word בוש is also used in the OT to express the sense of dismay, disillusionment, and despair. In Jer 49:23, for example, Hamath and Arpad are said to be בושה, because of a report of bad news (כי־שמעה רעה שמעו). The effect of the report (presumably the destruction of the city expressed in vv. 26–27) is then explained in terms of נמגו בים דאגה השקט לא יוכל ("swaying on the sea, anxiety not able to be quietened"). English translations render בושה variously as "ashamed" (NASB, JPSV) or, more helpfully "dismayed" (NIV) and "confounded" (ESV, RSV). That the latter renderings more accurately express the sense of the word in context is reinforced by the terms used in the following verse: "become feeble" (רפתה . . . . הפנתה, that is, "courage failing"),[7] "turning to flee," "gripped by panic."

The word בוש also expresses the concept of despair, as in Joel 1:11. There the farmers are told הבישו, which is then paralleled by the vinegrowers "howling" (הילילו) for the wheat and barley. The cause is then explicated in full: the harvest of the field is destroyed. Simkins has argued for an honor/shame reading of Joel and accordingly attempts to fold this instance (as in all the other instances in Joel) under the umbrella of shame.[8] However, it seems rather more straightforward to see the use of בוש in 1:11 as a play on words, with its examples in 1:12 and 1:17 and the very similar roots יבש ("to dry up," v. 12) and עבש ("to shrivel," v. 17). In 1:12, the joy of humankind has turned to despair (בוש) as a result of the withering (יבש) of the produce of the land. Likewise in 1:17, the seeds are shrivelled (עבש) and the grain is

---

5. Ibid., 302.
6. Ibid., 309.
7. S.v. בוש, *HALOT*.
8. Simkins, "Return to Yahweh."

dried up (בוש). [9] It is likely that the ambiguous use of בוש in 1:11 thus reflects a concomitant response to such ruin and misery. In other words, there is despair over the withering of the harvest joy due to the locust plague that has come on the land, rather than a loss of status in the eyes of other nations.

In Job 6:15, Job describes the support of his friends as seasonal desert springs, which are available in the wet season, but dry up in the heat. In 6:18–20, the metaphor continues on in terms of the caravans that traverse the desert: "The caravans of Tema look for water, the travelling merchants of Sheba look in hope (קוה). בשו, because they had been confident (בטח); they arrive there, only to be disappointed (חפר)." In a similar sense to Joel 1, בוש conveys the sense of distress and despair arising from the dashed hope of finding water.

The word בוש is also used to convey dismay in Ps 119:116, and is a particularly interesting example of how attempting to maintain shame as the primary meaning of בוש is a problematic exercise. The ESV, for example, translates Ps 119:116 as "Uphold me according to thy promise, that I may live, and let me not be put to shame in my hope!" As Avrahami notes, the translation has two major difficulties: first, the context lacks any of the typical associations with shame adumbrated in the anthropological model; feminine characteristics, sexual misbehavior, or public condemnation. Second, perhaps even more compellingly, the translation borders on absurdity. Avrahami instead opts for "Let me not be disillusioned in my hope." [10] In examples such as these, the advantages of seeing the basic meaning of בוש as the gap between reality and expectations, over the more restrictive and loaded term *shame*, becomes quite clear.

Failure/Frustration/Embarrassment

I have already noted the use of בוש in Joel 1:12, in association with plants withering or drying up. The word can thus also carry a sense of "failure to come to fruition," an idea that is particularly easy to transfer to concepts such as (failed) prosperity and trust in an entity, already outlined above. In a similar vein, Ps 14:6 says that evildoers "frustrate (תבישו) the plans of the poor," that is, cause them to fail to come to fruition. Avrahami also notes that Ezra 8:22 likely falls under this category. Rather than "being ashamed" to ask the king of Persia for reinforcements (which makes little sense in the flow of the passage), Ezra's confession of Yhwh's protection before him led to him "failing" to ask the king., that is, not asking the king at all, seeing as, with Yhwh's protection, a further escort was deemed unnecessary. [11]

---

9. Adding further to the play on words is the fact that the Hiphil form הביש used in 1:12 and 1:17 could be derived from either בוש or יבש.

10. Avrahami, "בוש in the Psalms," 308.

11. Alternatively, this instance of בוש could convey a sense of embarrassment, given Ezra's prior insistence to the king of Yhwh's protection over the convoy.

A further aspect of failure comes in the use of בוש, to indicate waiting for lengthy period of time (commonly occurring in the *polel* stem or the construction עד־בוש). While sometimes conveying a sense of embarrassment, which may be broadly related to shame (e.g., Judg 3:25; 2 Kgs 2:17; 8:11), the phrase can also have the more innocuous sense of simply being a long time (Exod 32:1; Judg 5:28). Avrahami suggests that the construction עד־בוש has the meaning "to the point of despair," while the Polel בשש, coupled with an infinitive construct, means "failed to descend" (Exod 32:1) or "failed to come" (Judg 5:28).[12]

Shame

Finally, בוש can be used in setting where "shame" is an appropriate translation. This is the case both in terms of SSA shame, especially in contexts of public or national humiliation (for example, 2 Chr 32:21; Ezra 9:7), and also psychological/emotional shame, in the context of parallel emotional responses (example, כלם and תועבה in Jer 6:15; 8:12). However, there are three qalifications that are necessary to bear in mind in understanding this sense of בוש.

The first is to bear in mind that when בוש does mean shame, it is often difficult to distinguish between anthropological and psychological shame in the clear-cut manner that many scholars do. Rather, the concepts seem to overlap fairly significantly in some instances, with בוש being used in a multivalent manner, as in the example of Saul's tirade against Jonathan, in 1 Sam 20:30: "You son of a perverse and rebellious woman! Don't I know that you have sided with the son of Jesse to your own shame (לבשתך) and to the shame (ולבשת) of your mother who bore you?" I have discussed some of the reasons for this overlap above, in ch. 3. In these instances, perhaps "embarrassment" may helpfully capture the span of meaning across emotional and social categories.

Second, בוש rarely means shame without another significant shame term also occurring in near proximity—כלם, חרף, and so on. This suggests that בוש is invested with shame concepts mainly by contextual factors, rather than being necessarily encoded into the meaning of the root. This observation in turn lends support to the strength of Downing's thesis that honor and shame *may be* significant in biblical passages but that this needs to be substantiated as primary clearly from the context.[13]

Third, it should be noted that shame—whether social, psychological, or both—can be seen to fall under the wider umbrella of disappointment, or the gap between expectations and reality.[14] Reflecting this fact, the term

---

12. Ibid., 311. One major advantage of Avrahami's suggestion is that it provides a way to integrate the three supposedly different but homonymic roots put forward in some lexicons: "to be ashamed," "to be scattered," and "to be slow/hesitant."

13. Downing, "Honor," 55.

14. Cf Avrahami, "בוש in the Psalms," 310.

shame can still be used in English to convey a sense of disappointment, without any psychological or anthropological baggage (for example, as I hear far too often, "You didn't catch any fish on your trip? What a shame!").[15]

The Use of בוש in Ezekiel

There are five instances of בוש and its cognates in Ezekiel, all of which appear in parallel, paired or clustered with other terms: the noun בושה in 7:18, and verbal forms in 16:52, 16:63, 32:30, and 36:32. I will analyze each in turn.

Ezekiel 7:18

In Ezek 7:18, after prophesying "the end" (הקץ, Ezek 7:2) for the land of Israel, Ezekiel describes the grief of the Israelites to the impending sacking of Jerusalem, using a chiastic, voluntary-involuntary-involuntary-voluntary, order: "They will put on sackcloth and be clothed with terror. Their faces will be covered with shame and their heads will be shaved" (Ezek 7:18, NIV).[16]

The emphasis in the verse lies on physical displays of mourning, which find parallels in other parts of the OT—sackcloth, shaved heads,[17] shuddering, and בושה. Block observes that the term often denotes a veil of mourning (Obad 10; Mic 7:10; Ps 89:46), but here describes a physical, facial response.[18] The chiastic structure of the cola can be represented as follows:

Voluntary/External		*Involuntary/Physiological*
Body	וחגרו שקים	(they will put on sackcloth)
Body	וכסתה אותם פלצות	(and terror will clothe them)
Head	ואל כל־פנים בושה	(and on all faces forlornness)
Head	ובכל־ראשיהם קרחה	(and on all their heads baldness)

In this context, having בושה on one's face is one of the results of the disaster that has befallen Israel. While most often translated "shame" (NIV, NASB, KJV, RSV), the cluster of terms that lie around בושה do not have so much to do explicitly with shame—whether defined psychologically or social-scientifically—so much as *grieving or mourning great loss*.[19] As such, בושה seems

---

15. On further reflection, perhaps this sort of comment in the face of sustained failure to bring home any piscatorial delights does create psychological baggage of sorts.

16. Block, *Ezekiel 1–24*, 261–62.

17. Sackcloth: e.g., Gen 37:34 over a death, Lam 2:10 over national disasters, or 1 Kgs 19:1–2 for penitence for sins. Shaved heads: e.g., Isa 3:24; 15:2 as an expression of grief.

18. Block, *Ezekiel 1–24*, 262.

19. Greenberg translates בושה as "confusion": "They shall gird sackcloth, and shuddering will cover them; confusion on every face, hair plucked from every head." In his commentary he does, however, also suggest that the word is associated particularly with (public) mourning rites (Greenberg, *Ezekiel 1–20*, 144, 152).

most intuitively to have to do with the looks of sadness and disappointment that would have accompanied the grief of Jerusalem's sacking.

It is possible to overstate the distinction between shame and grief at this point. Indeed, one could argue out that shame is one of the results of disaster, whether "natural" or sociopolitical (as the nation "loses face" before its enemies).[20] In response to these, one carries an expression of "shame-facedness"—either figuratively, or physiologically (lowering of the eyes, blushing, or the like), as an expression of loss of status. In other words, grief *may* be one response to being shamed (perhaps in lamenting the loss of social standing). On this front, it should be noted that some of the consequences of the exile *are* put in terms of loss of wealth (Ezek 7:19–21) and status (Ezek 7:27).[21]

However, while this may be a plausible suggestion due to the significant conceptual overlap between grief and shame, in context the majority translation is an instance of reading shame concepts "into the text" more than out of it. Indeed, it would be rather disingenuous to automatically assign such a reponse to the realm of shame, given that *anyone* would probably find being forcibly removed from their home and land an occasion for trauma and grief.

In fact, to translate בושה as "shame" in this instance runs into grammatical, syntactical, and conceptual difficulties. In terms of grammar and syntax, three issues stand against understanding בושה as shame. First, it undermines the symmetry of the couplet. It seems out of place to have such a balanced expression of grief interrupted by the sudden insertion of social sanction, or even status. Second (as noted above), by its correspondence with פלצות, בושה denotes a *physical* facial expression of mourning, rather than a statement of social standing.[22] Third, no other significant honor/shame terminology appears explicitly in the rest of the section.

Perhaps more telling, however, are the conceptual associations in the chapter. The chapter repeatedly states the direct cause of mourning and grief—the fall of Jerusalem—in terms of justice and recompense: "I will judge you according to your conduct and repay you for all your detestable

---

20. E.g., Simkins, "Return to Yahweh"; Bechtel-Huber, "Perception of Shame."

21. Zimmerli draws some fairly wide assocations (including SSA shame) into his discussion on v. 18, although he retains the translation "shame": "In the shame which lies on their faces there is betrayed a humiliation which is more than the simple psychological reaction to the surrounding world. It is the specific loss of honor and all that this means in the way of righteousness, which alone makes life possible" (Zimmerli, *Ezekiel 1–24*, 208).

22. The closest association that can be suggested is with regard to affect theory. In other words, one could reasonably suggest that the physical expression of grief reflects the affect-level reaction that combines with behavioral-cognitive elements to form an emotion that arises in response to being shamed through divine abandonment and exile. This much is plausible but not necessitated by the text.

practices" (וּשְׁפַטְתִּיךְ כִּדְרָכַיִךְ וְנָתַתִּי עָלַיִךְ אֵת כָּל־תּוֹעֲבֹתָיִךְ; Ezek 7:3, cf. 7:4, 8, 9, 27). It is "because of their iniquity" (בַּעֲוֹנוֹ, Ezek 7:13), "by their own standards" that YHWH will judge them (וּבְמִשְׁפְּטֵיהֶם אֶשְׁפֹּט, Ezek 7:27). The emphasis is clear: the fall of the city is not described in terms of honor and shame, but explicitly in terms of "justice."

In light of the above, the direct association of בּוּשָׁה with shame is unwarranted. It seems far more likely that the word communicates the disappointment, grief, and mourning of the Jerusalemites over the loss of what they thought the unshakeable fortress-city of God.[23] As such, I opt for the translation "forlornness" for בּוּשָׁה in Ezek 7:18. What is commonly understood to be shame concepts may be in the passage, but they are implicit, rather than explicit, and do not seem to be communicated directly by בּוּשׁ. There are more grounds for sensing honor concepts in the recognition formula that follows judgment: "then they will know that I am YHWH" (Ezek 7:27), which I will expand on later in this chapter.

Ezekiel 16:52, 63

Ezekiel 16 and 23 have been viewed as central in SSA readings of Ezekiel, and it is not hard to see why. The themes of gender, sexuality, promiscuity, and disgust dominate the passage. Accordingly, the passages have been thoroughly mined by scholars of recent times, most often with a view to elucidating the rather alien (to Western minds) model of sexual competition, possessiveness, and aggressiveness of the (so-called) Mediterranean male, or to analyze the characterization and treatment of women in this "Text of Terror."[24] I do not wish to deny the manner in which this scholarship has advanced our understanding of the passages, or the cogency of feminist critiques of the controversial imagery in these chapters and some interpretations of it. However, these readings can overlook that the use of בּוּשׁ here goes beyond the powerful imagery, to play a more judicial function within the larger context of the book of Ezekiel.[25] As such, in order to grasp

---

23. Block's representation of "Israel's House of Pride" is helpful in highlighting the nexus of dashed hopes and false confidence that the people had in Jerusalem—their pride and false security thus turned to בּוּשָׁה; see Block, *Ezekiel 1–24*, 4–8.

24. To use Trible's famous formulation; Phyllis Trible, *Texts of Terror: Literary-Feminist Readings of Biblical Narratives* (Philadelphia: Fortress, 1984).

25. As Kim perceptively comments regarding the interpretation of Ezek 16: "We must certainly acknowledge that the biblical text has been put to some horrific uses over the centuries—to support the bloody crusades of the Middle Ages and to justify the enslavement and barbarous treatment of one people group by another in the early history of the United States, to give just a couple of examples. Events like these should compel us to be vigilant and not allow such atrocities to be committed in the name of God and the Bible. But the original audience of the prophetic marriage texts would not have viewed these passages as providing justification for men to abuse their wives. Indeed, both male and female hearers would have been compelled to identify with the adulterous wife, not

Ezekiel's use of בּוֹשׁ here, it may be necessary to review the impact of SSAs on the interpretation of the term in the chapter.

I have already noted Baruch Schwartz's article, in which he finds Ezekiel's God to be an enraged husband, whose provision for orphan Judah has been only to guarantee "her unending gratitude and unquestioning sexual fidelity."[26] Accordingly, his restoration of her after infidelity is totally without love and, in SSA terms, "to shame her in the eyes of all nations and to render her eternally speechless, her self-esteem gone forever (16:52–63). In Ezekiel, *Israel is never forgiven*; rather, she remains perpetually ashamed."[27]

In a similar vein, though with more focus on the sexuality aspect of SSA shame, Shields offers a study of how Ezek 16 both constructs and is constructed by gender and the female body.[28] Drawing on Galambush, Shields frames the relationship between Yhwh and Israel in this chapter in terms of Mediterranean (misogynistic) honor and shame: "Yahweh, as the one with authority over the woman's body and sexuality, is shamed and dishonored by her behavior. Her exposure and punishment restore Yahweh's honor."[29]

Furthermore, it is not simply the behavior of the "wife" that has to do with shame, but also her very being. Shields, drawing on Mary Douglas's work on defilement, contends that the references to blood and nakedness in the descriptions of juvenile, pubescent, and conjugal Israel "problematize" the woman's body, and associate it inextricably with shame.[30] Shields's interpretation of בּוֹשׁ in v. 63 is then given, in terms consistent with what

---

the faithful divine husband who is at the same time supreme God and judge. This identification would have forcefully impressed on such hearers how reprehensible it would be to abandon the God with whom they had entered into a marriage-like relationship, challenging both men and women to respond in humble repentance, not domination"; Brittany Kim, "Yhwh as Jealous Husband: Abusive Authoritarian or Protective Husband? A Reexamination of a Prophetic Image," in *Daughter Zion: Her Portrait, Her Response* (ed. M.J. Boda et al.; AIIL 13; Atlanta: SBL, 2012), 147.

26. Schwartz, "Dim View," 66.

27. Ibid., 64 (emphasis his).

28. Mary E. Shields, "Multiple Exposures: Body Rhetoric and Gender Characterization in Ezekiel 16," *JFSR* 14/1 (1998): 5. For further examples of this perspective on the chapter, see also Athalya Brenner, "Pornoprophetics Revisited: Some Additional Reflections," *JSOT* 70 (1996): 63–86; Katheryn Pfisterer Darr, "Ezekiel's Justifications of God: Teaching Troubling Texts," *JSOT* 55 (1992): 97–117; Julie Galambush, *Jerusalem in the Book of Ezekiel: The City as Yahweh's Wife* (Atlanta: Scholars Press, 1992). For responses to these perspectives, see, for example, Daniel I. Block, "The God Ezekiel Wants Us to Meet," in *The God Ezekiel Creates,* 162–92; Daniel Bodi, "The Inversion of Values in Ezekiel 16 and the Reminiscence of the Ištar Cult" (paper presented at SBL Annual Meeting, San Francisco, November 18–22, 2011); Andrew Sloane, "Aberrant Textuality? The Case of Ezekiel the (Porno) Prophet," *TynBul* 59 (2008): 53–76; Renz, *Rhetorical Function,* 145–48.

29. Shields, "Multiple Exposures," 6–7. Shields does draw attention to the fact that Galambush goes on to return from "metaphor" to "reality," seeing the device as a way of turning the destruction of the city and temple into victory for monotheistic Israel.

30. Ibid., 9.

precedes it: "The emphasis on the woman's ongoing shame . . . reminds the reader—as well as the woman in the narrative—that her body is the source of shame and uncleanness."[31]

Once again, it should be acknowledged that several of the observations above have highlighted previously unnoticed or underemphasized aspects of the text, some of which are of particular importance to this study (defilement, uncleanness and "shame" concepts). However, in light of the criticisms of SSAs raised earlier, we also have grounds for reconsidering certain aspects of Jerusalem's shame raised by the imagery of Ezek 16.

Ezek 16 explains the fall of Jerusalem via two main devices: the allegory of the adulterous wife, and a form akin to the ריב lawsuit speech.[32] Typically, the speech consists of:

1. Introductory commissioning formula for the prophet to speak for YHWH (16:1)
2. Summons to the defendant to hear the case against them (16:2)
3. Accusation and evidence against the defendant (16:3–34)
4. Sentence and declaration of punishment for the crime (16:35–58)
5. Conclusion, stating the divine origin and authority of the oracle (16:59–63)

A full exegesis of the passage here is beyond the scope of this study.[33] Instead, I will draw in discussion of the wider passage as it seems necessary to analyze the appearances of בוש. It is worth noting, however, that despite the emotive and offensive imagery, in the flow of Ezekiel the chapter is ultimately aimed at addressing the sociopolitical entities "Jerusalem" and "Samaria." Thus, primarily, "The emotion which is meant to be created is not sexual excitement, nor satisfaction about the deserved punishment, but outrage at Jerusalem's behavior. What the prophet has in view are idolatry and political alliances."[34]

The word בוש first appears in 16:52. There, the sin of Judah is compared to the regions surrounding it in familial terms: Samaria to the north and Sodom to the south.[35] The particular indictment against Jerusalem in this section (16:44–58) is expressed in 16:47: "You not only walked in their ways

---

31. Ibid., 13.

32. Block, *Ezekiel 1–24*, 459–67; Michael de Roche, "Yahweh's *rîb* Against Israel: A Reassessment of the So-Called 'Prophetic Lawsuit' in the Preexilic Prophets," *JBL* 102 (1983): 563–74. For the use of ריב in prophetic literature see Hos 2:4; 4:1–3; Mic 6:1; Jer 2:5–9. Greenberg (*Ezekiel 1–20*, 292) sees the chapter structured in three sections (vv. 3–43, 44–58, 59–63) around the declarative formula "declares (Lord) YHWH."

33. For a full treatment, see Block, *Ezekiel 1–24*, 459–522; Iain M. Duguid, *Ezekiel* (NIVAC; Grand Rapids: Zondervan, 1999), 209–20; Leslie C. Allen, *Ezekiel 1–19* (WBC 28. Dallas: Word, 1994), 223–48; Greenberg, *Ezekiel 1–20*, 270–306; Zimmerli, *Ezekiel 1–24*, 322–53.

34. Renz, *Rhetorical Function*, 146.

35. Ezek 16:46. The words שמאל (left/north) and ימין (right/south) can do "double duty," given the standard easterly orientation of the OT.

and copied all of their detestable practices (תועבה), but in all your ways you soon became more depraved (שחת) than they." The reference to Sodom, both genealogically and temporally removed from Jerusalem and Samaria, makes it clear that the "sisterhood" that is referred to in the chapter is not ethnographic, but pragmatic.[36] It is "their ways" (דרכיהן) and "their detestable practices" (תועבותיהן עשית) that marks the three entities as belonging to the same family.

The substance of Jerusalem's offenses in this section completes the total sweep of her crimes. In 16:15–22, the particular relationship in view is that between Jerusalem and Yhwh; in 16:23–42 the focus turns Jerusalem's conduct before the nations. Here, the spotlight is turned inward to the Jerusalemites' treatment of each other, highlighted especially in 16:49. Sodom's sin (עון) is identified as the arrogance (גאון), gluttony (שבעת־לחם) and complacency (שלות השקט היה), leading to a complete lack of concern for the poor (ויד־עני ואביון לא החזיקה).[37] These combined indictments leave Jerusalem completely without defense.

The thrust of the passage, however, is not simply to liken Jerusalem to Sodom and Samaria. Rather the indictment is structured around a *qal wa-homer* argument: Sodom was "done away with" (ואסיר אתהן), as was Samaria, and yet in Yhwh's eyes Jerusalem had "done more detestable things than they" (ותרבי את־תועבותיך).[38] It was therefore completely fitting that Jerusalem should suffer the destruction it now faced. It is in this context that she is told: בושי (Ezek 16:52).

Superficially, it would seem that here "be ashamed" is a fairly natural translation of בוש in this verse. However, it is worth working through the conceptual network informing the meaning of the word, rather than coming to this sort of conclusion too quickly. Here I raise three considerations that are particularly relevant in moving toward a meaning of the word in this context.

First, as already noted, the overarching theme of the passage is Jerusalem's עון, her "sin," or "iniquity" (16:49).[39] Although the term only appears once in Ezek 16, it is dominant in the book, with the root עוה not only used frequently (appearing 44 times throughout Ezekiel), but concentrated at

---

36. Block uses the term *sociological* (*Ezekiel 1–24*, 508).

37. The close link between cause (arrogance, and so on) and effect (lack of concern, an so on) is indicated by the disjunctive *waw*, which mirrors the disjunction between the rich and the responsibility given to them to care for the vulnerable in society; cf. Deut 15:7, 11, 24:14–15.

38. Cf. Greenberg, *Ezekiel 1–20*, 288: "[Sodom's sin] is exploited for the invective." See also Zimmerli, *Ezekiel 1–24*, 350.

39. A full discussion of the meaning and significance of עוה is the focus of the next chapter. However, as it is integral to understanding the meaning of בוש in Ezek 16, and given that the concepts are closely related, it is necessary to begin an examination of its meaning here.

critical points in the book (for example, the commissionings of Ezekiel in chs. 3 and 33, and the initial indictment on Jerusalem in ch. 4). Moreover, it is a key term in the OT, and is foundational to the character creed in Exod 34:6–7: Yʜᴡʜ is the God who "forgives wickedness, rebellion, and sin" (נשׂא עון ופשע והטאה).[40] However, he also "will not leave the guilty unpunished" (ונקה לא ינקה פקד עון).[41]

The covenantal basis of עון is essential to bear in mind in Ezekiel, for it denotes a specificity of relationship that conditions the meaning of the word. Under the terms of the Mosaic covenant, עון does not seem to refer, in the first instance, to a universal "natural law" of justice that has been broken; rather, it connotes a twisting, distortion, or violation of the specific terms of the covenant established between Yʜᴡʜ and Israel.[42] In this regard, the contribution of SSAs is valuable in highlighting that עון operates within a social structure that has some affinities to a suzerain-vassal treaty, or, in SSA terms, a patron-client relationship.[43]

That עון should be understood in the context of covenant in Ezek 16 is indicated by the earlier sections of the passage:

> I passed by you, and I looked at you and you had come to the time for love. And I spread my garment-corner over you and covered your nakedness. I swore an oath to you and entered into a covenant with you, declares the Lord

---

40. For an intriguing suggestion regarding the "double meaning" of the construction עון + נשׂא, see Joseph Lam, "Metaphor, Lexicalization and Diachronic Change: The Case of the Biblical nāśāʾ" (paper presented at SBL Annual Meeting, San Francisco, November 18–22, 2011).

41. Cf. Exod 20:5.

42. עון can be used to indicate a "universal" law of justice in the OT (to which nations not specifically in a covenant relationship with Yʜᴡʜ are also subject, e.g., Gen 15:16), although even in such cases the sense of the term may require more nuance. However, its use in the introduction to the covenant in Exod 20:5 and in the theophany in Exod 33–34, in the form of the character creed, link its meaning, as applied to Israel, primarily with the terms of the covenant. See further s.v. עון, *NIDOTTE, TDOT, HALOT*; John Barton, *Understanding Old Testament Ethics: Approaches and Explorations* (Louisville: Westminster John Knox, 2003); Klaus Koch, "Is There a Doctrine of Retribution in the Old Testament?" in *Theodicy in the Old Testament* (ed. J. L. Crenshaw; Philadelphia: Fortress, 1983), 57–87. I will discuss the relationship between Yʜᴡʜ, the term עון, and the notion of justice at length in the next chapter.

43. The classic work on affinities to a suzerain-vassal treaty is Mendenhall, *Law and Covenant*. See also Meredith G. Kline, *Treaty of the Great King: The Covenant Structure of Deuteronomy, Studies and Commentary* (Eugene, OR: Wipf & Stock, 2012); K. A. Kitchen and Paul J. N. Lawrence, *Treaty, Law and Covenant in the Ancient Near East* (3 vols; Wiesbaden: Harrassowitz, 2012); K. A. Kitchen, *On the Reliability of the Old Testament* (Grand Rapids: Eerdmans, 2003). On an patron-client relationship, bear in mind the warnings of Schwartz, *Mediterranean People*, and, surprisingly, Crook, "Reciprocity," that the reciprocity of the patron-client relationship does not fit the solidarity-based social structures expressed in the OT. Given the importance of this for understanding "shame," I will return to this issue in the conclusion to this chapter.

YHWH, and you became mine. . . . [But] You took some of your garments and made colorful high places . . . you also took the beautiful things I gave you, made of my gold and silver which I gave you, and you made for yourselves male images and played the harlot with them. . . . And my food which I had given you—the fine flour, oil and honey I gave you to eat—and you set it before them (Ezek 16:8, 16–19).

The recount of Jerusalem's sin goes on to include what would be regarded as "immoral" activity; for example, shedding blood (Ezek 16:20–21, 35, including child sacrifice), and lack of regard for the poor (Ezek 16:49). However, as Ezek 16:8, 16–19 indicates, the passage is framed by the establishment of the covenant with YHWH. Thus, Jerusalem's "whoredom" consists of taking YHWH's covenant gifts and blessings and using them to run after the nations and their gods (that is, twisting, distorting, and violating the covenant they had agreed to).

The reprehensibility of Jerusalem's actions (as presented by Ezekiel), however, is made all the more worthy of condemnation when it is borne in mind that the suzerain-vassal/patron-client relationship is in fact not the vehicle of the covenantal allegory. Rather, it is the deeply personal and far more intimate covenant between husband and wife that has been repeatedly and flagrantly ruptured by one party.[44]

For Ezekiel then, the allegory, for all its extreme and violent imagery, communicates a straightforward but central and critical point: Judah's (repeated) violation of the covenant has brought the covenant curses on them, *according to the terms they themselves agreed to* (cf. Exod 19:8). Thus, Renz notes that the metaphor of ch. 16 (and ch. 23) is not designed to legitimize or enshrine violence against women. It is, rather, to cut through the exilic community's self-justification, and to arouse in them anger over the reality of their flagrant disloyalty to YHWH. Only by coming to such a realization will they recognize the fittingness of its destruction by the Babylonians, and acknowledge the culpability of the Jerusalemites in failing to keep faith with YHWH's faithfulness to them.[45]

Second, however, although the concept of "covenant" was widespread in the ANE, when it comes to Israel as presented in the OT, we cannot be content with understanding it in generic terms. As I have already observed in regard to Exod 33–34 and Lev 19:1–2, the Sinai covenant depended on the specific character of YHWH—his חסד ואמת as פקד עון . . . אל נשא עון—for its substance and detail. Accordingly, Kathryn Darr has highlighted some key theological bases arising from it that lie behind texts such as Ezek 16. Her final two are critical in this regard: that YHWH's actions in the chapter are

---

44. For discussion on the terminology of "vehicle" and "tenor" in metaphor, see Peggy L. Day, "The Bitch Had It Coming to Her: Rhetoric and Interpretation in Ezekiel 16," *BibInt* 8 (2000): 231–54. For further reflection on how the marriage metaphor may be understood in a "positive" light, see Kim, "Yhwh as Jealous Husband," 127–47.

45. Renz, *Rhetorical Function*, 147.

not capricious or abusive but come in response to human sin and, consequently, that Ezekiel produced such "troubling texts" because of his unwav-
ering conviction that Yнwн was just. Such a severe punishment, then, does
not indicate a disproportionate recompense. Instead, it indicates that the
sin must have been equally grievous. [46]

Although her own argument does not extend in this direction, Darr's
observations highlight that Ezekiel's perspective depends for its coherence
and defensibility on *theological*, rather than sociological, grounds. In other
words, Ezekiel contends that Yнwн is consistent rather than capricious,
just rather than unfair. As such, Jerusalem's עון is not measured by an incon-
sistent standard, and thus their judgment, while expressed in a provocative
image, is in reality meted out in accordance with its bounds. [47] Indeed, in
the city's destruction, the reality of the punishment coheres with the terms
of the covenant relationship between Yнwн and Jerusalem, rather than
those of the allegory.

Third, raising the concept of justice draws attention to the most immediate issue affecting the meaning of בוש: its relation to righteousness (צדק).
In 16:51, Jerusalem is told, "[you] have made your sisters seem righteous
(תצדקי) by all the things you have done." That the *piel* should be understood
comparatively ("seem righteous") rather than absolutely ("justified") is confirmed by the parallel phrase in 16:52: "Because your sins were more vile than
theirs (התעבת מהן), they appear more righteous than you (תצדקנה ממך)." בוש
then appears in the conclusion to the verse: "So then, בושי and bear your
disgrace, for you have made your sisters appear righteous."

Of note is that the verse's initial construction, גם־את שׂאי כלמתך ("So
then, bear your disgrace") is repeated in its conclusion, but this time with
the inclusion of בוש: וגם־את בושי ושׂאי כלמתך. While it is possible that בוש
may simply intensify כלם, it is equally, if not more likely that, given its pivotal position in the chapter (16:53 will begin the section on the restoration),
there is something distinctive in the meaning of בוש. This is reinforced by
the fact that נשׂא is used in conjunction with כלמה but not with בוש throughout the OT. כלמה is what is borne, but בוש stands outside the construction.
We must therefore be careful of too quickly lumping the two together as
synonyms, as Block does: "[Jerusalem] will have to bear the shame and disgrace of having made those, whom Judeans had traditionally viewed as the
epitome of evil, appear innocent." [48]

Rather, the context strongly expresses Jerusalem's insensitivity to her
vile, disgraceful state (expressed primarily by כלם), which is exposed only
by unfavorable comparison with those whom the Jerusalemites would have

---

46. Darr, "Ezekiel's Justifications," III.

47. Cf. Ezek 18:23; 33:II: "'Do I take any pleasure in the death of the wicked?' declares
the Sovereign Lord. 'Rather, am I not pleased when they turn from their ways and live?'"

48. Block, *Ezekiel 1–24*, 510; as does Jacqueline E. Lapsley, *Can These Bones Live? The
Problem of the Moral Self in the Book of Ezekiel* (Berlin: de Gruyter, 2000), 143 n. 95.

condemned without question. Thus, "be (utterly) disappointed" seems a better choice of translation for בּוּשׁ in 16:52. In other words, the essential prerequisite for Judah to accept the appropriateness of the call to "bear your disgrace" was בּוּשׁי: to be made painfully aware of how utterly they had failed their covenant obligations. The Judahites are called on to realize and be utterly disappointed in the disconnection between the deluded smugness of their self-righteousness and the reality of their wickedness, as they are confronted with the destruction of their superficial security, the city of Jerusalem.

When understood in this manner, translating בּוּשׁ as "shame" perhaps misses the thrust of the passage. If the meaning of בּוּשׁ is primarily "disappointment," then the description of their failure in such stark terms functions as a tool to free the addressees from a deluded self-righteousness. It is designed to bring them to an appropriate humility and repentance, whereby the pride that blinded her to her need of YHWH's favor in all things is prevented from rearing its head again (16:53–58). In this regard, even though it is associated here with *bringing down* Jerusalem's self-perception, and the imagery is highly provocative, it does seek to motivate a corrective response from Jerusalem's society at large.[49]

At this point, the value of Cairns's work on how the Greek shame term αἰδώς can have both negative and positive senses (or indeed both simultaneously), comes again to the fore. As he notes regarding the relationship of ἀιδώς to τιμή ("honor"):

> The link between *aidōs* and *timē* is, of course, fundamental, but the crucial point is that *aidōs* includes concern both for one's own *timē* and for that of others. As a result, part of the function of *aidōs* is to recognize the point at which self-assertion encroaches illegitimately upon the *timē* of others, and this means that *aidōs* . . . is concerned not only with one's own prestige, but also with the concepts of moderation and appropriateness in the pursuit of prestige.[50]

In a similar vein, the use of בּוּשׁ in Ezek 16:52 suggests an appropriate self-disappointment on Jerusalem's part that will enable its people to recognize the reality of their depravity, and with this renewed perspective, divested of the pride that led them to wander into wickedness, to turn back in repentance and humility to YHWH.[51]

---

49. Which is, in fact, a conceptual possibility of shame that I have already made note of in ch. 3, although one that requires a radical reconfiguration of concepts traditionally associated with shame. *For Shame.*

50. Cairns, *Aidōs*, 432.

51. As Zimmerli notes: "If the legal explanation of the fact of guilt should properly be set out in the indicative or jussive third person style . . . the declaration in the prophet's speech here has been changed into an impassioned appeal, which demands the recognition of guilt and the acceptance of the disgrace attaching to it by those who are guilty and under judgment" (Zimmerli, *Ezekiel 1–24*, 350).

The second example of בּוֹשׁ, in Ezek 16:63 has a similar sense to its use in Ezek 16:52. However, where Ezek 16:52 focused on the renewed self-perception precipitated by the fall of Jerusalem, Ezek 16:63 involves Jerusalem's self-perception following the renewal of the covenant and the restoration of the people. In some ways, this latter reference has been seen to be even more problematic than Ezek 16:52, for it suggests that Jerusalem continues being "shamed" by YHWH forever. As we have seen, this is exacerbated by the promise that Jerusalem will never open her mouth again, which only seems to reinforce some sort of perpetual pattern of abuse. The NIV translation exemplifies this sort of understanding: "you will remember and be ashamed and never again open your mouth because of your humiliation."

Given the above reflections on shame, however, the verse can be seen to communicate something quite different. This is even more so when we consider that vv. 59–63 form the conclusion to the oracle. As such, they may not communicate actions that follow chronologically on from the previous sections. In fact, it seems best to take them as a recapitulative summary of the whole chapter (as indicated by the oath formula in v. 59), in which case v. 63 reflects a continuation of Jerusalem's self-perceptive "return to reality" in the restoration.[52]

Understanding בּוֹשׁ in this way provides a potential resolution to several of the difficult features of the verse. That בּוֹשׁ follows זכר ("to remember") simply indicates, then, that the bringing down of Jerusalem's self-perception that occurred in v. 52 will not be forgotten, such that they should lapse back into an overinflated view of themselves that leads to rejection of YHWH. Likewise, the promise that Jerusalem will never open its mouth again, tied as it is to מפני כלמתך, may be communicating something other than an oppressive command of silent subservience or perpetual humiliation.

Odell suggests that the phrase מפני כלמתך refers to formal complaints made by the Judeans against YHWH for having betrayed them, and this is certainly plausible.[53] However, it may be rather more straightforward to take the phrase as reflecting not the status of humiliation, but rather the disgraceful haughtiness that characterized Jerusalem's iniquity. It is the proud and presumptuous speech of the wicked that is silenced, once they gain a true recognition of who YHWH is via their restoration, and hence their utter unworthiness to be in covenant with him.[54]

---

52. Zimmerli sees the verses as a final explanatory oracle to the chapter (ibid., 352.). Joyce views it as a secondary addition, which presents "a positive hope not found elsewhere in authentic Ezekiel material before the fall of Jerusalem (Joyce, *Ezekiel*, 134).

53. Odell, "Inversion of Shame," 104–5.

54. Joyce notes that, in the historical-social context of Ezekiel, this indictment would have actually had a "positive" effect on the psyche and morale of the Babylonian captives: "It is important to remember that Ezekiel is not a leisured work of systematic theology but rather an example of crisis literature written in an extreme situation. Ezekiel's theological message of judgment offered at least a glimmer of theological light to a people

Before proceeding to Ezek 32, it is also worth mentioning that the occurrence of בוש in Ezek 16:63 (as well as in 36:32), does not sit comfortably within the honor/shame model, given that the restoration should *remove* Jerusalem's shame, rather than perpetuate it. However, in at least these references, it is specifically its elevation to a place of rank among the nations that is the catalyst for בוש. I will focus further on the issue of shame after restoration in more detail in my analysis of Ezek 36:32.

Ezekiel 32:30

Ezekiel 32:17–32 follows on from the explicit קינה form in 32:1–16, and describes Egypt sharing the fate of the various other nations going down to *Sheol* via their defeat in battle. Strong has recently argued that the passage has its counterpart in the "resurrection" of Israel in Ezek 37:1–14, and that the entire package should be viewed in terms of honor and shame.[55] As the superscript to the article states (quoting from the introduction to *Semeia* 68): "Honor entitled a household to life . . . Shame sentenced a household to death." Strong suggests that the interpretive key to Ezek 32:17–32 lies in the descriptions of Egypt's associates in *Sheol*, and that the low and disgraced status of them emphasizes Egypt's now shameful state. Strong then argues that Ezek 37:1–14, with its emphasis on the recognition formula, should be seen in terms of a "new Exodus" that reverses the nation's shame and makes honor—especially YHWH's honor—apparent to all.[56]

Strong's article has much to commend it, and his attention to the social and associative terminology in Ezek 32, as well as the recognition formula in Ezek 37 is enlightening in appreciating the passage. On the other hand, there is a major issue with his argument. While in broad sweep, the generalizations about honor, shame, and status are evident, Strong fails to analyze the actual instances of shame terminology in the passages closely enough. Specifically, he does not mention the use of בוש in 32:20, nor in 36:32, an example that we will see simply does not fit within the model of honor and shame Strong endorses as the driving hermeneutic framework.[57]

---

who had lost it all; it made possible an initial assimilation of the traumatic disaster, which could eventually become the basis of subsequent more positive lessons" (Joyce, *Ezekiel*, 18). Cf. the proposal of Deonna et al. regarding shame as a virtue.

55. Strong, "Egypt's Shameful Death."

56. Ibid., 501.

57. It should be noted that we need to be aware of the word-concept fallacy, even in its negative form, such that a concept may be present in a passage even where the key word(s) indicating it do not appear. Equally important, however, we need to heed Avrahami's warning regarding the Context Group: "Scholars do not attempt to explain the nuanced 'shame roots,' or the possible contribution of such explanation to the alleged cultural notions of honor and shame" ("בוש in the Psalms," 297). This balance of constraints ties back in to the emic/etic discussion raised in the methodological section of the current study.

In Ezek 32:30, בוש appears in a significant place, as the final statement assigning the various nations to their defeated and defiled state in *Sheol*. Throughout the passage, the nations are associated by repeated phrases, each appearing in almost every verse emphasizing their previous, powerful state: "who spread terror in the land of the living," and their current place: "slain, fallen by the sword," "with the uncircumcized," "among the slain." Strong, drawing on Lipiński, helpfully observes that ancient funeral rites are in view, and in that sense, that honor or dishonor is present in the context.[58]

However, it is an overstatement to conclude from this alone that a system of honor and shame provides the explanation for every aspect of the passage, as a concern for dignity or disgrace in death seems to be fairly universally acknowledged across cultures (though in various forms), even in those that are usually characterized as "individualistic," or even "materialistic."[59] The more obvious contrast that is drawn in the passage is that between the former power of each nation, expressed particularly in terms of their reigns of terror, and the present reality of their fallen and defeated state. In other words, the critical issue in the chapter has more to do with *power* and *powerlessness* than social status (although this is in the background, as Strong correctly infers from the Exodus parallels, and the repeated recognition formulas in chs. 32 and 37).

The construction in 32:30, מגבורתם בושים (lit., "from their capability being disappointed/failing"), then, likely reflects this emphasis. As stated previously, while defilement concepts are present, the passage most immediately communicates the failure of the warriors' seeming strength to be able to keep them from being defeated and slain, and hence "failure" seems to capture the sense of בוש best. This also fits well with the wider context of Ezek 29–32, in which Egypt has already been characterized as "a staff of reed" to Israel (Ezek 29:7). This is an obvious reference to Israel's appeal to Egypt (despite YHWH's warnings) for aid against Babylon, an appeal that was of no avail to them. בוש thus indicates that the princes of the north and the Sidonians had failed Israel, just as would be the case with Egypt. In this case, the translation "failure" fits the construction and the context far better than "shame."

Ezekiel 36:32

Ezekiel 36 (along with Ezek 37) is considered the key restoration oracle in the book.[60] It is also an important chapter in the context of this study,

---

58. S.v. בוש, *TDOT*.

59. In my native Australia, for example, the concern over the recovery and proper burial of the bodies of Anzac soldiers, especially who lie in unmarked graves, is a given, despite it being a Western, "individualistic" culture. The obvious corollary of this is that honor is universal across cultures but also it need not always be the primary social value.

60. As Block states, "[the literary unit] is unmatched for its theological intensity and spiritual depth"; Daniel I. Block, *The Book of Ezekiel: Chapters 25–48* (NICOT; Grand Rapids: Eerdmans, 1998), 365.

for the reason that its details both *support* and *undermine* the honor/shame model. In this section, I will explore the manner in which it does so, and the reasons for this phenomenon.[61]

Ezek 36:16–23 is especially significant in the context of this study. In this passage, the history of Israel is once again recounted in terms of defilement and its counterpart, holiness. Israel's pattern of life is described in terms of the now loaded term "their way" (דרכם) and "their wantonness" (עלילותם), which is then likened to the defilement of menstrual blood (cf. Lev 15:19). The reason for this particular example of defilement is given in v. 18: "because they had shed blood in the land." Block suggests that the imagery is both appropriate, as well as incongruous, with the reality it refers to—the characterization of Jerusalem as a woman in chs. 16 and 23 and the (grammatically) feminine gender of אדמה suggest a fairly normal association with menstrual defilement. On the other hand, it is also (perhaps intentionally) a significantly *unnatural* association, as the land is not considered culpable for its defilement due to the voluntary bloodshed of the people, just as a menstruating woman is not morally guilty by virtue of her menstruation.[62]

In the background of the passage is also the theme of the land's sabbath in Lev 26:23–46. There, the covenant curse of expulsion and dispersal is to give the land its "sabbath years," in lieu of the rest denied to it by Israel in its sin.[63] Block notes that Ezekiel links the the two themes here: the menstruous woman's seven-day period of uncleanness, before being considered clean and fit to return to YHWH's house (Lev 15:19–30), is applied to the calculation of the land's "uncleanness," on the basis of unobserved Sabbaths while the people lived there.[64]

The passage is also significant in demonstrating that, in the context of YHWH's covenant with Israel/Judah, the (nonmoral) cultic-symbolic/defilement simile of menstruation and the moral/juridical reality of voluntary bloodshed are inherently capable of a "category transfer." This in turn confirms the theoretical problem in polarizing guilt and shame, characteristic of both psychological approaches and SSAs (as discussed in ch. 3). I will expand further on this issue ch. 5, as I survey recent research into cultic categories. In the rest of this section, however, I will consider the phenomenon of shame after restoration, and the manner in which Ezek 36 both exhibits aspects of the SSA model, but also undermines both SSA and psychological definitions of shame.

Shame, according to the SSA model, has to do with loss of status or position (honor) within the social context under consideration, and this accords

---

61. Ezekiel 36 is also important for the attention it gives to the themes of holiness and defilement, as well as their relationships to כבד and בוש. It is difficult to discuss these concepts without reference to the work of Mary Douglas. I discuss this further below.

62. Block, *Ezekiel 25–48*, 346.

63. For more on the importance of the Sabbath, see Andrew G. Shead, "An Old Testament Theology of the Sabbath Year and Jubilee," *RTR* 61 (2002): 19–33.

64. Block, *Ezekiel 25–48*, 347.

with the thrust of Ezek 36. One of the sustained themes in Ezekiel, which comes to the fore in the present chapter, is the perception of Judah among the nations (Ezek 36:3, 4, 6, 15, 30). The emphasis is especially strong in the earlier parts of the chapter. In Ezek 36:1–15, Judah's restoration to the land is motivated, at least in part, by her being "the scorn of the nations" (כלמת גוים, Ezek 36:6), while in Ezek 36:16–23 Israel's conduct is repeatedly described in terms of its effect on Yhwh's reputation: "my great name, which has been profaned (חלל) among the nations, which you defiled in their midst" (Ezek 36:23; cf. 20–22, 37).

Tucker, in his careful and sensitive SSA study of the psalms, finds a similar phenomenon at work there. He suggests that the psalmist's cries to Yhwh for vindication against his enemies presupposes and is predicated on the honor/shame model. In an agonistic culture, where the notion of limited good is so pervasive, the ascription of shame that forms the subject of the psalm must be redressed. The psalmist's appeal to this end is then articulated within the relational triangle of patron (Yhwh), client (the psalmist), and the antagonist (the enemy). The scorn poured on the client thus ultimately constitutes a challenge to the honor of the patron which, if left unanswered, would impugn his honor.[65]

Tucker goes on to explore how the dynamics of the SSA patron-client relationship provides substantial explanatory power in the relationship between Yhwh and the psalmist.[66] He first states the patron-client relationship as his basic model: the patron has the resources that the client gains access to through relationships of reciprocity. However, should the patron fail to produce the necessary resources for the client, both the patron (in the first instance), and the client (via association) suffer loss of honor and accumulation of shame.[67]

According to Tucker, this sort of model has significant implications for understanding the communal laments. He suggests that the psalmist's cries recount the divine patron's failure to act in a manner reflective of the reciprocity involved in the relationship. As such, both the client (the community) and, even more, the patron, become subject to shame. The psalms, then, are an attempt to restore honor to the client (the community) by first recognizing that the patron has failed them, and then calling on the patron to act according to his reciprocal responsibility to earn honor back. Once the patron's honor has been restored, it can then be extended to the client once more.[68]

---

65. W. Dennis Tucker, Jr., "Is Shame a Matter of Patronage in the Communal Laments?" *JSOT* 31 (2007): 468.

66. Tucker helpfully raises two caveats to using the patronage model: first, understanding that it is an etic construct; second, that attention needs to be given to particularization in the given social context; ibid., 473–74.

67. Ibid., 474.

68. Ibid., 475 (referring to Ps 74).

The parallels with Ezek 36 are clear, and the SSA model is at this point very helpful in dealing with the particulars of the passage. Tucker's application of the patronage model helpfully elucidates the interconnectedness of the reputations of YHWH and his people (cf. Ezek 36:20) and frames the insistence in Ezekiel on YHWH's vindication of his name. It also reflects the occasions where Judah's complaints of her treatment by YHWH are noted in Ezekiel (for example, Ezek 18:2, 25).

On the other hand, Tucker's call for particularization in the application of the model is also welcome and necessary, for Ezekiel's perspective presents a reversal of roles of the dynamics operating in the Psalms. In Ezekiel's prophetic utterances, YHWH is not called on to enact his part of the reciprocity bargain, but Judah.[69] In Ezek 36, the growing motif of "radical theocentricity" reaches its peak: the failure is completely and utterly Judah's, and her failure has brought YHWH's name into disrepute.

At this point, however, the model inverts to its original orientation. For rather than the client-community (that is, Judah) making reparation for the patron's damaged honor, YHWH takes the entire burden of responsibility on himself. Indeed, it must be so, for he is the only one with the resources available to effect such a reversal of fortunes.

As the above analysis demonstrates, SSA models at this point prove extremely helpful in giving an understanding of the passage that redressing the excesses of vitriolic assessments of YHWH's motivations in Ezekiel. In addition, the model provides a framework within which we may discern in Ezekiel the theme of grace, even if the explicit term is absent from the book. As Joyce notes, both YHWH's judgment and deliverance depend on the continuity of his providential activity. As such, "though the word *Hēn*, 'grace' is not used, the concept is central."[70] Ezekiel 36, then, provides an example where the SSA models are of great value in illumining the ancient text.

On the other hand, paradoxically, the chapter also undermines the dynamics of the SSA model in the appearance of בוש (Ezek 36:32), for under its terms restoration should remove shame, rather than result in it. As Lapsley comments, "[The SSA] definition of shame does not apply well to Ezekiel's presentation of shame."[71] It should also be noted that neither do psychological definitions, which tend to view shame as inherently pathological.[72]

Various attempts to resolve this problem of shame after restoration have been attempted. Odell, for example, notes three: ignoring the issue,

---

69. Ibid.

70. Joyce, *Ezekiel*, 27.

71. Jacqueline E. Lapsley, "Shame and Self-Knowledge: the Positive Role of Shame in Ezekiel's View of the Moral Self," in *The Book of Ezekiel: Theological and Anthropological Perspectives*, 148; see also Eric Ortlund, "Shame in Restoration in Ezekiel," *SEEJ* 2 (2011), n.p. [cited January 10, 2012]. Online: http://www.see-j.net/index.php/SEE-J/article/view/121/108.

72. So Schwartz.

rejecting it as inferior theology, or explaining it in terms of the paradox of divine grace and human unworthiness.[73] Odell herself adopts the SSA model in viewing Judah being shamed in their relationship to YHWH and thus having no further warrant for complaint against him.[74]

Lapsley also uses SSA models in her suggestion, but seeks to nuance the models by making distinctions (outlined in ch. 3 of this study) between both "public" vs. "private" shame, as well as "shame as dishonor/disgrace" vs. "shame as honor/discretion." The shame of ch. 36, she argues, is tied to a renewed self-perception of their failures before YHWH, resulting in a painful, yet cathartic new moral self, that is now able to feel appropriate shame (i.e. shame-discretion), and thus leads to a restored relationship with YHWH.[75]

Ortlund regards Lapsley's suggestions positively, but notes two weaknesses in them. First, there is a lack of clarity that such shame is not directed towards a personal deficiency in the audience. Second, Lapsley has misconstrued the important order of events. For Ezekiel, shame does not lead to restored relationship. Rather, it occurs only *after* restoration.[76]

Ortlund's own suggested resolution comes in the radical theocentricity of YHWH's desire to be known as both Judge and Deliverer. For Ortlund, shame in restoration must be understood as inextricably linked to the recognition of YHWH. In other words, YHWH cannot be known apart from a perpetual remembrance of standing both condemned under his just judgment, and saved by his grace alone. Such a view of shame, for Ortlund, is "deliberately recalcitrant" and is "impossible to fit into any systematic pattern of thought, being rather intentionally designed to confound all systems."[77]

Ortlund is to be commended for seeking a solution that accords with the absolute centrality of YHWH expressed in Ezekiel's oracles. Moreover, Ortlund helpfully links the nature of shame to the specific content of YHWH's character in the restoration oracles, and demonstrates how this renders both anthropological and psychological views of shame problematic in accounting for the phenomenon in Ezekiel.

Unfortunately, Ortlund remains unable to escape the definitions (and therefore conceptual associations) of shame he wishes to critique, which leads to a curious attempt to justify how Judah's shame continues perpetually. Ortlund suggests that, while painful, such shame gives a measure of emotional relief, as it "colored" the exiles' knowledge of YHWH in an appropriate way, while not dominating it. As such: "To have been unable to respond with shame to the reality of their unmerited restoration may, in fact, have been even more painful for the exiles."[78]

---

73. Odell, "Inversion of Shame," 102.

74. Ibid., 105–6.

75. Lapsley, "Shame and Self-Knowledge," 148.

76. Ortlund, "Shame in Restoration," 11.

77. Ibid., 17.

78. Ibid., 15.

Fig. 5. Block's "spectrum of shame."

Ortlund concludes his argument by drawing on Bonhoeffer's dialectic analysis of Ezek 16 and 36: "Shame can only be overcome by enduring an act of ultimate shaming, namely, inevitable exposure before God . . . by being put to shame through the forgiveness of sin."[79] However, it is difficult to see how Ortlund's own proposal differs greatly from Lapsley's, and thus his critique could be applied to his own position. In chief, this is because Ortlund, like Lapsely, continues to understand בוש as "shame," with all its conceptual baggage. As the analysis of Ezek 16 and 36 demonstrate, taking בוש to mean the broader concept of "disappointment" provides a simpler and more satisfying explanation that appropriates Ortlund's observations, and incorporates the validity of shame concepts, but without being so susceptible to the difficulties of shame in restoration in both psychological and anthropological formulations.

Other "Shame" Terminology in Ezekiel: קוט, כלם, חרף

I will examine three other shame-related roots that appear in Ezekiel (קוט,כלם,חרף). חרף appears seven times, all in the nominal form הרפה (Ezek 5:14, 15; 16:57; 21:33; 22:4; 36:15, 30). In Ezekiel, the word uniformly means "derision" and refers to to the reponse of the nations to Judah's fall. It appears in absolute form three times as a predicate, describing Judah herself; for example, "I will make you a ruin and derision (ולחרפה) among the nations" (Ezek 5:14; cf. 5:15; 22:4), and three times in construct, describing the taunts; for example, "the derision of the peoples (וחרפת עמים) you will no longer bear" (Ezek 36:15; cf. 16:57; 21:33; 36:30).

The use of חרף in Ezekiel has some points of contact with SSA definitions of shame as a loss of status in the eyes of the observing other (in this case, the surrounding nations). As Simkins suggests in his reading of Joel, for example, "The people of Judah were shamed before the nations [by the devastation of the locust plague]."[80] The broader issues with the honor/shame model notwithstanding, "the derision of the nations" *is* significant in Ezekiel, both its presence as an aspect of Judah's punishment, and its removal as an aspect of her restoration.[81]

---

79. Ibid., 17; Dietrich Bonhoeffer, *Ethics* (ed. C. J. Green; trans. R. Krauss et al.; vol. 6; Minneapolis: Fortress, 2005), 303.

80. Cf. Simkins, "Return to Yahweh," 51.

81. See, e.g., Chance, "The Anthropology of Honor and Shame," 144–45; Stiebert, *Construction of Shame*, 78–79.

כלם appears 19 times in Ezekiel, 6 times in its verbal/participial form (all *niphal* stem), and 13 times in its nominal form כלמה. The usage shows a broader semantic sweep than that of חרף. The sole example of the Niphal participle (Ezek 16:27) is used of the Philistine's revulsion toward Israel's lewd behavior (הנכלמות מדרכך זמה).[82] In some instances, כלמה could be used interchangeably with הרפה, "derision" (usually with regard to the nations), particularly when it appears in construct with נשא (Ezek 34:29; 36:6, 7, 15).

On the other hand, other appearances of the construction כלמה + נשא, as well as the instances of finite verbal forms, do not have the nations in view. In these instances, כלם conveys a sense of self-realization of disgrace or humiliation, on account of or with the realization of sinful/defiling conduct under the terms of the covenant (for כלמה + נשא, Ezek 16:52 (2×), 54, 61, 63 (in the construction מפני כלמתך, "in view of your disgrace"); 44:13; for כלם, Ezek 16:54, 61; 36:32, 43:10, 11).

The three examples of כלמה + נשא in Ezek 32—the "lament" (נהה) for Egypt—could also have the sense of "bear derision," but this is disputable. In each case, the warriors of Elam and Sidon are described first in terms of their power while living and the terror they caused their victims, before their ultimate fate of "going down to the pit"; a sentence that includes וישאו כלמתם. A case could be made for each of the meanings "derision" or "(SSA) shame," as the effect of the Elamites and Sidonians on their victims is clearly on view. However, it is also possible that כלמה has the broader sense of "failure," a possibility that is strengthened by the similar sense of בוש as "disappointment" in the same chapter (as analyzed above). If this is the case, then the contrast in view is not so much the perception of these warriors by the other nations (from fear/awe to derision/shame), as the change in their capability to impose their will on others (from power to powerlessness)—their great strength has come to an end, and in their defeat "they bear their failure."

One final instance of כלמה warrants brief discussion. Ezek 39:26 comes at the climax of the Gog prophecy, in a section recounting Jerusalem's exile and restoration. Several translations render the verse as "They will forget their shame" (NIV; cf. ESV, NASB, YLT). This reading takes the construction in the verse כלמה + נשא as adopting the syntax of עון + נשא, which can mean both "to bear (reponsibility/punishment for) sin" and "to forgive sin."

I will discuss the syntax of נשא + עון in the next chapter; here all I will note is that the reading "They will forget their shame" depends on the legitimacy of taking the construction in this way. The difficulty with the position is that the construction כלמה + נשא appears only in Ezekiel, and in every other instance (11 times) it clearly means "bear derision."[83] The main impetus for

---

82. Zimmerli suggests that זמה, which *BHS* sees as an addition, "appears in the sense of a permuative qualification of דרכך, expressing the evil of a way of conduct of which even the 'heathen' Philistine women would be ashamed" (Zimmerli, *Ezekiel 1–24*, 345).

83. The only occurrence outside Ezekiel that has a similar construction is Ps 69:8, which has the meaning "bear (derision)": כי־עליך נשאתי חרפה כסתה כלמה פני.

taking נשא to mean "to forget" in Ezek 39:26 seems to be its context after restoration. However, as shame after restoration is a consistent feature of Ezekiel's prophecies (most prominently, Ezek 16 and 36, where נשא + כלמה means "to bear disgrace"), there is little reason why the translation "to forget" should be favored.

The word כלם thus demonstrates a similar range of meaning to בוש in Ezekiel. However, its semantic associations (in contexts of sinful conduct, and in construction with נשא) situate its "center of gravity" in Ezekiel more toward an emotional response of disgrace or humiliation. These spring particularly from a new awareness of moral/relational failure. In the terms of this study, then, the usage of כלם in Ezekiel tends toward "psychological" shame concepts, although SSA shame concepts are at least present in several instances. [84]

The word קוט appears three times in Ezekiel (Ezek 6:9; 20:43; 36:31), and in each case it is associated with "remembering" (זכר) and the people's conduct before YHWH (זנה, רעה, תועבה, Ezek 6:9; דרך, עלילה, טמא, רעה, Ezek 20:43; תועבה, עון , לא-טובים,מעלל,רע, דרך, Ezek 36:31). The list is emotionally overwhelming, to say the least. Accordingly, קוט conveys a sense of (self) loathing and worthlessness before YHWH, on account of past evils committed. [85]

Drawing the threads of discussion together, Block suggests that Ezekiel's shame terms constitute a continuum from חרף, as "external" shame, due to loss of status in the eyes of an observing world, to קוט, as "internal" shame, due to someone's self-perception of their conduct and status (fig. 5). [86]

While the representation may require some modification to reflect that both בוש and כלם can occupy the entire spectrum, it is a helpful visualization of the interrelatedness of the terms, especially with regard to the semantic "center of gravity" of each of the outliers (חרף and קוט).

In summary, other shame-related language in Ezekiel covers a similar semantic range to בוש, with a particular concentration around the perception of failure in the people's conduct before YHWH (although the perception of both Jerusalem and YHWH among the nations is also present). Several concepts associated with both psychological/emotional and anthropological/social shame are thus present. However, there are also instances that may not sit comfortable under either umbrella, carrying a broader sense of failure, confirming the basic sense of the concept, "disappointment."

Constructing an Emic View of בוש *in Ezekiel*

The Range of Meaning of בוש *in Ezekiel*

From the analysis above, בוש in Ezekiel spans several aspects of the overall semantic study. With respect to Jerusalem, this includes mourning and

---

84. Bearing in mind, of course, the conditions and caveats on these categories that have been established in this study.

85. Block, *Ezekiel 1–24*, 232.

86. Idem, "The God Ezekiel Wants Us to Meet," 183–84.

loss of a funeral rite in response to Jerusalem's destruction (Ezek 7:18). It also involves a "bringing down" of Jerusalem's previously deluded and over-inflated self-perception before YHWH, such that they are able to truly perceive his holiness, their utter failure to keep covenant, and hence acknowledge that their restoration is not due to any merit on their part, but completely dependent on YHWH's character, initiative, and actualization (Ezek 16:52, 63; 36:32).

The word בוש is also used with respect to the failure of Egypt's strength to save from her defeat, death and defilement. The context includes a further indictment on Jerusalem for not looking to YHWH for deliverance from Babylon, but to Egypt, a "disappointing" object of trust (Ezek 32:30).

Wider Reflections: Shame and Defilement

Given Ezekiel's priestly concerns, it is no surprise that the cultic terminology of "holiness" (קדש, 83×), "profanation" (חלל, 71×), "clean" (טהר, 17×) and "defiled" (טמא, 44×) are dominant in the book. Biblical research into these categories has been indebted to the work of Mary Douglas, particularly her early work on Leviticus, *Purity and Danger*. Douglas's basic thesis was that all societies seek to structure and take control of their worlds via a system of order and classification. In this system, "dirt" or "impurity" is "matter out of place," while the system as a whole serves to define what is fitting and, consequently, what is not fitting within a society.[87]

In Douglas's view, holiness pertained to "wholeness," both physical and ethical. Undergirding this view was her suggestion that YHWH's holiness was found in his power to bless or curse, thus creating and confirming the order of the universe through which humanity could prosper.[88] The Torah, accordingly, emphasized physical and ritual "perfection," with humanity prospering by conforming to holiness, via the commandments.[89]

There are clear parallels between the categories of shame and defilement under such a classification, and Douglas's work has been appropriated enthusiastically by SSA research to explain and augment views of shame to do with, for example, gender.[90] While Douglas's work has met with significant

---

87. Douglas, *Purity and Danger*, 35; cf. idem, *Natural Symbols: Explorations in Cosmology* (London: Barrie & Rockliff, 1970). Douglas has since modified her proposal to a more "positive" view of how the Levitical system urged the Israelites to pursue "a chance to live by the principles that undergird the cosmos . . . [and] uphold the action of the Creator by their own enactment of the law"; idem, *Jacob's Tears: The Priestly Work of Reconciliation* (Oxford: Oxford University Press, 2004), 169. However, it is her early work that remains the most influential in biblical studies, and so I will focus on this.

88. Idem, *Purity and Danger*, 50.

89. Ibid., 67.

90. As in the example of Ezek 16, analyzed above. Malina devotes an entire chapter to expounding Douglas's purity system and connecting it to the culture of patronage that he sees as evident in the Bible. See further Malina, *New Testament World*, 149–83; for application of Douglas's purity system to shame and sexuality, see Kamionkowski, *Gender Reversal and Cosmic Chaos*.

criticism, it has been a valuable contribution to biblical studies and remains a helpful tool for understanding key concepts in the Bible. [91]

In the context of this study, Douglas's thesis that "dirt" is matter out of place in the symbolic social system gives further insight into the use of בוש. This is so, for example, in the case of Ezek 36, where Israel's conduct "profanes" Yʜwʜ's holy name. [92] To use Douglas's terms, for Ezekiel, Yʜwʜ's name (tied to his holy character), was put "out of place" by the people's conduct. Bound to him by the Mosaic covenant (with Judah's priestly character enmeshed in its terms; cf. Exod 19:3–6), the Jerusalemites failed to reflect an appropriate response to his character before the nations; their pattern of life did not accord with his חסד ואמת to them (cf. Ezek 16).

A similar vein of thought is found in the explanation of the siege sign-act in Ezek 5:5–17. Jerusalem was placed at the center of the nations as a beacon, pointing to Yʜwʜ and his ways. [93] As per the terms of the Mosaic covenant (cf. Deut 4:5–11), their conduct was intended to display Yʜwʜ's great and honorable character to the surrounding nations. However, their conduct so rebelled against his standards (משפטי) that Yʜwʜ's image among the nations was distorted and clouded by the extent of their wickedness (ותמר ... לרשעה מן־הגים, Ezek 5:6). In Douglas's framework, the effect of Jerusalem's actions could be put as "out of place" with Yʜwʜ's כבד, thus putting the nations's perception of him "out of place" with its reality. It is in this sense that Yʜwʜ declares, "You have profaned my holy name" (Ezek 36:21–23). [94]

In this respect, the motivation for Yʜwʜ's actions—"for the sake of my holy name" (Ezek 36:20)—also becomes clearer. *Pace* Schwartz, to see Yʜwʜ's concern for his name *solely* as a cold, ruthless obsession for his own aggrandizment is rather one-sided. Douglas is correct, to some extent, to suggest that the end goal of Yʜwʜ's holiness is to bring blessing, but in Ezekiel this needs supplementing with an appreciation for the integral relationship between Yʜwʜ's holiness and his כבד. [95] As the analysis in the previous chapter demonstrates, "blessing" (especially in the Priestly

---

91. See, e.g., Trevaskis, *Holiness*; Jonathan Klawans, *Impurity and Sin in Ancient Judaism* (New York: Oxford University Press, 2000).

92. Ironically, Ezek 36 also demonstrates the shortcomings of Douglas's model, as "holiness" in the passage cannot be taken to mean "power to bless and curse."

93. Zimmerli (*Ezekiel 1–24*, 174) suggests that the language stresses Jerusalem's exaltation as the "center" of the world nations. Greenberg, on the other hand, prefers the sense "amidst the nations" and rejects the possibility that later Jewish cosmogeny, with Jerusalem as the "navel of the earth," is meant. Instead, "the intent of the sentence is: set amidst the gentiles, Jerusalem learned from them, but surpassed them in corruption" (Greenberg, *Ezekiel 1–20*, 110). Allen argues, however, argues that the use of סביב in conjunction with בתוך emphasizes Judah's priestly role toward the nations, as custodians of Torah (Allen, *Ezekiel 1–19*, 72–73).

94. Cf. Kalinda Rose Stevenson, *The Vision of Transformation: The Territorial Rhetoric of Ezekiel 40–48* (Atlanta: Scholars Press, 1996), 11–47.

95. Douglas, *Purity and Danger*, 66.

conception) comes in the uninhibited expression of Yhwh's כבד throughout the entire creation.[96] The holiness, or hallowing, of Yhwh's name—
that is, the proper recognition and acknowledgement of his כבד—is an essential precondition of the world obtaining this blessing.

Thus, in Ezekiel's thought world, Yhwh's acting for his name's sake
alone may not be simply due to his spite or malice, but rather out of the
necessity that has arisen due to Jerusalem's failure. Granted, Yhwh does
not act "on their account" (למענכם, Ezek 36:22), but perhaps this is because
to do so would result in their utter destruction. Indeed, this seems to be the
rationale behind the restoration envisioned in Ezek 20:44: "You will know
that I am Yhwh, when I deal with you for my name's sake (למען שמי), not
according to your evil ways (לא כדרכיכם הרעים), nor according to your cor-
rupt doings (וכעלילותיכם הנשחתות)." He acts, rather, because what is unholy
cannot make itself holy again, it must be made so by what is still holy (cf.
Ezek 36:23).[97]

In this regard, the command for Jerusalem, בושי, communicates a call,
not so much for her to "feel shamed" (in the first instance), but for her to
recognize the depth of her failure to properly respond to Yhwh's holiness,
her utter unworthiness of his deliverance and thus the appropriateness of
his taking sole action on her behalf. Emotions associated with failure and
betrayal of relationship are, of course, appropriate. They are also often in-
tensely strong, as is evidenced by the tone of the passage and the buildup of
terms sharing the semantic sphere of בוש. It is important, however, to keep
in mind the order of concepts (that is, awareness of reality to appropriate
emotional response).

Douglas's work raises one further area of importance for this study, which
I will explore in full in the next chapter. As Douglas herself recognized, her
work on the cultural universality of purity and pollution systems meant that
older dichotomies needed to be dissolved. Especially relevant at this point
is the dichotomy between cultic or mystical categories as representative of
primitive conceptions of God, and ethical or rational categories as representative of a more advanced view. This in turn parallels the dichotomy between Priestly and deuteronomic categories on which some insist.[98]

In this regard, Ezekiel has always been an anomaly that has needed explanation, for a prophet who is so Priestly does not fit well in this sort of
schema. However, Douglas argues that the notion of "pollution," or "dirt,"

---

96. Cf. Gordon J. Wenham, "Sanctuary Symbolism in the Garden of Eden Story," in "*I
Studied Inscriptions before the Flood": Ancient Near Eastern, Literary, and Linguistic Approaches
to Genesis 1–11* (ed. R. S. Hess and D. T. Tsumura; SBTS 4; Winona Lake, IN: Eisenbrauns,
1994), 399–404.

97. Cf. Greenberg's comment on the similar 20:41: "By his marvellous restoration of
them in the future his holy majesty will be affirmed before all men" (Greenberg, *Ezekiel
1–20*, 376).

98. See, e.g., the discussion in Levitt Kohn, *A New Heart and a New Soul*, 6–29.

as matter out of place, set right through patterns of order, is universal across all cultures. Furthermore, it applies across sacred and secular categories with no clear-cut distinction, and thus the same principles operate in both primitive and modern cultures. According to Douglas, the difference is simply that primitive culture conceives of life as a unified whole, while modern culture views things in disjointed, separate areas of existence.[99]

With our postmodern sensibilities, we may choose to take exception to some of Douglas's phraseology.[100] Her point, however, remains true. This, then raises the question whether Priestly and Prophetic categories are as discrete as they have sometimes been taken to be. As I will demonstrate in the next chapter, in the case of עון—one of the main biblical words for "sin"—the distinction becomes impossible to maintain; for עון denotes a "twisting," or distortion of the covenant stipulations. In other words, עון is not simply a breach or violation of moral imperatives. It is ultimately what is "out of place" in the covenant with YHWH. In the terms of this study, this again indicates that shame concepts cannot be separated as cleanly from from guilt concepts as SSA models and their accompanying dichotomous tables sometimes suggest.[101] Furthermore, it demonstrates that both guilt and shame concepts cannot be separated from honor concepts. As I have also attempted to make clear, critical to an accurate understanding of each term, however, will be a proper exploration of their relationship.

Imposed Etic and Emic B Part 2:
Agreement and Disagreement

Areas of Agreement
Human and Divine Relationships in the ANE

Contemporary SSAs, such as the Context Group's honor/shame model, have helpfully drawn attention to the importance and and shape of patterns of relationships in the ancient world, including that of the Bible. In so doing, they have built on previous work, particularly research into ancient suzerain-vassal treaties as parallels to the biblical ברית, and extended this by appropriating the newer model of patron-client relationships. As with most aspects of the research, this development has both strengths and weaknesses. Here I focus on the strengths, before highlighting the weaknesses below.

I have already drawn on the work of Tucker in relation to בוש in Ezek 36. Here I will reflect further on the benefits of his SSA. Building on the insights of Hobbs, as well as Eisenstadt and Roniger, Tucker suggests that

---

99. Douglas, *Purity and Danger*, 50.

100. By this I mean particularly the terminology and associated categories of "primitive" and "modern."

101. E.g., Malina, *New Testament World*, 82–87 (table 2).

the patronage model is a step forward from the suzerain-vassal treaty in describing covenant relationships in the OT, especially that between Yнwн and his people. For Hobbs, it better reflects the intimacy, trust, and spiritual involvement of the parties involved, over and above a simply institutionalized, contractual view. Furthermore, it is a model that more naturally lends itself considerations and conflicts of power and interest.[102] Tucker also notes that sensitive application, which includes particularization, leads to the recognition that, in practice, "goods and services are exchanged according to the traits of the social actors involved rather than on the basis of what they would be entitled to as members of social categories."[103]

On the other hand, Tucker also notes, helpfully, that patronage and covenantal treaty model are not inherently mutually exclusive but may significantly intersect and overlap.[104] The "openness" of Tucker's model to particularization makes his work an example of positive application of an SSA model to the OT that is highly fruitful in understanding the relational dynamics of the biblical text.

In terms of Ezekiel, a patronage model such as that applied by Tucker, helpfully articulates five interrelated aspects of the relationship between Yнwн and his people. First, the exchange of goods and services is based on the traits of the actors, rather than established social entitlements. Second, the relationship involves exchanges of a wide variety of resources, under the unifying banner of loyalty (or faithfulness). Third, there is a strong element of unconditionality, voluntarism, and "relational credit," built into the model. Fourth, there is a strong notion of solidarity inherent in the relationship. This often extends to conceptions of personal identity, including a drive to maintain both personal honor and the honor of the other party in the relationship. Fifth, the relationship is based on a strong sense of social inequality and difference in power. [105]

This sort of model has several points of clear resonance with the biblical text, and great explanatory power, for example, in enabling the interpreter to reconcile the relational dynamics of the Yнwн in Ezek 16 and 36, for example, with the Yнwн of the rest of the canon. As a tool for investigating heretofore underappreciated biblical themes, Tucker's application of the patronage model serves as a good example of how SSAs may benefit biblical scholars and theologians.

---

102. Tucker, "Patronage," 472; T. Raymond Hobbs, "Reflections on Honor, Shame, and Covenant Relations," *JBL* 116 (1997): 501–3; S. N. Eisenstadt and L. Roniger, *Patrons, Clients and Friends: Interpersonal Relations and the Structure of Trust in Society* (Cambridge: Cambridge University Press, 1984).

103. Tucker, "Patronage," 472; citing L. Roniger, *Hierarchy and Trust in Modern Mexico and Brazil* (New York: Praeger, 1990), 3.

104. Tucker, "Patronage," 473.

105. Detailed on pp. 473–74. My reproduction is slightly summarized.

בוש as Reflective of Pivotal Values

The use of בוש in Ezekiel confirms that its conceptual sphere is of great significance in the social script, or story, from which the biblical documents are built. While not identical to shame (whether defined psychologically or by SSAs), or an inherent pivotal value (as formulated in the honor/shame model), it nonetheless plays a critical part in the Bible's storyline.

As such, בוש *could* be seen as a pivotal value of sorts, inasmuch as it reflects the fundamental importance of right relationship to YHWH in the OT. Attention to particularization allows us to observe that the main communicative force of בוש in Ezekiel is to express the gap between the expectations of Judah as YHWH's holy people, and the reality of their sinful state. בוש thus expresses that the system of blessing and harmonious relationships established by YHWH (in accordance with his כבד) has been fundamentally disrupted by humanity's (and especially Judah's) failure to respond appropriately to him.

Avrahami has also noted that the relationship between בוש and honor (כבד) is indirect, owing to its wider semantic field of worthlessness/lightness, rather than a binary pair (honor/shame) as in SSA formulations.[106] As I will explore in the next chapter, this is a critical observation, because the indirect relationship of כבד and בוש in the Bible provides one key to understanding the connections between the concepts of honor, shame, and guilt.

Areas of Disagreement:
Patronage, Covenant, and Shame

While the patron-client relationship, as articulated by Tucker, is a helpful tool, we must also note its limits and dangers. Application has not always been done with sufficient sensitivity to particularization. In this regard, I have already outlined some less-sophisticated applications of patronage models.[107]

Application of the patronage model to Ezekiel must be further disciplined and conditioned (that is, particularized) by consideration of the other relational metaphors that are significantly employed in the book. For example, the most appropriate relational phenomenon in developing a model with which to understand Ezek 16 is not the divine patron but the divine husband. Although bearing affinities to the patron-client relationship, biblical marriage is not the same thing, and therefore great care must be taken to ensure that these models do not distort perceptions of the data.

Furthermore, even in Tucker's case, the persistence of problematic definitions and models basic to the Context Group still remain. This is most obviously the case in Tucker's retention of the standard "social script" generated by SSAs: the binary model of honor/shame, agonistic culture, and

---

106. Avrahami, "בוש in the Psalms," 302.
107. Especially Crook, *Reconceptualising Conversion*; idem, "Honor Revisited."

limited good, as well the equation of בוש and so on with shame.[108] As a result, his reading of the psalms still seems ill-fitting at points.

For example, his analysis of Ps 74:1–2, which for Tucker represents the patron-client relationship, undermines the model he attempts to use. In these verses, the appeal for divine help is *not* best explained in terms of an agonistic appeal to a patron-client relationship (though it may bear affinities to it). Rather, as the verse Tucker cites states (Ps 74:2), the appeal is based on YHWH's *purchase* (קנה) of his people, who became his *possession* (נחלה). A model of redemption/slavery is thus a more appropriate parallel than patronage.[109]

Finally, in conjunction with this, though Hobbs and Tucker argue that patronage is closer to ancient patterns of relationship in the Bible, there are SSA voices arguing in the other direction. Perhaps surprisingly, Crook has argued against Hobbs that covenant concepts more accurately reflect the social dynamics of YHWH's relationship with Israel than patronage concepts. As such, those who adopt patronage as their primary model have mistakenly conflated the two.[110] These reservations from "within the camp" of SSAs reinforces the care required to utilize the model. In other words, we must remember that these models are not simply etic but an *initial* etic.

בוש *in Restoration*

That בוש appears *after* Jerusalem's restoration simply does not fit well in either SSA or psychological formulations. With regard to SSAs, Jerusalem's shame should be removed by her restoration. With regard to psychology, the persistence of an inherently negative and damaging emotion indicates that full reconciliation (and restoration of human dignity) has not taken place.

The analysis of בוש in this chapter has explored how the concept of disappointment far more easily allows the term to be appropriate in the context of restoration. YHWH's restoration of Judah—not on their account, but due alone to his grace and holiness—should lead to a renewed, accurate self-perception. בוש thus communicates the (positive) gap between Jerusalem's previous self-righteousness and the reality of their true state before him. For Ezekiel, this humble acknowledgment of their utter need for him lays the necessary foundation for proper recognition of and relationship to YHWH. בוש is needed for sinful people to "know that I am YHWH."

Conclusion

The analysis conducted in this chapter has demonstrated that בוש and its synonyms may certainly communicate shame concepts that have been traditionally associated with both psychological and SSAs. However, like כבד

---

108. Tucker, "Patronage," 466–69.

109. Not only so, but the Psalm incorporates the additional concept of YHWH's kingship over his people (v. 12).

110. Crook, "Reciprocity," 78–91.

and honor, בוש covers a broader semantic range than shame, and bearing this in mind enables more accuracy in analyzing specific appearances of the term. In this chapter I have argued that disappointment, as the term's semantic center of gravity, captures these wider associations. It also resolves several issues with definitions of shame in both psychology and SSAs.

Disappointment, or failure, also better captures the indirect association of בוש with honor in the biblical material. This is true of Ezekiel, especially given that its most significant relationship, between Yhwh and his people, is in view. In such contexts, rather than a binary opposition (honor/shame), בוש in Ezekiel denotes their failure to reflect a pattern of covenant relationship with Yhwh appropriate to his holy character (that is, his כבד).

On the other hand, shame concepts are clearly present in Ezekiel. From an SSA perspective, the reputation of Yhwh and Jerusalem before the nations is an important consideration, as he is the creator of the world. It is thus imperative that the reputation of his name be restored from its defiled state, via the elevation of his people's status, in the eyes of the nations. From a psychological perspective, Jerusalem's restoration includes a call to perceive herself as a failure of her ideal self, and to therefore consider herself with a certain self-loathing.

While sharing several shame concepts in common with both SSA and psychological definitions, however, the concept of shame in Ezekiel cannot be satisfyingly accounted for under either model. For Ezekiel, shame, primarily, is directed neither toward loss of status before a human PCR nor toward an abstract ideal self. Rather, shame in Ezekiel is the recognition Judah's failure to conform to Yhwh's ideal relational pattern, expressed in the terms of his covenant with his people. In other words, shame in Ezekiel is not defined by the PCR (as in SSAs), nor the individual (as in psychology), but the *DCR*—the person, character, and values of Yhwh himself.

Following on from this, it can also be seen that, for Ezekiel, shame concepts cannot be sharply distinguished from guilt concepts, for the covenant stipulations form the objective, concrete expression of an appropriate (that is, ideal) relationship between Yhwh and his people. This is all the more so when Tucker's insights, into the breadth and depth of relational commitment involved in ancient patronage structures, are taken into account.

As such, even if we take shame as having primarily to do with being, and guilt as having primarily to do with act, in Ezekiel's conceptual framework the two are aspects of the one whole. In this regard, the people's acts (their breaches and distortions of Yhwh's covenant) are therefore simply symptomatic of their failure to give him the כבד due his name (that is, hallow it) in their relationship with him. To put it in biblical terms, Judah's sinful acts (עון) are symptomatic of the fact that, in Yhwh's eyes, they have failed (בוש) to be people who live in a relationship of appropriate response to his glory (כבד). In other words, they have failed to respond to his חסד ואמת toward them, with חסד ואמת toward him. I will now explore the relationships between these terms further, in analyzing עוה.

Chapter 6

Guilt in Ezekiel: Emic B Part 3

עוה *in the Old Testament*

There are several words used in the OT for concepts associated with the English catch-all term "sin." These include פשע (Gen 31:36), שגה (Lev 4:13), אשם (Lev 6:4), חטא, and עוה. Of these, by far the two most common are חטא (appearing 593 times) and עוה (appearing 232 times). In some instances, the two seem interchangeable, and both were used as a catch-all term for Israel's overall failure to keep the covenant. However, the concentrated use of חטא in legislative and cultic settings to indicate particular transgressions or failures, as well as being the term used uniquely for the "sin/purification offering" (חטאת), suggests that חטא was used as a technical term in a manner that עוה was not.[1] However, given its prevalence in Ezekiel and its association with Priestly conceptions of defilement, I will take עוה as the focal point of the concept sphere associated with "guilt."[2]

Many have noted that the usages of both עוה and חטא in the OT span the spectrum of a misdeed-consequence process (deed-consequence-completion).[3] To this may be added that the completion of the process, most often indicated by the construction נשא + חטאת/עון, can mean either "to bear one's own sin" (for example, Lev 5:1) or "to forgive" (for example, Exod 10:17). In the semantic analysis that follows, I will provide brief discussion on the attempts that have been made to make clear the relationships of the seemingly opposite meanings, expressed by the one word/phrase.

Bend/Twist/Distort

While עוה most commonly appears in explicit contexts of sin and guilt, occasionally the verb indicates the basic physical concept, "to bend/twist/

---

1. As Milgrom has argued, the term should probably be listed lexically as "purification offering" given its range of usage (which includes situations where there no particular "sin" has been committed). On the other hand, as has been raised already in this study (see especially chs. 3 and 5), and will be discussed further in this chapter, "purification" retains a significant conceptual overlap with "sin." As a result, the change in translation may signal a shift in semantic center of gravity, rather than a complete dichotomization of meaning. See further Jacob Milgrom, "Sin-Offering or Purification-Offering," *VT* 21 (1971): 237–39

2. Cf. s.v. בוש, *TDOT*, 566: "Almost one-fifth of all occurrences of . . . [עון] are in the book of Ezekiel."

3. S.v. בוש, *TLOT*.

distort." This can be seen in Ps 38:7, "I am bowed down (נעויתי)." See also Isa 21:3, "At this my body is racked with pain, pangs seize me, like those of a woman in labor; I am doubled over (נעויתי) by what I hear." However, even in these cases, sin and punishment form the backdrop to the passages. עוה in Ps 38:7 corresponds to the earlier nominal form in v. 5: "My guilt (עונתי) has overwhelmed me," while in Isa 21, it is plausible that "the prophet's own shattered condition has resulted from the sin and guilt of those whom he is to denounce."[4] Thus, there seems to a connection between the so-called nontheological instances of the word and the concept of sin, although the exact nature of the association is unclear.

The idea of bending, or distorting, also lends itself to more metaphorical uses, such as in Isa 24:1: "See, Yнwн will lay waste the earth and devastate it; he will ruin (ועוה) its face and scatter its inhabitants." Yнwн's judgment leaves the earth in a twisted and distorted state, barren and uninhabitable in contrast to the life-sustaining purpose for which it was created (Isa 45:18).[5] In Lam 3:9, the writer likens the destruction of Jerusalem to an inescapable prison, in which Yнwн in his wrath "has barred my way with blocks of stone; he has made my paths crooked (עוה)."[6] Connected to this idea, Ben-Mordecai suggests in his provocative article that עון may include the idea of "hazard" (with regard to the danger involved in priestly service, namely, Num 18:22–23), or "trouble" (for example, Ps 59:5, "they run without mishap"), without necessarily involving a crime, moral failure, or punishment.[7]

Extending into the moral realm, עוה in 1 Sam 20:30 has the meaning "perverted," as is made clear by its construction with מרדות in Saul's accusation of Jonathan's perceived betrayal, in protecting David: "Son of the perverted (one) of rebellion (בן־נעוה המרדות)." Another important example is Jer 9:4, which has the specific sense of twisted (that is, deceptive) speech: "They have taught their tongues to speak lies, wearying themselves with deception (העוה)." In 1 Kgs 8:47, Solomon's prayer envisions Israel's confession as חטאנו והעוינו רשענו ("We have sinned and committed iniquity, we have done what is wicked").

As the last examples make apparent, there is a clear conceptual bridge between the concrete sense of עוה as "bending," or "twisting," and its occurrences in covenantal/hamartiological settings for "sin" or "iniquity" (by

---

4. S.v. "עון," *TDOT*.

5. Koch (ibid., 549) considers the meaning "ruined" to be semantically distant from "twisted," and draws on Moran's suggestion of an alternative, undocumented Hebrew root as a possible explanation. However, once it is observed that the earth/land had a particular *telos* of habitation, the suggestion of an alleged alternate root seems rather needless; the distance is not so great after all.

6. Cf. Jer 3:21.

7. C. A. Ben-Mordecai, "The Inquity of the Sanctuary: A Study of the Hebrew Term עָוֹן," *JBL* 60 (1941): 311–14. Admittedly, the Hebrew of Ps 59:5 is difficult: בלי־עון ירוצון ויכוננו, and Ben-Mordecai's interpretation of the verse is debatable.

far the main use in the OT). Furthermore, the association with "weariness" (לאה) in Jer 9:4 also raises another significant aspect of עוה in the OT, that of sin as a burden, or weight. I will explore this connection below, in my analysis of נשא + עון.

Sin/Iniquity/Offense (Against)

The concept "twisting," then, leads naturally to the major use of עוה in the OT, sin and punishment. Basically, עוה has the sense of "offense" or "iniquity," in terms of behavior or motives that have gone awry of appropriate standards (or, perhaps more accurately, appropriate patterns of relationship).[8] Also, as stated in the introduction to this chapter, עוה can be both a collective noun and indicate specific or individual sin(s).

In Gen 15:16, for example, it is used in the collective sense of "the sin of the Amorites," which will eventually result in their destruction. Interestingly, in this case it is explicitly quantified (לא־שלם), perhaps suggestive both of the pervasive use of the metaphor of sin as a weight/burden, as well as the notion of retribution that is often entailed in its use (which would in turn encompass both the idea of sin as a "debt" that needs to be "accounted/paid for," and the use of עון to mean "punishment").[9] This sense of עוה is also common in prophetic literature, where the term is often used as a summary term for Israel's rebellion against Yʜwʜ. In examples such as these, the sense goes beyond mere action to include the attitude of the heart, and as such includes moral, emotional, and relational overtones (for example, Isa 1:4; 43:24; 57:17; Jer 3:21).

In terms of specific sin, עוה is used, for example, in Gen 44:16. When the "theft" of Joseph's cup is discovered, Judah states, "God has found out the sin (עון) of your servants." In Josh 22:17 and 20, עון appears in construct, again referring to specific sins—Israel's prostitution at Peor (22:17) and Achan's theft of the devoted things (22:20). More explicitly, in Isa 30:13 עון is coupled with the pronoun זה, indicating the particular group of sins referred to in the previous verse: "Because you have rejected this message and trusted in extortion and leaned on crookedness, *this* sin will become for you like a high wall, cracked and bulging, that collapses suddenly, in an instant" (emphasis mine).

Excursus: הוע and Covenant

Most OT examples of עוה with the meaning "sin" are found in contexts where Yʜwʜ's covenant with Israel forms the parameters that construct

---

8. S.v. עון, *TLOT*, 863.

9. Gen 15:16 also raises several important, related issues, such as the perspective of the writer on the universality of Yʜwʜ's rule, the notions of justice and theodicy, and so on. I will discuss these issues later in this chapter, but for further discussion specifically on Gen 15:16, see Gerhard von Rad, *Genesis: A Commentary* (London: SCM, 1972), 188; Walter Brueggemann, *Genesis* (Atlanta: John Knox, 1982), 148–49.

and constrain its meaning, a consideration that I will discuss further below. However, the example of Gen 15:16 provides a counterpoint, in that "the sin of the Amorites," as well as their judgment, is assessed outside of an explicit covenant with YHWH.

The passage exemplifies a perspective in which YHWH is considered to have lordship over a nation other than Israel/Judah. It should be noted that the sense here extends beyond YHWH as a warring God, conquering foreign nations.[10] Rather, YHWH is pictured as universal "judge," with nations held accountable to his standard, even in the absence of an explicit, covenantal relationship with them. This sort of perspective finds resonance with Ezekiel, in which the nations surrounding Judah are culpable for their part in, or response to, her downfall (Ezek 25–32).[11]

The emphasis in the OT, however, falls on Israel as YHWH's covenant partner. As noted in ch. 4, the Sinai theophany plays an important role in much of the OT. עוה serves an important function in the declaration of YHWH's character, which in turn forms the basis of the covenant. It thus provides the particular focus of meaning for עוה in the OT. It appears in Exod 20:5 as the rationale for Israel's exclusive loyalty to YHWH: the prohibitions for making or serving any other gods are because "I, YHWH your God, am a jealous God (אל קנא), bringing the iniquity (פקד עון) of the fathers upon the sons." Likewise, I have already made much of the Exod 33–34 theophany and the importance of the character creed in determining the pattern of relationship between YHWH and Israel.

עוה can thus be viewed as extending beyond a strictly legal "breach of covenant terms," to include a strong sense of relational orientation against YHWH, as can be seen, for example, in Lev 26:40: "If they confess את־עונם ואת־עון אבתם—their treachery (מעל) and hostility (אף) toward me. " Likewise, in Ps 51:6, the psalmist declares: "Against you, you alone (לך לבדך) I have sinned, and done what is evil in your sight (בעיניך)."[12] However, the terms of the covenant provide the concrete parameters of right relationship with YHWH (cf. Exod 19:3–6).[13] As such, "guilt," in most biblical contexts

---

10. As seen in several ANE divine warrior texts, for example, *Enuma Elish*, the *Baal Cycle*. For further discussion on the divine warrior motif, see Tremper Longman III and Daniel Reid, *God Is a Warrior* (Grand Rapids: Zondervan, 1995).

11. Cf. von Rad, *Genesis*, 188: "Characteristic [of the paragraph's theology] is first the universal aspect: God rules over world history in the sense of a *providentia generalis*."

12. Cf. s.v. עון, *TLOT*, 865: "[The theological] usage of the term . . . dominates completely in the prophets (Hos, Isa, Deutero-Isa, Trito-Isa, Jer, Ezek), in the Psa. and in P. where either the relationship between person and God *per se* is the chief concern, or is used in cultically-oriented texts . . . in the final analysis, there is no nontheological understanding of an *'āwōn* process when Yahweh's all-encompassing influence on the world is confessed"; Katchadourian, *Guilt*, also argues cogently for the importance of relationship in understanding the concept of guilt.

13. As Childs puts it with regard to Exod 20:2: "[The self-introductory formula] makes absolutely clear that the commands which follow are integrally related to God's

concerning Israel/Judah, refers specifically to culpability for judgment, due
to a rejection of YHWH, expressed as a breach in the appropriate patterns of
relationship established by the covenant.[14] This conclusion leads naturally
to the next category: עוה as responsibility (for sin).

Responsibility/Guilt (for Sin)

The majority of instances of עוה in the OT have the meaning "to bear/
bear responsibility for sin." In these instances, עוה usually appears in construction with נשא, suggesting the appropriateness of the metaphor of sin
as a weight. Most often, there is a straightforward relationship between the
sin committed and the responsibility incurred: the transgressor is said to
נשא עונו (for example, Lev 5:1, 17; 7:18; Num 18:1), to bear the responsibility
for their actions (or failure to act appropriately). Even more explicit is Ps
38:5: "For my iniquity has come over my head, like a burden too heavy for me
(עונתי עברו ראשי כמשא כבד יכבדו ממני)."

There has been much discussion arising out of the use of "sin" language
in the Priestly material in particular, revolving mainly around the closely
related meanings of עוה, חטא, and אשם. Most famously, Milgrom proposed
that where אשם appears in cultic texts without the preposition ל and a personal object, its meaning was "to feel guilt," rather than "to be guilty."[15] Milgrom assumed Koch's misdeed-consequence process, with its tight cause-
and-effect view of sin and punishment, as common to ancient perceptions.[16]
This, accordingly, is the reason why "sin" words can mean both the transgression *and* its consequences. Moreover, there is an interchangeability of
protasis and apodosis in this schema: sin results in feelings of guilt and fear
of punishment, and suffering is interpreted as punishment for sin and thus
creates feelings of guilt.[17]

Milgrom thus defined these instances of אשם as "the consequential
asham," which he took to mean the suffering brought on by guilt—*feeling*
guilty (rather than being in an objective state of guilt).[18] Milgrom used Lev

---

act of self-revelation" (Childs, *Exodus*, 401). Cf. Koch, "Doctrine of Retribution," 68;
commenting on Hosea's presentation of YHWH's judgment: "Whoever acts wickedly is
not just hurting oneself but transgresses the covenant (6:7) and threatens the very existence of the covenant."

14. Cf. Duguid, *Ezekiel*, 68: "The essence of the people's transgression lies in their rebellion, that is, their refusal to recognize God's sovereignty over them"; Renz, *Rhetorical
Function*, 147: "Chapters like 16 and 23 are designed to arouse in the readers an anger over
Israel's disloyalty by portraying it as the disloyalty of a spouse, that is, a variety of unfaithfulness which is more easily and more strongly condemned than political or cultic
unfaithfulness."

15. Jacob Milgrom, *Cult and Conscience: The Asham and the Priestly Doctrine of Repentance* (Leiden: Brill, 1976), 3.

16. Ibid.

17. Ibid., 8.

18. Ibid., 9.

5:17 (where נשא עונו appears with אשם) to argue that אשם must mean "to feel guilty," otherwise it is rendered tautological by נשא עונו. This is reinforced by the fact that people were unaware of their specific transgression (לא ידע). Milgrom concluded that, therefore, people could only suspect they had done wrong, that is, they felt guilty.[19]

While Milgrom's work אשם has been widely criticized, several aspects of it are helpful in advancing our understanding of sin in the OT, especially in light of the anthropological dichotomy between so-called guilt and shame cultures.[20] Here, I note two. First, Sklar's work on the meaning of כפר affirms that there *are* instances in which "to feel guilty" is clearly part of the semantic payload of אשם.[21] That this is a legitimate aspect of the concept indicates that the category of individual psychological awareness may not have been as foreign to the ancient mind as is often suggested by some proponents of anthropological approaches to biblical studies.

Numbers 5:15 may be an example where עוה connotes a similar "sense of guilt," indicated by the construction זכרון מזכרת עון, literally, "remembrance of iniquity," which stands in apposition to קנאת, "(a gift of) jealousy." Another example comes in the description of David, after taking the census of fighting men, as "heartstruck" (ויך לב־דוד אתו), leading to his plea: "Now, O Lord, I beg you, take away the guilt of your servant" (העבר־נא את־עון עבדך; 2 Sam 24:10). While it would be overstating the case to say that guilt "feelings" were the sum total of the meaning of עון in this instance, they are clearly included.

Second, Milgrom's work draws attention to the close connection between sin, guilt, and punishment that characterizes the ancient worldview, the so-called consequential view of sin. In other words, the undergirding worldview of the OT (and the ANE in general) is that sin is always attended by some sort of consequence or penalty. This is evident from a plethora of references in the OT,[22] but it is also made clear by the construction נשא + עון. As Koch notes, "the term *ʿāwōn* ... [refers] to an almost thing-like substance," in which the transgressor "bears" his transgression and its consequences.[23]

The quasi-substantial nature of this aspect of עון leads to a further implication of the word's meaning. That is, while sin can have a psychological component of guilt feelings, it does so *in correspondence with*, rather than in distinction from an actual sin committed. The one who "feels guilty" does so because there has been a corresponding action that has rendered them

---

19. Ibid.

20. E.g., Jay Sklar, *Sin, Impurity, Sacrifice, Atonement: The Priestly Conceptions* (HBM 2;Sheffield: Sheffield Phoenix, 2005); N. Kiuchi, *The Purification Offering in the Priestly Literature: Its Meaning and Function* (JSOTSup 56; Sheffield: JSOT Press, 1988).

21. Sklar, *Sin ... Atonement*, 24–39.

22. See, for example, the represetative list in ibid., 11 n. 1.

23. S.v. בוש, *TDOT*.

guilty in fact. This is indicated by examples such as 1 Sam 20:8, in which עון is coupled with the preposition ב "If there is iniquity in me (ואם־יש־בי עון)."[24]

This stands somewhat at odds with Freudian psychological formulations. These see guilt as a purely negative, illegitimate, and oppressive emotion that needs to be done away with. As Kiuchi states in his analysis of Lev 5:17, "the law presupposes as an objective fact that a person has committed a sin. In other words, the law does not envisage a case in which the person suspects either unnecessarily or wrongly that he has done wrong. Rather *since* he has done wrong, he feels guilty: when he feels guilty, he knows what the sin was."[25]

However, the "objective fact" that Kiuchi refers to must be carefully nuanced, lest the idea of objectivity be taken to be the same as in most post-Enlightenment formulations. Guilt in the OT does not correspond exactly to the laws of nature in and of themselves, or any other impersonal principle, but is defined in relation to the figure of authority appropriate to the context. This can be seen, for example, in 2 Sam 19:20, where Shimei appeals to David: "May my lord not hold me guilty (אל־יחשב־לי אדני עון). Do not remember how your servant committed iniquity (ואל־תזכר את אשר העוה עבדך) on the day the king left Jerusalem." Shimei recognizes that his עון has been committed *against* David, and that it is the right of the king to hold him responsible for his offense.

Similarly, the "objective" nature of the more generic sense of עוה as "sin" needs to be seen as sin *against* Yhwh as the king/judge of creation, *according to the various terms he sets in relation to those under his authority*. It is due to this perspective that David, as a further example, understands his sin in the Bathsheba/Uriah incident as committed ultimately against Yhwh: "Before you, you alone, I have sinned (חטא) and done evil in your eyes" (cf. Gen 39:9). Likewise, as previously stated, all nations are accountable to Yhwh for their עון (Gen 15:16) by virtue of his creation of them, but Israel is especially so under the more specific conditions of the Sinai covenant (cf. Exod 19:1–6; Deut 6:25).

Debt

Closely related to the category of responsibility, עוה also appears with the sense of a debt that requires payment. The metaphor can appear obliquely, as in the case of Lev 7:18, in which the consequence of eating the meat of the fellowship offering on the third day is that it is "not credited/reckoned (לא יחשב לו)" to the offerer; instead, they are held responsible (עונה תשא) for it becoming "a foul thing" (פגול יהיה). While not directly described as a "debt," the idea is clearly present in the use of חשב. A similar sense of ac-

---

24. See also Num 15:31; 1 Sam 25:24; 2 Sam 14:32.
25. Kiuchi, *Purification Offering*, 33; cf. Sklar, *Sin . . . Atonement*, 32–39, for a critical appraisal of Kiuchi.

counting is expressed in Ps 130:3: "If you kept (a record of) sins, O Yₕ(wₕ) (אם־עונות תשמר־יה), who could stand?"[26]

The idea of payment is more explicit in Lev 22:16, where the priests bear "guilt requiring payment" (השיאו אותם עון אשמה) for allowing sacrificial meat to be illegitimately consumed. Perhaps most clear, however, are references such as Lev 26:41, where the purpose of Israel's expulsion from the land is expressed in terms of debt and payment (ירצו את־עונם). Significantly, the concept is further explicated two verses later in covenantal terms: "They will pay for their sins because they rejected my laws and abhorred my decrees" (ירצו את־עונם יען וביען במשפטי מאסו ואת־חקתי געלה נפשם; Lev 26:43).[27]

Perhaps the most pronounced economic metaphor involving עוה appears in Ps 49:6–13. The psalmist poses the key rhetorical question of the psalm: "Why should I fear when evil days come, when the iniquity of my deceivers (עון עקבי) surrounds me, those who trust in their wealth and boast of their great riches?" The reason why they are not to be feared is then given in monetary terms: "No man can redeem the life of a brother, or give his ransom to God. Because the ransom-price for their life is costly, and the underworld is forever" (ויקר פדיון נפשם וחדל לעולם).[28]

Gary Anderson has recently argued strongly for a "history" of the notion of sin, in which he argues for a diachronic change in the way the concept was understood.[29] Anderson suggests that between the First and Second Temple periods a fundamental shift occurred, from the metaphor of sin as a "burden" (which characterizes the use of the term in earlier OT documents) to sin as a "debt" (in later OT, intertestamental, NT, and early Christian texts), fundamentally through the influence of Aramaic in the Second Temple period.[30]

Anderson's overall argument has several helpful elements in the broad conceptualization of sin in Jewish and Christian thought, and he marshalls impressive evidence to support his case. There are, however, some issues that cut against the thrust of his suggestions. Of particular note, Anderson recognizes that the appearance of רצה ("to pay") in Lev 26:41–43 creates a problem for his thesis of a marked diachronic change in the conceptualization process from sin as burden to sin as debt.

---

26. As a caveat, this could also be translated "If you guarded (i.e., observed) sin."

27. For a detailed discussion of the notion of sin as debt, with an extended analysis of Lev 26, see Gary A. Anderson, *Sin: A History* (New Haven, CT: Yale University Press, 2009), 27–94.

28. The translation of the last phrase is notoriously difficult, but the connection between iniquity and debt is clear. I have opted for repointing the text to read וחדל, "the underworld" (s.v. חדל, *HALOT*), as a word-play with חלד, "earth(ly inhabitants)," in v. 2; cf its similar use in Isa 38:11, where it is explicitly contrasted with "the land of the living" (בארץ החיים). For further discussion on wordplay in Ps 49, see Daniel J. Estes, "Poetic artistry in the expression of fear in Psalm 49," *BibSac* 161 (2004): 55–71.

29. Anderson, *Sin*, 3–14.

30. Ibid., 27–31.

Anderson attempts to resolve this issue by recourse to dating of the texts, arguing that P (Lev 1–16, which contain most of the references to sin as burden) should be dated in the First Temple Period, while H (Lev 17–26, which contain the notion of sin as debt) comes from a later date.[31] At this point, however, his argument becomes rather circular. Anderson suggests that Lev 25 and 26 were originally preexilic, but then redacted in the exile or beyond.[32] This later redaction includes the insertion of רצה in Lev 26:41–43. However, Anderson's proof for the late redaction of Lev 26 is that there, sin is conceived of as debt.[33] This, to say the least, seems to be assuming the conclusion Anderson wishes to reach.[34]

Furthermore, by the time that Lev 25 and 26 in the final form of the book, it must have been considered appropriate to place the notion of sin as a debt that needed payment alongside the notion of sin as a burden. This implies either that it was felt that either there was no danger of confusing or illegitimately transferring connotations from one to the other, or else (in my opinion) that the overlap between the two was fairly well understood, at least by the time of canonization.

When recent research on the meaning of כפר, especially in terms of its use in both cultic and atonement contexts, is added to the mix, the need to delineate the concepts of sin as burden and as debt along chronological lines seems to overplay the evidence. Perhaps seeing a shift in emphasis within a shared concept sphere, whereby "older" texts mainly make use of the metaphor of weight but also on occasion have recourse to economic terminology, and vice versa, would be a better way forward. After all, even in contemporary settings (both secular and theological), the metaphors have a fairly natural connection.[35] It would seem rather unlikely that only contemporary thinkers were capable of such multifaceted thinking.

The previous paragraph brings us to a further conclusion, particularly relevant to our study of the book of Ezekiel and its close connection to both P and H. That sin can be thought of in terms of debt obviously has implications for the relation between atonement and purification. I will begin to adress this issue at the conclusion of this chapter and more fully in the next.

Punishment

As this semantic study confirms in accordance with previous studies on the topic, the OT uses "sin" to cover the whole range of misdeed-

---

31. Ibid., 55.

32. Ibid., 56.

33. Ibid.

34. For a fuller critique of Anderson, see Joseph Lam, "Review of Gary A. Anderson, *Sin: A History*," *RBL* (2010), n.p. [cited October 30, 2012]. Online: http://www.bookreviews.org/pdf/7556_8254.pdf.

35. E.g., the idea of a financial debt as a burden.

consequence concepts, and thus in several instances עוה primarily means "punishment." This is the case in Gen 4:13, where Cain says to Yhwh, "My punishment (עוני) is more than I can bear."[36] Punishment also seems to be in view in 2 Kgs 7:9, where the lepers plundering the abandoned Aramean camp say, "We should not be doing this on this day. It is a day of good news, but we are being silent. And if we wait until daylight, punishment will find us out (ומצאנו עוון)." It is possible, indeed likely, that "feeling guilty" is included in the concept here, but the coupling with the *weqatal* ומצאנו suggests that a looming punishment is the predominant focus of the word's meaning in this instance.

The word עוה also appears with the sense of punishment in 1 Sam 28:10, in a manner that reveals the thought process involved in spanning the misdeed-punishment spectrum. There, Saul attempts to reassure the medium in bringing up the spirit of Samuel from *Sheol*, that "As surely as Yhwh lives, you will not be punished (lit., "meet with iniquity," אמ־יקרך עון) for this thing." That punishment (or consequence of action) is in view is made clear by the protests of the medium that elicit Saul's words in the previous verse: "Why have you set a trap for my life to bring about my death?"

Punishment is also significant in key occurrences of the covenant formulations. Most prominently, it appears with the double sense of (forgiveness of) sin and punishment, in Exod 34:6–7 (cf. 20:5): "Yhwh, Yhwh, the compassionate and gracious God ... bearing/forgiving iniquity, transgression and sin (נשא עון ופשע וחטאת), but by no means acquitting, bringing the iniquity of the fathers upon the sons (פקד עון אבות על־בנים)." Similar instances include Lev 18:25; Isa 26:21; Jer 14:10; 25:12; 36:31; Lam 4:22; Hos 8:13; 9:9; and Amos 3:2. In this formulation, Yhwh's punishment of sin is presented as corresponding to his just character: the עון that is visited on people is in accordance with their עון against him.

Noting the close correspondence between act and punishment, Koch put forward the influential (and, at the time, radical) argument that, although there was indeed a consequential relationship between sin and punishment, that this was not due to divine retribution but rather was the end point of an inevitable process (which Koch called *schicksalwirkende Tatsphäre*). Koch's favored analogies for this relationship were planting seed (act) and harvesting fruit (consequence),[37] and Yhwh's role in punishment as a midwife

---

36. Koch gives good reason for not limiting the sense of עון to Cain's punishment (that is, death) alone, but rather to understand it in terms of a more holistic sweep of misdeed-consequence, as "an enduring burden" (s.v. עון, *TDOT*, 551). However, it would seem that, even if this is borne in mind, the emphasis (in the context of Yhwh's pronouncement of the penalty for the murder of Abel) is indeed on the punishment that Cain will undergo. This is confirmed by the mitigation of the penalty that occurs in Gen 4:14–16.

37. Koch, "Doctrine of Retribution," 61, 65, 72.

(rather than a judge), *"facilitating the completion of something which previous human action has already set in motion."*[38]

While Koch's thesis found acceptance by some prominent OT scholars (including von Rad)[39] it has been strongly criticized. Among others, Knierim, Miller, Hubbard, and, more recently, Wong, have produced extended interactions that seek to acknowledge the close relationship between deed and consequence endorsed by Koch, yet demonstrate the shortcomings of viewing YHWH as a largely passive figure in references to punishment in the OT.[40]

From a different angle, John Barton has argued that Koch's view seems to have been derived from (or at least heavily influenced by) deism.[41] As such, the likelihood of it being an accurate reflection of an ancient understanding of the workings of the cosmos is questionable, especially when van der Toorn's comparative study of sin in ANE cultures is also taken into account.[42]

However, despite its shortcomings, Barton recognizes the usefulness of Koch's work in moving forward in the discussion of the close connection between sin and punishment. In particular, Barton suggests that, while the prophets did hold to such a connection, this was not due to a mechanistic worldview. Rather, their views derived from the particular moral character of the God for whom they claimed to speak.[43]

The real value in Koch's work, then, is to alert readers that OT ethics are not simply a self-contained theonomy, in which "justice" is tautological to "what God does or commands."[44] Rather, there is an agreed moral standard by which YHWH's character is able to be publicly recognized and confirmed as just in his punishment of sin. The chief function of the prophet, in this regard, was to ensure that people would have no excuse for misinterpreting his actions as unjust or capricious. Barton uses Ezek 18 (especially vv. 25–29) as the prime example of this phenomenon: YHWH's justice is not inscru-

---

38. Ibid., 61 (emphasis original).

39. Gerhard von Rad, *Old Testament Theology*, vol. 1: *The Theology of Israel's Historical Traditions* (trans. D. M. G. Stalker; New York: Harper & Row, 1962), 384–86; Hans Walter Wolff, *Hosea: A Commentary on the Book of the Prophet Hosea* (ed. P. D. Hanson; trans. G. Stansell; Hermeneia; Philadelphia: Fortress, 1974), 68.

40. Rolf Knierim, *Die Hauptbegriffe für Sünde im Alten Testament* (Gütersloh: Mohn, 1965); Patrick D. Miller, *Sin and Judgment in the Prophets: A Stylistic and Theological Analysis* (Chico, CA: Scholars Press, 1982); Robert L. Hubbard, "Dynamistic and Legal Processes in Psalm 7," *ZAW* 94 (1982): 267–79; Ka Leung Wong, *The Idea of Retribution in the Book of Ezekiel* (VTSup 87; Leiden: Brill, 2001). For a representative list of verses supporting YHWH's active punishment of sin, see Sklar, *Sin . . . Atonement*, 11 n. 1.

41. Barton, *Old Testament Ethics*, 40.

42. Karel van der Toorn, *Sin and Sanction in Israel and Mesopotamia: A Comparative Study* (SSN 22; Assen: Van Gorcum, 1985), 41–55, 67–70.

43. Barton, *Old Testament Ethics*, 42.

44. Ibid.

table, but is available to human reason, and thus accountable: "God really is just as people would like God to be—just according to human standards of justice."[45]

Barton thus provides an important contribution toward understanding how עוה functions as both sin and punishment in the OT, by tying it to Yʜᴡʜ's just character, plainly apprehendable to all, in the prophetic declarations of judgment. This will have obvious and important implications for the analysis of עוה in Ezekiel, especially given that the "radical theocentricity" of his book is sometimes taken as a sign of a "wholly theonomic," inscrutable and unaccountable—that is, *unjust* ethical basis to Yʜᴡʜ's treatment of Judah.[46]

Excursus: נשׂא + זון *and Forgiveness*

Before examining the occurrences of עוה in Ezekiel, it is worth mentioning some recent research into the construction "נשׂא + sin terminology" (most often עון)[47] and its meanings, given the instances of the construction in Ezekiel (Ezek 4:4–6; 14:10; 18:19–20; 44:10, 12). As stated previously, the construction can mean completely opposite things; either "to bear sin" (that is, to be held responsible and punished for sin) or "to forgive sin" (that is, not to be held responsible and punished for sin). In attempting to resolve this apparent contradiction, two main suggestions have been offered. One is that the meaning is to be found in the relationship of the verb נשׂא to its subject and the sin in question. Thus, for example, Morgenstern argues that the meaning turns on whether the subject of the verb is the sinner himself (in which case the sinner "bears" his sin), or someone other than the sinner (in which case the expression means "to forgive").[48]

The second attempt is put forward by Baruch Schwartz.[49] Schwartz accepts Morgenstern's basic distinction, but seeks to advance the position by suggesting that critical to resolving the issue is to grasp the significance of the underlying metaphor of sin as a burden. According to Schwartz,

---

45. Ibid., 43–44.

46. As, for example, in Schwartz, "Dim View."

47. I discussed this construction briefly in the previous chapter, in my analysis of Ezek 16:52, and also the use of כלם as another shame term in Ezekiel. Given the prevalence of the construction עון + נשׂא in Ezekiel, a fuller discusion is warranted here. I am indebted for the reviews of previous scholarship to Lam, "Metaphor." These are more fully developed in idem, *The Metaphorical Patterning of the Sin Concept in Biblical Hebrew* (Ph.D. diss.: University of Chicago, 2012).

48. Julian Morgenstern, "The Book of the Covenant, Part 3: The Huqqim," *HUCA* 8–9 (1931–32): 17.

49. Baruch J. Schwartz, "The Bearing of Sin in the Priestly Literature," in *Pomegranates and Golden Bells: Studies in Biblical, Jewish, and Near Easter Ritual, Law, and Literature in Honor of Jacob Milgrom* (ed. David P. Wright, David Noel Freedman, and Avi Hurvitz; Winona Lake, IN: Eisenbrauns, 1995), 3–22.

this means that the phrase נשא + עון "has two *uses*, but only one *meaning*."[50] Rather than meaning either "to bear sin" or "to forgive sin," the phrase can be used with the senses "to bear sin" or "to bear sin (away)."[51]

Schwartz's solution is certainly attractive in many respects. Lam, however, contends that the solution is ultimately unsatisfactory. He grants that Schwartz's highlighting of sin as burden does in fact lie behind the original meaning, but does not think that this resolves the ambiguity of opposite meanings or cut to the heart of the issue. Rather, for Lam, the key is the recognition that there are two distinct meanings for the same phrase, and that they cannot be distinguished on contextual morphosyntactic factors.[52]

Lam's own solution revolves around a more developed understanding of the "life cycle" of a metaphor. In this, he draws on the work of Josef Stern, whose work focuses on the process of "lexicalization"—the transformation of a metaphor from highly context-dependent for its meaning, to a "literal" linguistic entity, whose meaning is largely context-independent.[53] Lam uses the example of the term "backhanded" as an illustration of his point, noting that its use in association with non-physical nouns such as "compliment" indicate that it has been lexicalized, bypassing the original domain of its metaphorical roots.[54]

Lam's goes on to analyze the occurrences of נשא + sin in the OT and demonstrates, with a few exceptions, a striking overall pattern of distribution: virtually all occurrences of נשא meaning "bear sin" occur in P, H, and Ezekiel.[55] Lam also observes that in occurrences outside those corpora, נשא seems to adopt the same syntax of the more specific term for forgiveness, סלח. He concludes that the meaning "forgive sin" has become highly lexicalized, bypassing the metaphor and coming simply to mean "the act of an offended party to relieve the offender of the effect of a sin."[56]

The critical element in Lam's argument is the suggestion that, on the evidence of the linguistic analysis, the meaning of נשא as "bear sin" is a Priestly innovation. On the other hand, its more "lively" meaning should place it earlier in the metaphor "life-cycle," than the lexicalized "forgive sin." Lam tentatively suggests that this striking "backward move" was due to borrowing from the Akkadian verb *našû(m)* in legal contexts, associated with the sharp social dislocation of the Babylonian exile. As such, this new, "vivified" meaning of נשא generated a new, Priestly notion of sin, exemplified by Lev 16, Isa 53, and, significantly, Ezek 4.[57]

---

50. Ibid., 9.
51. Ibid., 10.
52. Lam, "Metaphor," 4.
53. Ibid., 6.
54. Ibid., 7.
55. Isa 53:12 is also included in this list, which Lam explains as "a post-exilic text occurring in a very rich poetic context containing other Priestly material" (ibid., 9.).
56. Ibid., 12.
57. Ibid., 13.

Lam's work on the distinctive use of נשׁא for "bearing" sin in Priestly material is extremely valuable with regard to establishing the likely parameters in analyzing the use of עוה in Ezekiel: the dominant concept behind sin is that of burden, whose consequences must be borne by someone in order for it to be dealt with properly. To this I now turn.[58]

The Use of עוה *in Ezekiel*

There are 44 examples of עון, and an additional 3 of the noun עוה in Ezekiel. Given the abundance of the term, I will not attempt to analyze each instance in full, but seek to examine them in appropriate groups. In brief, Ezekiel's use of עוה in relation to the rest of the OT is conceptually conventional, but at points syntactically idiosyncratic. As such, I will survey the appearances of עוה according to the various forms and constructions used by Ezekiel, under the categories of "conventional" and "idiosyncratic," focussing attention on exegetically significant instances, or those that present challenges to interpretation.[59]

"Conventional" Constructions

עוה/עון

Ezekiel 4:5a. The word עון appears without modifiers (that is, not in dependent construction with another syntactic entity) 4 times (Ezek 4:5a; 9:9; 16:49; 32:27). עון in Ezek 4:5a appears in the fivefold cluster (Ezek 4:4–6) and establishes the proportions of Ezekiel's representative sign-act of "bearing" Israel's iniquity: "I have given you the years of their iniquity for the number

---

58. One minor caveat worth mentioning is that Lam does concede: "One needs to recognize that a continuum exists between metaphoricity on one end and literality on the other" (ibid., 7.), and hence a measure of fluidity applies to the stratification of occurrences. To this we might add that, although some metaphors do undergo a fairly complete process of lexicalization (as in Lam's example of "backhanded") and are most appropriately visualized over a continuum, others can remain capable, over extended periods, of both retaining their original metaphorical sense, while at the same time also being able to be used in a lexicalized manner. A contemporary example of this may be the metaphor of "warming up," which may be used in senses that are both metaphorical (for example, a person playing a competitive sport whose performance gets better as the game goes on), and lexicalized (as in the phrase, "I'm warming up to him").

As an adjunct to Lam's argument, this may contribute to explaining how, in the final form of the text, both "metaphoricized" and "lexicalized" meanings of עון + נשׁא sometimes appear in the same context, both in cases where there are apparently "mixed" sources/traditions combined, (e.g., Num 14:18–34) as well as cases where there do not appear to be (e.g., Gen 50:17).

59. It should also be noted in passing that the occurrences tend to occur in "clusters" (3:18–19 [2 times], 4:4–6 [5 times], 7:13–19 [3 times], 14:3–10 [5 times], 18:17–30 [6 times], 21:28–34 [7 times], 33:6–9 [3 times], 36:31–33 [2 times], 44:10–12 [3 times]), and are especially prominent in the commissioning and "quasi-legal" sections of Ezekiel. This is not an exclusive pattern, however, as several instances occur individually.

of days (עוֹנָם לְמִסְפַּר יָמִים)." Thus, Ezekiel is to lie on his left side for 390 days, then on his right side for 40 days, to symbolize, respectively, the עֲוֹן of "Israel," and the עֲוֹן of Judah (Ezek 4:4, 6).[60] I will examine the nature of Ezekiel's representative "bearing" of עֲוֹן further when I analyze the instances of עֲוֹן + נשׂא in Ezekiel. Here, I will focus on the manner in which עֲוֹן in 4:5a functions as the centerpoint of a play on the word's range of meaning in Ezek 4:4–6.

Despite the initial difficulty of the references and mathematics, most contemporary commentators agree that the 390 "years" refer to the sins of the unified entity "Israel" in the first temple period. The 40 "years," correspondingly, are symbolic of a generation—referring to the period of Judah's exile, in a manner highly evocative of the wilderness generation.[61]

The cluster of examples of עֲוֹן in Ezek 4:4–6 is illuminative of the meaning(s) and significance of the concept in several regards. First, if the resolution proposed by commentators is correct, this indicates *both* that the breadth of the semantic range (from "sin" in 4:5 to "punishment" in 4:6), *and* that the specificity of meaning in each instance was clearly meant to be understood.[62] The critical element in such an understanding is the ambiguity of עֲוֹן in 4:4–5a, which is bifurcated and defined in 4:5b–6 by the numerical referent attached to each. The principle "a day for a year" refers equally to both Israel's 390 year period of "sin" (4:5), and Judah's 40 year period of "punishment" (4:6).

This analysis offers a further insight into the strengths and weaknesses of Koch's thesis regarding act and consequence in the OT. In terms of strengths, the close, almost inseparable relationship between act and consequence is reflected in the range of meanings spanned by עֲוֹן in Ezek 4:4–6. The same word is used in almost identical constructions to mean "sin" and "punishment," and the instance in 4:4 confirms the continuity between the meanings.

On the other hand, that עֲוֹן must specifically mean "punishment" in 4:6 undermines Koch's argument that there is no Hebrew word with that meaning, and that therefore the concept is absent from ancient thought patterns.[63] We may grant Koch's recognition that there is no Hebrew word

---

60. Block helpfully notes that it is unlikely that Ezekiel spent the entire periods lying on his side. Rather, he probably performed various aspects of the sign-acts described in Ezek 4–5 at times during the day; Block, *Ezekiel 1–24*, 184.

61. Joyce, *Ezekiel*, 85–86; Block, *Ezekiel 1–24*, 174–80; Greenberg, *Ezekiel 1–20*, 104–6, 117–28; Zimmerli, *Ezekiel 1–24*, 166–68. On the difficulty of the mathematics, Greenberg, *Ezekiel 1–20*, 105: "ancient and medieval attempts to interpret the numbers in vss. 5 and 6, and the phrase *naśa 'awon* in both, within a single frame of reference have not succeeded."

62. For a review and critique of various attempts to interpret the references, see Block, *Ezekiel 1–24*, 176–81.

63. Koch, "Doctrine of Retribution," 77.

with the *dedicated* meaning "punishment," as there is in English (and German), but עון in Ezek 4:6 clearly carries this meaning. Koch's thesis in this regard is therefore an instance of the (lack of) word-concept fallacy.[64]

Greenberg offers another intriguing perspective on Ezek 4:4–5:4. On the basis of the interweaving of the siege sign-act and the sign-act of Ezekiel lying on his side to "bear" the עון of Israel, Greenberg argues that Ezekiel drew on the particular expression of the covenant curses in Lev 26:13–49. The common factors between the two passages includes continual sin, punctuated by staged, escalating punishment; interweaving of sin and punishment, ending with devastation of the land; and confluence of the siege sign-act and sin-bearing sign act, representing the First Temple period as one long age of wrath.[65]

Greenberg's suggestion, if correct, adds a further depth of meaning to what is expressed by עון, the one instance of the word now doing (at least) "double duty," if not an even more multifaceted polysemy.[66] There are, however, some challenges to this view, which Greenberg himself grants. Specifically, the issues of how the 40 days of the עון בית־יהודה, and how the exile-specific sign acts relate to the First Temple period present significant problems to this reading. As Greenberg admits, it "defies integration from the aspect of its content." Greenberg suggests that these may be secondary additions, made as an editorial afterthought to the main body of sign-acts.[67]

There does not seem to be an easy resolution to the problem. Integrating 4:9–13, where Ezekiel is to eat "siege ration" bread (corresponding to the exile; cf. Ezek 4:13), with the 390 days in which he is to eat it (corresponding to the First Temple period, cf. Ezek 4:5) seems impossible. Block suggests that the various sign-acts may not have been performed continuously or, necessarily, sequentially, but rather aspects of each would have been done for certain parts of the day, for the duration of the 390-day period.[68] Extending this line of thought, perhaps the sign-acts themselves do not correspond exactly to each other, but contain an amalgamation of the entire communicative package, from which explanatory points are highlighted as

---

64. Cf. Barr, *Semantics of Biblical Language*, 36; Carson, *Exegetical Fallacies*, 45, 55; Wong, *Idea of Retribution*, 22–23.

65. Greenberg, *Ezekiel 1–20*, 124–25. For more on Ezekiel's use of Lev 17–26 (H), see Michael A. Lyons, *From Law to Prophecy: Ezekiel's Use of the Holiness Code* (LHBOTS 507; New York: T. & T. Clark, 2009).

66. For more on polysemy and facets (or aspects) of the meaning of words, see Croft and Cruse, *Cognitive Linguistics*. For a fuller application of this area of linguistics to the biblical notion of sin, see Lam, *Sin Concept*, 142–51.

67. Greenberg, *Ezekiel 1–20*, 125–26.

68. Block, *Ezekiel 1–24*, 184. Block (ibid., 169) also puts forward a possibility that the section is structured chiastically around *two* diets: the siege diet (Ezek 4:9–11, 16–17) and the exilic diet (4:12–13). This is certainly true, but does not resolve the ambiguity of the number of days.

appropriate. On balance, however, it seems best to retain a relatively distinct semantic weighting between the 390 days of Israel's "sin" (that is, the reason for punishment) and the 40 days of Judah's "punishment" (that is, the result of sin), and to see them "held together" by the initial ambiguity of the references in 4:4–5a.[69]

The particular nuances of meaning in each instances aside, one thing the analysis does indicate is that עוֹן in this context must also include in its sweep notions of guilt, at least in the sense of some sort of "objective" responsibility for sin. The term *objective* is used to indicate that the עוֹן is viewed as something *external* to Ezekiel, determined by someone external to Ezekiel (that is, YHWH), that is laid on him in a quasi-physical manner (sin as burden), rather than a subjective feeling or emotion.[70] It is also "objective" in that there is a clear sense of *proportionality* or *justice* expressed in the formula of 4:5a: "I have given you the years of their עוֹן for the number of days [that you will bear their עוֹן]."

On the other hand, there is also a sense of *disproportionality* expressed in the passage, for the 390 days/years of "sin" are only accorded 40 days/years of "punishment." At this stage, however, whether this is a statement of grace (in alleviating the penalty) or of finality is left unsaid.[71] The full answer is only finally given in the sweep of the whole book's message.

Ezekiel 9:9; 16:49. The appearances of עוֹן in Ezek 9:9 and 16:49 can be dealt with together, because they both carry the same sense, and are also associated with shame/defilement concepts in their contexts. In Ezek 9:9, the עוֹן of the Israelites and Judeans is described as "very very great" (גדול במאד מאד), then spelled out in terms of bloodshed and injustice, due ultimately to a lack of regard for YHWH's awareness of his people's actions. In Ezek 16:49, the עוֹן of Sodom—characterized as the sister of Judah—was pride in her plenty and peace, while disregarding the poor and those in need. In both cases, עוֹן simply means those actions, with their underlying attitudes, that have occasioned the judgment and punishment of YHWH, the judge. However, these examples are worthy of further mention due to their association with shame/defilement concepts. I have already examined the relationship between בוש and עוֹן in Ezek 16:49 in the previous chapter. Here I will focus on Ezek 9:9.

---

69. For further suggestions on the various aspects of Ezekiel's sign-acts in Ezek 4, see Hayyim Angel, "Ezekiel: Priest—Prophet," *JBQ* 39 (2011): 39–40.

70. An emotional response, of course, may well have been involved—performing the sign-act might have made Ezekiel "feel guilty" for his own perceived failures, inasmuch as he was part of the "house of Israel." However, this is clearly not the emphasis or sense of the passage.

71. Compare the use of כלה, "to finish," and קץ, "the end," in Ezek 5–7. Mein's reflection on the opening vision in Ezekiel is also helpful on this front: "The significance of God's dwelling among the exiles is not yet clear . . . [it] may mean reassurance . . . but it may also mean judgment." Andrew Mein, *Ezekiel and the Ethics of Exile* (OTRM; Oxford: Oxford University Press, 2001), 236.

There is a clear juxtaposition of cultic and legal categories in Ezek 9. The most obvious indicator of this is the sustained focus, from Ezek 8, on the idolatrous activity taking place in the temple, encapsulated particularly by the repeated term "abominations" (תועבות). Correspondingly, in Ezek 9, judgment is expressed in heavily cultic terms, revolving around a play on words with חלל 1—"to profane," and חלל 2—"to begin," together with the key cultic term טמא: in v. 6, the executioners are ordered to kill (הרג) all who do not have not been marked out as belonging to Yhwh, and instructed to "begin at my sanctuary (וממקדשי תחלו)," which they proceed to do (ויחלו). In v. 7, the order is augmented: "Defile (טמאו) the temple, and fill the courts with the slain (חללים)."[72]

On the other hand, as Block notes, the passage also has a juridical, prophetic style, indicated by the legal vocabulary "bring on" (קרבו), "administrators/executioners" (פקדות), the accusation of "injustice" (מטה),[73] the report in v. 11 that the sentence had been carried out "according to all you commanded me," and Ezekiel playing a "quasi-legal" role as a witness in Yhwh's case against his people.[74]

It is widely recognized that Ezekiel combines Prophetic and Priestly terms and themes in a distinctive manner, but mainstream study has tended to emphasize the priestly aspect of the book, even tending towards a polarization.[75] For example, Clements claims: "Whereas all the theological connections of the book of Jeremiah are with the Deuteronomic movement, those of Ezekiel are to be found in the work of the emergent Priestly school."[76] However, such a sharp distinction seems rather forced; for although Ezekiel does indeed place great importance on cultic language and

---

72. For more on Ezekiel's use of this wordplay, see Block, *Ezekiel 1–24*, 308 n. 45; Zimmerli, *Ezekiel 1–24*, 187 (commenting on Ezek 6:4–5): "The judgment which Yahweh brings upon the land by the sword has, by a deep inner logic of righteousness, the consequence that the cult places of the mountains of Israel, which are outwardly places of venerable sanctity, although in Yahweh's eyes they are places of abomination, are to be publicly desecrated by the dead of Israel lying there." Although חלל by and large means "slain," Ezekiel's use of the term is both concentrated (according to *HALOT*, 34 of the 90 instances of the term are in Ezekiel) and, at times, idiosyncratic. Cf. Ezek 21:30, for example, where Zedekiah is called חלל רשע, and "profane wicked (one)" is at least a possibility.

73. A *hapax* Hophal of נטה, "to stretch out," and obviously reminiscent of the ruler's staff (המטה), hence the rendering "injustice."

74. Block, *Ezekiel 1–24*, 303.

75. For a range of perspectives and review of this topic, see Iain M. Duguid, "Putting Priests in Their Place: Ezekiel's Contribution to the History of the Old Testament Priesthood," in *Ezekiel's Hierarchical World*; Baruch J. Schwartz, "A Priest out of Place: Reconsidering Ezekiel's Role in the History of the Israelite Priesthood," in *Ezekiel's Hierarchical World*; Corrine L. Carvalho, "Priest, Prophet, and Exile: Ezekiel as a Literary Construct," in *Ezekiel's Hierarchical World*.

76. Ronald E. Clements, "The Ezekiel Tradition: Prophecy in Time of Crisis," in *Israel's Prophetic Tradition* (ed. J. Coggins et al.; Cambridge: Cambridge University Press, 1982), 126.

concepts, Deuteronomic concerns are by no means less prominent. The examples of Ezek 9:9 and 16:49 illustrate this, and they are representative of Ezekiel's overarching rhetorical strategy. Cult and ethics do not stand at odds with each other; they are interwoven and interdependent, a fact that been increasingly recognized in biblical scholarship, at least since the work of Douglas.[77]

Mein, for example, helpfully appropriates the work of Douglas and Milgrom on the relationship between ritual and ethics into his study of Ezekiel. Importantly, he sees the unifying factor being found in the person of Yhwh himself. Mein suggests that the notion of holiness may bridge the two categories, and that as Yhwh makes both ritual and ethical demands, the distinctions, in practice, are blurred.[78]

At a broader level, Sklar's study of כפר in relation to both sin and impurity also demonstrates the high degree of overlap between the two categories, even if the distinction between them can sometimes be clearly maintained. He suggests that while the cause of each is distinguishable—impurity beginning from amoral causes, sin from moral wrongdoing—the endpoint is the same. Both endanger, and so require כפר, and both defile, and so require purgation. As such, in either case, the person presenting the sacrifice requires both, and this dual event is described in the verb כפר.[79]

In the case of Ezekiel, even this distinction is sometimes blurred. In Ezek 36:17–18, for example, culpability for shed blood is expressed in both cultic and ethical/moral categories; fused together, as it were, into the one indictment: "Son of man, when the house of Israel lived in their land, they defiled (ויטמאו) it by their ways and wantonness. Like the uncleanness of menstruation (כטמאת הנדה) were their ways before me. So I poured out my anger upon them because of the blood (על־הדם) they had poured out in the land, and because by their dung/idols they defiled it (ובגלוליהם טמאוה)."[80]

Recognition of the importance of ritual in human life and behavior have been very helpful on this front, and when held together with the shaping of the covenant ethics around the character of Yhwh, provide powerful tools for integrating the categories of sin and defilement in Ezekiel, as well as having significant implications for the broader interaction between guilt and shame in anthropology and theology.

Ezekiel 21:32. The three instances of the noun עוה, "ruin, twistedness," appear together in Ezek 21:32, and they may be commented on only briefly. The hapax form is unusual, but its meaning is clear. The threefold repe-

---

77. See further the discussion of Douglas's work in the previous chapter, as well as Trevaskis, *Holiness*; Sklar, *Sin . . . Atonement*.

78. Mein, *Ethics of Exile*, 152. Mein also helpfully surveys the close relationship between Ezekiel and the concerns of the so-called Deuteronomists, ibid., 101–36. Levaskis, *Holiness*, argues for a similar synthesis of ritual and ethics, via holiness, in Leviticus.

79. Sklar, *Sin . . . Atonement*, 159.

80. See further the discussion on Ezek 36 in the previous chapter.

tition is emphatic, expressing a superlative sense—Jerusalem is to be utterly ruined.[81] Block also notes that עוה forms a play on words with עון in Ezek 21:30, once again highlighting the close connection between the elements in the deed-consequence process—here, the declaration of impending judgment (בעת עון קץ), and its expression (עוה). We may also note that Ezek 21:32 is one example that undermines Koch's thesis of YHWH playing the role of midwife in the process of punishment—there is no passivity expressed here: "A ruin! A ruin! A ruin I will make it!" (עוה עוה עוה אשמינה). As Block puts it, "The anarchy in Jerusalem is not merely the result of social or political incompetence; it is Yahweh who turns the world upside down."[82]

Ezekiel 32:27. The appearance of עונתם in Ezek 32:27 likewise needs only brief treatment. Ezek 32 presents the final lament (נהה) for Egypt, a description of the fellows she is ultimately to join in שאול, and in vv. 26–27, the warriors of Meshech and Tubal are described as being buried with their "swords (חרבותם) under their heads, and their iniquity (עונתם) upon their bones." As most commentators observe, despite its attestation in the manuscripts, this makes little sense in the context, and a slight emendation to צנתם, "their shields," is a more likely reading.[83] Given the textual issue, it is hard to give this instance any weight in the discussion.

עון + *Preposition* (כ/מן/על/ב)

There are 21 examples of עון attached to a preposition, 18 of which fall under the banner "conventional" constructions—that is, those that match the regular syntactical constructions expected to appear with עון. Of these, 12 appear with the preposition ב, 3 with מן, 2 with כ, and 1 with על. The remaining 3 (Ezek 18:19, 20 [2×]), in which the prepositional construction בעון appears with the verb נשא, I have classified as "idiosyncratic." Exegetically, the most significant categories are עון + ב and עון + על. I will focus attention on them, with brief coverage to the rest.

ב + עון

The 12 examples of עון + ב (3:18, 19; 4:17; 7:13, 16; 18:17, 18; 24:23; 33:6, 8, 9; 39:23) are concentrated around the quasi-legal passages (Ezek 3; 18; 33), and in these contexts are most often closely connected with the death sentence of the person in view (מות, דמו). This is not always the case, however; other associated verbs include "(not) strengthening" (חזק; Ezek 7:13),[84] "wasting away" (נמק; Ezek 7:16; 24:23), and "being exiled" (גלה; Ezek 39:23).

---

81. GKC §133 i.

82. Block (*Ezekiel 1–24*, 691) helpfully notes the parallels with Esarhaddon's descriptions of Marduk's fury against the crimes of the Babylonians twisting nature out of shape; cf *CAD* 10/2, 135.

83. Idem, *Ezekiel 25–48*, 220 n. 55; Greenberg, *Ezekiel 21–37*, 666; Zimmerli, *Ezekiel 25–48*, 168.

84. In context, preservation of life is in view.

It should be noted, however, that in these cases the shadow of death remains. Recent research into the biblical concept of death has highlighted the depth of the notion beyond physical expiration. In his study of שאול, Johnston, for example, argues convincingly that the divine name is related to "being" or "life." Thus, to be removed from Yhwh, or under his judgment, is to be removed from life itself.[85] Wright, likewise, has made much of the association of the Exile with death.[86] Accordingly, the occurrences not explicitly associated with death should still be understood as operating "on the path" or "within the sphere" of death.[87]

The key exegetical issue this raises with regard to the use of עון + ב, then, is whether the preposition should be understood *statively*—"*in* [the sphere of] (his) עון," or *causally*—that is, "*because of* (his) עון." The former category seems more reflective of Priestly conceptions while the latter is more Deuteronomistic. While a causal sense may seem initially more intuitive, there are contextual factors that push toward viewing the preposition as communicating an overarching stative sense, under which the causal (or symptomatic) sense sits. I will consider the instances of עון + ב in Ezek 3:18, 19 as a test case.

First, it should be noted that although "deeds" are in view in Ezek 3, they are not finally determinative of life or death for the person involved. Instead, deeds are indicative of eventual *states* or *locations*, and it is these that ultimately determine destiny. Judgment is *not* on the balance of "righteousness" and "wickedness" accumulated by the person involved, but rather, in which "direction" they have turned towards. Indeed, in Ezek 3:20, if a righteous man (צדיק) turns "from" his righteousness (ובשוב . . . מצדקו) and does evil, his righteous deeds will not be remembered (לא תזכרן צדקתו אשר עשה)." The sustained language of Israel/Judah's "ways" (דרך) reinforces this perspective. Acts are important, but they are so because they are indicative of the state, or realm, toward which the person is oriented.[88]

Second, the use of "stumbling block" (מכשול), a favored term for Ezekiel,[89] in 3:20 is significant. Given that its appearance in construct with עון is so prominent, and unique to Ezekiel, I will reserve the main discussion of this difficult term for the "idiosyncratic" section. Here, I simply note that the

---

85. Philip Johnston, *Shades of Sheol: Death and Afterlife in the Old Testament* (Leicester: Apollos, 2002); cf. Peter Bolt, *Jesus' Defeat of Death: Persuading Mark's Early Readers* (SNTSMS 125; Cambridge: Cambridge University Press, 2003).

86. Especially in Wright, *NTPG*.

87. There is here, then, support for something akin to Koch's concept of a *schicksalwirkende Tatsphäre*, although it is more accurate to view the sphere revolving around *destiny*, rather than *deeds*. See further Robert L. Hubbard, "Is the 'Tatsphäre' Always a Sphere?" *JETS* 25 (1982): 257–62.

88. The same sense is reflected in Ezek 18, although there acts play a more prominent role.

89. Eight of the 14 instances appear in Ezekiel.

use of מכשול lends support to the suggestion that ב should be understood as stative. It is instructive to note the logical sequence involved in the verse. When the righteous person *turns* and *does* evil, and YHWH *places* the מכשול before him, he *will die*.[90] It is the next phrase, however, that is the critical one for our purposes. There, the twofold consequences of Ezekiel's failure to warn the person is spelled out, the first of which is relevant: "Because you did not warn him, he will die בחטאתו."[91] Although often translated "because of/for his sin,"[92] the metaphor suggests a destination, or realm, that the person "trips" and falls headlong into, and as a result, experiences death.[93]

A further indication that this is the most likely intended force of עון + ב may be the instance in Ezek 39:23, where ב appears along with the more transparently causal על: "And the nations will know that בעונם the house of Israel went into exile, על־אשר they acted faithlessly towards me." The use of the different prepositions, rather than simply restating the cause of the Exile, indicates a broader sense of "realm" for ב, of which Israel's faithless actions are symptomatic.

Before proceeding, it should be noted that in the discussion above I am not seeking to set up a dichotomy between ב as "cause" and as "state." If the study of עון so far has demonstrated anything, it is that such strict delineations are by and large unhelpful, and that in order to be understood accurately, words must (perhaps counterintuitively) be allowed to retain a sense of ambiguity in meaning. In the case of ב, the two senses are clearly and closely related.[94] The purpose of the preceding discussion, then, has been to alert the reader to an underrepresented sense (at least in terms of mainstream translations and commentaries) of meaning, that has recently began to be rediscovered, and adds much to the richness of the concepts involved.

If, indeed, ב indicates that one aspect of the meaning of עון is that of a "realm" or "state" that leads to death, this may in turn reinforce the strong theocentricity that so transparently characterizes Ezekiel. Ultimately, the only hope for those בעונם—in their helpless state—comes from YHWH himself. As Joyce concludes in his study of Ezekiel: "the insight that humankind

---

90. The colon begins with an infinitive construct (ובשוב), followed by a *weqatal* chain (ועשה . . . ונתתי), and ends with an *x-yiqtol* (הוא ימות).

91. Here, חטאת is synonymous with עון.

92. Block suggests that the ב is a *beth pretii*, indicating a price paid or exchanged; Block, *Ezekiel 1–24*, 139.

93. Cf. Zimmerli, *Ezekiel 1–24*, 306 (commenting on the construction מכשול עון in Ezek 14:3): "The man who "bears guilt" (נשא עון) is excluded from the cultic community, and thereby from "life." The description of idolatry as מכשול עון enables us to see that the man who chooses idols chooses death."

94. As a humorous parallel, consider the famous words of the movie character, Forrest Gump: "My momma always says, 'Stupid is as stupid does.'" More seriously, the appearance of עון in Ezek 24:23 is plural: בעונתיכם, which must include activity, and thus suggests at least some sense of cause.

is ultimately impotent without God remains one of the central truths about human existence."[95]

עון + על

The single example of עון + על in Ezek 36:31 is critical for the present study. The meaning of the construction is fairly clear: "because/on account of your עון." Its importance lies in the manner it brings together guilt and shame vocabulary and concepts in a fairly seamless integration. Here, עון is linked in its immediate context to the חרפה (v. 30), תועבה, קוט (v. 31), כלם, and בוש (v. 32) that Israel either has or will experience in the sweep of exile-restoration.[96] Coming as it does in perhaps *the* theocentric chapter *par excellence* in Ezekiel, it is no wonder that the stress lies on the unworthiness of Israel/Judah in her restoration. The wider passage (Ezek 36:24–33) is worth reproducing in full (with vv. 31–33 in italic type):

> And I will take you from the nations and gather you together from all the lands, and I will bring you to your land. I will sprinkle clean water on you (מים טהורים), and you will be clean (וטהרתם). From all your uncleanness (טמאותיכם) and from all your dung pellets/idols I will cleanse (אטהר) you. And I will give you a new heart (לב חדש) and a new spirit I will put in you. I will take away your heart of stone (לב האבן) from your flesh and give you a heart of flesh (לב בשר). And I will put my Spirit in you and make it so you walk in my statutes (בחקי תלכו) and keep my judgments (ומשפטי תשמרו), and will you do them.

> You will dwell in the land that I gave to your fathers, and you will be my people, and I will be your God. And I will deliver you (והושעתי) from all your uncleanness (טמאותיכם), and I will call for the corn and I will make it plentiful, and I will not bring upon you famine. And I will multiply the fruit of the trees and the produce of the field, in order that you may not receive any longer the reproach of famine (חרפת רעב) among the nations.

> *And you will remember your evil ways (דרכיכם הרעים) and wantonness (מעלליכם), which were not good. And you will feel loathing in your faces (ונקטתם בפניכם) על עונתיכם and because of your abominations (תועבותיכם). Not for your sake am I doing this, declares the Lord Y*HWH*, let it be known to you. Be disappointed (בושו) and humiliated for your ways (מדרכיכם), house of Israel!*

> *Thus says Lord Y*HWH*: "On the day I cleanse (טהרי) you מכל עונתיכם, I will re-populate the cities, and the ruins will be built."*

In this passage the overlap of Deuteronomistic and Priestly categories is again evident. What is distinctive here, though, is the manner in which specific expressions associated with each concept sphere (or tradition) are integrated to such an extent that they virtually blur into one another.[97] Priestly language includes טהר, טמא, תועבה, and עון, while Deuteronomistic

---

95. Joyce, *Divine Initiative*, 129.

96. I analyze these terms in the previous chapter.

97. For a full analysis of shared terminology between Ezekiel, P/H, and D, see Risa Levitt Kohn, *A New Heart and a New Soul: Ezekiel, the Exile and the Torah* (JSOTSup 358; London: Sheffield Academic Press, 2002), esp. pp. 139–46.

language includes מְשׁפט ... שׁמר, ישׁע, לב, דרך, and מעלל, and על, "on account of." The fact that Ezekiel fuses the categories together so naturally
indicates that "Ezekiel evaluates the people's past behavior using the legal
standards of both P and D."[98]

Although a *direct* parallel between Deuteronomistic and Priestly traditions cannot be drawn with "moral" and "cultic," or with "guilt" and "shame"
(as the concepts cannot be equated with the traditions), there is more than
enough conceptual overlap to support the close and intertwined relationship of all three sets of concerns in Ezekiel. I will outline the implications
of this in the conclusion to the chapter.

עון + מן/כ

The remaining examples of עון + preposition do not require as much exegetical legwork to appreciate. עון + מן appears 3 times (Ezek 28:18; 36:33;
43:10) and means either "because of/arising from your iniquity" (28:18;
43:10), or "being cleansed from your iniquity" (36:33).[99] עון + כ appears twice
(both in Ezek 14:10), and communicates the shared condemnation of the
false prophet and the idolatrous enquirer.

There is one interesting aspect to, related to the conceptualization of
עון. The instance in Ezek 36:33, "I will cleanse you from all your iniquities"
utilizes the image of sin as "stain." As there are only three examples of עון +
טהר in the OT (as well as eight of טהר + חטאת), it hardly qualifies as a dominant image but it is still worthy of mention for its connections to the purgation ritual of Lev 16.[100] Greenberg notes that the shift from "uncleanness"
(טמאות) in Ezek 36:25 to "iniquities" (עונות) in Ezek 36:33 mirrors "the identical exchange of terms in the annual purgation ritual of Lev 16, vss. 16 and
21."[101]

עון + שׂים/נשׂא

The construction שׂים/נשׂא + עון appears seven times in Ezekiel (4:4 [2×],
5, 6; 14:10; 44:10, 12). I have already made note of Joseph Lam's work on the
construction עון + נשׂא in the semantic study of the OT above, where he
observes that Ezekiel uniformly uses the construction to mean "bear sin,"
in common with the Priestly material. Further, in my analysis of Ezek 4:5a
I suggested that the three examples of עון in Ezek 4:4–6 form a play on
words, from bearing "responsibility" (that is, accumulated culpability) to
"punishment" for sin. Here I will briefly note one further scholarly attempt
to understand the significance of the sign-act.

---

98. Ibid., 113.

99. In both contexts עון is associated with a sense of "distortedness." In Ezek 28:18, it
appears in conjunction with Tyre's with "unjust trade practices," while in Ezek 43:10 it is
used in the context of Israel's former idolatrous behavior in the temple.

100. Besides Ezek 36:33, עון + טהר appears in Josh 22:17 and Jer 33:8, while in Ps 51:4 they
appear in successive cola in parallel with חטאת and כבס, respectively.

101. Greenberg, *Ezekiel 21–37*, 732.

Some have taken Ezekiel's actions to indicate some form of atonement for Israel, perhaps due to similarities to the priest's actions in the *Yom Kippur* ceremonies (Lev 16:21–22).[102] However, it is difficult to see how such an understanding holds in light of Ezekiel's other prophecies of judgment on Israel/Judah. As Block notes, "Ezekiel's action cannot be interpreted as expiatory."[103] Rather, the sign-acts constitute a *mimesis* of Yhwh's judgment on Jerusalem via the Babylonian siege and exile. Within this framework, as we have already seen, sin is primarily conceived as a "weight" or "burden" with the gravest of consequences.

"Idiosyncratic" Constructions

נשא + ב + עון

The construction נשא + ב + עון appears only in Ezekiel, where it appears three times, all in close proximity (Ezek 18:19, 20 [2×]). The construction is difficult syntactically, rather than exegetically.[104] The LXX renders בעון with τὴν ἀδικίαν, reading the construction simply as נשא + עון. Lam, on the other hand, suggests that ב functions partitively and thus reads, "share in any of the guilt."[105] Either way, neither the meaning of עון nor the verses overall are greatly impacted by the idiosyncratic construction.

מכשול + עון

The word עון appears seven times in the construction מכשול עון (usually translated "stumbling block") in Ezekiel (7:19; 14:3, 4, 7; 18:30, 44:12 x2). מכשול is a favored term for Ezekiel, especially its appearance in construct with עון.[106] The idea of the term seems fairly straightforward—a "stumbling block"[107]—and is reminiscent of the use of עוה in Lam 3:9, "He has barred my way with hewn stones (גזית), he has twisted (עוה) my paths." Its use in Ezekiel, however, has proven difficult in interpretation. Derived from כשל, "to stumble, stagger," it first appears in Ezek 3:20 with Yhwh as the active agent: "When a righteous person turns away from his righteousness and does evil, and I place מכשול before him, he will die." Yhwh is also the causative agent in Ezek 21:20: "In order that heart(s) may melt and the

---

102. *B. Sanh.* 39a; cf. William H. Brownlee, *Ezekiel 1–19* (WBC 28; Waco, TX: Word, 1986), 66.

103. Block, *Ezekiel 1–24*, 177.

104. Although it does come in the theological storm-center of Ezek 18. For discussion of the theological issues and their resolutions, see the review of scholarship on Ezek 18 in ch. 2, pp. 4–8

105. Lam, *Sin Concept*, 198–99.

106. Eight of the 14 appearances of מכשול in the OT are in Ezekiel (3:20, 7:19, 14:3, 4, 7, 18:30, 21:20, 44:12), with six of those in the construction (pron. suff. +) מכשול עון, a construction unique to Ezekiel. The other instances of מכשול are Lev 19:14; 1 Sam 25:31; Ps 119:165; Isa 8:14; 57:14; and Jer 6:21.

107. From כשל; cf. Zimmerli, *Ezekiel 1–24*, 306.

stumbling blocks be made many (והרבה המכשלים), I have set at all the gates the slaughter of the sword."[108]

That YHWH is the one who puts the מכשול in place has raised exegetical and theological difficulties for some interpreters. Exegetically, in both of the above instances, it is not clear what the "stumbling block" exactly is. Theologically, it raises the issue of whether or not Ezekiel presents YHWH as in some way responsible for human sin, and the attendant questions concerning his character.[109] On this front, Blenkinsopp tentatively suggests that "the phrase has perhaps been added in explanation of what is involved in the mysterious impulse that leads a person to embrace evil (is it heredity, environment, or a combination of both? Is there a certain predestination to evil?)."[110] Block, on the other hand, attempts to resolve the theological issue by arguing that the LXX rendering βάσανον, "torment, suffering punishment" (as opposed to the more direct equivalent σκάνδαλον) is an intentional decision on the part of the translators, such that the מכשול "signifies a concrete equivalent to the death sentence,"[111] which avoids the implication that God is directly responsible for sin. In a similar vein, Allen suggests that the term was borrowed from Jer 6:21 and denotes "a fatal 'accident' that leads to [the sinner's] premature death."[112]

There is no doubt that the two references where מכשול appears in an absolute state have close association with death, but judging by the provisionality of all the explanations offered above, we are no closer, at this stage, to determining if the metaphor refers to something specific or remains ambiguous and evocative. Nor does it seem that the theological issue raised has as straightforward an answer from the text itself as Block suggests. In this regard, Blenkinsopp helpfully notes that "biblical statements about divine causality do not make the logical and philosophical distinctions—for example, between the absolute and the permissive will of God—which we would deem necessary."[113] Joyce also suggests that there is a sense in which a complete resolution is beyond our grasp: "The major contribution of Ezekiel consists in the fact that here [in the dynamic between divine sovereignty

---

108. The LXX has οἱ ἀσθενοῦντες, "the stumblers," while Targ. *mtqljhwn* likewise repoints to המכשולים.

109. Blenkinsopp calls it "theologically perplexing," while Block says, "Modern sentimental perceptions of God make Ezekiel's attribution of stumbling blocks in the paths of backsliders to Yahweh difficult to understand." He does go on, however, to note that the concept is not unique (or even original) to Ezekiel, citing similar examples from Isa 8:14 and Jer 6:21. See Joseph Blenkinsopp, *Ezekiel* (Louisville: John Knox, 1990), 30; Block, *Ezekiel 1–24*, 147.

110. Blenkinsopp, *Ezekiel*, 30.

111. Block, *Ezekiel 1–24*, 147.

112. Allen, *Ezekiel 1–19*, 49. Allen does not engage as explicitly with the theological issue as Block and Blenkinsopp.

113. Blenkinsopp, *Ezekiel*, 30.

and human responsibility] everything rests ultimately on the mysterious nature of the God who acts that it might be known that 'I am Yahweh.'"[114]

The theological issue notwithstanding, Block and Allen are correct to note the close association of the מכשול with death, and thus to view it (at least in part) as consequential (or responsive) to "the righteous [person] turning from their righteousness."[115] Furthermore, as Block points out, the primary focus of ch. 3 is "not on the fate of the *nouveau méchant* but the response of the sentry,"[116] which entails warning the wicked in order that they might not encounter the stumbling block.

In contrast to the difficulties of מכשול in the absolute state in Ezekiel, its use in the construction מכשול עון is much clearer. In four of the instances in Ezekiel, the construction is the predicate of a specific subject: מכשול עון refers to the now useless silver and gold of the dispossessed Judahites (7:19); the sins (פשעים) of the Judahites potentially rendering them liable to YHWH's judgment (Ezek 18:30) and; "the Levites who went far" from YHWH and led the Israelites astray via their idolatrous worship (Ezek 44:12).

The three examples in Ezek 14 do not predicate an explicit subject, but the implied subject is reasonably clear from the context. In Ezek 14 the "elders of Israel" (זקני ישראל, presumably the elders of the Judean exiles) come to Ezekiel seeking a word from the prophet.[117] In response, Ezekiel is given a two-part answer; in v. 3 he is privately given YHWH's insight into the state of the elders before him, and in v. 4–11 he is given the statement he is to report to the elders, which takes the form of the quasi-legal language akin to the commissioning narratives (Ezek 3, 33) and the so-called "individual responsibility" narrative in Ezek 18. The three appearances of מכשול עון (Ezek 14:3, 4, 7) have the same sense each time and serve as an interesting counterpoint to the use of מכשול in the absolute state analysed above.

While in Ezek 3:20 YHWH places the מכשול before the Israelites (ונתתי מכשול לפניו), in Ezek 14 the human actors themselves are responsible (ומכשול עונם נתנו נכח פניהם). Further, where Ezek 3:20 leaves the exact nature of the מכשול ambiguous, two factors in the instances in Ezek 14 suggest a more explicit meaning. First, there is a clear association with idolatry, by virtue of the parallel with the phrase "set up idols in their inner selves (העלו

---

114. Joyce, *Divine Initiative*, 129.

115. The syntax of the verse (inf. cst. + *weqatal* chain) supports this conclusion. The *weqatal* chain continues the sense of the initial inf. cst. clause and is interrupted by the final, resultant *x-yiqtol* clause, הוא ימות.

116. Block, *Ezekiel 1–24*, 147.

117. Exactly what issue was at hand is left unstated in the text. Block, however, notes that the phrase ישב לפני elsewhere indicates an official meeting with regard to a specific communal concern (ibid., 425). Zimmerli suggests that Ezek 14 is a continuation of the similar episode in Ezek 8:1: "Is it the expectation of a turning point for the 'house of Israel,' completely defeated after 587, which brings them to the prophet? Or do they expect, as in 8:1; 20:1, an assurance of deliverance for the still intact Jerusalem?" (Zimmerli, *Ezekiel 1–24*, 306).

(גלוליהם על־לבם)."[118] Second, the construct relationship indicates some form of genitival relationship that closely associates the meaning of the two concepts: it is "the stumbling block of their iniquity (מכשול עונם)."

In this regard, Block translates מכשול עון taking עון with an adjectival force: "his/their iniquitous stumbling block,"[119] while Allen suggests a causative relationship between the two terms: "that which has made them fall into iniquity."[120] It seems, however, more straightforward to take the construct chain in an epexegetical or appositional sense — "the stumbling block of (that is) their/his iniquity."[121] In other words, in Ezek 14:3–7 the stumbling block here *is* the iniquity of the people, which they themselves are the active agents in setting up before their own faces. Any stumbling that occurs, if Yнwн either chooses not to answer (Ezek 14:3), or answers in judgment (Ezek 14:7), is entirely their own responsibility.

The appearance of מכשול עון in Ezek 14:4, while having the same meaning and following the same structure as in Ezek 14:3 and Ezek 14:7 (that is, person/people . . . set up idols . . . put stumbling block . . . consultation episode . . . Yнwн's response), nonetheless seems to be used in a slightly different sense. Where all three of Yнwн's responses have a strong sense of indictment, in Ezek 14:3 and 7 it is pervasive. By contrast, in Ezek 14:5–6 the intent of Yнwн's answer is "to lay hold of the hearts of the house of Israel," which issues further in a call to repentance. In the shadow of judgment, the exilic community is promised a place and Yнwн's future but also is warned that by no means does this exempt them from the need to turn back to him.[122]

In summary, the use of מכשול עון is mutually illuminative of Ezekiel's use of both terms individually. In terms of מכשול, whatever the theological challenges that appear in its meaning, it is used in the book to denote a significant "barrier" to positive relationship with Yнwн and hence to life and blessing. As such, it holds a close association with "death." As Zimmerli argues, the phrase confirms that, for Ezekiel, עון was the "great problem upon which life turns," as stumbling into guilt excluded one from the cultic comminity, and therefore from "life."[123]

זכר + עון

There are three examples of עון + זכר in Ezekiel (21:28, 29; 29:16, all Hiphil). There are slightly different nuances in the nature of "remembering"

---

118. For further reflection on the use of גלולים in Ezekiel, see idem, *Ezekiel 1–24*, 187.

119. Block, *Ezekiel 1–24*, 421.

120. Allen, *Ezekiel 1–19*, 187.

121. Cf. *GKC* §130e, Bill T. Arnold and John H. Choi, *A Guide to Biblical Hebrew Syntax* (Cambridge: Cambridge University Press, 2003), 10–11; Bruce K. Waltke and Michael Patrick O'Connor, *An Introduction to Biblical Hebrew Syntax* (Winona Lake, IN: Eisenbrauns, 1990), 151. For an extended discussion of nominal genitive relationships in general, see Daniel B. Wallace, *Greek Grammar Beyond the Basics: an Exegetical Syntax of the New Testament* (Grand Rapids: Zondervan, 1996), 95–100.

122. On this front, see further Renz, *Rhetorical Function*, 73.

123. Zimmerli, *Ezekiel 1–24*, 306.

(זכר) between the appearances in Ezek 21 and the single example in Ezek 29:16. The last is fairly straightforward and can be dealt with briefly. There, Ezekiel declares that Egypt's ruin will be "a reminder of iniquity" for Israel because they put their trust (מבטח) in Egypt. Greenberg suggests that the verse is an application of Ps 40:5: "Blessed is the man who makes Yнwн his trust, and does not turn to רהבים ["the arrogant," a play on words with Egypt, רהב]."[124] In terms of the meaning of עון, of interest here is its conception in highly relational terms, as "misplaced trust." Israel had "twisted" its gaze away from Yнwн, its true lord (cf. אדני יהוה, Ezek 29:13), and turned (פנה) instead to Egypt for deliverance.

In both instances in Ezek 21, the construction conveys the "exposure" of culpability in the impending destruction of Jerusalem by Nebuchadnezzar. Ezek 21:28 concerns the Jerusalemites' sham orthodoxy. They scoffed at Nebuchadnezzar's pagan divination practices and his resulting decision to come against Jerusalem rather than Rabbah (כקסום־שוא בעיניהם והיה להם),[125] believing themselves to be under Yнwн's protection. In reality, however, Nebuchadnezzar was Yнwн's sword against Jerusalem (Ezek 21:1–28). His successful campaign exposed their culpability before God.[126]

In Ezek 21:29, the same thought is revisited, but this time the agent of exposure is the Jerusalemites themselves (יען הזכרכם עונכם; cf. Ezek 21:28 והוא־מזכיר עון, i.e., Nebuchadnezzar). As Block notes, "The cumulative effect of their crimes is emphasized by heaping up four designations for the offenses" (עלילות, חטאות, פשעים, עון),[127] as well as three verbs reflecting the manner in which these offenses reveal the reality of their state before Yнwн (ראה, גלה, זכר).

The construction is instructive for several reasons. First, in this context there are clear connections between the meaning of זכר + עון and shame, whether defined in terms of psychology or SSAs. Chiefly, this is because central to both definitions are the notions of (unwanted) exposure and failure. In psychological shame, the exposure concerns a revelation of an individual psyche's failure to live up to its ideal self. In SSA shame, it concerns exposure/humiliation before a PCR. The meaning of the construction in this context thus lies closer to contemporary definitions of shame than several of the instances that are normally considered shame vocabulary.

Second, although the construction's *meaning* lies closer to contemporary definitions of shame, its *terminology* lies in the realms of guilt. Guilt is usually classified in terms of agency and the transgression of legal standards, and both חטאת and פשע are prominent in the Deuteronomistic "quasi-legal" passages in Ezekiel (Ezek 18, 33). As such, the construction further supports the necessity of understanding the interconnectedness of guilt and shame,

---

124. Greenberg, *Ezekiel 21–37*, 607.
125. *Qere* כקסם.
126. Cf. Greenberg, *Ezekiel 21–37*, 431.
127. Block, *Ezekiel 1–24*, 689.

in both ancient and contemporary contexts. Furthermore, it is indicative of the relationship between the two in Ezekiel's conception: shame occurs when guilt (that is, transgression) is exposed. The exposure of the people's rebellion results in an exposure of their true state before YHWH.[128]

This last observation finds significant points of contact with the tendency in contemporary formulations to distinguish between shame and guilt on the basis that shame concerns the whole person, while guilt concerns the act.[129] This distinction is helpful to a degree, but as I have argued throughout this study, only if the two (act and being) are held together as aspects of a unified whole.

Additionally, and critically, the passage reinforces (in distinction to contemporary formulations) that YHWH is the determiner of the content of both guilt and shame. In terms of guilt, the transgressions of YHWH's statutes, rather than an individualized moral code or "conscience," are condemned. In terms of shame, YHWH, rather than the individual psyche or the PCR, is the observing other and the determiner of what is ideal and honorable. As Greenberg notes, "the tribunal before whom 'iniquity is brought to mind' is God."[130]

Finally, it is important to note that the consequence of shame in this context does not have primarily to do with emotions or feelings (although these may be expected to be included). Rather, the consequence of shameful exposure is YHWH's judgment (that is the punishment of exile).

עת + עון + קץ

The construction עת + עון + קץ, unique to Ezekiel, appears three times, in Ezek 21:30, 34 (also in association with יום) and 35:5, In each case, it means "the time for punishment has (finally) come." Block notes that the phrase "is pregnant with meaning, speaking not only of the moment of . . . punishment but also the termination of . . . iniquitous behavior."[131] The multivalency of the phrase supports the straightforward view of "guilt" and "justice" that undergirds the OT, as noted in the discussions of Koch and Barton reviewed above: that which is עון will be met with עון.

Other Guilt-Related Terms in Ezekiel: חטא, אשם, פשע

There are 43 examples of חטא in Ezekiel (16 verbal forms, חטאת 26 times, and חטא once). In Ezek 1–39 all verbal forms are in the *qal* stem and

---

128. Ibid.

129. E.g., the influential presentations in Gerhart Piers and Milton B. Singer, *Shame and Guilt: A Psychoanalytic and a Cultural Study* (American Lecture Series 171; American Lectures in Psychiatry; Springfield: Norton, 1953); Helen B. Lewis, *Shame and Guilt in Neurosis* (New York: International Universities Press, 1971). See further the literature review throughout ch. 3 above.

130. Greenberg, *Ezekiel 21–37*, 431.

131. Block, *Ezekiel 1–24*, 690.

all instances refer to "sin," while in Ezek 40–48 all verbal forms are in the Piel and refer to purification rituals. The nominal חטאת refers to the sin offering. In Ezek 1–39, the verb חטא can refer to both specific sins (for example, "the sin of your idolatry," Ezek 23:49), and as a general term for "sin" (which stands in contrast with צדק/צדקה, "righteousness," e.g., Ezek 3:20). The nominal form חטאת shares a similar semantic range to עון (for example, חטאת also appears with ב, indicating its conception as a "realm" associated with death, in Ezek 3:20; 18:24).[132]

The word אשם appears eight times in Ezekiel, four verbal instances (all *qal*) and four nominal instances. The four nominal forms (אשם) appear in Ezek 40–48 and refer to the "guilt/reparation offering." Three of the four verbal forms (Ezek 22:4; 25:12 [twice]) mean "become guilty," that is, become culpable for punishment. The final verbal form (ויאשמו), occurring in Ezek 6:6, refers to "desecration" of Israel's altars, although some have suggested that the word should be taken as וישמו, from שמם ("to devastate").[133]

The word פשע appears 13 times in Ezekiel, and shares a similar semantic sphere to חטאת (in Ezek 1–39) and עון. Its semantic "center of gravity" possesses the sense of "rebellion" (for example, Ezek 2:3; 20:38, appearing with מרד, "to rebel") and "offense against" (for example, Ezek 37:23, appearing with שקוץ, "vile things," and גלול, "feces/idols").

Overall, there is a great deal of overlap and sharing of semantic spheres in Ezekiel's "guilt" terminology, although they may sometimes be used in close proximity to each other, presumably having distinct nuances in those cases (for example, Ezek 21:29). However, all have in common that they are "actual" offenses (that is, primarily "objective," over and above "subjective"), and that they are offenses "before YHWH" (in relation to his observation, standard, and verdict).

Constructing an Emic View of עוה *in Ezekiel*

From the above analysis, I have observed that עוה in Ezekiel incorporates a range of associated concepts and metaphors to express that which does not accord with patterns of relationship appropriate to YHWH's character, expressed especially with regard to Israel/Judah in terms of the covenant stipulations. Ezekiel's main use of עוה, as vocabulary characteristic of P/H, utilizes the Priestly conceptions of sin as "burden," "defilement," and "realm (of death)." As such, Ezekiel views עוה as that which is contrary to holiness, leading to the climactic punishment/restoration oracle in Ezek

---

132. It should be noted, however, that its "center of gravity" possesses the activity of transgression (e.g., Ezek 16:51) or faithlessness to YHWH (e.g., Ezek 18:24).

133. *BHS* apparatus; Greenberg, *Ezekiel 1–20*, 133; cf. Jacob Milgrom, *Leviticus 1–16: A New Translation with Introduction and Commentary* (AYB 3; New York: Doubleday, 1991), 339–341, who defends אשם.

36, with its expression of radical theocentricity *par excellence*. YHWH acts in restoration for his holy name alone.

However, Ezekiel also utilizes terms and concepts drawn from D, indicting Israel for her "ways and deeds." Thus his conception of עוה includes that which we would term "moral," or "ethical." However, Ezekiel's "radical theocentricity" leaves no room for YHWH to be subject to any other authority in his judgment. For Ezekiel, then, עוה is ultimately what YHWH deems it to be, punishment meted out according to his standard. On the other hand, great care is taken to qualify this with an important controlling factor: YHWH is not capricious or malicious in his judgment; rather, YHWH's way is just, and he takes "no pleasure in the death of the wicked" (cf. Ezek 18:23, 25), in accordance with his own character.

Ultimately, then, according to Ezek 36, although YHWH acts for the holiness of his name alone, and although עון must be met with עון in his determination and thus eliminated, the ultimate end for which YHWH acts is not the elimination of his people, but in order that whatever *prevents* relationship with him may be eliminated. As such, in Ezekiel's final grand vision of restoration, covenant relations are reestablished (as the temple is rebuilt and the sacrificial system reinstated, Ezek 40–44), creation (beginning from the renewed temple) is restored (Ezek 45:1–48:29) and, finally, YHWH is able to dwell permanently with his people (Ezek 48:30–35). For all its severity, then, Ezekiel ends on a triumphant note: עון has been properly dealt with, the city and its people cleansed and restored, the glory has returned: יהוה שמה.

Imposed Etic and Emic B Part 3: Points of Contact and Divergence

SSAs have tended to focus on shame rather than guilt in their research. As a result, the theme of guilt does not usually feature highly in their models of social construction. Rather than weigh up the SSA model in terms of "agreement and disagreement," then, I will use the more appropriate categories of "points of contact and divergence." I will also engage with the distinction between guilt and shame in psychology where appropriate.

Points of Contact: Guilt and the Problem of Objectivity

I have noted the insight of Zeba Crook into the notion of the PCR with regard to the honor/shame model, and the manner in which, in a "collectivistic" culture it "becomes the first, last and, only arbiter of honorable and shameful behavior."[134] I have also noted the ascerbic nature of his concluding reflection: "The PCR attributes honor to those with inherent honor, and distributes honor to those who stand out honorable. It is the final

---

134. Crook, "Honor Revisited," 599.

arbiter of all things honorable and shameful; it is answerable to no one. It is, ironically, not a democracy but a tyranny."[135]

What I wish to observe here, though, is how transferrable the idea of the PCR is to the notion of "guilt." Guilt, as we have seen, is often taken as characteristic of "individualistic" societies, is guided by "conscience" and, as alluded to by Crook, seems a more "democratic," "objective," or autonomous ethical basis by which to live, independent of the assessments of others. However, as explored in ch. 3, this distinction is somewhat an illusion, for even the internal "conscience" is generated in response to the moral code of an external authority; in other words, a PCR (in the standard psychological formulations, the imposition of the parents' moral standards). Moreover, as some recent fights for human rights expose (for example, the debate concerning "marriage equality"), the concept of "objective rights" is often simply a clash of differing moral/ethical codes; in other words, competing PCRs.

This in turn cannot help but demand a modification in our understanding of guilt. The tendency to assign it to the realm of objectivity (in opposition to subjective shame) is reflective of a worldview in which natural law—impartial and impersonal—reigns supreme. In this chapter I have briefly reviewed the work of two OT scholars in this area (i.e. Koch and Barton) who, although differing from each other in substantial ways, both share in common a form of natural law holding sway even over YHWH. However, a closer analysis of guilt terminology in the Bible, and especially in Ezekiel's radically theocentric world, indicates that to make sense of guilt in the Bible, it must be seen in relation to YHWH's standards, to the DCR. Biblically speaking, guilt is relational, and the reference of its relativity is YHWH's judgment.[136] In this way, Crook's analysis of the allocentric nature of shame can be equally applied to guilt. In Ezekiel's world, guilt is what YHWH, the DCR, says it is.

On the other hand, Ezekiel's presentation—especially in light of Barton's argument regarding natural law in Ezek 18—may also challenge Crook's rather inescapably negative assessment of the PCR: a "tyranny," by definition can never be just. Ezekiel, however, claims both that YHWH is completely sovereign (that is the DCR/true PCR), *and* that his ways are publicly just (תכן, e.g., Ezek 18:25, 29). In attempting to understand how this may be resolved in the mind of Ezekiel (or his editors), the logical ordering of the concepts is critical in understanding the relationship between YHWH and justice: the priority lies in YHWH's own character in determining what justice and, consequently, guilt are. However, once so determined, YHWH can be seen to be true to his own standards. In this manner, guilt can be construed as objective.

---

135. Ibid., 611.
136. See further Wong, *Idea of Retribution*; di Vito, "OT Anthropology."

Face-to-Face Communities

As an extension of the above point, SSAs have also drawn attention to the distinctive relational patterns of "face to face" communities, and the importance of nonjuridical factors in establishing and maintaining community relations in these contexts. As Peristiany states, in these contexts: "relations are of paramount importance and . . . the social identity of the actor is as significant as his office." [137] To adopt the phraseology used in this study, appropriate patterns of relationship include complex dynamics of relationship. Applied to the notions of justice and retribution, these considerations helpfully demonstrate that they cannot be completely encapsulated in or subsumed under juridical categories.

On this front, Wong, Joyce, and Mein have all helpfully explored the complexity of Ezekiel's ethical framework and its relationship to the figure of YHWH in the book. [138] Wong, in particular, has highlighted three conceptual frameworks for retribution evident in the book: covenant, impurity, and poetic justice. That these can all be conceived of as "justice" indicates that moving toward a more satisfying understanding of biblical ethics and guilt will require a reexamination of so-called Western notions of these ideas that undergirds much contemporary biblical scholarship.

Points of Divergence: The Universality of Guilt

SSAs have tended to drive a strong wedge between ancient and modern, mediterranean and Western cultures, although some more recent and sensitive studies have improved in this area. As with most new methodologies, initial excitement in discovery leads to an overenthusiastic application, before a more balanced perspective is stimulated by discussion and critique.

Unfortunately, the initial honor/shame model developed by Malina, although it has been adjusted and refined, persists in unhelpful polarities (honor vs. shame, shame vs. guilt), and definitions that cloud the interconnectedness of these important concepts. The broad adoption of the model (that is, "The Bible was written in an honor/shame culture") by mainstream scholarship, although superficially helpful in describing social dynamics that are different from contemporary Western culture, is ultimately a misleading one.

After all, shame is not unique to Eastern/Mediterranean cultures, as even the writers of *Honour and Shame* recognized, "as all societies evaluate conduct by comparing it to ideal standards of action, all societies have their own form of honor and shame." [139] The statement, however, also betrays the fact that all societies have their own form of guilt: of determining what is wrong action (that is, transgression of ideal standards of action). Different

---

137. Peristiany, "Introduction," 11.

138. Wong, *Idea of Retribution*; Joyce, *Divine Initiative*; Mein, *Ethics of Exile*.

139. Peristiany, "Introduction," 10.

cultures simply construe the values according to their different social norms and ideals, and impose correspondingly different forms of penalty and praise.

Conclusion

The analysis in this chapter demonstrates that the meaning of עוה in Ezekiel cannot be equated with guilt, any more than בוש can be equated with shame, or כבד can be equated with honor. Rather, in common with its use elsewhere in the OT, its meaning spans the entire range of the sin-consequence spectrum, revolving around its foundational notion of twistedness, or perversion.

To be sure, עוה can be used to convey the concept of guilt, including the emotional response to awareness of transgression (real or imagined) in contemporary psychological formulations. However, when עוה designates, or includes this emotional dimension, it both converges and diverges with psychological definitions at critical points. From the review of shame and guilt in ch. 3, I observed that Freud was, in a sense, correct to view guilt as the imposition of the moral code of the parents/God (superego) on the id-driven ego. It is not difficult to see how formulations, driven by the individualistic ideal of self-realization, would thus construe guilt as inherently negative, needing to be cast aside for wholeness and fulfillment.

Ezekiel, by contrast, calls on his audience to *reclaim* a proper sense of guilt, by lining themselves up against God's standard. This is because in the biblical material, as we have seen, "moral competence belongs only to Yhwh...[thus] only a species of heteronomy can be the basis for morality."[140] Since this is the case, in the biblical estimation a person (or community/nation) *should* be aware of and feel guilty in their עון, but only Yhwh himself establishes what עון is and what it is not.

At its heart, then, עוה is that which is twisted, that is, what does not accord with the character of Yhwh. This can be expressed as a general term (especially singular), or in specifics. It is also dependent on the particular relationship established between Yhwh and the subject (nations, and more specifically Israel). At its core, though, because Yhwh is life, עוה is that which distorts or rejects life, hence its conceptualization as a realm, and that particularly associated with death.

Furthermore, the analysis in this chapter demonstrates that עוה also spans both guilt and shame concepts. In this sense, the delineation of two distinct categories of psychological or sociological concepts, usually formulated with polarizing terminology (that is, why guilt *isn't* shame and vice versa), is a largely unhelpful development. Creating categories for distinguishing aspects of the concept cluster may be a helpful way to further understanding, but not at the expense of their essential unity.

---

140. Di Vito, "OT Anthropology," 235.

To return to the analogical terminology in BH, it is clear that עוה and בוש in reference to Yнwн's relationship with his people, are very closely related. בוש tends slightly more toward the category of emotion, given its base meaning of "disappointment" or "failure." Also, we can grant that עוה is more associated with particular acts than בוש, but this is not always the case. What we have then, is perhaps best conceptualized as overlapping polysemic entities that have slightly different semantic centers of gravity. Accordingly, the concepts that accompany them (guilt and shame) likewise share a common bond—their relation to Yнwн and his character as פקד עון חסד ואמת; אל נשא עון . . .; or, to put it in other words, כבוד יהוה.

Chapter 7

Conclusion: Derived Etic

We are now in a position to draw the threads of this study together. The aim of this monograph has been to examine the concepts of honor, shame, and guilt in the OT, with a special focus on Ezekiel. To this end, I appropriated recent SSAs in a critically appreciative manner: incorporating the benefits of honor/shame models, while also examining how these approaches might be strengthened.

A method was developed from the categories of emics and etics (ch. 2), in order to examine Ezekiel's key terms for honor (כבד), shame (בוש), and guilt (עון). Incorporating the researcher's own perspective in the process, the main elements in method were identified as "emic A" (the researcher's own cultural context and concepts), the "imposed etic" (the interpretive framework and models initially used to approach the object of study), "emic B" (the cultural context and concepts of the object of study), the "derived etic" (the modified interpretive framework and models resulting from interaction with the object of study), and "emic A1" (the impact of the process and derived etic on the researcher's own cultural context and conceptualities). The advantages of a recursive, or iterative, application of the method were also noted.

The study first examined the development of the honor/shame model (that is, the imposed etic) in its contexts of modern psychological and anthropological research on shame and guilt (that is, emic A, ch. 3). The main body of the study consisted of three iterations of the method, each analyzing a key term in the study (ch. 4: כבד; ch. 5: בוש; ch. 6: עון) in light of the imposed etic. Each chapter began with an OT-wide survey of the meanings of the term, followed by close examination of its instances in Ezekiel, and then coverage of other terms sharing its semantic sphere.[1] This analysis provided the basis to move toward the meaning of the term in its context (emic B). Wider reflection and engagement with the gains and dangers in the honor/shame and psychological models facilitated development of the derived etic, and its affect on emic A1. A brief summary of the results of each chapter follows.

---

1. Ch. 4 also included a restatement and further examination of the meaning and significance of honor in SSA formulations, as the main focus in the previous chapter lay on the other two key terms, *shame* and *guilt*. Chapter 4 also included justification for a canonical interpretive framework for approaching the text of Ezekiel.

כבד (*Chapter 4*)

The basic meaning of כבד in the OT is "to be heavy." כבד was observed to have both substantive and responsive aspects to its meaning. Substantively, כבד can denote weight, posessions, significance, splendor, and character.[2] "Responsively, כבד can denote reverence, reward, and repute. There may also be several facets of each aspect of meaning intertwined in particular occurrences. The analysis also demonstrated that in the biblical material, Yʜwʜ was held to be the ultimate owner, assessor, and distributor of כבד.[3] Furthermore, the theophany in Exod 33–34 was examined for its place as the nexus of כבד in the OT.

In the analysis of Ezekiel, the occurrences of כבד (along with other OT honor terms) spanned several of the categories in the overall semantic sphere. However, the main use of the term revolved around the person of Yʜwʜ, and most often occurred in the theophanic construction כבוד יהוה which (as also in the foundational Exod 33–34 theophany) formed the nexus of כבד in Ezekiel, and indicated the source and nature of its content: Yʜwʜ himself. The work of Hamilton was appropriated as aptly summarizing the Yʜwʜ-centric nature of כבד in Ezekiel, its centrality in the message of the book, and the particular notion of honor that it generated: "The center of Ezekiel's theology is the glory of God in salvation through judgment as Yahweh acts for the sake of his name, saving to show mercy and judging to show holiness, that all might know that he is Yahweh."[4]

In light of the analysis of Ezekiel, I then returned to note areas of agreement and disagreement with the imposed etic, the honor/shame model. I noted in agreement that Yʜwʜ's honor, and its acknowledgement by all, was of central importance to Ezekiel and that SSAs have thus been helpful in highlighting honor in the context of the book as a pivotal value, drawing attention to and reflecting fruitfully on the nature of the concept. I also noted that the SSA stress on the social nature of human beings formed an important critique of modern cultures in which the individual is viewed as an independent, isolated entity.

However, I also noted prominent areas of disagreement. Primarily, SSA models of honor have not accounted very well for the figure of Yʜwʜ and his place in the honor system, as the systems are both anthropologically (rather than theologically) defined, and (in Herzfeld's terms) are not particularized according to indigenous definitions. In the case of Ezekiel, that means in regard to Yʜwʜ and his character of חסד ואמת as the source and

---

2. Weight, with the associated concepts substance, density, and severity. Posessions, with the associated concepts wealth and abundance. Significance, with the associated concept status. Splendor, with the associated concept magnificence. Character, with the associated concept (good) name.

3. Cf. Stiebert, *Construction of Shame*, 88.

4. Hamilton, *God's Glory*, 106.

definition of כבד. Further, SSA models did not account well for types of honor (primarily to do with honor before YHWH) ill-fitted to a zero-sum, agonistic view. Finally, SSA models fell short in accounting for aspects of YHWH's honor not being subject to any human PCR but standing over and against them (that is, the DCR).

The chapter concluded by noting כבד covered a broader range of concepts than honor, which was one aspect of its semantic range. I also observed that honor is ultimately a vague notion, needing its content filled out and defined according to the values of authoritative body in the context (that is, the PCR/DCR). In Ezekiel's conception, the answer to the question "what is honor/worth?" was simply YHWH himself, and the appropriate response of his creatures to him.

בוש (*Chapter 5*)

In ch. 5, I turned to analysis of בוש. Drawing on the insights of Avrahami, I noted that the basic concept behind the word, rather than shame, was "disappointment." Under this umbrella, the range of meaning of בוש spanned "dismay," "failure,"[5] and also "shame," although it was noted that the concept was often more strongly communicated by contextual factors than by בוש itself.

The analysis of Ezekiel demonstrated that, although בוש appears infrequently in Ezekiel, its placement at critical points made it an important term in the description of the Israelites relationship with YHWH. The main sense of בוש in Ezekiel (Ezek 16:52, 63; 36:32) concerned the prediction (Ezek 16:63) or command of YHWH (Ezek 16:52, 36:32) for the Jerusalemites to "be disappointed" in themselves, bringing down a previously overinflated self-perception before YHWH. Other shame terminology demonstrated a similar range of meaning to בוש, expressing anything from public humiliation to the emotion of self-loathing due to an awareness of falling short of an ideal.

After the analysis of Ezekiel, I turned to consider some wider associations of בוש in formulating a derived etic. Drawing on Douglas's work on defilement, along with Avrahami's on semantics, it was observed that בוש was indirectly, rather than directly linked to כבד by virtue of Israel's covenant with YHWH, the holy God. Douglas's key concept, "dirt is matter out of place," was appropriated to explain the manner in which YHWH's name had been put out of its proper place by Israel's conduct. Israel had failed to reflect YHWH's holiness (expressed in his כבד) to the nations by her conduct, instead defiling YHWH's name and distorting his image before the world. I also suggested that עוה functions as a link between כבד and בוש, indicating by analogy that shame concepts could not finally be separated from guilt concepts.

---

5. Dismay, with the associated concepts disillusionment or despair. Failure, with the associated concepts frustration and embarrassment.

עוה *(Chapter 6)*

In ch. 6, I examined the third key term in the study, עוה. Analysis of the OT explored its semantic range, built around the concept of "twistedness:" "bending," "sin," "guilt,"[6] "debt," and "punishment (for sin)." I also explored the manner in which עוה in the biblical material is defined primarily by the terms of YHWH's covenant with his people, and the use of עון + נשא to denote both "to bear responsibility for sin" and "to forgive sin."

Analysis of עוה and other guilt terminology in Ezekiel demonstrated that the word is primarily used in the book to express that which does not accord with patterns of relationship appropriate to YHWH's character, expressed particularly with regard to Jerusalem in the terms of the Sinai covenant. Ezekiel's use of עוה also integrated both P/H and D traditions and thus, analogously (although not completely parallel terms), cultic and moral categories, and shame and guilt concepts.

After analysis of Ezekiel, I moved toward constructing a derived etic view of guilt. I noted the points of contact and divergence with contemporary formulations of both guilt and shame, and concluded that both of the key terms עוה ("iniquity") and בוש ("disappointment") in Ezekiel were associated with (but not limited to) shame and guilt concepts and were unified by their determination according to YHWH's character, his כבד.

Statement of Derived Etic:
The Relationship of Honor, Shame, and Guilt in Ezekiel

In the development of this study's methodology, I noted the manner in which the interests emic to the researcher impacted the etic models used and the particular focus they brought to the analysis of the object of study. One of the main stimuli for this study—personal fascination with SSAs due to a mixed cultural heritage—has helped determined the parameters for this study. Beginning with an imposed etic that appropriated the psychological model of the distinction between shame and guilt and the SSA model of honor/shame, the study has demonstrated that a more appropriate, derived etic requires a different articulation of the relationship between the three concepts. This may be stated as follows.

I begin with the concept of honor. Honor may be best described as the value or worth of an entity in the eyes of the determining body of authority.[7] Biblically speaking, honor is one aspect of the broader semantic sweep of כבד. As YHWH is the source, owner, and giver of כבד (that is, the ultimate determining body of authority), honor is ultimately defined and measured

---

6. Bending, with the associated concept distortion. Sin, with the associated concepts iniquity and offence against. Guilt in the sense of culpability or responsibility for sin.

7. As adumbrated in terms of the PCR in Crook, "Honor Revisited"; deSilva, *Despising Shame*.

according to his standards. Thus, while there may be many (human) PCRs with different, perhaps competing definitions of what is honorable, in the worldview expressed across the OT they are all finally subject to the DCR. Y HWH alone determines what is finally and truly honorable.[8]

However, כבד is also a description of Y HWH's own person and character. He is, in the terms of Exod 34:6–7, אל נשא עון ... רב־חסד ואמת; פקד עון, and as Creator and Lord, his actions express his substantive כבד to his creation. The goal of creation, in turn, is to respond, that is, receive and return, Y HWH's כבד, being blessed by him and blessing him in return. Honor, from this perspective, is those patterns of relationship and activity that confirm or augment Y HWH's כבד and its blessings in his creation. Understood in this manner, honor *can* be taken as a pivotal value in the biblical documents, by virtue of its association with and definition by Y HWH.

Shame is also a concept of critical importance in human and human-divine relationships. However, in biblical conceptuality shame does not stand in binary opposition to either honor or guilt. Rather than being defined primarily with regard to the individual self, as an emotion (the pain and embarrassment of failing to attain to the ideal self), or with regard to the community, as a social state (being demoted in status or socially excluded by the PCR), shame, like honor, is defined with regard to Y HWH.

Thus, though shame may include both emotion and social state, it is better seen as an aspect of the broader semantic category of בוש, best described as disappointment, or "the experience of a disconnection between expectations and reality."[9] As such, בוש is indirectly (but still closely) related to כבד, and especially Y HWH's כבד. בוש appears when there is a fundamental disruption to Y HWH's intended goal for creation, to receive and return his כבד.

Within this framework, it can be seen why Y HWH can never truly be shamed in the OT.[10] When there is any disruption to Y HWH's intended state of affairs for creation, the failure is never his, because he is the God of חסד ואמת, who is always true to his word and his people. Granted, there are instances where there seems to be some danger of Y HWH failing in his obligations (for example, some of the lament psalms), and were this to eventuate in reality, it seems reasonable to infer that Y HWH might experience בוש as a "disappointing entity."[11] However, as Avrahami has demonstrated (at least for the psalms, although her examples range beyond that corpus), the

---

8. Stiebert, *Construction of Shame*, 88. Cf, 1 Cor 4:3–5.

9. Avrahami, "בוש in the Psalms," 308.

10. Cf. Stiebert, *Construction of Shame*, 96–98.

11. Avrahami, "בוש in the Psalms," 309. For example of scholars who suggest that Y HWH is (or at least is susceptible to) shame, see Bechtel, "Perception of Shame"; Yvonne Sherwood, *The Prostitute and the Prophet: Hosea's Marriage in Literary-Theoretical Perspective* (JSOTSup 212; GCT 2; Sheffield: Sheffield Academic Press, 1996); Hobbs, "Reflections on Honor." For a response, at least regarding the character of Y HWH in Isaiah, see the discussion in Stiebert, *Construction of Shame*, 96–98.

thrust of the appeals that are expressed are undergirded by "the absolute trust of the psalmist in the divine aid . . . [in] the summons to Yahweh."[12]

Shame, then, where it is actually ascribed or commanded, refers to YHWH's disappointment at his people's failure to respond appropriately to his כבד, in their ways and deeds.[13] Furthermore, as his כבד also establishes the patterns and parameters for what is appropriate, their failure renders them "out of place" in his social system—defiled, and thus unable to participate in YHWH's blessing.[14]

YHWH's כבד is also critical in determining the nature of guilt and its relationship to shame. Although Ezekiel's presentation of YHWH is often characterized as unique among—even at odds with—the other portraits of him in the OT, in the final analysis, the strong connections between Ezekiel and the foundational interactions between Moses and YHWH in the Torah have been cogently argued. Thus, Ezekiel's YHWH is presented as the same God of חסד ואמת, of "love and faithfulness," as the one who passed by Moses (Exod 34:6). He is also the judge of creation by virtue of his position as Lord and Creator. Justice, therefore, is critical in understanding the person of YHWH and his relationship to creation. Moreover, as YHWH himself is the source of כבד, it is his to determine what is true and just.

Importantly, however, although YHWH is the sole determiner of justice, this does not entail capriciousness. Rather, it stresses the relational nature of justice—YHWH is just because he acts in accordance with his own character, and he judges justly because his judgments are in accordance with his character (cf. Ezek 18). However, as Barton has demonstrated, YHWH's justice (as presented by the prophets) is not a "wholly theonomous system" and thereby a closed hermeneutical circle. Rather, "the moral principles which rational people can recognize are not other than the principles on which God works when judging human actions."[15]

The word עוה, of which guilt (in terms of culpability or responsibility for iniquity) is an aspect, denotes transgressions or distortions of the patterns of relationship and conduct deemed appropriate, in YHWH's eyes, for the particular relational context in view. With the particular focus of the OT (YHWH's covenant with Israel), the main relational axis to which עוה applies is that between YHWH and his people. As such, with regard to the prophetic indictment on Israel/Judah, such as we see in Ezekiel, the meaning of עוה is primarily derived from the terms of the Sinai covenant and its stipulations and requirements. However, it is also important to keep in mind that, especially in light of the emotive imagery utilized by the prophets in their indictment of Israel/Judah, the sense of עוה extends beyond

---

12. Avrahami, "בוש in the Psalms," 305.

13. Or a call for his people to be accordingly disappointed in themselves.

14. Cf. Douglas, *Purity and Danger.*

15. Barton, *Old Testament Ethics,* 43.

the impersonal, mechanistic, cause and effect view of sin-punishment suggested, for example, by Koch. Rather, it involves a rejection of Yhwh, the
lawgiver, himself.[16]

In the prophetic presentation, then, guilt does not refer, in the first instance, to the *feeling* of having transgressed an internalized moral code, so
much as the *fact* of having transgressed Yhwh's moral code, in Yhwh's eyes.
Moreover, guilt is highly relational, because in the covenant Yhwh did not
simply give Israel a moral code but rather gave *himself* to them (as indicated
by the marriage metaphor that forms the introduction to the Sinai covenant
in Exod 19). Sustained rejection of the covenant terms, then, was indicative
of rejection of Yhwh himself.

As with shame, however, feelings *should* follow facts. Thus, awareness of
guilt before Yhwh ought to lead to feelings of guilt (and shame) for iniquity, as an appropriate emotional response. Placed in the context of relationship with a God whose כבד is to be חסד ואמת, the necessity of this sort
of realization and its personal impact becomes clear: to be reconciled to
God requires a disclosure of that which, in God's eyes, is a barrier to truth.
Thus, Ezekiel insists that a necessary aspect of Judah's restoration was the
recognition of the extent of their עוה and an acceptance of their בוש (for
example, Ezek 36).

In summary, then, this study of Ezekiel within the context of the OT
canon argues that honor is what Yhwh deems of worth, is indicative of
right relationship with him, and is defined in accordance with and in appropriate response to his כבד, which is in turn derived from his own character
of חסד ואמת. Shame is what in Yhwh's eyes fails/falls short of an appropriate
response to his כבד and thus consitutes a fundamental breach of relationship with him. Guilt is the concrete expression of that failure, the transgression or distortion of the covenant terms that express and enable right
relationship with the God of חסד ואמת.

Implications for Applying SSAs to Biblical and Theological Studies

Throughout this study, I have attempted to demonstrate that the fundamental distinction between shame and guilt (in terms of both basic concepts as well as cultural characterization) used in most contemporary SSAs
can be a helpful entry point into discussion of different cultures but is ultimately problematic and deeply flawed. I have explored this both in the
theoretical literature (ch. 3), as well as in the biblical example of Ezekiel. As
Cairns has demonstrated, the distinction between shame and guilt, psychologically speaking, amounts to "little more than a shift in ideation from '*I*
should not have done that,' to 'I should not have done *that*.' It certainly does
not amount to a distinction between a concept that is fundmentally non-

---

16. Koch, "Doctrine of Retribution"; s.v. עון, *TDOT.*

moral and one that is, or between one that is solely concerned with external sanctions and one that is based on individual conscience."[17] The simplicity of the statement belies its profundity, as it is rather something of a fly in the ointment of models built on the shame/guilt distinction.

I will give three examples of how this affects the use of these SSA models in biblical and theological studies and exposes the caveats that need to be borne in mind in utilizing them. First, although Benedict's work has been regarded as foundational in distinguishing between shame and guilt cultures, her own descriptions undermine the classifications. Benedict gives ample evidence of internalized conscience (that is, of guilt) in Japanese people. This leads to the eventual conclusion that Japan is not a "true shame culture" but a shame culture with an admixture of guilt.[18] In light of this, how can the conclusions derived from the bipolarity of the classification be maintained? If a shame culture was so easily distinguished from a guilt culture, it would be reasonable to expect more clear-cut lines. The fact that lines are blurred, no matter what culture is in view, speaks against the usefulness of the classifications.

The second example is drawn from Zeba Crook, perhaps the most developed presentation of the Context Group's formulations of honor and shame (or at least the most forcefully argued).[19] I have already engaged with some of Crook's arguments, but here I will briefly assess his attempt to define an honor culture. After noting several honor culture areas besides the Mediterranean (for example, Japan, and South America), Crook observes that honor cultures also appear "within subcultures in non-honor cultures." He cites several North American examples of this phenomenon: sports teams, the military, the police, and gangs. These lead to his definition: "An honor culture is defined by the seriousness with which the people who inhabit it protect their honor and fight to retrieve it if it has been lost."

Key to this definition is the notion of honor as a limited good, for this is what distinguishes an honor culture from a nonhonor culture. While honor (and shame) may be known and operate to some extent in a nonhonor culture, there is enough to go around, and thus it is not contested with the same intensity as in an honor culture.[20]

---

17. Cairns, *Aidōs*, 26–27; cf. Lasch, *For Shame*.

18. Benedict states, for example, "Japanese sometimes react as strongly as any Puritan to a private accumulation of guilt." However, she then mitigates the statement by defaulting to the definition: "[The Japanese tendency to] extreme statement [in their reactions] nevertheless point out correctly where the emphasis falls in Japan. It falls on the importance of shame rather than on the importance of guilt" (Benedict, *Chrysanthemum and Sword*, 222). As Cairns observes: "The rigidity with which the criterion in terms of external and internal sanctions is applied thus prevents the recognition that the presence of internalized standards of behavior may be all of a piece with those phenomena which are classified in terms of shame" (Cairns, *Aidōs*, 28).

19. Crook, "Honor Revisited."

20. Ibid., 593.

Crook is to be applauded for the manner in which he sees "honor culture" operating in non-Mediterranean/nonhonor culture settings, and there is much more fruitful exploration to be done in this regard. Like Benedict's formulation, however, the examples given actually illustrate the opposite point. Far from more clearly marking the "line in the sand" between honor cultures and nonhonor cultures, they blur them.

For example, do the existence of clear social pecking order, peer pressure, fights for status, status-determining cross-gender pairings (and fights over these as well), and the like, indicate that the social dynamics of a North American high school or college are, in fact, an instance of an honor culture?[21] If so, and if the majority of North Americans have been through this, should it not indicate that North America is largely made up of people who have inhabited and been shaped by an honor culture for a significant part of their lives, and thus modify the classic characterization of North America as a guilt culture?

Likewise, does a North American sporting team who meet for primarily social reasons and thus pay little regard to their success on the sporting field, still qualify as an honor subculture within a nonhonor culture? Or does their lack of concern to "protect their honor" mean that their team is a nonhonor subculture within an honor subculture within a nonhonor culture? At what point does the intensity to which a culture fights to preserve its honor qualify it to be deemed as viewing honor as a limited good, and where are we to draw the limits as to the classifications? At death? Physical violence? Psychological violence? Withdrawal of favor or resources? A vague dislike or dissociation? Until the answers to questions such as these can be clearly articulated and applied, the usefulness of the SSA honor/shame model as a heuristic tool remains doubtful.

The third example comes from an essay by John Elliott in the Context Group's volume *Ancient Israel: The Old Testament in Its Social Context*.[22] Elliott provides a stimulating discussion on the nature and function of euphemism in the biblical material, and provides a helpful reading of the difficult

---

21. An anecdotal case could be made for the truth of this from popular films, based on North American high school experience, for example, *Grease* (motion picture, Paramount Pictures: United States, 1978), or its contemporary equivalent, *High School Musical* (motion picture, Buena Vista Home Entertainment: United States, 2006). Despite the seeming triviality of these examples, the social dynamics that drive their plots are highly reminiscent of the main pillars of the SSA honor/shame model. Further, while they are fictional works of entertainment, there do seem to significant points of resonance with the real experience of a Western high school. Alternatively, it might be more accurate to say that the characterization of a clear distinction between honor and nonhonor cultures simply introduces a dichotomy that is not there.

22. John H. Elliott, "Deuteronomy: Shameful Encroachment on Shameful Parts. Deuteronomy 25:11–12 and Biblical Euphemism," in *Ancient Israel: The Old Testament in Its Social Context* (ed. P. F. Esler; London: SCM, 2006), 161–76.

Deut 25:11–12 from a cultural perspective. That it provides an illustration of the shame/guilt culture distinction, however, is rather questionable. Elliott suggests that changing the translation of מבשים, from "shameful parts" to "private parts," reflects the the waning of group orientation, with shame as its social sanction, and a growing focus on the individual, with its attendant privileging of guilt over shame. [23]

While Elliott's presentation does have some resonance with cultural trends, the counter-example of shame in the garden of Eden is hardly an example of modern Western culture. [24] However, even there shame (cf. ולא יתבששו, Gen 2:25), when it inserts itself into the relationship between Adam and Eve, prompts them to "make *coverings* for themselves" (ויעשו להם חגרת); that is, to make their parts private. If this does indeed indicate the waning of group orientation, and a growing focus on the individual, perhaps Western culture is not as much of a watershed in cultural classifications as is sometimes portrayed.

Once again, the above examples are not given to denigrate the use of SSAs in biblical and theological studies but rather so that a more consistent and accurate application can be made. It can be *very* useful to distinguish between act and being (and even to focus primarily on one rather than the other), but positing a fundamental opposition or dichotomy between the two is as misleading as it is powerful. SSAs are of immense value in exploring value systems held by different groupings, the notion of PCR highly applicable in alerting researchers to the different and sometimes competing notions of honor at play in various characters and groups.

As such, SSAs have helped to advance our understanding of the complexity of human existence and motivations, as well as that of spirituality and the divine, as expressed in the biblical documents. In this regard, this study has sought to explore how the SSA highlighting of shame has served to advance the theological framework that undergirds much of the prophetic proclamation of Yhwh's character, and his relationship to his creation and especially to his people. These caveats, however, remind us that as the broader anthropological research on shame and guilt have demonstrated the need to hold the two concepts together, so also this applies to biblical and theological studies.

Final Conclusions

For all its difficult imagery, the book of Ezekiel has a clear message: Yhwh's כבד will be acknowledged throughout his creation. Neither his people's עון (their iniquity) nor their בוש (their failure that it constitutes)

---

23. Ibid., 176.

24. Even here, Avrahami's challenge to the default translation "shame" for בוש is relevant; as the translation "the man and his wife were both naked, and were not disappointed [i.e. with each other]," may perhaps be argued.

will finally prevent Yhwh from dwelling with them and bringing blessing to the renewed creation. I have explored how SSA models may be fruitfully applied to the biblical material, to further our understanding of these foundational themes. Such studies, built on the social values of honor and shame are a valuable (one might even argue, central) addition to the interpretive framework of the reader of the Bible. However, the models utilized need more care and sensitivity in construction and application than has largely been the case. Specifically, the values of honor and shame ought not to be seen in opposition to guilt, either in psychological concept or in models of social and cultural interaction. Rather, they need to be held together as key parts of the rich mixture of what it means to be human—individually and socially.

In essence, then, this study may best be summed up in the following terms: there are no guilt cultures or shame cultures. Or, perhaps more accurately, *all* cultures are shame cultures, and *all* cultures are guilt cultures. Thus, what differs between them (and their individual members) is not which of these dynamics they operate on, but how these concepts are variously configured, related, and articulated. Central to this are the various P/DCRs that operate to determine and dispense what honor *is* for the cultural group in view—what is ultimately esteemed and valued in the eyes of the group—and hence what constitues both shame (as a failure or disappointment of honor) and guilt (as a transgression or twisting of its terms).

In the case of Ezekiel, this model is particularized, primarily, by the character of Yhwh. His substantive כבוד, focused particularly in his חסד ואמת, determines what honor is. His covenant with Israel determines what Judah's honor should have been in response. However, they have transgressed and distorted its terms (עוה), and thus have failed (בוש) to relate appropriately, either to him, or each other, or the nations. In Ezekiel's terms, they do not "know" Yhwh.

This failure on Judah's part has brought on them the covenant curse of the exile to Babylon. While this is an expression of Yhwh's faithfulness to the terms of the covenant, it also forms an obstacle to a greater end, that all will respond appropriately to Yhwh's כבוד. Yhwh thus acts to restore his people, not simply in status before the nations, but into a renewed relationship with himself, so that nothing will hinder his honor filling the world.

In summary, for Ezekiel, the whole exercise of Judah's experience of blessing, exile, and restoration, have a single goal in mind: "that they may know that I am Yhwh."

כבוד to whom כבוד is due.

Appendix

Implications of This Study for Models of Atonement Theology

Introduction

In this monograph, I explored how the concepts "honor," "shame," and "guilt" function in the book of Ezekiel, in the wider contexts of their general use in SSAs. My aim was to examine the meanings of key terms and concepts as they appear in Ezekiel, in light of both the wider context of the OT, and contemporary definitions in psychology and anthropology. Here, I explore the implications of the study for contemporary atonement debates in Christian theology.

SSAs and the Atonement Debates

While this study is situated within the field of OT, as mentioned previously, its initial impetus came from debates concerning the nature of the atonement in Christian theology, especially within contemporary Evangelicalism. The issues raised in the doctrinal debates thus formed the outer framework of this study (that is, emic A and emic A1), and are organically related to SSAs. I will therefore begin this appendix by briefly outlining recent developments in atonement theology that are particularly relevant to SSAs (emic A), before applying the results of the main study to the topic (emic A1). In so doing, I am seeking to integrate several aspects of biblical and theological study into a unified presentation that holds together well.[1]

Author's note: As noted previously, this appendix is an integration of the original introduction and conclusion to the study, as a self-conscious attempt to follow the model and method constructed in ch. 2 (emic A and emic A1). I have retained them to preserve the integrity of the model, although they have been integrated into a single, retrospective, application.

1. For broader discussion on debates surrounding the atonement, see James K. Beilby and Paul R. Eddy eds., *The Nature of the Atonement: Four Views* (Downers Grove: IVP Academic, 2006); Anthony W. Bartlett, *Cross Purposes: The Violent Grammar of Christian Atonement* (Harrisburg, PA: Trinity Press International, 2001); Christian Eberhart, *The Sacrifice of Jesus: Understanding Atonement Biblically* (Minneapolis: Fortress, 2011); Stephen Finlan, *Problems with Atonement: The Origins of, and Controversy about, the Atonement Doctrine* (Collegeville, MN: Liturgical Press, 2005); René Girard, *I See Satan Fall Like Lightning* (Maryknoll, NY: Orbis, 2001); idem, *Things Hidden Since the Foundation of the World* (trans. S. Bann and M. Metteer; Stanford: University Press, 1987); Colin E. Gunton,

Gustaf Aulén, Christus Victor, *and Penal Substitution*

Contemporary debates surrounding the atonement in Christian theology are indebted to Gustaf Aulén's *Christus Victor.*[2] Aulén presented the atonement as a series of competing theories, or models of atonement: the moral influence theory (championed by Peter Abelard), the satisfaction theory (associated with Anselm); and the ransom theory, which Aulén called the classical view of the Church Fathers. The oft-quoted summary of this is, "Christ—Christus Victor—fights against and triumphs over the evil powers of the world, the 'tyrants' under which mankind is in bondage and suffering, and in Him God reconciles the world to Himself."[3]

For Aulén, however, this classical theory had been obscured in Western Christendom by the satisfaction theory, and its development into the dominant view of the Reformed tradition, of penal substitutionary atonement (hereafter, PSA).[4] The chief reason for this, according to Aulén, is that Anselm fixes the atonement into a legal straitjacket: "God receives compensation for man's default."[5] As a result, where the Christus Victor model presents the atonement as a *"continuous* Divine work," the "Latin" view becomes a *"discontinuous* work."[6]

The determining factor in characterizing an approach as "continuous" or "discontinuous" lies in which "direction" the atonement works. In the classical view, Christ acts as God's representative, and the work of the atonement is directed toward the powers under which humankind is held. In the Latin view, Christ acts as man's representative and the work of the atonement is directed toward God, whose wrath and justice are satisfied in the death of

---

The Theology of Reconciliation (Edinburgh: T. & T. Clark, 2003); S. Mark Heim, *Saved from Sacrifice: A Theology of the Cross* (Grand Rapids: Eerdmans, 2006); Henri Blocher, "Biblical Metaphors of the Atonement," *JETS* 47 (2004): 629–45; Charles E. Hill et al., *The Glory of the Atonement: Biblical, Historical and Practical Perspectives, Essays in Honor of Roger Nicole* (Downers Grove: InterVarsity, 2004); Alister E. McGrath, *What Was God Doing on the Cross?* (Grand Rapids: Zondervan, 1992); Darby Kathleen Ray, *Deceiving the Devil: Atonement, Abuse, and Ransom* (Cleveland: Pilgrim, 1998); S. W. Sykes, *The Story of Atonement* (London: Darton, Longman, & Todd, 1997); Steve Chalke, et al., *The Atonement Debate: Papers from the London Symposium on the Theology of Atonement* (Grand Rapids: Zondervan, 2008); Steve Chalke and Alan Mann, *The Lost Message of Jesus* (Grand Rapids: Zondervan, 2003); Thomas F. Torrance and Robert T. Walker, *Atonement: The Person and Work of Christ* (Downers Grove: IVP Academic, 2009); J. Denny Weaver, *The Nonviolent Atonement* (Grand Rapids: Eerdmans, 2011); Hans Boersma, *Violence, Hospitality, and the Cross: Reappropriating the Atonement Tradition* (Grand Rapids: Baker Academic, 2006).

    2. Gustaf Aulén, *Christus Victor: A Historical Study of the Three Main Types of the Idea of the Atonement* (London: SPCK, 1931).

    3. Aulén, *Christus Victor,* 4.

    4. Ibid., 14–15, 123–33.

    5. Ibid., 90.

    6. Ibid., 5 (emphasis mine).

Christ, the righteous man. Furthermore, this continuity and discontinuity revolves, critically, around the notions of justice and rationality.

The Latin theory is built on the refrain of *nihil rationabilius*—nothing is more reasonable than God's demand for satsifacation and the manner in which it is met. The classical view, by contrast, "defies rational systematization," because the antinomy created by God being both Reconciler and Reconciled cannot be resoved by rational equation. In Aulén's summation, the Latin theory demonstrates a *legal consistency*, but *discontinuity in divine operation*; while the classical view demonstrates a *continuity in divine action* but *discontinuity in the order of justice.*[7]

Of particular note for this study is the relation of God to justice. For Aulén, the OT is built on law/justice as the basis of God's relation to humanity. In the NT, God's love "breaks through" the order of justice, triumphs over evil, and establishes a new relationship between God and the world.[8] The Latin view, by contrast, perpetuates the ("legalistic") outlook of the OT, due largely to Anselm's unquestioning adoption of the moralistic penitential system of the Middle Ages as the *sine qua non* of right standing before God.[9] As such, God's love is straight-jacketed by his justice in a manner incongruent with the teaching of the NT.[10] Instead, Aulén argues, God justifies without any satisfaction of divine justice.[11]

Aulén's work has five significant points of contact with honor/shame studies:

1. Aulén clearly associates the Latin theory with a Western framework, built predominantly on justice and guilt, in line with contemporary psychological and anthropological cultural definitions.

2. These are largely negative concepts, especially in terms of God's relationship to humanity. Justice and satisfaction stand opposed to grace, reconciliation and the continuity of divine action in the atonement.

3. In the classic idea, the main culprit in the rift between God and humanity is not humanity but "the powers." Hence, the primary need for humanity is not that satisfaction be made for them, but that "the powers" be overcome and humanity liberated and given victory.

4. Accordingly, sin must be understood in a wider sense than in the Latin view, which reduces it to the level of morality. It is, rather, part of the package of evil powers opposed to God and his people: the realm of death, the devil, law, the curse, and so on.[12]

---

7. Ibid., 91.
8. Ibid., 79.
9. Ibid., 147.
10. Ibid., 156.
11. Ibid., 155.
12. Ibid., 149.

5. Aulén's resulting framework contains more than a hint of shame concepts, which are endorsed in contrast to the guilt concepts of the Latin theory: "God, the all-ruler, the Infinite, yet accepts the lowliness of the Incarnation," so that he can defeat the enemy, free the enslaved captives and give them victory and vindication. [13]

Green and Baker: Recovering the Scandal of the Cross

Green and Baker have appropriated Aulén's work, and are representative of highly cogent, contemporary objections to PSA. They also stand within the Evangelical tradition and thus their critiques are closely attuned to PSA. Further, they explicitly connect the doctrinal debates with cross-cultural studies, and particularly with honor/shame.

Green and Baker follow a similar pattern to Aulén in their presentation by critiquing contemporary Evangelicalism's focus on a singular model of the atonement (i.e., PSA) which, in their understanding, is "deficient and disturbing," both biblically and according to the church's theological tradition. [14] They do, however, separate Anselm's satisfaction model (built on medieval feudalism and honor concerns) from PSA (built on legal concerns), which they treat as a separate, fourth model.

Green and Baker summarize what they perceive to be the shortcomings of PSA and, hence, its unsuitability to be counted amongst the legitimate "metaphors" for making sense of the cross of Christ. They argue that PSA

- has engendered forms of Christian faith and practice that are suspect
- has been construed by persons within and outside the church as a form of "divine child abuse," and so at the very least invites more careful articulation
- has not been heard as "good news" in contemporary cultures in and outside of the West that are not guilt based
- may well have increasingly less relevance among 21st century Christians
- at the very least, constrains overmuch the richness of biblical thinking concerning the death of Jesus [15]

Green and Baker's argument is mainly a restatement of Aulén, although they develop the critique by including contemporary objections (for example, the notion of "divine child abuse") sometimes seen as implicit in PSA. Green and Baker also seek to analyze Anselm's position more sensitively,

---

13. Ibid., 159.

14. Joel B. Green and Mark D. Baker, *Recovering the Scandal of the Cross: Atonement in New Testament and Contemporary Contexts* (2nd ed.; Downers Grove: IVP Academic, 2011), 117.

15. Ibid., 49–50.

by articulating how his medieval, feudal framework shaped the main meta-phor used in *Cur Deus Homo*. In Green and Baker's assessment, Anselm's presentation concerns sin as a "debt of honor," rather than the strictly legal, courtroom verdict of PSA. Green and Baker applaud Anselm for attempting to formulate atonement concepts in the cultural thought-forms of his day (a principle endorsed throughout the book, and apparently modeled by the NT authors), and are more positive than Aulén in acknowledging the importance of relationship in Anselm's theory.

Despite these concessions, the critique is sustained: Anselm was too influenced by feudalism and a narrow view of sin, resulting in atonement being understood exclusively as "remission of debt." The picture of God as an offended feudal lord necessarily distorted the biblical picture of the God of love.[16] In summary, Anselm was entangled in a worldview that rendered it unbefitting for a feudal lord simply to forgive a vassal who had offended him, and his view of the atonement was accordingly bound by this foundational premise.[17] As such, God is recast as something of a "cruel and bloodthirsty judge, bound and determined to exact the last farthing owed by any debtor in justice."[18]

When Green and Baker turn to Hodge's articulation of PSA, their assessment is almost universally negative. They follow similar contours to their review of Anselm but characterize Hodge as reading the Bible from a framework of "universal moral law." This legal framework drives Hodge's understanding of "blood sacrifice," which is used to interpret Jesus' death on the cross. Thus, although Hodge's explication of PSA appears to be biblically based, the reality is that the concepts are supplied by a faulty framework, derived from a 19th-century American criminal justice system, which is then "read in" to the biblical material.[19]

As such, despite some substantial differences between them, Hodge's presentation ultimately suffers from the same fundamental flaw as Anselm—a cold, forensic concept of justice, rather than a more biblical, covenantal one, "almost synonymous with faithfulness."[20] Consequently, Green and Baker see little that is salvageable in PSA as a legitimate understanding of the atonement.[21]

---

16. Ibid., 156–61.

17. Ibid., 158.

18. Ibid., 159. Green and Baker derive this point from Leonardo Boff, whom they cite approvingly. See further Leonardo Boff, *Passion of Christ, Passion of the World: The Facts, Their Interpretation, and Their Meaning Yesterday and Today* (trans. R. R. Barr; Maryknoll, NY: Orbis, 1987), 97.

19. Green and Baker, *Recovering the Scandal*, 172–73.

20. Ibid., 173.

21. Green and Baker do acknowledge some more recent and positive articulations of PSA, e.g., Boersma, *Violence, Hospitality, and the Cross*; Stephen R. Holmes, *The Wondrous Cross: Atonement and Penal Substitution in the Bible and History* (London: Paternoster, 2007);

In the place of PSA, Green and Baker suggest that, for contemporary Evanglicals, the urge to find a single, overarching "model" of the atonement needs to be resisted. This is especially true for one built on an abstract notion of "justice," and in which God's anger is understood to be vengeful or retributive or actively directed toward humans. Rather, the saving *significance* of the cross needs to be emphasized, while its exact *meaning* (that is, logical explanation) remains rather elusive, being best expressed in a "kaleidoscope" of images according to differing cultures and concepts. This, according to Green and Baker, is exactly what the NT writers themselves did as they "cast about for metaphors" and "struggled to make sense of Jesus' crucifixion." A similar search for "culturally appropriate" metaphors should be the template for contemporary atonement theology.[22]

Green and Baker stress that this task, however, must be conducted between two nonnegotiable points: God's eternal purpose, and *the ancient Mediterranean world* within which Jesus was crucified.[23] The interface between these provides the rich backdrop for the many metaphors and models of the cross that we find in the pages of the NT. As Green and Baker conclude, "So infinite is the mystery of God's saving work that we need many interpretive images, many tones, many voices."[24]

Importantly, however, not all models are equally suitable. Some may be better suited to different times and locales, while others may fail to be faithful to the apostolic witness to the gospel. The latter, Green and Baker argue, should be left aside.[25]

After a considerable review section, Green and Baker go on to suggest several alternatives to PSA (that is, "rearrangements" of the kaleidoscope) in a series of case studies in various "cultural" settings (including feminist theology, a Tanzanian tribe, and college students in the U.S.A.), carefully locating each in their contemporary geographic, ethnic, and social contexts. Of particular relevance to this study, however, is their devotion of an entire chapter to the presentation of Norman Kraus's experience as a missionary in Japan, entitled "Removing Alienating Shame: The Saving Significance of the Cross in Japan." In this chapter, Green and Baker bring SSA considerations to the fore that are directly related to this study.

The chapter begins by relating a Japanese church leader telling Kraus of his dissatisfaction with the standard explanation given by missionaries as to why Jesus had to die (that is, PSA). Kraus realised that these missionaries had practiced "suitcase theology"—simply restating the doctrines learned in North America and European institutions without any recontextualiza-

---

and esp. Kevin Vanhoozer, "The Atonement in Postmodernity: Guilt, Goats and Gifts," in *The Glory of the Atonement*, 367–404.

    22. Ibid., 113, 140–41.

    23. Ibid., 139.

    24. Ibid.

    25. Ibid. PSA is presumably a key example of such a model.

tion. As a result, their explanations of the atonement "were difficult for the Japanese people, even Japanese believers in Christ, to understand."[26]

Green and Baker then go on to outline an incident that illustrated to Kraus the difficulties that the Japanese had in accepting PSA. They report on a case in which a young man driving a lorry accidentally hit and killed two women. According to Kraus (via Green and Baker),[27] the critical element in what followed was that "the police and court demonstrated more concern for relationships and people's responses than to written codes. They handled the case in a way markedly different from American legal processes."[28] The young man, for example, immediately confessed that he was at fault as he had been speeding (a move, it later became clear, designed to take responsibility for his company). Although the judge ordered his incarceration, the young man was released to attend the women's funerals, with the judge being present and observing the young man's responses. The police, meanwhile, investigated the situation and found that that the young man could not in fact have been speeding and that the cause of the accident was in fact a steering defect in the company truck. The young man's sentence was lightened to community service for a year, after which he was released and rehabilitated into the community.[29]

According to Kraus, this incident demonstrated a concept of justice different from that of the USA; he later ascertained that, to the Japanese, "Justice is what the judge says it is."[30] For Kraus, this was indicative of the gulf between the Western image of justice as the blindfolded goddess, determining guilt or innocence based on an abstract law, and the Japanese image of the male judge with eyes wide open, so that he could do what would best preserve human relationships.[31]

Kraus concluded that the differences derived from Japan being "a *shame-based culture*, very much *unlike the guilt-based culture* in which most North Americans live." As such, there was a pronounced difference in the concept and practice of justice in these two contexts. Consequently, it was entirely understandable that the Japanese church elders found penal satisfaction theory of the atonement rather unsatisfactory, as it was built on a penal approach to justice alien to them.[32]

As can be seen from the above quotation, Green and Baker (via Kraus) introduce the SSA shame/guilt culture dichotomy as the critical element in

---

26. Green and Baker, *Recovering the Scandal*, 193. See further C. Norman Kraus, *Jesus Christ Our Lord: Christology from a Disciple's Perspective* (Scottdale: Herald, 1987).

27. The authors state that the main discussions in the chapter "were reported in a phone conversation with C. Norman Kraus, May 12, 1999" (Green and Baker, *Recovering the Scandal*, 192 n. 1).

28. Ibid.

29. Ibid.

30. Ibid.

31. Ibid.

32. Ibid., 194 (emphasis mine).

the dynamics of the episode, and the main reason why PSA is an unsatisfactory explanation of the atonement. Green and Baker go on to explore how atonement might work in a shame culture, as distinct from a guilt culture. However, this is not presented simply as an alternative based on cultural concerns. Rather, an emphasis on shame in particular is, in their assessment, a move *closer* to the cultural milieu of the Bible and hence a "better" explanation of the cross than PSA.[33]

In support of their suggestion, Green and Baker cite Malina's work as key in articulating honor and shame as pivotal values, not simply in Japanese culture, but for the social settings of Old and New Testaments. As such, they argue that, as threatening as the move away from PSA to honor and shame may be for Western Evangelicals, "far from 'compromising the gospel' by inquiring how it might be located on Japanese soil, our questions about the significance of the cross for the Japanese people might actually bring us *closer to the pages of the New Testament*."[34]

The Place of SSAs in the Debate: Gains and Dangers

Gains

The above review demonstrates the important place that awareness of cultural context and boundedness plays in contemporary theological debates concerning the atonement. Moreover, as the review also shows, these considerations have long been part and parcel of biblical and theological study. However, the explicit application of anthropological research has been a recent and welcome innovation.

As the review of Green and Baker demonstrates, much of the impetus for the contemporary atonement debates is built on the foundation of the Context Group's SSA. This is also an area of particular personal resonance. As someone who was born and raised in a Western context (Australian), but with Eastern heritage (Chinese), I find the new appreciation of honor and shame concepts a welcome move. I also agree with Green and Baker that recognizing the importance of these concepts moves us closer to the Bible.

Further, as someone whose theological background (Reformed Evangelicalism) includes regarding PSA as the foundational model of the atonement, I find the critique somewhat uncomfortable and challenging. It is

---

33. As Green and Baker put it: "The Old Testament concepts of ritual purity and uncleanness, views of death and disease, exile as a form of punishment—'these point toward a shame rather than guilt orientation. . . . To a greater extent than is often recognized, the problem of sin in Israel was the problem of purifying the nation of its pollution without permanently expelling the unclean person.'" (Green and Baker, *Recovering the Scandal*, 196; citing Kraus, *Jesus Christ*, 214).

34. Green and Baker, *Recovering the Scandal*, 200–201 (emphasis original). Green and Baker cite Malina, *New Testament World*, as the main support for their suggestion (p. 200 n. 6).

healthy to have one's presuppositions and beliefs challenged, refined, and even corrected.

Recognizing the importance of the area, and its potential to challenge such a fundamental tenet of Evangelical theology, then, this study has attempted to delve behind the atonement debates to the SSA research that underlies their critique of PSA. It has assessed the model's strengths and weaknesses in light of the biblical material, while also seeking to enrich understanding of the biblical material through appropriating its concepts and parameters into the areas of both biblical studies and theological reflection.

The atonement debates expose the importance of being aware of one's own cultural heritage in approaching the Bible. Hence, in this study I have tried, where relevant, to be as transparent as possible in this regard. The intent in so doing, of course, is that the researcher may be more self-aware, self-critical, and open to other modes and models of understanding.

Dangers

On the other hand, there is also an inherent danger in proclaiming oneself as "aware." To do so assumes a certain authoritative stance in and of itself; not to mention a tendency to pillory and dismiss those who may disagree as being blind, or bound to presuppositions, which those who are aware have managed to miraculously transcend.

The method I developed for use in the main study was an attempt to navigate carefully between the Scylla and Charybdis of "unawareness" and "awareness." The atonement debates challenged the legitimacy of PSA on SSA grounds, and suggested that Mediterranean honor and shame provided a more accurate interpretive framework for understanding the death of Jesus than Western guilt. Having assessed the honor and shame model in the main study, I now apply the results of the analysis to the atonement debates.

The Valid Concerns in Critiques of PSA

There are several positive benefits in the challenges to PSA in advancing our understanding of the atonement. Aulén, for example, has helpfully identified how an excessive regard for one aspect of God's character ("justice") at the expense of a holistic understanding of his person obscures the framework within which the atonement works. Further, imposing onto the text concepts of justice alien to biblical categories exacerbates the problem.[35] This in turn can indeed lead to a reductionistic view of sin, cast *exclusively* in juridical or economic terms and a distorted view of God's character, either as an unyielding legalist or incensed tyrant.[36] The Christus Victor model helpfully places the cross within its broader framework of God's purpose to

---

35. Aulén, *Christus Victor*, 84–95.

36. Cf. Colin E. Gunton, *Actuality of Atonement: A Study of Metaphor, Rationality and the Christian Tradition* (London: Continuum, 2003),

reconcile the world to himself, an important correction to some presentations of PSA that focus simply on the mechanics of vicarious substitution,
and view the atonement solely in terms of "getting right with God."

Green and Baker raise the further issues of reductionism (the urge to
find a single, overarching model of the atonement) and cultural context in
appropriately expressing the significance of the atonement. In so doing,
they have helpfully drawn attention to the multiplicity of images and metaphors used to communicate, and have thus stimulated further work on the
relationship between them. They have also drawn the concepts of honor,
shame, and human relationality into discussion on the atonement, and in so
doing have directed attention to these important themes in the Bible and
in contemporary cultures.

The Weaknesses in Critiques of PSA

Despite the valuable gains and stimuli to a deeper understanding of the
centerpiece of the Christian faith, there are also significant weaknesses in
the critiques of PSA examined in this study. Several of the fundamental
flaws have been adequately covered elsewhere;[37] here, I will focus on the
critiques of Anselm's satisfaction theory, and Green and Baker's flawed use
of SSAs.

Weaknesses in Aulén's Critique of Anselm

Aulén's critique of Anselm has set the terms in which his presentation of
the atonement is understood. However, this study has highlighted two areas
of weakness in Aulén's critique that raise questions over its validity.

First, Aulén suggests that Anselm's presentation of sin as a debt requiring payment is grounded in medieval feudalism, rather than the Bible.[38]
However, the analysis of עוה demonstrated that the metaphor of debt *is*
biblical, and centrally so. Further, for Aulén, sees the atonement operating
within the "strict requirements of justice" as problematic.[39] God "is not,
indeed, unrighteous, but He transcends the order of justice."[40] For Aulén,
this statement is motivated by a desire to see God's grace as central to the
atonement, and in this he is biblically correct.

However, Aulén also drives a wedge between God's grace and his justice, seeing the two as fundamentally incompatible. As the biblical study
has shown, however, such a polarization posits a fundamental split in God's
nature (as expressed in the character creed). YHWH is the God of חסד ואמת,

---

37. See S. Jeffery et al., *Pierced for Our Transgressions: Rediscovering the Glory of Penal
Substitution* (Leicester: Inter-Varsity, 2007); Vanhoozer, "The Atonement in Postmoder-
nity"; Blocher, "Biblical Metaphors." For a more moderate defense of PSA see Boersma,
Violence, Hospitality, and the Cross.

38. Aulén, *Christus Victor*, 84–95.

39. Ibid., 90.

40. Ibid., 91.

the God of *both* steadfast love *and* justice, the God who both *forgives iniquity* and *visits iniquity*. Accordingly, salvation does not occur outside the context of justice, but in harmony with it. Aulén's critique is in part drawn from a misunderstanding of the relationship between God and justice, in a manner reminiscent of Koch's characterization. As this study has demonstrated, this is an inadequate view of YHWH's justice.

Second, Anselm's presentation of the atonement is often criticized for its characterization of God as a feudal lord, to whom his vassals owe a debt for his injured honor in their sin. This sort of metaphor, it is argued, arises more from Anselm's medieval context than the Bible.[41] Brown, however, has raised significant questions over the validity of the charges. He demonstrates that the bases and logic of Anselm's atonement theology *were* drawn from biblical categories and concepts, and that he was far less tied to the feudal system than most presentations suggest.[42] Further, it is more than a little curious that Green and Baker, who follow Aulén in his stinging criticism of Anselm's presentation in terms of God's honor,[43] endorse Japanese and SSA conceptions of honor and shame (some of which demonstrate remarkably similar patterns to medieval feudalism) so heartily as "moving us *closer to the pages of the New Testament.*"[44]

Weaknesses in Green and Baker's Use of SSAs

Green and Baker make much of honor and shame in relation to the cross, both as the native culture of the NT, and in relation to mission in contemporary Japan. Their fundamental argument is that PSA, as a guilt-culture-based view of atonement, simply did not "work" in a Japanese context and, further, that a shame culture was in fact a move closer to the conceptual world of the NT. The main study highlighted the shortcomings of SSA honor and shame model adopted to explain Japanese and biblical culture throughout this study. However, here I will make the additional observation that Green and Baker's case study of the Japanese truck driver confirms the very point they are attempting *not* to make.

Fundamental to the account being a positive example is the *actual innocence* of the truck driver. As a counter example, if the driver had been a relative of the judge and in fact negligent in his driving, or if the judge had received a bribe from a powerful relative of the driver, it would have hardly done to endorse the judge for his actions to minimize the sentence. For the case to support a positive example of human relationships *assumes the presence of juridical innocence.*

---

41. Ibid., 86.

42. David Brown, "Anselm on Atonement," in *The Cambridge Companion to Anselm* (ed. B. Davies and B. Leftow; Cambridge: Cambridge University Press, 2004), 279–302.

43. Green and Baker, *Recovering the Scandal*, 156–161.

44. Ibid., 214 (emphasis original).

The true point of the case study, then, is not the characterizations of shame/guilt culture or a demonstration of the shortcomings of the Western legal system. Rather, it emphasizes the relational nature of justice. The so-called Japanese view that "Justice is what the judge says it is,"[45] only brings us closer to the pages of the Bible if YHWH as judge is truly just—forgiving wrongdoing *and* not leaving the guilty unpunished—according to his כבד.

Green and Baker's suggestion that the Japanese "would not find a penal satisfaction theory of the atonement helpful, for it was built on a penal approach to justice alien to them," rests on the false dichotomy between shame and guilt cultures.[46] For example, Green and Baker suggest that rather than viewing jail time as "serving their debt to justice . . . Japanese criminals are imprisoned as a shameful act of exclusion from society."[47] As Downing has so convincingly demonstrated, however, such polarities often mask the common elements in both sets of cultural concepts.[48]

It is difficult to see much conceptual difference, for example, between the (apparent) Japanese view of imprisonment as "exclusion from society" and the common Western parental practice of sending a misbehaving child to their room for "time out." More soberly, most criminals in the West can hardly be considered to have paid their debt to justice in full by the length of their jail sentence. The stigma of having been in prison continues to affect the way they are perceived, and their acceptance into society is often hampered. It is difficult to see how this is vastly different from the shameful exclusion of Japanese criminals.

The Impact of the Study on
Biblical and Theological Reflection on the Atonement

The preceding critiques do not indicate that these studies are worthless. Quite the reverse. Works in the vein of Aulén and Green and Baker have provided highly valuable insights for understanding the atonement, which this current study supports. However, agreeing with their affirmations does not require accepting their denials.

This study has demonstrated that, in line with the centrality of YHWH's כבד in the Bible, the Christus Victor model resonates significantly with the Bible's emphases. The triumph of God over all that stands opposed to him is the central story of the Scriptures. It is the ultimate honor/victory theme. Conceptions of the atonement that fail to situate themselves within this context indeed risk distortion of God and his ways. Aulén's work, then, has catalyzed a broadening of horizons beyond simply articulating the mechanism of the atonement. It saw the cross in its ultimate context, in relation to the person of God and his plan to reconcile the world to himself (cf.

---

45. Ibid., 192.
46. Ibid., 194.
47. Ibid.
48. Downing, "Honor."

2 Cor 5:19). SSAs have supplemented this and drawn helpful attention to the importance of the themes of honor and shame in the biblical documents, as well as their central place in the biblical concepts of relationship with God.

However, the Christus Victor model needs to be articulated in light of the specific character of Y HWH as רב־חסד ואמת . . . . נשׂא עון . . . פקד עון. As a result, both Aulén's and Green and Baker's formulations require significant conceptual realignment if a positive appropriation is to be made to bring us closer to a biblical emic of atonement. Aulén is mistaken to set grace against justice, while Green and Baker are mistaken to set shame against guilt.

This study has demonstrated that the concepts of honor, shame, and guilt are fundamental categories in God's relationship with his creation, by virtue of his character and the manner in which his character affects his creatures. Although there are a multiplicity of images and metaphors of atonement in the Bible, they revolve around these three central ideas.

My goal, then, has been to delve behind the atonement debates, to explore the conceptual foundations behind the cross in the book of Ezekiel. It has confirmed the central place of honor in the biblical material, defined in terms of Y HWH's כבד, and that shame and guilt concepts stand at the heart of expressing the fundamental disruption to Y HWH's plan for creation to receive and return his כבד. Although the book of Ezekiel does not have an explicit atonement theology in its pages, the foundational conceptual structures and relationships are central to its message: Y HWH's people have committed עון and are בושׁ before him, but he will act for his name's sake to remove any and every obstacle to his כבד.

The importance of this matrix of concepts to atonement theology can be illlustrated from two critical NT passages regarding the person and work of Christ that that have significant parallels to the conceptual framework that undergirds the message of Ezekiel. First, in John 1:14, the *logos*, who came into the world to reconcile it to its maker, is described: "And the Word became flesh and dwelt among us, and we saw his *glory*, *glory* of the only one of the Father, full of *grace* and *truth*." Second, in Rom 3:23–26, the atonement is expressed in relation to both sinful humanity and the glory of God: "For all have *sinned* and fall short of the *glory* of God, and are justified freely by his grace through the redemption that came by Christ Jesus. God presented him as a sacrifice of atonement, through faith in his blood. He did this to demonstrate his *justice*, because in his forbearance he had left the sins committed beforehand unpunished. He did it to demonstrate his *justice* in the present time, so as to *be just* and the one who justifies those who have faith in Jesus Christ."

Conclusion

To conclude, I will present a summary of the atonement that seeks to integrate the overall findings of the study. The glory and honor of Y HWH (that is, Christus Victor) is the central rationale and driving force for the atonement. However, Yhwh's honor (כבד) is his love and faithfulness (חסד ואמת), through which he both forgives sin (נשא עון) and judges and punishes sin (פקד עון). Thus, to speak of Yhwh's honor, leads immediately to human guilt (עון) before him, and the need for it to be overcome (that is, humanity is בוש before him, symptomatic of which is their עון).

The death and resurrection of the incarnate Christ is the means by which the victory of Yhwh's honor is realized. This is the display, *par excellence*, of his חסד ואמת. His אמת is displayed in the just judgment on human עון. His חסד is displayed in the forgiveness that flows from it. Both of these are required for humanity's בוש to be overcome, so that Yhwh's כבד may be met with an appropriate response of restored, human כבד. Honor to whom honor is due. As such, PSA is the mechanism by which atonement "works." However, it is far from cold, legalistic, or impersonal. It is the very expression of the חסד ואמת of Yhwh, and the only means by which love and faithfulness may flow, uninhibited, between God and humanity. This, in the end, is the victory of God.

To be sure, this is not a full and final statement. Other important doctrinal and scriptural considerations must be taken into account for that, for example, the Trinity, the incarnation, the two natures of Christ, and the doctrine of total depravity. I also have not included how such a view of the atonement may also enable the moral influence model to be fruitfully integrated into Evangelical theology. However, the examination of honor, shame, and guilt in Ezekiel has also been, I hope, a helpful stimulus toward further understanding the central tenet of the Christian faith: the death of Christ for us.

Soli Deo Gloria.

Bibliography

Adkins, A. W. H. *Merit and Responsibility: A Study in Greek Values*. Oxford: Clarendon, 1960.

Aguilar, Mario I. "Changing Models and the 'Death' of Culture: A Diachronic and Positive Critique of Socio-Scientific Assumptions." Pp. 299–313 in *Anthropology and Biblical Studies: Avenues of Approach*. Edited by Louise Joy Lawrence and Mario I. Aguilar. Leiden: Deo, 2004.

Aichele, George. "Canon as Intertext: Restraint or Liberation?" Pp. 139–56 in *Reading the Bible Intertextually*. Edited by Richard B. Hays, Stefan Alkier, and Leroy A. Huizenga. Waco: Baylor University Press, 2009.

Aichele, George and Gary A. Phillips. "Intertextuality and the Bible." *Semeia* 69–70 (1995): 1–305.

Alexander, T. D. *From Paradise to the Promised Land: An Introduction to the Pentateuch*. 2nd edition. Grand Rapids: Baker Academic, 2002.

Alexander, T. D., and D. W. Baker. *Dictionary of Old Testament: Pentateuch*. Downers Grove: InterVarsity, 2002.

Allen, Leslie C. *Ezekiel 1–19*. WBC 28. Dallas: Word, 1994.

Alter, Robert. *The David Story: A Translation with Commentary of 1 and 2 Samuel*. New York: Norton, 1999.

Anderson, Gary A. *Sin: A History*. New Haven: Yale University Press, 2009.

Angel, Hayyim. "Ezekiel: Priest—Prophet." *JBQ* 39/1 (2011): 35–45.

Archer, Margaret S. *Critical Realism: Essential Readings*. New York: Routledge, 1998.

Aristotle. *Art of Rhetoric*. Translated by J. H. Freese. *LCL* 193. Cambridge: Harvard University Press, 1926.

Attridge, Harold W. "God in Hebrews." Pp. 197–209 in *The Forgotten God: Perspectives in Biblical Theology: Essays in Honor of Paul J. Achtemeier on the Occasion of His Seventy-Fifth Birthday*. Louisville: Westminster John Knox, 2002.

Augustine. *The City of God*. Translated by Marcus Dods. Peabody: Hendrickson, 2009.

Aulén, Gustaf. *Christus Victor: A Historical Study of the Three Main Types of the Idea of the Atonement*. London: SPCK, 1931.

Avrahami, Yael. "בוש in the Psalms: Shame or Disappointment?" *JSOT* 34 (2010): 295–313.

Bailey, D. R. S., ed. and trans. *Martial: Epigrams*. 3 volumes. Cambridge: Harvard University Press, 1993.

Bal, Mieke. *Death and Dissymmetry: The Politics of Coherence in the Book of Judges*. Chicago: University of Chicago Press, 1988.

_____. *Narratology: Introduction to the Theory of Narrative*. 2nd edition. Toronto: University of Toronto Press, 1997.

Barr, James. *History and Ideology in the Old Testament: Biblical Studies at the End of the Millennium*. Oxford: Oxford University Press, 2000.

_____. *The Concept of Biblical Theology: An Old Testament Perspective*. London: SCM, 1999.

_____. *The Semantics of Biblical Language*. London: Oxford University Press, 1961.

_____. *The Scope and Authority of the Bible*. London: SCM, 1980.

Bartlett, Anthony W. *Cross Purposes: The Violent Grammar of Christian Atonement*. Harrisburg: Trinity Press International, 2001.

Barton, John. *Oracles of God: Perceptions of Ancient Prophecy in Israel after the Exile*. London: Darton Longman & Todd, 2007.

_____. *Reading the Old Testament : Method in Biblical Study*. 2nd edition. London: Darton Longman & Todd, 1996.

_____. *Understanding Old Testament Ethics: Approaches and Explorations*. Louisville: Westminster John Knox, 2003.

Baumgarten, Albert I. "Prologue: How Do We Know When We Are on to Something?" Pp. 3–20 in *Sects and Sectarianism in Jewish History*. Edited by Sacha Stern. ISJSJ 12. Leiden: Brill, 2011.

Beardslee, William A. "Poststructuralist Criticism." Pp. 253–67 in *To Each Its Own Meaning: An Introduction to Biblical Criticisms and Their Applications*. Edited by Stephen R. Haynes and Steven L. McKenzie. Louisville: Westminster John Knox, 1993.

Bechtel, Lyn M. "Shame as a Sanction of Social Control in Biblical Israel: Judicial, Political, and Social Shaming." *JSOT* 49 (1991): 47–76.

_____. "The Perception of Shame within the Divine-Human Relationship in Biblical Israel," Pp. 79–92 in *Uncovering Ancient Stones: Essays in Memory of H. Neil Richardson*. Winona Lake, IN: Eisenbrauns, 1994.

Beilby, James K., and Paul R. Eddy, eds. *The Nature of the Atonement: Four Views*. Downers Grove: IVP Academic, 2006.

Ben-Mordecai, C. A. "The Inquity of the Sanctuary: A Study of the Hebrew Term עָוֹן." *JBL* 60 (1941): 311–14.

Benedict, Ruth. *The Chrysanthemum and the Sword: Patterns of Japanese Culture*. Boston: Houghton Mifflin, 1946.

Bergant, Dianne. "'My Beloved Is Mine and I Am His' (Song 2:16): The Song of Songs and Honor and Shame." *Semeia* 68 (1994): 23–40.

Berry, J. W. "Imposed Etics-Emics-Derived Etics: The Operationalization of a Compelling Idea." *IJP* 24 (1989): 721–35.

Bertholet, Alfred. *Das Buch Hesekiel Erklärt*. KHZAT 12. Tübingen: Mohr Seibeck, 1897.

Bhaskar, Roy. *Dialectic: The Pulse of Freedom*. New York: Verso, 1993.

_____. *Reflections on Meta-Reality: Transcendence, Emancipation, and Everyday Life*. Thousand Oaks: Sage, 2002.

Blenkinsopp, Joseph. *Ezekiel*. Louisville: John Knox, 1990.

Blocher, Henri. "Biblical Metaphors of the Atonement." *JETS* 47 (2004): 629–45.

Block, Daniel I. "Divine Abandonment: Ezekiel's Adaptation of an Ancient near Eastern Motif," Pp. 15–42 in *The Book of Ezekiel: Theological and Anthropological Perspectives*. SBLSymS 9. Atlanta: SBL, 2000.

_____. "Text and Emotion: A Study in the 'Corruptions' in Ezekiel's Inaugural Vision (Ezekiel 1:4–28)." *CBQ* 50 (1988): 418–442.

_____. *The Book of Ezekiel: Chapters 1–24*. NICOT. Grand Rapids: Eerdmans, 1997.

_____. *The Book of Ezekiel: Chapters 25–48*. NICOT. Grand Rapids: Eerdmans, 1998.

_____. "The God Ezekiel Wants Us to Meet." Pp. 162–92 in *The God Ezekiel Creates*. Edited by Paul M. Joyce and Dalit Rom-Shiloni. LHBOTS 607. London: Bloomsbury, 2015.

Blois, R. de and E. R. Mueller, eds. *A Semantic Dictionary of Biblical Hebrew.* No pages. Cited 10 November 2011. Online: http://sdbh.org.

Bockmuehl, Markus. "Review of Bruce Malina, *the New Testament World: Insights from Cultural Anthropology (Third Edition, Revised and Expanded),*" *Bryn Mawr Classical Review* (2002). No Pages. Cited 26 August 2011. Online: http://ccat.sas.upenn.edu/bmcr/2002/2002–04–19.html.

Bodi, Daniel. "The Inversion of Values in Ezekiel 16 and the Reminiscence of the Istar Cult." Paper presented at SBL Annual Meeting. San Francisco, 18–22 November, 2011.

Boersma, Hans. *Violence, Hospitality, and the Cross: Reappropriating the Atonement Tradition.* Baker Academic, 2006.

Boff, Leonardo. *Passion of Christ, Passion of the World: The Facts, Their Interpretation, and Their Meaning Yesterday and Today.* Translated by Robert R. Barr. Maryknoll, NY: Orbis, 1987.

Bolt, Peter. *Jesus' Defeat of Death: Persuading Mark's Early Readers.* SNTSMS 125. Cambridge: Cambridge University Press, 2003.

Bonhoeffer, Dietrich. *Ethics.* Edited by Clifford J. Green. Translated by Reinhard Krauss, Charles C. West, and Douglas W. Stott. Vol. 6. Minneapolis: Fortress, 2005.

Borg, Marcus J., and N. T. Wright. *The Meaning of Jesus: Two Visions.* 1st edition. San Francisco: Harper, 1998.

Botha, P. J. "Isaiah 37.21–35: Sennacherib's Siege of Jerusalem as a Challenge to the Honour of Yahweh." *OTE* 13 (2000): 269–82.

Botterweck, G. J., and H. Ringgren. *Theological Dictionary of the Old Testament.* Translated by J. T. Willis, G. W. Bromiley, and D. E. Green. 8 volumes. Grand Rapids: Eerdmans, 1974-.

_____. *Theologische Wörterbuch zum Alten Testament.* Stuttgart: Kohlhammer, 1970-

Bourdieu, Pierre. *Outline of a Theory of Practice.* New York: Cambridge University Press, 1977.

Brenner, Athalya. "Pornoprophetics Revisited: Some Additional Reflections." *JSOT* 70 (1996): 63–86.

Brichto, Herbert. *The Names of God: Poetic Readings in Biblical Beginnings.* New York: Oxford University Press, 1998.

Broome, Edwin C., Jr. "Ezekiel's Abnormal Personality." *JBL* 65 (1946): 277–92.

Broughton, Geoff. *Restorative Christ: Jesus, Justice, and Discipleship.* Eugene: Pickwick, 2014.

Brown, David. "Anselm on Atonement," Pp. 279–302 in *The Cambridge Companion to Anselm.* Edited by Brian Davies and Brian Leftow. Cambridge: Cambridge University Press, 2004.

Brown, F., S. R. Driver, and C. A. Briggs. *A Hebrew and English Lexicon of the Old Testament.* Oxford: Clarendon, 1907.

Brownlee, William H. *Ezekiel 1–19.* WBC 28. Waco: Word, 1986.

Brueggemann, Walter. *An Introduction to the Old Testament: The Canon and Christian Imagination.* Louisville: Westminster John Knox, 2003.

_____. *Genesis.* Atlanta: John Knox, 1982.

Cairns, Douglas L. *Aidōs: The Psychology and Ethics of Honour and Shame in Ancient Greek Literature.* Oxford: Clarendon, 1993.

Carasik, Michael. *Theologies of the Mind in Biblical Israel.* New York: Peter Lang, 2005.

Carroll, Robert P. "The Myth of the Empty Land." *Semeia* 59 (1992): 79–93.

_____. "Textual Strategies and Ideology in the Second Temple Period." Pp. 108–124 in *Second Temple Studies: 1. Persian Period*. Edited by Philip R. Davies. JSOTSup 117. Sheffield: JSOT Press, 1991.

Carson, Donald A. *Exegetical Fallacies*. 2nd edition. Grand Rapids: Baker, 1996.

_____. *The Gagging of God: Christianity Confronts Pluralism*. Grand Rapids: Zondervan, 1995.

Carter, Charles E. "A Discipline in Transition: The Contributions of the Social Sciences to the Study of the Hebrew Bible." Pp. 3–36 in *Community, Identity, and Ideology: Social Science Approaches to the Hebrew Bible*. Edited by Charles E. Carter and Carol L. Meyers. SBTSOTS 6. Winona Lake, IN: Eisenbrauns, 1996.

Carvalho, Corrine L. "Priest, Prophet, and Exile: Ezekiel as a Literary Construct." Pp. 73–89 in *Ezekiel's Hierarchical World: Wrestling with a Tiered Reality*. Edited by Stephen L. Cook and Corrine Patton. SBLSymS 31. Atlanta: SBL, 2004.

Chalke, Steve and Alan Mann. *The Lost Message of Jesus*. Grand Rapids: Zondervan, 2003.

Chalke, Steve, Derek Tidball, David Hilborn, and Justin Thacker. *The Atonement Debate: Papers from the London Symposium on the Theology of Atonement*. Grand Rapids: Zondervan, 2008.

Chance, John K. "The Anthropology of Honor and Shame: Culture, Values, and Practice." *Semeia* 68 (1994): 139–51.

Chatman, Seymour. *Story and Discourse: Narrative Structure in Fiction and Film*. Ithaca, NY: Cornell University Press, 1978.

Childs, Brevard S. *Old Testament Theology in a Canonical Context*. Philadelphia: Fortress, 1986.

_____. *The Book of Exodus: A Critical, Theological Commentary*. OTL. Philadelphia: Westminster, 1974.

Choi, John H., and Bill T. Arnold. *A Guide to Biblical Hebrew Syntax*. Cambridge: Cambridge University Press, 2003.

Clements, Ronald E. "The Ezekiel Tradition: Prophecy in Time of Crisis." Pp. 119–136 in *Israel's Prophetic Tradition*. Edited by J. Coggins, A. Phillips, and M. Knibb. Cambridge: Cambridge University Press, 1982.

Clines, David J. A. *Interested Parties: The Ideology of Writers and Readers of the Hebrew Bible*. JSOTSup 205. Sheffield: Sheffield Academic Press, 1995.

_____, ed. *Dictionary of Classical Hebrew*. Sheffield: Phoenix, 1993-

Cogan, Morton. *Imperialism and Religion: Assyria, Judah and Israel in the Eighth and Seventh Centuries B.C.E.* Missoula, MT: SBL, 1974.

Cole, Graham A. *God the Peacemaker: How Atonement Brings Shalom*. Nottingham: Apollos, 2009.

Conn, Harvie M. *Eternal Word and Changing Worlds: Theology, Anthropology, and Mission in Trialogue*. Grand Rapids: Zondervan, 1984.

Conrad, Edgar W. *Reading the Latter Prophets: Toward a New Canonical Criticism*. JSOTSup 376. London: T. & T. Clark, 2003.

Cook, Stephen L. "Cosmos, *Kabod*, and Cherub: Ontological and Epistemological Hierarchy in Ezekiel." Pp. 179–197 in *Ezekiel's Hierarchical World: Wrestling with a Tiered Reality*. Edited by Stephen L. Cook and Corrine Patton. SBLSymS 31. Atlanta: SBL, 2004.

Cooper, Alan. "In Praise of Divine Caprice: The Significance of the Book of Jonah," Pp. 144–163 in *Among the Prophets: Language, Image and Structure in the*

Prophets. Edited by Philip R. Davies and David J. A. Clines. Sheffield: Sheffield Academic Press, 1993.

Craffert, Pieter F. "Is the Emic-Etic Distinction a Useful Tool for Cross-Cultural Interpretation of the New Testament?" *RT* 2 (1995): 14–37.

Creighton, M. R. "Revisiting Shame and Guilt Cultures: A Forty-Year Pilgrimage." *Ethos* 18 (1990): 279–307.

Crews, Frederick. *Postmodern Pooh*. Evanston, IL: Northwestern University Press, 2006.

_____. *The Pooh Perplex*. Chicago: University of Chicago Press, 2003.

Croft, William, and D. A. Cruse. *Cognitive Linguistics*. CTL. Cambridge: Cambridge University Press, 2004.

_____. *Lexical Semantics*. CTL. Cambridge: Cambridge University Press, 1986.

Crook, Zeba A. "Honor, Shame, and Social Status Revisited." *JBL* 128 (2009): 591–611.

_____. "Method and Models in New Testament Interpretation: A Critical Engagement with Louise Lawrence's Literary Ethnography." *RelSRev* 32 (2006): 87–97.

_____. "Reciprocity—Covenantal Exchange as a Test Case," Pp. 78–91 in *Ancient Israel: The Old Testament in Its Social Context*. Edited by Philip F. Esler. London: SCM, 2005.

_____. *Reconceptualising Conversion: Patronage, Loyalty, and Conversion in the Religions of the Ancient Mediterranean*. BZAW 130 Berlin: De Gruyter, 2004.

_____. "Reflections on Culture and Social-Scientific Models." *JBL* 124 (2005): 515–520.

_____. "Structure Versus Agency in Studies of the Biblical Social World: Engaging with Louise Lawrence." *JSNT* 29 (2007): 251–75.

Cserháti, Márta. "The Insider/Outsider Debate and the Study of the Bible." *CV* 50 (2008): 313–322.

Darr, Katheryn Pfisterer. "Ezekiel's Justifications of God: Teaching Troubling Texts." *JSOT* 55 (1992): 97–117.

Davies, Philip R. *Whose Bible Is It Anyway?* 2nd edition. London: T. & T. Clark, 2004.

Day, Peggy L. "The Bitch Had It Coming to Her: Rhetoric and Interpretation in Ezekiel 16." *BibInt* 8 (2000): 231–54.

Dembski, William A. "The Fallacy of Contextualism." *Themelios* 20 (1995): 8–11.

Deonna, Julien, Fabrice Teroni, and Raffaele Rodogno. *In Defense of Shame: The Faces of an Emotion*. Oxford: Oxford University Press, 2011.

Derrida, Jacques. *Of Grammatology*. Baltimore: Johns Hopkins University Press, 1998.

_____. *Writing and Difference*. Translated by Alan Bass. London: Routledge, 2001.

Derrida, Jacques, Alan Bass, and Henri Ronse. *Positions*. Chicago: University of Chicago Press, 1981.

Derrida, Jacques, and John D. Caputo. *Deconstruction in a Nutshell: A Conversation with Jacques Derrida*. New York: Fordham University Press, 1996.

DeSilva, David Arthur. "Despising Shame: A Cultural-Anthropological Investigation of the Epistle to the Hebrews." *JBL* 113 (1994): 439–61.

_____. *Despising Shame: The Social Function of the Rhetoric of Honor and Dishonor in the Epistle to the Hebrews*. Atlanta: Scholars Press, 1996.

_____. "Honor and Shame." Pp. 518–22 in *DNTB*. Edited by Craig A. Evans and Stanley E. Porter. Downers Grove: InterVarsity, 2000.

_____. "Honor and Shame." Pp. 431–36 in *DOTPe*. Edited by David W. Baker and T. Desmond Alexander. Downers Grove: InterVarsity, 2003.

Dickson, John P. *How Christian Humility Upended the World*. Australian Broadcasting Association. No Pages. Cited 27 October 2011. Online: http://www.abc.net .au/religion/articles/2011/10/27/3349673.htm.

_____. *Humilitas: A Lost Key to Life, Love, and Leadership*. Grand Rapids: Zondervan, 2011.

Douglas, Mary. *Jacob's Tears: The Priestly Work of Reconciliation*. Oxford: Oxford University Press, 2004.

_____. *Leviticus as Literature*. Oxford: Oxford University Press, 1999.

_____. *Natural Symbols: Explorations in Cosmology*. London: Barrie & Rockliff, 1970.

_____. *Purity and Danger: An Analysis of the Concepts of Pollution and Taboo*. London: Routledge and Kegan Paul, 1966.

Downing, F. Gerald. "'Honor' among Exegetes." *CBQ* 61(1999): 53–73.

Dozeman, Thomas B. "Inner-Biblical Interpretation of Yahweh's Gracious and Compassionate Character." *JBL* 108 (1989): 207–23.

Duguid, Iain M. *Ezekiel*. NIVAC. Grand Rapids: Zondervan, 1999.

_____. "Ezekiel." Pp. 229–32 in *NDBT*. Edited by T. Desmond Alexander and Brian S. Rosner. Leicester: Inter-Varsity Press, 2000.

_____. "Putting Priests in Their Place: Ezekiel's Contribution to the History of the Old Testament Priesthood." Pp. 43–59 in *Ezekiel's Hierarchical World: Wrestling with a Tiered Reality*. Edited by Stephen L. Cook and Corrine Patton. SBLSymS 31. Atlanta: SBL, 2004.

Eberhart, Christian. *The Sacrifice of Jesus: Understanding Atonement Biblically*. Minneapolis: Fortress, 2011.

Eilberg-Schwartz, Howard. *The Savage in Judaism: An Anthropology of Israelite Religion and Ancient Judaism*. Bloomington: Indiana University Press, 1990.

Eisenstadt, S. N. and L. Roniger. *Patrons, Clients and Friends: Interpersonal Relations and the Structure of Trust in Society*. Cambridge: Cambridge University Press, 1984.

Elliger, K., and W. Rudolph, eds. *Biblia Hebraica Stuttgartensia*. Stuttgart: Deutsche Bibelgesellschaft, 1998.

Elliott, Charles. *Memory and Salvation*. London: Darton, Longman & Todd, 1995.

Elliott, John H. "Deuteronomy—Shameful Encroachment on Shameful Parts: Deuteronomy 25:11–12 and Biblical Euphemism." Pp. 161–76 in *Ancient Israel: The Old Testament in Its Social Context*. Edited by Philip F. Esler. London: SCM, 2006.

_____. "On Wooing Crocodiles for Fun and Profit: Confessions of an Intact Admirer." Pp. 5–20 in *Social Scientific Models for Interpreting the Bible: Essays by the Context Group in Honor of Bruce J. Malina*. Edited by Bruce J. Malina and John J. Pilch. Leiden: Brill, 2001.

Erikson, Erik H. *Childhood and Society*. Revised edition. London: Vintage, 1995.

Esler, Philip F., ed. *Ancient Israel: The Old Testament in Its Social Context*. London: SCM, 2006.

_____. *Sex, Wives, and Warriors: Reading Old Testament Narrative with Its Ancient Audience*. Eugene: Cascade, 2011.

_____. "The Context Group Project: An Autobiographical Account." Pp. 46–61 in *Anthropology and Biblical Studies*. Edited by Louise Joy Lawrence and Mario I. Aguilar. Leiden: Deo, 2004.

_____. *The First Christians in Their Social World: Social-Scientific Approaches to New Testament Interpretation*. London: Routledge, 1994.

Estes, Daniel J. "Poetic Artistry in the Expression of Fear in Psalm 49." *BSac* 161 (2004): 55–71.

Evans, C. A. and S. E. Porter, eds. *Dictionary of New Testament Background*. Downers Grove: InterVarsity, 2000.

Evans, John Frederick. ""You Shall Know That I Am Yahweh:" Ezekiel's Recognition Formula as a Marker of the Prophecy's Intertextual Relation to Exodus." Th.D. dissertation, University of Stellenbosch, 2006.

Evans-Pritchard, E. E. *Theories of Primitive Religion*. Oxford: Clarendon, 1965.

Feldman, Louis H. "Jewish Proselytism." Pp. 372–408 in *Eusebius, Christianity and Judaism*. Edited by Harold W. Attridge and Gohei Hata. Detroit: Wayne States University Press, 1992.

Finlan, Stephen. *Problems with Atonement: The Origins of, and Controversy About, the Atonement Doctrine*. Collegeville, MN: Liturgical Press, 2005.

Fish, Stanley. *Is There a Text in this Class? The Authority of Interpretive Communities*. Cambridge: Harvard University Press, 1980.

Fishbane, Michael A. *Biblical Interpretation in Ancient Israel*. Reprinted with corrections. Oxford: Oxford University Press, 1988.

Foucault, Michel, Lysa Hochroth, and Sylvere Lotringer. *The Politics of Truth*. New York: Semiotext(e), 1997.

Frame, John M. *The Doctrine of the Knowledge of God*. Grand Rapids: Presbyterian and Reformed, 1987.

Freeman, Derek. *Margaret Mead and Samoa: The Making and Unmaking of an Anthropological Myth*. Canberra: Australian National University Press, 1983.

_____. *Paradigms in Collision: The Far-Reaching Controversy over the Samoan Researches of Margaret Mead and Its Significance for the Human Sciences: A Public Lecture Given at the Australian National University on October 23, 1991*. Canberra: Research School of Pacific Studies, Australian National University, 1992.

_____. *The Fateful Hoaxing of Margaret Mead: A Historical Analysis of Her Samoan Research*. Boulder: Westview, 1999.

Freud, Sigmund. *The Ego and the Id*. Edited by James Strachey. Translated by Joan Riviere. Rev. ed.. IPAL 12. London: Hogarth Press and the Institute of Psycho-Analysis, 1962.

Galambush, Julie. *Jerusalem in the Book of Ezekiel: The City as Yahweh's Wife*. Atlanta: Scholars Press, 1992.

Geertz, Clifford. *The Interpretation of Cultures*. New York: Basic Books, 1973.

Gemeren, Willem A. van, ed. *New International Dictionary of Old Testament Theology and Exegesis*. 5 volumes. Grand Rapids: Zondervan, 1997.

Gibson, J. C. L. *Davidson's Introductory Hebrew Grammar—Syntax*. Edinburgh: T. & T. Clark, 1994.

Giddens, Anthony. *The Constitution of Society: Outline of the Theory of Structuration*. Berkeley: University of California Press, 1984.

Girard, René. *I See Satan Fall Like Lightning*. Maryknoll, NY: Orbis, 2001.

_____. *Things Hidden since the Foundation of the World*. Translated by Stephen Bann and Michael Metteer. Stanford: University Press, 1987.

Glatt-Gilad, David A. "Yahweh's Honor at Stake: A Divine Conundrum." *JSOT* 98 (2002): 63–74.

Gnuse, Robert Karl. *No Other Gods: Emergent Monotheism in Israel.* JSOTSup 241. Sheffield: Sheffield Academic Press, 1997.

Goldsworthy, Graeme. *Christ-Centred Biblical Theology: Hermeneutical Foundations and Principles.* Nottingham: Apollos, 2012.

_____. *Gospel and Kingdom: A Christian Interpretation of the Old Testament.* Rydalmere: Crossroad, 1994.

Green, Joel B. and Mark D. Baker. *Recovering the Scandal of the Cross: Atonement in New Testament and Contemporary Contexts.* 2nd edition. Downers Grove: IVP Academic, 2011.

Greenberg, Moshe. *Ezekiel 1–20: A New Translation with Introduction and Commentary.* Anchor Bible 22. New York: Doubleday, 1983.

_____. *Ezekiel 21–37: A New Translation with Introduction and Commentary.* Anchor Bible 22A. New York: Doubleday, 1997.

_____. "The Thematic Unity of Exodus 3–11." *WCJS* 4 (1967): 151–154.

Gruber, Mayer I. *Aspects of Nonverbal Communication in the Ancient near East.* Rome: Pontifical Biblical Institute, 1980.

Gundry, Robert H. *Mark: A Commentary on His Apology for the Cross.* Grand Rapids: Eerdmans, 1992.

Gunton, Colin E., ed. *The Cambridge Companion to Christian Doctrine.* Cambridge: Cambridge University Press, 1997.

_____. *Actuality of Atonement: A Study of Metaphor, Rationality and the Christian Tradition.* London: Continuum, 2003.

_____. *The Theology of Reconciliation.* Edinburgh: T. & T. Clark, 2003.

Hagedorn, Anselm C., Zeba A. Crook, and Eric Clark Stewart, eds. *In Other Words: Essays on Social Science Methods and the New Testament in Honor of Jerome H. Neyrey.* Sheffield: Phoenix, 2007.

Halperin, David J. *Seeking Ezekiel: Text and Psychology.* State College: Pennsylvania State University Press, 1993.

Halpern, Baruch. "Jerusalem and the Lineages in the Seventh Century BCE: Kinship and the Rise of Individual Moral Liability." Pp. 11–107 in *Law and Ideology in Monarchic Israel.* Edited by Baruch Halpern and Deborah W. Hobson. *JSOTSupp.* Sheffield: Sheffield Academic Press, 1991.

Hamilton, James M. *God's Glory in Salvation through Judgment: A Biblical Theology.* Wheaton: Crossway, 2010.

Harris, Marvin. *Cultural Materialism: The Struggle for a Science of Culture.* New York: Random House, 1979.

Hasel, Gerhard F. "Polemic Nature of the Genesis Cosmology." *EQ* 46 (1974): 81–102.

Hays, Richard B. *Echoes of Scripture in the Letters of Paul.* New Haven: Yale University Press, 1989.

_____. "Foreword." Pp. xi–xv in *Reading the Bible Intertextually.* Edited by Richard B. Hays, Stefan Alkier, and Leroy Andrew Huizenga. Waco: Baylor University Press, 2009.

Heim, S. Mark. *Saved from Sacrifice: A Theology of the Cross.* Grand Rapids: Eerdmans, 2006.

Herntrich, Volkmar. *Ezechielprobleme.* Giessen: Alfred Topelmann, 1933.

Herzfeld, Michael. "Honour and Shame: Problems in the Comparative Analysis of Moral Systems." *Man* 15 (1980): 339–351.

Hess, Richard S. *Israelite Religions: An Archaeological and Biblical Survey.* Grand Rapids: Baker Academic, 2007.

Hiebert, Paul G. *Missiological Implications of Epistemological Shifts: Affirming Truth in a Modern/Postmodern World.* Harrisburg: Trinity Press International, 1999.

Hill, Charles E., Frank A. James, and Roger R. Nicole eds. *The Glory of the Atonement: Biblical, Historical & Practical Perspectives, Essays in Honor of Roger Nicole.* Downers Grove: InterVarsity, 2004.

Himmelfarb, Gertrude. *Marriage and Morals among the Victorians: Essays.* London: Faber, 1986.

Hobbs, T. Raymond. "Reflections on Honor, Shame, and Covenant Relations." *JBL* 116 (1997): 501–3.

Holmes, Stephen R. *The Wondrous Cross: Atonement and Penal Substitution in the Bible and History.* London: Paternoster, 2007.

Hubbard, R. L. "Dynamistic and Legal Processes in Psalm 7." *ZAW* 94 (1982): 267–79.

_____. "Is the "Tatsphäre" Always a Sphere?" *JETS* 25 (1982): 257–62.

Hundley, Michael. "To Be or Not to Be: A Reexamination of Name Language in Deuteronomy and the Deuteronomistic History." *VT* 59 (2009): 533–55.

Hutton, Rodney R. "Are the Parents Still Eating Sour Grapes? Jeremiah's Use of the Māšāl in Contrast to Ezekiel." *CBQ* 71 (2009): 275–85.

Hymes, Dell H. "Emics, Etics, and Openness: An Ecumenical Approach." Pp. 120–26 in *Emics and Etics: The Insider/Outsider Debate.* Edited by Thomas N. Headland, Kenneth L. Pike, and Marvin Harris. Newbury Park: Sage, 1990.

Idestrom, Rebecca G.S. "Echoes of the Book of Exodus in Ezekiel." *JSOT* 33 (2009): 489–510.

Jeffery, S., Michael Ovey, and Andrew Sach. *Pierced for Our Transgressions: Rediscovering the Glory of Penal Substitution.* Nottingham: InterVarsity, 2007.

Jenni, E., and C. Westermann, eds. *Theological Lexicon of the Old Testament.* Translated by M. E. Biddle. 3 volumes. Peabody: Hendrickson, 1994.

Jobes, Karen H. "Shame and Honor in the Book of Esther." *RBL* 2 (2000): 273–75.

Johnston, Philip. *Shades of Sheol: Death and Afterlife in the Old Testament.* Leicester: Apollos, 2002.

Jones, E. Michael. *Degenerate Moderns: Modernity as Rationalized Sexual Misbehavior.* San Francisco: Ignatius, 1993.

Joüon, P. *A Grammar of Biblical Hebrew.* Subsidia Biblical 27. Translated and revised by T. Muraoka. 2 volumes. Rome: Pontifical Biblical Institute, 2006.

Joyce, Paul. *Divine Initiative and Human Response in Ezekiel.* Sheffield: JSOT Press, 1989.

_____. *Ezekiel: A Commentary.* New York: T. & T. Clark, 2007.

_____. "Ezekiel and Individual Responsibility," Pp. 317–21 in *Ezekiel and His Book: Textual and Literary Criticism and Their Interrelation.* Edited by J. Lust. BETL. Leuven: Leuven University Press, 1986.

_____. "Individual Responsibility in Ezekiel 18?" Pp. 185–96 in *Studia Biblical 1978: Papers on Old Testament and Related Themes.* Edited by E. A. Livingstone. Sheffield: JSOT Press, 1978.

_____. "The Individual and the Community." Pp. 77–93 in *Beginning Old Testament Study.* Edited by J. W. Rogerson. London: SPCK, 1998.

Kaminsky, Joel S. *Corporate Responsibility in the Hebrew Bible.* Sheffield: Sheffield Academic Press, 1995.

_____. "The Sins of the Fathers: A Theological Investigation of the Biblical Tension between Corporate and Individualized Retribution." *Judaism* 46 (1997): 319–32.

Kamionkowski, S. Tamar. *Gender Reversal and Cosmic Chaos: A Study on the Book of Ezekiel.* London: Sheffield Academic Press, 2003.

Kamper, Angela. "Child-Sex Fiend Dennis Ferguson Promises to Return." *The Daily Telegraph* (22/10/2009). No Pages. Cited 22 October, 2012. Online: http://www.dailytelegraph.com.au/news/child-sex-fiend-dennis-ferguson-promises-to-return/story-e6freuy9-1225789557953.

Katchadourian, Herant A. *Guilt: The Bite of Conscience.* Stanford: Stanford General Books, 2009.

Kautszch, E., ed. *Gesenius' Hebrew Grammar.* Translated by A. E. Crowley. 2nd edition. Oxford: Oxford University Press, 1910.

Kemp, Stephen. "Critical Realism and the Limits of Philosophy." *European Journal of Social Theory* 8 (2005): 171–91.

Kim, Brittany. "Yhwh as Jealous Husband: Abusive Authoritarian or Protective Husband? A Reexamination of a Prophetic Image." Pp. 127–47 in *Daughter Zion: Her Portrait, Her Response.* AIIL 13. Edited by Mark J. Boda, Carol Dempsey, and LeeAnn Snow Flesher. Atlanta: SBL, 2012.

Kirkpatrick, Shane. *Competing for Honor: A Social-Scientific Reading of Daniel 1–6.* Leiden: Brill, 2005.

Kitchen, K. A. *On the Reliability of the Old Testament.* Grand Rapids: Eerdmans, 2003.

Kitchen, K. A., and Paul J. N. Lawrence. *Treaty, Law and Covenant in the Ancient Near East.* 3 Volumes. Wiesbaden: Harrassowitz Verlag, 2012.

Kiuchi, N. *The Purification Offering in the Priestly Literature: Its Meaning and Function.* JSOTSup 56. Sheffield: JSOT Press, 1988.

Klawans, Jonathan. *Impurity and Sin in Ancient Judaism.* New York: Oxford University Press, 2000.

Kline, Meredith G. *Treaty of the Great King: The Covenant Structure of Deuteronomy: Studies and Commentary.* Eugene, OR: Wipf & Stock, 2012.

Knierim, Rolf. *Die Hauptbegriffe Für Sünde Im Alten Testament.* Gütersloh: G. Mohn, 1965.

Koch, Klaus. "Is There a Doctrine of Retribution in the Old Testament?" Pp. 57–87 in *Theodicy in the Old Testament.* Edited by James L. Crenshaw. Philadelphia: Fortress, 1983.

Koehler, L., W. Baumgartner, and J. J. Stamm, *The Hebrew and Aramaic Lexicon of the Old Testament.* Translated and edited by M. E. J. Richardson. 5 volumes. Leiden: Brill, 1994–2000.

Konstan, David. "Shame in Ancient Greece." *SR* 70 (2003): 1031–60.

———. *The Emotions of the Ancient Greeks: Studies in Aristotle and Classical Literature.* Toronto: University of Toronto Press, 2006.

Kraus, C. Norman. *Jesus Christ Our Lord: Christology from a Disciple's Perspective.* Scottdale: Herald Press, 1987.

Kressel, Gideon M. "An Anthropologist's Response to the Use of Social Science Models in Biblical Studies." *Semeia* 68 (1994): 153–161.

Kristeva, Julia. *Desire in Language: A Semiotic Approach to Literature and Art.* Colombia: Columbia University Press, 1980.

Kutsko, John F. *Between Heaven and Earth: Divine Presence and Absence in the Book of Ezekiel.* Winona Lake, IN: Eisenbrauns, 2000.

Laato, Antti. *Josiah and David Redivivus: The Historical Josiah and the Messianic Expectations of Exilic and Postexilic Times.* Stockholm: Almqvist & Wiksell International, 1992.

Lam, Joseph. "Metaphor, Lexicalisation and Diachronic Change: The Case of the Biblical Nāśā'." Paper presented at SBL Annual Meeting. San Francisco, 18–22 November, 2011.

_____. "Review of Gary A. Anderson, *Sin: A History*." *RBL* (2010). No Pages. Cited October 30 2012. Online: http://www.bookreviews.org/pdf/7556_8254.pdf.

_____. "The Metaphorical Patterning of the Sin Concept in Biblical Hebrew." Ph.D. dissertation. University of Chicago, 2012.

Lane, William L. *The Gospel According to Mark*. Grand Rapids: Eerdmans, 1974.

Laniak, Timothy S. *Shame and Honor in the Book of Esther*. Atlanta: Scholars Press, 1998.

Lapsley, Jacqueline E. *Can These Bones Live? The Problem of the Moral Self in the Book of Ezekiel*. Berlin: de Gruyter, 2000.

Lapsley, Jacqueline E. "Shame and Self-Knowledge: The Positive Role of Shame in Ezekiel's View of the Moral Self." Pp. 143–73 in *The Book of Ezekiel: Theological and Anthropological Perspectives*. SBLSymS 9. Edited by Margaret S. Odell and John T. Strong. Atlanta: SBL, 2000.

Lasch, Christopher. "For Shame: Why Americans Should Be Wary of Self-Esteem." *NR* 207 (1992). No Pages. Cited June 7 2012. Online: http://www.newrepublic.com/book/review/shame-why-americans-should-be-wary-self-esteem#.

_____. *The Culture of Narcissism: American Life in an Age of Diminishing Expectations*. New York: Norton, 1991.

Lawrence, Louise Joy. *An Ethnography of the Gospel of Matthew: A Critical Assessment of the Use of the Honour and Shame Model in New Testament Studies*. WUNT 2/165. Tübingen: Mohr Siebeck, 2003.

_____. "'For Truly, I Tell You, They Have Received Their Reward' (Matt 6:2): Investigating Honor Precedence and Honor Virtue." *CBQ* 64 (2002): 687–702.

_____. "Structure, Agency and Ideology: A Response to Zeba Crook." *JSNT* 29 (2007): 277–86.

Lemos, T. M. "Shame and Mutilation of Enemies in the Hebrew Bible." *JBL* 125 (2006): 225–41.

Lessing, Gotthold. *Lessing's Theological Writings: Selected and Translated by Henry Chadwick* LMRT. Edited and translated by Henry Chadwick. Stanford: Stanford University Press, 1957

Leung Lai, Barbara M. *Through the 'I'-Window: The Inner Life of Characters in the Hebrew Bible*. HBM 34. Sheffield: Phoenix, 2011.

Levenson, Jon Douglas. *Theology of the Program of Restoration of Ezekiel 40–48*. Missoula, MT: Scholars Press, 1976.

Levi-Strauss, Claude. "Structuralism and Ecology." *SSI* 12 (1973): 7–23.

Levitt Kohn, Risa. *A New Heart and a New Soul: Ezekiel, the Exile and the Torah*. JSOTSup 358. London: Sheffield Academic Press, 2002.

Lévy-Bruhl, Lucien. *Primitive Mentality*. Translated by Lilian A. Clare. London: Allen & Unwin, 1923.

Lewis, Helen B. *Shame and Guilt in Neurosis*. New York: IUP, 1971.

Lindars, Barnabas. "Ezekiel and Individual Responsibility." *VT* 15 (1965), 452–67.

Lindbeck, George. *The Nature of Doctrine: Religion and Theology in a Postliberal Age*. Philadelphia: Westminster, 1984.

Ling, Timothy J. "Virtuoso Religion and the Judean Social World." Pp. 227–58 in *Anthropology and Biblical Studies: Avenues of Approach*. Edited by Louise Joy Lawrence and Mario I. Aguilar. Leiden: Deo, 2004.

Lonergan, Bernard. *Method in Theology.* 2nd edition. London: Darton, Longman & Todd, 1973.

Longman, Tremper, III, and Daniel Reid. *God Is a Warrior.* Grand Rapids: Zondervan, 1995.

Luc, Alex. "A Theology of Ezekiel: God's Name and Israel's History." *JETS* 26 (1983): 137–143.

Lyons, Michael A. *From Law to Prophecy: Ezekiel's Use of the Holiness Code.* LHBOTS 507. New York: T. & T. Clark, 2009.

Maine, Henry Sumner, and Carleton Kemp Allen. *Ancient Law: Its Connection with the Early History of Society and Its Relation to Modern Ideas.* World's Classics 362. London: Oxford University Press, 1931.

Malina, Bruce J. "Review of *Despising Shame: Honor, Discourse, and Community Maintenance in the Epistle to the Hebrews.*" *RBL* 116 (1997): 378–79.

_____. *The New Testament World: Insights from Cultural Anthropology.* Rev ed. Louisville: Westminster John Knox, 1993.

_____. *Windows on the World of Jesus: Time Travel to Ancient Judea.* Louisville: Westminster John Knox, 1993.

Malina, Bruce J., and John J. Pilch, eds. *Social Scientific Models for Interpreting the Bible: Essays by the Context Group in Honor of Bruce J. Malina.* Boston: Brill, 2001.

Martial. *Epigrams, Volume 1: Spectacles, Books 1–5.* Edited and translated by D. R. Shackleton Bailey. *LCL* 94. Cambridge, MA: Harvard University Press, 1993.

Matthews, I. G. *Ezekiel.* AACOT. Philadelphia: Amerian Baptist Publication Society, 1939.

Matties, Gordon H. *Ezekiel 18 and the Rhetoric of Moral Discourse.* SBLDS 126. Atlanta: Scholars Press, 1990.

McConville, J. Gordon. "God's 'Name' and God's 'Glory'." *TynBul* 30 (1979): 149–63.

McCutcheon, Russell T. *Studying Religion: An Introduction.* London: Equinox, 2007.

McGrath, Alister E. *What Was God Doing on the Cross?* Grand Rapids: Zondervan, 1992.

McKeating, Henry. "Ezekiel the 'Prophet Like Moses.'" *JSOT* 61 (1994): 97–109.

Mead, Margaret. *Coming of Age in Samoa: A Study of Adolescence and Sex in Primitive Societies.* Melbourne: Penguin, 1954.

_____. *Cooperation and Competition among Primitive Peoples.* London: McGraw-Hill, 1937.

Mein, Andrew. *Ezekiel and the Ethics of Exile.* OTRM. Oxford: Oxford University Press, 2001.

Mendenhall, George E. *Law and Covenant in Israel and the Ancient near East.* Pittsburgh: Presbyterian Board of Colportage of Western Pennsylvania, 1955.

Mettinger, Tryggve N. D. *The Dethronement of Sabaoth: Studies in the Shem and Kabod Theologies.* Lund: Gleerup, 1982.

Milbank, John. *Theology and Social Theory: Beyond Secular Reason.* 2nd edition. Oxford: Blackwell, 2006.

Milgrom, Jacob. *Cult and Conscience: The Asham and the Priestly Doctrine of Repentance.* Leiden: Brill, 1976.

_____. "Sin-Offering or Purification-Offering." *VT* 21 (1971): 237–39.

_____. *Leviticus 1–16: A New Translation with Introduction and Commentary.* AB 3. New York: Doubleday, 1991.

Miller, Patrick D. *Sin and Judgment in the Prophets : A Stylistic and Theological Analysis.* Chico, CA: Scholars Press, 1982.

Miller, Susan. "Shame as an Impetus to the Creation of Conscience," *IntJPsychoanal* 70 (1989): 231–43.

Miller-Naudé, Cynthia, and Ziony Zevit, eds, *Diachrony in Biblical Hebrew.* LSAWS 8. Winona Lake, IN: Eisenbrauns, 2012

Morgenstern, Julian. "The Book of the Covenant, Part 3: The Huqqim." *HUCA* 8–9 (1931–32): 1–150.

Nathanson, Donald L. *Shame and Pride: Affect, Sex and the Birth of the Self.* New York: Norton, 1992.

_____, ed. *The Many Faces of Shame.* New York: Guilford, 1987.

Nevader, Madhavi. "Creating a *Deus Non Creator*: Divine Sovereignty and Creation in Ezekiel." Pp. 55–70 in *The God Ezekiel Creates.* Edited by Paul M. Joyce and Dalit Rom-Shiloni. LHBOTS 607. London: Bloomsbury, 2015.

Neyrey, Jerome H. "Despising the Shame of the Cross: Honor and Shame in the Johannine Passion Narrative." *Semeia* 68 (1994): 113–37.

_____. *Honor and Shame in the Gospel of Matthew.* Louisville: Westminster John Knox, 1998.

_____. *Paul, in Other Words: A Cultural Reading of His Letters.* Louisville: Westminster John Knox, 1990.

Nietzsche, Friedrich Wilhelm, Walter Arnold Kaufmann, and R. J. Hollingdale. *The Will to Power.* New York: Vintage, 1968.

Nogalski, James. "Recurring Themes in the Book of the Twelve: Creating Points of Contact for a Theological Reading." *Interpretation* 61 (2007): 125–36.

Odell, Margaret S. *Ezekiel.* Macon: Smyth & Helwys, 2005.

_____. "The Inversion of Shame and Forgiveness in Ezekiel 16.59–63." *JSOT* 56 (1992): 101–12.

Ortlund, Eric. "Shame in Restoration in Ezekiel." *SEEJ* 2 (2011): 1–17.

Ostrofsky, Richard. *Affect Theory, Shame and the Logic of Personality.* No Pages. Cited June 6 2012. Online: http://www.secthoughts.com/Misc%20Essays/Shame%20and%20Personality.htm.

Otto, Rudolf. *The Idea of the Holy: An Inquiry into the Non-Rational Factor in the Idea of the Divine and Its Relation to the Rational.* Harmondsworth: Penguin, 1959.

Overholt, Thomas W. *Cultural Anthropology and the Old Testament.* Minneapolis: Fortress, 1996.

Pembroke, Neil. *The Art of Listening: Dialogue, Shame, and Pastoral Care.* Grand Rapids: Eerdmans, 2002.

Peristiany, John G., ed. *Honour and Shame: The Values of Mediterranean Society.* London: Weidenfeld & Nicolson, 1965.

Peristiany, John G., and Julian Alfred Pitt-Rivers. *Honor and Grace in Anthropology.* CSSCA 76. Cambridge: Cambridge University Press, 1992.

Petersen, David L. "Creation and Hierarchy in Ezekiel: Methodological Perspectives and Theological Prospects." Pp. 169–78 in *Ezekiel's Hierarchical World: Wrestling with a Tiered Reality.* Edited by Stephen L. Cook and Corrine Patton. SBLSymS 31. Atlanta: SBL, 2004.

_____. "The Ambiguous Role of Moses as Prophet." Pp. 311–24 in *Israel's Prophets and Israel's Past: Essays on the Relationship of Prophetic Texts and Israelite History in Honor or John H. Hayes* LHBOTS 446. Edited by Brad E. Kelle and Megan Bishop Moore. London: T. & T. Clark, 2006.

Piers, Gerhart and Milton B. Singer. *Shame and Guilt: A Psychoanalytic and a Cultural Study.* American Lectures in Psychiatry 171. Springfield: Norton, 1953.

Pike, Kenneth L. *Language in Relation to a Unified Theory of the Structure of Human Behaviour.* 2nd edition. Janua Linguarum Series Maior 24. The Hague: Mouton, 1971.

Pike, Kenneth L., Thomas N. Headland, and Marvin Harris. *Emics and Etics: The Insider/Outsider Debate.* Frontiers of Anthropology 7. Newbury Park: Sage, 1990.

Pippin, Tina. "Ideology, Ideological Criticism, and the Bible." *Currents in Research* 4 (1996): 51–78.

Pitt-Rivers, Julian Alfred. "Honour," in *IESS.* Edited by David Sills and Robert Merton. No Pages. Cited 4 October, 2011. Online: http://www.encyclopedia.com/doc/IG2-3045000526. Print Edition: New York: MacMillan, 1968.

———. *The Fate of Shechem: Or, the Politics of Sex: Essays in the Anthropology of the Mediterranean.* Cambridge: Cambridge University Press, 1977.

Polzin, Robert M. *Samuel and the Deuteronomist: A Literary Study of the Deuteronomic History. Part Two—I Samuel.* San Francisco: Harper & Row, 1989.

Porter, J. R. "Legal Aspects of the Concept of Corporate Personality in the Old Testament." *VT* 15 (1965): 361–80.

Porter, Stanley E. "Peace." Pp. 682–83 in *New Dictionary of Bibilcal Theology.* Edited by T. Desmond Alexander and Brian S. Rosner. Leicester: Inter-Varsity, 2001.

Ray, Darby Kathleen. *Deceiving the Devil: Atonement, Abuse, and Ransom.* Cleveland: Pilgrim, 1998.

Renz, Thomas. *The Rhetorical Function of the Book of Ezekiel.* Boston: Brill Academic, 2002.

Reynolds, Jack. "Jacques Derrida (1930–2004)." *Internet Encyclopedia of Philosophy.* No Pages. Cited December 17 2012. Online: http://www.iep.utm.edu/derrida/

Richter, Sandra L. *The Deuteronomistic History and the Name Theology: ləšakkēn šəmô šām in the Bible and the Ancient Near East.* Berlin: de Gruyter, 2002.

Robinson, H. Wheeler. *The Christian Doctrine of Man.* 3rd edition. Edinburgh: T. & T. Clark, 1926.

———. "The Hebrew Conception of Corporate Personality." Pp. 49–62 in *Werden und Wesen des Alten Testaments: Vorträge gehalten auf der internationalen Tagung alttestamentlicher Forscher zu Göttingen vom 4.–10. September 1935.* Edited by P. Volz, F. Stummer and J. Hempel. BZAW 66. Berlin: de Gruyter, 1936)

Roche, Michael de. "Yahweh's Rîb against Israel: A Reassessment of the So-Called "Prophetic Lawsuit" in the Preexilic Prophets." *JBL* 102 (1983): 563–74.

Rogerson, J. W. *Anthropology and the Old Testament.* Oxford: Basil Blackwell, 1978.

———. "The Hebrew Conception of Corporate Personality: A Re-Examination." *JTS* 21 (1970): 1–16.

Roniger, L. *Hierarchy and Trust in Modern Mexico and Brazil.* New York: Praeger, 1990.

Rosner, B. S. et al., eds. *New Dictionary of Biblical Theology.* Downers Grove: Inter-Varsity, 2000.

Roth, M. T. et al., eds. *The Assyrian Dictionary of the Oriental Institute of the University of Chicago.* Chicago: Oriental Institute, 1956–2011.

Runge, Steven. *Discourse Grammar of the Greek New Testament: A Practical Introduction for Teaching and Exegesis.* Peabody: Hendrickson, 2010.

Scheff, Thomas J. *Microsociology: Discourse, Emotion and Social Structure.* Chicago: University of Chicago Press, 1994.

Schwartz, Baruch J. "A Priest out of Place: Reconsidering Ezekiel's Role in the History of the Israelite Priesthood," Pp. 61–71 in *Ezekiel's Hierarchical World: Wres-*

tling with a Tiered Reality. Edited by Stephen L. Cook and Corrine Patton. SBLSymS 31. Atlanta: SBL, 2004.

——. "Ezekiel's Dim View of Israel's Restoration." Pp. 43–67 in *The Book of Ezekiel: Theological and Anthropological Perspectives.* Edited by Margaret S. Odell and John T. Strong. SBLSymS 9. Atlanta: SBL, 2000.

——. "The Bearing of Sin in the Priestly Literature." Pp. 3–21 in *Pomegranates and Golden Bells: Studies in Biblical, Jewish, and Near Easter Ritual, Law, and Literature in Honor of Jacob Milgrom.* Edited by David P. Wright, David Noel Freedman, and Avi Huritz. Winona Lake, IN: Eisenbrauns, 1995.

Schwartz, Seth. *Were the Jews a Mediterranean Society? Reciprocity and Solidarity in Ancient Judaism.* Princeton: Princeton University Press, 2010.

Shead, Andrew G. "An Old Testament Theology of the Sabbath Year and Jubilee." *Reformed Theological Review* 61 (2002): 19–33.

Shead, Stephen L. *Radical Frame Semantics and Biblical Hebrew: Exploring Lexical Semantics.* Leiden: Brill, 2011.

Sherwood, Yvonne. *The Prostitute and the Prophet: Hosea's Marriage in Literary-Theoretical Perspective.* JSOTSup 212. GCT 2. Sheffield: Sheffield Academic Press, 1996.

Shields, Mary E. "Multiple Exposures: Body Rhetoric and Gender Characterization in Ezekiel 16." *JFSR* 14 (1998): 5–18.

Sills, David L., ed. *International Encyclopedia of Social Sciences.* New York: Macmillan, 1968.

Simkins, Ronald A. "'Return to Yahweh': Honor and Shame in Joel." *Semeia* 68 (1994): 41–54.

Simkins, Ronald A., Stephen L. Cook, and Athalya Brenner, eds. "The Social World of the Hebrew Bible: Twenty-Five Years of the Social Sciences in the Academy." *Semeia* 87 (1999).

Simmel, Georg. "The Metropolis and Mental Life," Pp. 174–86 in *Simmel on Culture: Selected Writings.* Edited by Mike Featherstone, Georg Simmel, and David Frisby. London: Sage, 1997.

Sklar, Jay. *Sin, Impurity, Sacrifice, Atonement: The Priestly Conceptions.* HBM 2. Sheffield: Sheffield Phoenix, 2005.

Sloane, Andrew. "Aberrant Textuality? The Case of Ezekiel the (Porno) Prophet." *Tyndale Bulletin* 59 (2008): 53–76.

Smith, John Merlin Powis. "The Rise of Individualism among the Hebrews." *The American Journal of Theology* 10 (1906): 251–66.

Smith, Mark S. *The Origins of Biblical Monotheism: Israel's Polytheistic Background and the Ugaritic Texts.* New York: Oxford University Press, 2001.

Sommer, Benjamin D. "Reflecting on Moses: The Redaction of Numbers 11." *JBL* 118 (1999): 601–24.

——. *The Bodies of God and the World of Ancient Israel.* New York: Cambridge University Press, 2009.

Stansell, Gary. "Honor and Shame in the David Narratives." *Semeia* 68 (1994): 55–79.

Stead, Michael R. *The Intertextuality of Zechariah 1–8.* London: T. & T. Clark, 2009.

Steinem, Gloria. *Revolution from Within: A Book of Self-Esteem.* London: Corgi, 1993.

Stendahl, Krister. "The Apostle Paul and the Introspective Conscience of the West." *HTR* 56 (1963): 199–215.

Stevenson, Kalinda Rose. *The Vision of Transformation: The Territorial Rhetoric of Ezekiel 40–48.* Atlanta: Scholars Press, 1996.

Stiebert, Johanna. "Shame and Prophecy: Approaches Past and Present." *BibInt* 8 (2000): 255–75.

_____. *The Construction of Shame in the Hebrew Bible: The Prophetic Contribution.* London: Sheffield Academic Press, 2002.

Stone, Ken. *Sex, Honor and Power in the Deuteronomistic History.* JSOTSup 234. Sheffield: Sheffield Academic Press, 1996.

Strong, John T. "Egypt's Shameful Death and the House of Israel's Exodus from Sheol (Ezekiel 32.17–32 and 37.1–14)." *JSOT* 34 (2010): 475–504.

_____. "God's *Kabod*: The Presence of Yahweh in the Book of Ezekiel," Pp. 69–96 in *The Book of Ezekiel: Theological and Anthropological Perspectives.* Edited by Margaret S. Odell and John T. Strong. SBLSymS 9. Atlanta: SBL, 2000.

Sykes, S. W. *The Story of Atonement.* London: Darton Longman & Todd, 1997.

Taylor, Charles. "Rorty and Philosophy." Pp. 158–80 in *Richard Rorty.* Edited by Charles Guignon and David R. Hiley. Cambridge: Cambridge University Press, 2003.

_____. *Sources of the Self: The Making of the Modern Identity.* Cambridge: Harvard University Press, 1989.

Tomkins, Silvan S. and Bertram P. Karon. *Affect, Imagery, Consciousness.* 4 vols. New York: Springer, 1962.

Tooman, William A. "Ezekiel's Radical Challenge to Inviolability." *ZAW* 121 (2009): 498–514.

Toorn, Karel van der. *Sin and Sanction in Israel and Mesopotamia: A Comparative Study.* SSN 22. Assen: Van Gorcum, 1985.

Torrance, Thomas F. *Theological Science.* Edinburgh: T. & T. Clark, 1996.

Torrance, Thomas F., and Robert T. Walker. *Atonement: The Person and Work of Christ.* Downers Grove: IVP Academic, 2009.

Trevaskis, Leigh M. *Holiness, Ethics and Ritual in Leviticus.* Sheffield: Phoenix, 2011.

Trible, Phyllis. *Texts of Terror: Literary-Feminist Readings of Biblical Narratives.* Philadelphia: Fortress, 1984.

Tucker, W. Dennis, Jr. "Is Shame a Matter of Patronage in the Communal Laments?." *Journal for the Study of the Old Testament* 31, no. 4 (2007): 465–80.

Van Leeuwen, Raymond C. "Scribal Wisdom and Theodicy in the Book of the Twelve." Pp. 31–49 in *In Search of Wisdom: Essays in Memory of John G. Gammie.* Edited by L. G. Perdue, B. B. Scott, and W. J. Wiseman. Louisville: Westminster John Knox, 1993.

Vanhoozer, Kevin. "Human Being, Individual and Social." Pp. 158–88 in *The Cambridge Companion to Christian Doctrine.* Edited by Colin E. Gunton. Cambridge: Cambridge University Press, 1997.

_____. *Is There a Meaning in This Text? The Bible, the Reader, and the Morality of Literary Knowledge.* Grand Rapids: Zondervan, 1998.

_____. "The Atonement in Postmodernity: Guilt, Goats and Gifts." Pp. 367–404 in *The Glory of the Atonement.* Edited by Charles Hill and Frank James III. Downers Grove: InterVarsity, 2004.

_____, ed. *The Cambridge Companion to Postmodern Theology.* Cambridge: Cambridge University Press, 2003.

_____. *The Drama of Doctrine: A Canonical-Linguistic Approach to Christian Theology.* Louisville: Westminster John Knox, 2005.

Vito, Robert A. di. "Old Testament Anthropology and the Construction of Personal Identity." *CBQ* 61 (1999): 217–38.

Vogt, Peter T. "Centralization and Decentralization in Deuteronomy." Pp. 118–38 in *Interpreting Deuteronomy: Issues and Approaches*. Edited by David G. Firth and Philip Johnston. Downers Grove: IVP Academic, 2012.

_____. *Deuteronomic Theology and the Significance of Torah: A Reappraisal*. Winona Lake, IN: Eisenbrauns, 2006.

Von Rad, Gerhard. "Deuteronomy's Name Theology and the Priestly Document's "Kabod Theology."" Pp. 37–44 in *Studies in Deuteronomy*. London: SCM, 1953.

_____. *Genesis: A Commentary*. 3rd edition. London: SCM, 1972.

_____. *Old Testament Theology*, vol. 1: *The Theology of Israel's Historical Traditions*. Translated by D. M. G. Stalker. New York: Harper & Row, 1962.

_____. *Old Testament Theology*, vol. 2: *The Theology of Israel's Prophetic Traditions*. Translated by D. G. M. Stalker. San Francisco: Harper & Row, 1965.

Vries, Pieter de. *De Heerlijkheid Van Jhwh in Het Oude Testament En in Het Bijzonder in Het Boek Ezechiël*. Heerenveen: Groen, 2010.

_____. "Ezekiel: Prophet of the Name and Glory of Yнwн—The Character of His Book and Several of Its Main Themes." *JBPR* 4 (2012): 94–108

_____. "The Glory of Yhwh in the Old Testament with Special Attention to the Book of Ezekiel." *TynBul* 62 (2011): 151–54.

Wallace, Daniel B. *Greek Grammar Beyond the Basics: An Exegetical Syntax of the New Testament*. Grand Rapids: Zondervan, 1996.

Waltke, Bruce K. *The Book of Proverbs: Chapters 15–31*. NICOT. Grand Rapids: Eerdmans, 2005.

Waltke, Bruce K., and Michael Patrick O'Connor. *An Introduction to Biblical Hebrew Syntax*. Winona Lake, IN: Eisenbrauns, 1990.

Walton, John H. *Ancient Israelite Literature in Its Cultural Context: A Study of Parallels between Biblical and Ancient near Eastern Texts*. Grand Rapids: Zondervan, 1989.

_____. *Ancient Near Eastern Thought and the Old Testament: Introducing the Conceptual World of the Hebrew Bible*. Nottingham: Apollos, 2007.

_____. *Genesis*. Grand Rapids: Zondervan, 2001.

Warner, Sean M. "Primitive Saga Men." *Vetus Testamentum* 29 (1979): 325–35.

Watson, Francis. "Bible, Theology and the University: A Response to Philip Davies." *JSOT* 71 (1996): 3–16.

Weaver, J. Denny. *The Nonviolent Atonement*. 2nd edition. Grand Rapids: Eerdmans, 2011.

Webb, Barry G. *The Book of Judges*. Grand Rapids: Eerdmans, 2012.

_____. *The Message of Isaiah: On Eagles' Wings*. Leicester: Inter-Varsity, 1996.

Webster, J. B. *Holiness*. Grand Rapids: Eerdmans, 2003.

Webster, Richard. *Freud's False Memories: Psychoanalysis and the Recovered Memory Movement*. Southwold: Orwell, 1996.

_____. *Why Freud Was Wrong: Sin, Science and Psychoanalysis*. Rev ed. London: HarperCollins, 1996.

Wells, Jo Bailey. *God's Holy People: A Theme in Biblical Theology*. JSOTSup 305. Sheffield: Sheffield Academic Press, 2000.

Wenham, Gordon J. *Genesis 1–15*. Waco: Word, 1987.

_____. "Sanctuary Symbolism in the Garden of Eden Story." Pp. 399–404 in *"I Studied Inscriptions before the Flood": Ancient Near Eastern, Literary and Linguistic Approaches to Genesis 1–11*. SBTS 4. Edited by Richard S. Hess and David T. Tsumura. Winona Lake, IN: Eisenbrauns, 1994.

Whittaker, Molly. *Jews and Christians: Graeco-Roman Views.* Cambridge: Cambridge University Press, 1984.

Wikan, Unni. "Shame and Honour: A Contestable Pair." *Man* 19 (1984): 635–52.

Williamson, Paul R. "Promises with Strings Attached: Covenant and Law in Exodus 19–24." Pp. 89–122 in *Exploring Exodus: Literary, Theological and Contemporary Approaches.* Edited by Brian S. Rosner and Paul R. Williamson. Nottingham: Apollos, 2008.

Wilson, Ian. *Out of the Midst of the Fire: Divine Presence in Deuteronomy.* Atlanta: Scholars Press, 1995.

Witherington, Ben, III. *Is There a Doctor in the House: An Insider's Story and Advice on Becoming a Bible Scholar.* Grand Rapids: Zondervan, 2011.

Wolff, Hans Walter. *Hosea: A Commentary on the Book of the Prophet Hosea.* Edited by Paul D. Hanson. Translated by Gary Stansell. Philadelphia: Fortress, 1974.

Wong, Ka Leung. *The Idea of Retribution in the Book of Ezekiel.* VTSup 87. Leiden: Brill, 2001.

Woodhouse, John. *1 Samuel: Looking for a Leader.* Wheaton: Crossway, 2008.

Wright, N. T. *The New Testament and the People of God.* London: SPCK, 1992.

Wurmser, Léo. *The Mask of Shame.* Baltimore: Johns Hopkins University Press, 1981.

Wyatt-Brown, Bertram. *Southern Honor: Ethics and Behavior in the Old South.* New York: Oxford University Press, 1982.

Young, Ian, Robert Rezetko, and Martin Ehrensvärd. *Linguistic Dating of Biblical Texts.* 2 vols. London: Equinox, 2008.

Zimmerli, Walther. *Ezekiel: A Commentary on the Book of the Prophet Ezekiel, Chapters 1–24.* Edited by Frank Moore Cross, Klaus Baltzer, and Leonard J. Greenspoon. Translated by Ronald E. Clements. Hermeneia. Philadelphia: Fortress, 1979.

_____. *Ezekiel 2: A Commentary on the Book of the Prophet Ezekiel, Chapters 25–48.* Edited by Paul D. Hanson and Leonard J. Greenspoon. Translated by James D. Martin. Hermeneia. Philadelphia: Fortress, 1983.

_____. *I Am Yahweh.* Edited by Walter Brueggemann. Translated by Douglas W. Scott. Atlanta: John Knox, 1982.

Zimmerli, Walther, and K. C. Hanson. *The Fiery Throne: The Prophets and Old Testament Theology.* Minneapolis: Fortress, 2003.

Index of Authors

Index of Scripture

New Testament